DAUGHTER TO NAPOLEON

DAUGHTER TO

NAPOLEON

A Biography of

HORTENSE,

QUEEN OF HOLLAND

by Constance Wright

HOLT, RINEHART AND WINSTON

New York

Published simultaneously in Canada by Holt, Rinehart
and Winston of Canada, Limited.

First Edition

Library of Congress Catalog Card Number: 61–14680

Designer: Ernst Reichl

89565–0311

Printed in the United States of America

To M.E.H.,

in memory of long friendship.

"The poetry of history does not consist of imagination roaming at large, but of imagination pursuing the fact and fastening upon it . . . Just because it really happened, it gathers round it all the inscrutable mystery of life and death and time."

—GEORGE MACAULAY TREVELYAN

FOREWORD

HORTENSE DE BEAUHARNAIS has told her own story in the memoirs she wrote in the latter part of her life. In the pages that follow, most of the conversation quoted is a translation of Hortense's own words, taken from these memoirs. All other bibliographical references have been left to the commentary at the end of the book.

For help in preparing *Daughter to Napoleon*, the author is deeply grateful to the staff of the New York Public Library, the Library of Yale University, and the Public Library of Pleasantville, New York, through which many books, some rare and difficult to trace, were borrowed. She wishes also to thank warmly Miss Margaret Payson for permission to reproduce the portrait of Hortense as a young girl.

CONTENTS

PART

I

(April 10, 1783–January 4, 1802)

𝄞𝄞𝄞𝄞𝄞𝄞𝄞𝄞𝄞𝄞𝄞

㉕㉕㉕㉕㉕㉕㉕㉕㉕㉕㉕㉕㉕

I

DINNER AT THE LUXEMBOURG

HORTENSE DE BEAUHARNAIS, who one day would be a queen, had an obscure, but adventurous, childhood. She was born in Paris on April 10, 1783, and before she was more than a few months old had been accused of being a bastard. Her father, the Vicomte Alexandre de Beauharnais, knew, before he left France for Martinique, that his wife Joséphine was pregnant, but in the Antilles he had found a lady who was more to his taste. He wrote a searing, flamboyant letter, accusing Joséphine of multiple adulteries and repudiating this, her second, child. "I swear by the heavens that shine upon me that it belongs to another, that the blood of a stranger flows through its veins." Joséphine was ordered to retire to a convent, the traditional refuge for disgraced and distressed gentlewomen, there to wait for her husband's return.

A suit for a legal separation followed. Though Joséphine was declared innocent and all of Alexandre's relatives, including his father, the Marquis de Beauharnais, upheld her, she and her husband were never completely reconciled. Their marriage had been arranged for them by an aunt of Joséphine, who for many years was the mistress and later the wife of Alexandre's father. Both families involved in the connection were creole, Joséphine's family, the Taschers de la Pagerie, being far less wealthy and prominent than that of her husband.

For reasons best known to herself, Joséphine went back to visit her mother in Martinique in 1787, taking with her the four-year-old Hortense, a cherub, blue-eyed and golden-haired. Mother and daughter stayed for three years in the islands, leaving at an hour's notice when threatened with massacre by a slave uprising. On her second crossing of the Atlantic, Hortense narrowly escaped shipwreck off the coast of Africa. Later, she compared notes with her brother, Eugène, two years older than she, who all this time had been living in a boarding school at Paris; Eugène, generous boy that he was, admitted that Hortense had seen more of life in the raw than he.

Great excitements and great trials, however, lay ahead for the two children. The year was 1790. The Bastille had fallen, and the great Revolution, that was to toss so many up and toss so many down, had begun. Alexandre de Beauharnais was one of the leaders of reform and was president of the Constituent Assembly, that had undertaken to transform the absolute government of France into a constitutional monarchy, while at the same time waging a desperate foreign war against a coalition of European kings and princes. In 1791, De Beauharnais gave up lawmaking and joined the army as adjutant general. He failed to distinguish himself.

Meanwhile the daughter, whom he had tried unsuccessfully to repudiate and whom he now acknowledged as his own, had been with her grandfather at Versailles and for a short time at a convent school, the Abbaye-aux-Bois, where, as the youngest pupil, she became the pet of the Abbess and her nuns. In August of 1792, Hortense was hurried back to her mother's home in Paris. The monarchy had fallen; the Tuileries had been sacked; the King and Queen of France were prisoners. Joséphine was anxious for her children to be safe, but—once more for obscure reasons—did not want to go with them to safety. She put Hortense and Eugène in the keeping of some friends who were leaving for England. Before they had reached their port of embarkation, they were recalled to Paris by their father.

Alexandre, insensitive to danger, wanted his son and daughter to follow the educational scheme favored by the newly formed French Republic, which had decreed that all junior citizens should learn to work with their hands. Eugène was apprenticed to a carpenter; Hortense was apprenticed, after a fashion, to her governess, a Mademoiselle Lannoy, who had been a dressmaker.

While the children's education was being carried out along these lines, the early instigators of the Revolution were being liquidated under the dictatorship of Maximilien Robespierre. In March of 1794, Alexandre de Beauharnais was arrested at his country estate at La Ferté. A month later, Hortense and Eugène woke in their home in the rue Saint Dominique to be told that their mother was gone. Agents for the Committee of Public Safety had come during the night and had taken her away to prison.

Mademoiselle Lannoy was now in charge of the household. To the children she seemed very homely and very faultfinding, when compared to their exquisite, gentle-spoken mother, who never scolded or punished them, but only looked grieved when they did something that was wrong. Hortense and Eugène laughed behind the governess' back, because she was forever saying disapprovingly that this or that "could never have happened under the Old Regime," by which she meant, of course, the time when there had been a king and queen at Versailles. To the foreshortened memory of a girl of ten and a boy of twelve, this seemed an epoch as remote and romantic as a fairy tale.

Hortense and Eugène always went with Mademoiselle Lannoy, when she took a bundle of clean clothes to the Carmelite Prison in the rue de Rennes. The guard at the gate objected to their pinning a note to the bundle, so they took turns in copying the laundry list; thus their mother would know that they both were alive and well. An even better idea was to take *Maman's* little dog, Fortuné, with them and to fasten a note inside his collar where it was hidden by his shaggy coat. They would let Fortuné loose in the prison, and he would dart away between the guard's legs to find his mistress. When he returned, another twist of paper would be found attached to his collar. Once, the message brought by Fortuné was that the children should write a letter to the National Convention, asking for their mother's release. A friend of Joséphine, Jean Tallien, would see that the appeal was delivered. The letter was duly written and dispatched, but brought no reply.

Hortense and Eugène, however, would never admit to one another that their mother, the one point of stability in their threatened world, was gone for good. When it was reported that the children of prisoners might be sent to orphan asylums maintained by the state, Eugène reassured Hortense.

"Don't worry," he said. "I won't let them take you away. I will enlist as a soldier. Then no one will dare to hurt my mother or my sister. While I'm in the army and until *maman* comes home, you can stay at La Ferté-Beauharnais."

"What—all by myself!" Hortense cried in alarm. "I would never dare do that!"

"Then you could come with me. You wouldn't be afraid of the shooting, would you?"

"No—I promise," Hortense replied.

One day in July, a woman whom the children had never seen before came to the rue Saint Dominique, bringing a note that was written in their mother's hand. The governess told Hortense and Eugène that they were to go to the prison with the stranger, who led them, not to the rue de Rennes, but to a small, empty house in its rear, which had been a gardener's cottage when the prison was a Carmelite monastery. The children were stationed at an upper window and told to be perfectly quiet.

Presently, the shutters of a window, high up in the prison wall opposite, opened, and Hortense saw not only her mother, but also her father looking down at her. Hortense, the child of a broken home, had rarely seen the handsome, fair-haired Alexandre, and never before in such close proximity to her mother.

She stretched up her arms and cried out in her shrill child's voice.

There was an answering shout from a guard, who came hurrying around the corner of the building. The children were hustled away from the window by their guide, down the stairs, and out of the gardener's cottage, back by a circuitous route to the rue Saint Dominique. A few days later, Mademoiselle Lannoy told them that their father was dead. He was executed a short time after they had seen him.

For Hortense, there could be no sense of personal loss, but, ever impressionable, she wept for her father as she might have wept for the hero of one of her story books: for Roland, bursting his lungs to blow a last, despairing blast upon his horn at Roncesvalles. Alexandre de Beauharnais, of whose real life and character she knew so little, had, by dying, become a paladin. He had stepped back into the storied past, and his pale image would soon be replaced by another, by that of a prodigious personality, transforming Hortense's life and drawing it within the compass of recorded history.

Not long after the death of Alexandre, the Reign of Terror was brought to an end by the sudden and bloody death of Maximilien Robespierre. The Paris prisons emptied, and Joséphine de Beauharnais came back to the rue Saint Dominique. After an interim stay with her grandfather at Versailles, Hortense's home was once more a boarding school, the National Institution for the Education of Young Women, at Saint-Germain-en-Laye. On one of her rare holiday visits to her mother in Paris, Hortense saw for the first time Napoleon Bonaparte.

◫

That evening—it was the twenty-first of January, 1796—there was a dinner party at the Luxembourg Palace, its host, Paul Nicolas Barras, one of the five Directors of the French Republic. Having been born a count, Director Barras knew how to entertain in elegant, pre-revolutionary style. He was so much more important than his colleagues in office that he was sometimes called "the Uncrowned King of France." He was also called "the King of Stinkers" (*le roi des pourries*), for Barras, a tough and wily politician, had enriched himself on his way to the top. With the men who crowded his anteroom during business hours, begging for favors, he could talk the language of the streets; in his salon he reverted to the *grand seigneur*. Barras' taste in women was also atavistic. He liked them to be silken voiced and silken clad, with all the airs and graces of the Old Regime; many of his female friends were, like Joséphine de Beauharnais, widows of noblemen who had died during the Terror.

Through Barras' crowded reception rooms the daughter of Joséphine moved demurely in her mother's shadow, well aware that, for all her pink cheeks and golden curls, she was too young to receive much attention in her own right. Hortense was now twelve years old. Though her mother had sometimes taken her to dances in the public ballrooms that abounded in Paris, this was her first taste of a more formal social life. Hortense saw no one she knew, except one lady, Madame Tallien, wife of the Jean Tallien who had delivered the children's appeal for mercy to the Convention. The lady was tall and beautiful as a Greek statue; like a Greek statue, she was clad in flowing, diaphanous robes. These, in conjunction with bare, sandaled feet and an almost complete absence of underclothing, were the latest female fashion. Barras' male guests, on the other hand, were muffled to the ears in wide-lapelled coats, their necks swathed by goiterous cravats of silk or muslin.

At table—a table decorated with flowers and sparkling with silver—Hortense found herself seated between her mother and a stranger, a young man who wore the uniform of a major general. Not having seen his picture—it was on display in all the print shops of Paris—Hortense did not recognize General Bonaparte. If someone had thought of introducing her, she would have known his name; even in the National Institution for the Education of Young

Women someone must have spoken of the heroic defender of the National Convention.

Only three months earlier, on October 5, 1795, the de facto government of France was threatened by an armed force of thirty thousand. Bonaparte, an ex-officer of artillery, who was working obscurely as a clerk in the Topographical Office, collected all the big guns in Paris and its suburbs, stationed them strategically about the Convention Hall, and used the grapeshot with which they were loaded to murderous effect. Shortly thereafter the first elections, under a new constitution, were held, and the man who had had the bright idea of employing Bonaparte's talents, Paul Nicolas Barras, was elected to the Directory. At the same time, Bonaparte, in spite of his youth, was given command of the Army of the Interior.

The officer at Hortense's elbow was only twenty-six. He was lean and haggard, pale as a cadaver. His long hair hung almost to his shoulders and straggled across his brow, a fashion that had become popular during the Revolution. Hortense noted the classic outline of his features, his compelling eyes, but his eyes were not for her. He disregarded her completely. All his attention was fixed upon her mother. He spoke to no one else at the table, but spoke to Joséphine continually, ardently, in a low voice.

As he did so, Bonaparte leaned across Hortense. She grew tired of politely withdrawing her head, and being forced to peck at the food on her plate like a bird. Eventually, she gave up trying to eat altogether and pushed back her chair. She sat looking with growing disapproval at this intruder between her mother and herself.

Hortense had decided that she did not like this man, nor did she like his setting, this palace of a long dead Queen of France. Now it was crowded with people, who, for all their fine and fashionable clothes, seemed out of place. Instead of being pleased by the prospect of dining with a chief of state, Hortense had come to the Luxembourg rather unwillingly. She had even lodged a protest with her mother, when she heard what was scheduled for the evening.

"But, *maman*," she exclaimed in surprise, "is it possible that you actually associate with such people?"

Hortense was probably unfamiliar with the more unsavory details of Barras' career, but she knew that he and all of his fellow Directors had voted for the death of King Louis XVI, and this was enough to prejudice her against him. In 1796, even a twelve-year-old schoolgirl could have a political point of view; Hortense's politics had not been borrowed entirely from her elders, they had grown out of her own experience. She and her brother, Eugène, also present at the Luxembourg dinner, were royalists, not because Mademoiselle Lannoy had twittered of the Old Regime, but because the Republic had brought them insecurity and sorrow. It was something of a shock to learn that *maman* "actually associated" with regicides.

But now, only a few hours later, in Barras' palatial dining room, with her chair pushed back from Barras' table, a new, a much more real worry had developed. Hortense could hardly wait until the party was over, so that she could share her misgivings with Eugène, with whom she shared everything. She told her brother that she was sure the officer who had sat next to her at dinner, General Bonaparte, was determined to marry their mother.

"If *maman* should marry him," Hortense predicted—and she was close to tears—"she will not love us as much as she does now."

II

MARIE JOSEPHE ROSE

HORTENSE'S mother—she had been christened Marie Josephe Rose, but her latest admirer preferred to call her Joséphine—loved her children as she would love anything that was pretty and that belonged to her. She had a great fondness for personal possessions, a fondness starved during her down-at-heel youth in Martinique. Like many who have lived, not in actual want, but close to it, Joséphine saw in inanimate objects a wall against disaster and decay. Though she could be very generous to others, she was realistic in her approach to the problem of obtaining the luxuries she craved. When, for example, Hortense expressed her disapproval of their dining at the Luxembourg, her mother's face took on that look of grieved surprise she had always found so effective in dealing with her children.

"My dear little girl," she said very gently and sweetly, "you may not realize it, but ever since your father's death I have been trying to save as much of his fortune as I could—save it for you. Do you think I should be ungrateful to those who have helped and protected me?"

Hortense felt herself properly rebuked and begged her mother's pardon, though she was only dimly aware of what her mother's words implied.

11

On the day she walked out of the Carmelite Prison, Joséphine was free as never before in all of her thirty-one years. She was also better equipped than formerly to fend for herself. The Widow Beauharnais was a very different person from the unsophisticated, teen-age girl who had been imported from the Indies for Alexandre to marry, and whom he had treated so disdainfully and so cruelly. Marie Josephe Rose had never been exactly beautiful, but she had learned how to make the best of her good points. She was slim and graceful; she had curling chestnut hair and big violet eyes, beneath languorous lids. Because her teeth showed early signs of decay, she had practiced before her mirror a tight-lipped, fascinating smile. Even in the Carmelite Prison, Joséphine had found a man other than her husband to fascinate, a muscular young officer in the Republican army, General Lazare Hoche.

Hoche, as soon as released, returned to his command and offered to take Eugène with him, thus relieving Joséphine of one of her responsibilities. She had many others, and no money with which to meet them. The Beauharnais estate at La Ferté had been confiscated, the house in the rue Saint Dominique did not belong to Joséphine, and all of her clothes and furniture had been sequestered. While she was in prison, small sums had come occasionally from Martinique. These were used to feed and clothe the children, but Joséphine knew that she could expect little more from that quarter. Recently, the English fleet had snatched the colony from France. As for the old marquis and his wife, they had had to hide during the Terror and, almost as poor as Joséphine was now, were living in a very small way at Fontainebleau. The most that Joséphine could ask them to do was to give houseroom to Hortense, while she looked about for more substantial aid.

She found it first in Jean Tallien and his wife, the beautiful lady of the flowing robes and sandaled feet, who had come to call on Hortense and Eugène to reassure them before their mother's release. Teresa Tallien became Joséphine's closest friend. She could introduce Joséphine to men who had made money during the Revolution, among them—greatest boon of all—to Paul Nicolas Barras, the Uncrowned King of France. The various claims that were registered for the return of Alexandre de Beauharnais' property to his children and the return of personal property to his widow were promptly honored by the government. Even a pair of carriage horses was given to Joséphine to replace a team that her husband had donated several years earlier to the army, a milk cow and a carriage being thrown in for good measure.

But Barras was willing to do more—much more—than to act in an official capacity. At first there was a small villa at Croissy, just outside Paris, where Madame de Beauharnais, a born hostess with a faculty that amounted almost to genius for saying the right thing to the right person, entertained Barras and his friends over week ends. Later there was a house in town, in the rue Chantereine, a little gem of a house, standing between court and garden—what the French slyly term a *maison galante*. There were only five rooms, sparsely but tastefully furnished, on the first two floors, with the kitchen and service rooms below and an attic above, for the servants. The most completely appointed room in the house was the bedroom, with its many mirrors, its alcoved bed, and dressing table, laden with mysterious boxes and flasks containing the perfumes, the rouge, the powder, and make-up pencils Joséphine used with artistry.

Before she moved into the rue Chantereine, at about the same time that Barras moved into the Luxembourg, Joséphine made other arrangements for her children. Her liaison with General Hoche had ended almost at the door of the Carmelite Prison, and Eugène, whom Hoche had taken with him to the army, was soon recalled to Paris and entered at a boarding school at Saint-Germain-en-Laye. It was Barras who suggested that Hortense should be sent to the National Institution for the Education of Young Women, also at Saint-Germain. It was obvious that the house in the rue Chantereine was no place for a growing girl. Nor was there any need for Hortense to know the latest development in her mother's amorous career, the sultry and determined courtship of General Bonaparte.

That also was Barras' doing. He had introduced the young General to the widow, and at the time of the dinner party at the Luxembourg was fostering their intimacy. The Director had discovered that Joséphine as a mistress was a very expensive luxury. She accepted all that was given to her and continually hinted that further gifts would be welcome. She was forever speaking with a sigh of some pressing financial obligation that must be met. If Barras' protégé, Bonaparte, was foolish enough to want to provide for her permanently, and for her son and daughter, Barras was prepared to step aside and to give his blessing to the match.

A match—marriage? At the time of the Luxembourg dinner party, Joséphine had not yet made up her mind, though she had at first seemed to fall in with Barras' plans. She was so instinctively coquettish that she gave encouragement to any man who might be useful to her.

"You no longer come to see a friend who loves you," she wrote, soon after Bonaparte had become famous and comparatively rich, in October. "You neglect your friend—what a pity, for she is very fond of you! Come to have luncheon with me tomorrow— Thursday. I want to see you and to talk with you about everything that interests you. Good night, dear friend. I embrace you."

The reply to this letter was stiff and awkward, but Bonaparte presumably came to lunch on Thursday, and often thereafter to the rue Chantereine. He went everywhere in society where he was sure that he would meet Joséphine. Though he wanted to be married—early marriages were the rule in his native Corsica—and had made a few tentative moves in that direction, he had had little to do with women hitherto. He had been too poor, too shy, too wrapped up in his own concerns to make the necessary advances. This seductive, glamorous lady, this former vicomtesse, with her beautiful manners, her soft voice, and luxurious surroundings, embodied all that he had longed for. The love letters that he wrote in his untidy, bird-track handwriting, between visits to the rue Chantereine, were almost as incoherent as they were indecipherable: "Lovely, incomparable Joséphine, what strange effect you have upon my heart! . . . My soul is broken with sorrow; your lover can find no rest . . . I will see you in three hours time; till then, *mio dolce amor*, a million kisses—but give me none in return for they set my blood on fire!"

Joséphine had never been wooed in quite these terms before. She would have been satisfied with the sort of light-hearted and profitable alliance she had had with Barras, who was a married man and had a wife whom he kept in Provence; when Bonaparte spoke, and spoke again and again, of marriage, Joséphine temporized. Love was a private affair and could be terminated at will; marriage was forever and was so public, even in its initial stages, that her friends, Barras in particular, knew of Bonaparte's intentions almost as soon as she did, and urged her to accept.

There was much sound advice in favor of acceptance that Joséphine could give herself, unprompted. She would be thirty-three her next birthday. Women born in the tropics, it was said, matured early and faded prematurely. As she looked into her mirror in the rue Chantereine, Joséphine could see how many signs of age had to be concealed by her make up. After all, her chief stock in trade was her power to attract.

And there were those pressing financial obligations, her debts, to give them their true, ugly name. Barras did not know the tithe of them, nor did Joséphine herself know the exact amount. As soon as she had had the full management of her affairs, she began to buy widely on credit. She borrowed from everyone, not only from monied men, the bankers to whom Teresa Tallien introduced her, but even from Mademoiselle Lannoy, Hortense's governess, who was willing to sacrifice her small savings and to work for wages that were promised, never paid. Unless Joséphine married and was sure of a stable income, what would become of the household in the rue Chantereine during the next few years?

But on the other hand, how much there was to hold her back! Joséphine did not love Bonaparte—as she conceived of love. He was too strange, too alien. She recognized his brilliance, but why was he never gay? Why didn't he want to enjoy life, as she did? Just where his ambition tended she did not know, but she sensed and feared so strongly his determination to succeed and to dominate all with whom he came in contact, including herself, that she sometimes thought he must be a little mad.

Although he boasted that he came of the best blood in Corsica, he fell far short of her ideal of the well-born, well-bred man. "That queer Bonaparte," she would say with a smile and shake of the head. He was even a little ridiculous. Once when Bonaparte, a very indigent young lieutenant, appeared proudly in a new uniform, with his thin shanks and thighs thrust into a pair of enormous jackboots, a mischievous little girl cried out "Puss in Boots," and the nickname stuck. Joséphine had heard it and had heard him spoken of as "that little Italian." She did not relish the idea of being announced in a drawing room as the Citizeness General Bonaparte. She could not even bring herself to utter her lover's given name: "Nabulione," as it sounded when pronounced in Corsican dialect.

For almost two months after the dinner at the Luxembourg, Joséphine put off her decision and held her frenzied suitor at bay, though Barras spoke enticingly of a new appointment for the General that was in the offing: he might be put in command of the army that for years had been vainly battling the Austrians in Italy. This was the most important military post within the Directory's gift.

One day in March, Joséphine went to see a lawyer who had helped her in some of her business affairs and told him that she was going to marry General Bonaparte. Somewhat to her surprise, for all urgings hitherto had been pro rather than con, the lawyer warned her against taking such a step.

"The man is only an adventurer," he said drily. "He has nothing to offer you, Madame, but his cloak and sword."

It was too late to draw back. Bonaparte had gone with her to the lawyer's house, was waiting in the anteroom, and through the half-open door had overheard the conversation.

On the evening of March 9, 1796, the Mayor of the Second Arrondissement of Paris, who had retired early to bed, was routed out at ten o'clock to marry General Napoleon Buonaparte to the Widow Detascher (sic) Beauharnais, the entire ceremony consisting in drawing up and signing a legal document. The witnesses for the bride were Paul Nicolas Barras and Jean Tallien. Joséphine gave her age as twenty-eight, as did also Napoleon, he adding two years, she subtracting four. There were no guests and no festivities, except a little supper party for the principals and witnesses that Barras, the benevolent matchmaker, had arranged.

As for the wedding gift from the Directory, it had already arrived. Napoleon was General of the Army of Italy. He left for the south after only two days honeymoon in the many-mirrored bedroom of the house in the rue Chantereine.

III

A ROSE FOR VIRTUE

BETWEEN their first encounter and March 9, 1796, Hortense de Beauharnais had seen her prospective stepfather once or twice when she went to spend a day with her mother in Paris. Her opinion of Bonaparte had not improved. He no longer ignored her. On the contrary, he paid a great deal of attention to her and seemed to think that she would like to be teased. When he asked her about her life at school, she told him that she was being prepared to receive her first communion, religious instruction being part of the curriculum at the National Institution for the Education of Young Women.

Napoleon smiled derisively. "So you are a little bigot," he said.

"*You* were confirmed, weren't you?" Hortense shot back indignantly. "If you, why not I?"

This brought forth one of Bonaparte's rare, explosive bursts of laughter.

One evening the General was unusually talkative, though Hortense had noticed that when he was bored he was not polite enough to make the effort of keeping up a conversation. He told a ghost story and told it so effectively that she could not help squirming and looking uneasily into the dark corners of the room.

18

She felt sure that another bloodcurdling yarn was directed at her.

It was Madame Campan, the headmistress of Hortense's boarding school, who broke the news to her pupil that the marriage had taken place. Hortense wept while Madame Campan, trying to console her, said that the General's hands had not been bloodstained by the Terror; he had taken no active part in the Revolution. Because of his position, he would be able now to help Eugène to become a soldier.

Madame Campan was a sensible, intelligent woman, a gifted teacher. She had been lady-in-waiting to Marie Antoinette, and had found a hiding place outside of Paris during the dangerous days for all connected with the court. Only a month after the death of Robespierre, finding herself penniless with an invalid husband and a young son to educate, Madame Campan sent out one hundred prospectuses for the school she hoped to found, all written in her own hand to save the cost of printing.

The school was an immediate success. The convents, where young ladies had formerly been taught embroidery, the catechism, and little else, had disappeared. Madame Campan, who was well read and could speak two foreign languages, English and Italian, could offer courses in history, literature, mathematics, and the arts, with some training in home economics and physical education. There was a pleasant combination of the new with the old. The girls were taught how to make soup and were expected to keep the schoolrooms tidy, as well as to play games out of doors, but there was also heavy emphasis on good manners of the old-fashioned sort and on the art of conversation. One must not forget the past, Madame Campan said. On one of the walls of her study hung a portrait of her patroness, the martyred queen, of whom she often spoke with emotion to her pupils. On the back of the portrait was a summary of the ideals of the Republic, as expressed in *The Rights of Man*. In the early days, when the school was sometimes visited by prying government inspectors, the picture would be hastily reversed.

The National Institution for the Education of Young Women

had a student body of more than a hundred when Madame de Beauharnais drove out from Paris to enroll her daughter. It was housed
in the old Hôtel de Rohan, one of the splendid country houses that
the nobility had built at Saint-Germain during the last century.
Joséphine was acquainted with Madame Campan and was greeted
as an old friend. While Hortense was taken on a tour of the school
by two of the pupils, Joséphine asked deprecatingly for a reduc-
tion in fee, saying that her finances were still "disordered." She
hoped that she would soon be able to pay for Hortense's tuition
in full.

The request was granted. Madame Campan offered to take
Hortense at half-price and to provide her with a cast-off school
uniform. The headmistress had taken a fancy to this eager little
girl. She was just the sort of pupil of whom a teacher dreams but
seldom finds. Hortense had lived in so many places, had led such
a Gypsy life, that she settled into her new environment without a
pang of homesickness. She was wildly enthusiastic about everything that went on in the Hôtel de Rohan: the studies and amateur
theatricals within its walls, the games in its garden. She was not
at the head of her class in mathematics or dictation, that hardy
perennial of the French scholastic system, but she excelled in
music and drawing; she was the best dancer in the school.

The prim little report cards that were sent from time to time
to the rue Chantereine expressed only a small part of the affection
that Madame Campan felt for Hortense. "The Citizeness Hortense
Eugénie Beauharnais," she wrote, "is gifted with rare good
qualities. She is obedient, responsive, and always ready to oblige
her companions. She is very sweet tempered. She would have all
that is needed to succeed, if she were just a little less flighty."

For flighty, read over-impulsive. Madame Campan was used to
dealing with adolescents, and realized that Hortense, like many
other of her pupils, had survived some cruel experiences that
might have left their scars, but she was disturbed by her young
friend's emotional extremes. Hortense was very sensitive to
criticism, very anxious for approval. One moment she was in

despair, the next she was dancing with delight. Nothing was indifferent to her, everything affected her profoundly. Her violent
reaction to her mother's marriage was only a case in point. The
marriage, Madame Campan thought, was all to the good as far
as Hortense was concerned. What the child needed was a firmer
hand than her mother's to guide her, and this the General would
probably supply.

Soon news began to appear in the papers of the campaign that
Bonaparte was waging in Italy. He had found a sullen, starving
army; thousands barefoot, hundreds even without weapons.
"Soldiers," he harangued them, "you are famished and nearly
naked . . . I will lead you into the most fertile plains of the world.
There you will find great towns, rich provinces. There you will
find honor, glory, and riches. Soldiers of Italy, will you be wanting
in courage?"

Within six weeks Napoleon had defeated the Austrians repeatedly, had conquered all of Piedmont, and was riding into
Milan at the head of his still ragged, but fanatically loyal troops.

Madame Campan read the reports aloud to Hortense and cried,
"Do you realize that your mother has picked out an extraordinary
man as her husband? What talents! How remarkable he is!"

"Madame," Hortense said mournfully, "I will give him credit
for all his other conquests, but I will never forgive him for having
conquered my mother."

She was chiefly concerned because Joséphine had not come
out to see her recently at Saint-Germain. "I suppose it is the
General's victories that have kept you away," she wrote sadly.
"If that is what robs me of the joy of seeing my dear little *maman*,
I hope there won't be many more victories."

But this was absurd, Madame Campan said! She insisted that
Hortense should be reasonable and should write to her stepfather
to congratulate him.

Hortense thought deeply before she wrote the letter. She was
still hurt that she had not been told of the wedding in advance, and
from Napoleon's teasing she had gathered that he had a low opinion

of girls and of the entire female sex. "I have been told of your marriage with my mother," she wrote. "What surprises me is that you, whom I have so often heard speak badly of women, should have made up your mind to marry one of these creatures."

In time a reply came back from military headquarters at Milan, written on official letter paper. It was all that Madame Campan could have wished. Its tone was playful, but warmly affectionate.

I have received your charming letter . . . but you are a naughty —a very naughty girl! You wish to make me contradict myself. You should know, charming Hortense, that when we speak ill of men, we make exception in our own favor; when we speak ill of women, we except the one whose charm and gentle ways have captured our hearts and to whom we give all our love . . . As you know very well, your mother is not to be compared with anyone else on earth. No one else can unite so much sweetness with an indescribable something that draws everyone to her. If anything could add to the joy I feel in belonging to her, it is the welcome responsibilities it involves toward you. I will act as though I were your father, and you shall love me as though I were your best friend . . .

But I am cross with you and cross with your dear *maman*! She promised to come to see me and she has not yet come. Time goes slowly when we are far from those we love. Think of how glad I should be to see you in Paris, to argue with you and tell you terrible tales! Do not forget me entirely. A kiss to Eugène, to whom I ought to write.

Believe me, yours forever,

Bonaparte

P.S. You should have received a little box of perfume. I will bring you a hundred pretty things.

It would have taken a harder heart than Hortense's to reject this offer of friendship. The postscript also had its effect in breaking down her defenses. Hortense loved perfume, and, never having had any of her own, she also loved jewelry. She had sometimes thought that she could be perfectly happy if she had a full trinket box.

But Hortense did not want her mother to go to Italy. She didn't know that ever since Napoleon left Paris in March a torrent of anguished letters had flowed to the rue Chantereine, begging Joséphine to come to him. At first, the Directory was unwilling for reasons of safety to give the General's wife a passport, but after the capture of Milan that was no longer an obstacle. Joséphine pleaded ill health; she hinted that she might be pregnant. Bonaparte was frantic with worry, but overjoyed at the thought of a child.

The truth of the matter was, however, that Joséphine was not an expectant mother. She was in her usual state of excellent health and was enjoying every moment, every hour in Paris. She was so overwhelmed with attentions and invitations that she didn't have time to drive out the thirteen miles to Saint-Germain, much less to cross the Alps. Napoleon was sending back captured flags, wagonloads of Italian art treasures, and, what the Directory wanted most of all, large sums of money. When Milan was taken there was a holiday for the entire city of Paris, and a great fête was given at the Luxembourg, at which Joséphine was greeted as "Our Lady of Victory."

At last, when she could no longer find an excuse that would hold water, Joséphine set out, in June, for Milan. Hortense, though she had often had to say good-bye to her mother before, was desolate; all the more because Eugène, who was such a comfort to her, who had come every Sunday afternoon to visit her from his neighboring school in Saint-Germain, had already been called to Italy to join the General's staff.

Vacation time came. Hortense saw parents come to take their daughters home for the summer holiday. She was to stay with Madame Campan. Fond though she was of her teacher, she could not help feeling sorry for herself, though every bearer of dispatches from the southern front brought her letters and souvenirs from her mother, as well as the first installments of "the hundred pretty things" that Napoleon had promised: enameled watches, chains and necklaces of Venetian goldwork.

Madame Campan saw to it that Hortense was not entirely without companionship of her own age. The headmistress had three motherless nieces who were pupils at the school; one of them, Adèle Auguié, was Hortense's best friend. The Auguiés lived nearby at Grignon, and Hortense went there often to spend a few days. She was also invited for a visit by Madame Tallien, but this invitation was refused. Madame Campan had managed, without open criticism to suggest that the beautiful Teresa, even though a friend of Joséphine, was not a proper chaperone.

The founder of the National Institution for the Education of Young Women was too practical, too canny, not to realize how fortunate she was to have the stepdaughter of General Bonaparte in her school. But she had loved Hortense when she was only a half-pay pupil in a shabby uniform; now she wondered what effect Bonaparte's rising importance would have upon her darling's future. Hortense was beginning to grow up. When she first came to Saint-Germain she was so rosy and roly-poly that she was called *la petite bonne*, the little goody. The last few months had brought a great change in her appearance. The child was receding, the woman-to-be was emergent. Hortense would inherit her mother's slenderness and grace. Her nose was a little bit too long, her mouth a little bit too large; but with her vivacious coloring, her big blue eyes, and masses of golden hair, she would be very striking.

Sometimes Hortense surprised Madame Campan by her flashes of adult worldly wisdom. One summer afternoon they went together to Versailles, where Madame Campan had spent so many years as lady in waiting to the Queen. It was almost a ghost town now, with its many empty houses surrounding the Sun King's empty, dismantled palace. Relatives of Madame Campan entertained her and her pupil at tea. Among the guests was a poet, who devoted himself to Hortense, sitting beside her, trying to draw her out, paying her extravagant compliments.

A few days later some verses addressed to "la Belle Hortense" appeared in a newspaper. Madame Campan, when she read them, laughed and thought that Hortense would be amused also, but tears—unpredictable, angry tears—were the result.

"Just think, Madame," Hortense cried, "he's only a flatterer who is trying to get himself into favor with my stepfather—and he's hurting me! To be happy, a woman must never attract attention, but here's my name in print in a newspaper! Everyone will be talking about me. If I'm going to be famous I'll be perfectly miserable."

Madame Campan saw that this was no laughing matter. The visit to Versailles had perhaps brought back memories of Marie Antoinette and all the harm that notoriety and death-dealing talk had brought to the Queen.

Madame Campan put her arms about Hortense. "Yes, people will talk about you," she said prophetically. "That may be your fate. Remember, you must never do anything wrong, for everything you do will be known. The higher a person's rank, the more deadly the criticism. But," she added more lightly, "I am sure that you will be happy, because you will be good."

When summer was over and the Hôtel de Rohan was filled again with chattering girls, Hortense's moodiness disappeared. She plunged back with vigor into work and play. Madame Campan had instituted a special prize for virtue, an artificial rose that was to be worn for three months, but on Sunday only, by the "best girl" in the school, the winner to be chosen by secret ballot. Everyone in the Hôtel de Rohan was allowed to vote, the servants as well as the teachers and pupils. It was a tribute to Hortense's universal popularity that in the first election she carried off the prize, uncontested. While her stepfather was completing his conquest of Italy, Hortense was passionately absorbed in such questions as whether Monsieur Isabey, the art instructor, would approve of her latest drawing, or—even more important—which one of her schoolmates would be the next to wear Madame Campan's rose.

IV

THE CLAN

By April of 1797 all of Italy had been liberated from Austrian domination, a Cisalpine Republic had been established, a French army was advancing on Vienna through the Styrian Alps, and a truce was called preliminary to a peace treaty between Austria and France. Napoleon and Joséphine went to spend the summer months at the castle of Mombello near Milan. The castle, huge though it was, was not large enough to hold all of the people who flocked to pay court to the conqueror. A large tent was set up before the front entrance to accommodate the overflow of guests. Among those who were certain of the most comfortable quarters within the château itself were the members of Napoleon's family, whom he had invited to visit him.

He, his four brothers, and three sisters, had grown up in a harsh land and in poverty. Their father, Carlo Buonaparte, was one of the first to ally himself with the French when they took over Corsica from Genoa in 1768. He spent all his energy, until a cancer of the stomach cut him off in his prime, in trying to find some sort of profitable government appointment. He never succeeded, but at least he managed to wangle scholarships for his four older children to be educated in French schools and at government expense. The

Revolution came to Corsica with Pasquale di Paoli, the Corsican patriot and strong man, upheld by the British and taking the side of the crown against the local Jacobins. The Buonapartes sided with the Republican element; at a crucial moment they had to escape as refugees from the island to southern France, where they lived on a small pension granted them by the Convention.

And then the great opportunity: the defense of the Convention, the sudden rocketing to fame of Carlo's second son, the "little Nabulione," whom no one in Corsica had thought of as particularly promising. As soon as Napoleon began to soar, all of his kin panted to follow after him and to share in his good fortune. This was their right. This was the way that things were done in Corsica, where ties of blood were despotic, where it was a duty for brother to help brother, and where a large family connection was such an asset that the number of cousins possessed by bride and groom was sometimes listed in a marriage contract.

Napoleon, true to tradition, had been very generous. He had sent money; he had looked out for various family interests, even while he was frantically busy in Paris with his expanding military career and while he was courting Joséphine. The gathering at Mombello in the early summer of 1797 was intended to regulate certain family affairs and to allow Joséphine to become better acquainted with the Bonapartes.

She had been escorted to Italy by Joseph, eldest of the tribe. In Paris, she had met more or less casually the three other brothers, Lucien, Louis, and Jérôme, who was only thirteen and a pupil at the same boarding school as Eugène de Beauharnais. The women of the family, however, were new to Joséphine. With all her tact, with all her charm, with all her gift for easy sociability, she tried to make them her friends. Her chief efforts were directed toward her mother-in-law, Letizia Bonaparte, who, though she wore a widow's cap and considered herself an old woman, was still austerely beautiful at forty-seven.

But Madame Mère, as she would later be called in France, was glacially unresponsive. For one thing, Napoleon's mother was unable to express herself fluently in French and was too proud to risk blunders and absurdities. Letizia had ears to hear, however, and eyes to see. Everything about her aristocratic daughter-in-law displeased her: the sophisticated chic, the spendthrift trousseau of clothes and jewels, even the obnoxious lap dog that Joséphine had brought with her from Paris, the same little Fortuné who had once carried notes tucked in his collar back and forth to Joséphine in prison.

The abyss between the two women was too deep, too broad to be bridged, even if there had been a determined effort on either hand. Letizia could have only scorn for a wife who pretended pregnancy to escape coming to her husband. Was Joséphine pregnant now? Letizia saw no signs—and saw that Joséphine was much older than she pretended to be. She herself, in nineteen years of marriage, had borne twelve children and had raised the eight survivors by the strength of her own hand. She had knelt upon the rocks to wash their dirty clothes in the river; she had spent sleepless nights to nurse them when they were sick; she had also whipped them soundly when they transgressed her law.

Letizia's oldest daughter, who had been christened Maria Anna, but who preferred to call herself Elisa—Elisa was such a romantic name—was something of a bluestocking. She had spent several years at Saint-Cyr, the school for dowerless girls that had been established near Versailles by Madame de Maintenon and Louis XIV. Elisa had recently been married, without consulting Napoleon, to a dull and undistinguished Corsican, Félix Bacciochi. She and her husband had come to Mombello to get Napoleon's consent, *post facto*, to the marriage.

Joséphine extended herself in making the Bacciochis welcome and in reconciling them with the all-powerful elder brother, but her only thanks was a politely cold reserve on the part of Elisa.

With the two younger female Bonapartes, Joséphine was even less successful. Pauline (Maria Paulina) was the *enfant terrible* of the family. All of the Bonapartes were handsome, but she was incredibly beautiful. Though only seventeen, she had already had a torrid love affair with a man of whom Napoleon did not approve. The suitor was sent about his business, and Pauline was now engaged to one of her brother's staff officers. General Leclerc, who, though blond, closely resembled the dark-haired Bonapartes. Pauline was reconciled to this new alliance, but she secretly—and unjustly—held a grudge against Joséphine for being the prime mover in putting an end to her earlier romance.

While she waited for her fiancé to arrive at Mombello, Pauline flirted with the junior officers and listened, sometimes at keyholes, to their salty gossip, much of which had to do with the wife of their commander in chief: her past intimacy with Barras, her present presumed partiality for a young lieutenant, Hippolyte Charles, who, like Joseph and the dog Fortuné, had come with Joséphine from Paris. During the solemn family meals that were eaten in the great hall of the château, and to which the public was admitted to watch the Bonapartes dine as if they were royalty, Pauline whispered, nudged her neighbors, and laughed uproariously, setting a bad example to her younger sister, Maria Annunciata, and to Jérôme. When Joséphine was not looking, Pauline would make a face at her sister-in-law and run out her tongue.

The family business was soon accomplished. General Leclerc came from Milan. He and Pauline were married by a magistrate, and later a Nuptial Mass was performed for them and for the Bacciochis by an Italian priest, assisted by Abbé Fesch, yet another member of the family, a half-brother of Letizia Bonaparte. A handsome dowry was decided upon and settled on each of the married sisters.

Soon after the wedding ceremonies, the house party at Mombello dissolved. Except for Pauline's mischievous clowning, some show of decorum had been maintained; this coming together under a single roof had consolidated the attitude of the Clan Bonaparte toward Joséphine. The Bonapartes might quarrel ferociously among themselves, but when faced by an issue that concerned them all, they could present a united front.

They thought, as one, that Joséphine was a menace. For all her

show of friendliness, she might divert from them, the blood relatives, some of the golden flow of benefits that had only just begun.
She could do this now, because Napoleon was still passionately in
love with her.

How could they combat her? Only by showing her up to her husband for the lascivious woman that she was. If Joséphine should
produce a child, she would be still more difficult to dislodge, but
one of her major sins in the eyes of her newly acquired relatives
was the fact that she already had two children of her own. Surely
Joséphine would want Napoleon to do something substantial for
her son Eugène, for her daughter Hortense!

回

In time, all of the Bonaparte clan would converge on Paris, but
Napoleon was the first to return. The Treaty of Campoformio was
signed in October, and on December 7, 1797, the General was
once more in the French capital after an absence of a year and nine
months. Again it was vacation time for Madame Campan's schoolgirls. Hortense had gone to stay with her grandfather Beauharnais,
who had left Fontainebleau temporarily and come to Paris. With
her was one of her schoolmates, her cousin, Émilie de Beauharnais.

On the morning after the General's arrival, the Marquis drove
with the two girls to the rue Chantereine, which had been rechris-
tened rue da la Victoire, in Napoleon's honor. The street was
packed with people. Sentries had to clear a way for visitors to
enter the house, the interior of which was barely recognizable. Before she left for Italy, Joséphine had given orders for the *maison
galante* to be completely done over, using military motifs. Eagles
clasping thunderbolts were perched above the mirrors; the hang-
ings of the bed were in the form of a tent; stools were drum-
shaped.

Napoleon was breakfasting with some of his staff when the
guests were ushered in. He sprang up from table to kiss Hortense
and her cousin affectionately. But where was the person whom Hortense wanted most in all the world to see? To her sorrow she learned

that her mother was traveling slowly home, visiting many towns in Italy and France, bringing with her a rich cargo of acquisitions: cameos, statues, paintings, even some antiquities which had been recently discovered at Herculaneum. A month went by before Joséphine reached Paris, and then she was so occupied with the series of receptions that were given to celebrate her return, that Hortense saw little of her.

Hortense had other trials to endure. She had always been the friend, and somtimes the protector from teasing, of newcomers to the school; she had just encountered a newcomer who refused her advances and who seemed determined to be her enemy. The youngest of the Bonaparte sisters, Maria Annunciata, who had been renamed Caroline—this seemed to be almost a Bonaparte tradition—had had so little schooling that she could barely read and write. She was sixteen, a year older than Hortense. Before packing her off to the National Institution for the Education of Young Women, Napoleon told her what a charming companion and model student she would find in his stepdaughter.

This tactless puff of praise might in itself have been enough to disgust Caroline, but, in addition, Hortense was the daughter of Joséphine! And Caroline loathed the school. Since her visit to Mombello last summer, she had been in Rome with her brother Joseph, who had been appointed Minister to the Papal·States by the Directory. In the early part of their stay, the Bonapartes were much fêted. Caroline was surrounded by attractive young men. An Italian poet had dedicated a book, *The Adventures of Sappho, Poetess of Mytilene,* to her; Caroline's pretty face being used as a model for the picture of Sappho on the title page.

How dreary it was to find herself now in an institution to which the only men admitted were a few emasculated male instructors, or perhaps a brother who came to visit on Sunday afternoon! Caroline made no attempt to hide her boredom and was forever at the bottom of her class. She was particularly poor at art work. Hortense offered to help her with one of her drawings and Caroline exploded.

She accused Hortense of being a show-off, of trying to humiliate her.

Hortense was deeply—twice over—wounded. It was hard for her to understand how anyone could dislike Madame Campan's school, or, for that matter, how anyone could dislike her. Popularity had come so easily to Hortense that she had become a trifle smug.

She pressed hard for an explanation, in the course of which she learned that Caroline was trying to do so poorly at her lessons that Madame Campan would be discouraged and would send her home. Caroline's ambition was to be married as soon as possible. She was in love with a dashing young soldier, Joachim Murat, whom she had met at Mombello and later again in Rome. Hortense was so fascinated by this confession and was so sympathetic, that for the time being a rapprochement was established between the two girls.

Love and marriage were subjects that were much discussed in the National Institution for the Education of Young Women, but not in the classroom. The Revolution, which had brought so many changes to France, had not altered the megalithic pattern of French family life. Though they were supposed to be in a state of almost pathological innocence, Madame Campan's girls knew very well that soon after graduation their parents would select husbands for them. Hortense had once told her bosom friend, Adèle Auguié, Madame Campan's niece, how she would meet this situation.

"I want my husband, whoever he may be, to love me," she said. "I shall train myself to win his affection. If he is too frivolous, I shall know how to make him more serious minded: if he is jealous, I shall be ready to give up every social pleasure for his sake. In short, I shall cure him, whatever ailment he may have."

These were brave words!

That spring of 1798 there were flutterings and stirrings in Madame Campan's dovecote. Now that Caroline was an inmate, Caroline's two unmarried brothers, Louis and Jérôme, came often to visit her on Sunday. Louis was nineteen, a great favorite of Napoleon, who had brought him, a boy, from Corsica to France, tutored him, and shared with him the meager pay of a first lieutenant until a scholarship in a military school was available. During the Italian campaign, Louis was a member of his brother's staff. He was taller than the General, fine looking, melancholy. On his way back from Italy, Louis had been in a carriage accident that dislocated his knee. He seemed to be much worried about his health and to have little taste for soldiering.

Hortense liked cheerful, hearty people—in this respect her brother Eugène seemed to her to have the ideal temperament—and Louis' low spirits and hypochondria repelled her. She was glad that he seemed less interested in her than in her cousin, Émilie de Beauharnais.

Émilie also had a melancholy streak, but she, poor girl, had good reason to be sad. Sensitive and withdrawn, Hortense's senior by two years, Émilie was the daughter of a brother of Alexandre de Beauharnais, who had been, unlike Alexandre, a fervent royalist. He left France in 1792 to join the emigrant army on the Rhine; his wife divorced him and soon married a widower with four children. There was no place in this new home for Émilie. She was left in charge of a governess who neglected and even persecuted her, until she was rescued and sent to Saint-Germain by Joséphine, soon after Joséphine had become Madame Bonaparte. Napoleon was meeting the expenses of Émilie's education.

Émilie and Louis were often to be seen tête-a-tête in Madame Campan's drawing room. They found comfort, apparently, in telling their troubles to one another. A tenderness developed that the other girls were quick to notice. And then, suddenly, there were no more Sunday visits from Louis. He had been sent off to Toulon on a military mission. The reason for his disappearance was not immediately apparent.

Napoleon, during the past few months, had avoided publicity. He wished to divorce himself in the popular mind from the Directory. When he was forced to appear at a state function, he came late and left early. He realized how quickly his popularity might vanish without further exploits. With compass and ruler in hand, he spent hours bending over large-scale maps of England and of Egypt. Now that Austria had been humbled, France's chief enemy was England. Would it be better to attack the mother island, or the dependency guarding the approach to India?

The East had always had a fascination for Bonaparte. When he was very young and unsuccessful, he had dreamed of taking service as a soldier of fortune under an Eastern potentate. He now inspected the northern ports that would have to be used in an invasion of Great Britain, found them inadequate, and presented his plan for an Egyptian campaign to the Directory. It was promptly authorized.

Napoleon was to leave in May. He would take Eugène de Beauharnais with him and, of course, Louis. But Louis was reluctant to leave France; he pleaded ill health. His brother discovered that there was a heart attraction at Saint-Germain and took immediate action. Napoleon did not want his favorite sibling to marry the daughter of a royalist *émigré* and of a divorced woman. It was not enough to send Louis to the south of France en route to Egypt; Napoleon must make doubly sure.

One day he and Joséphine drove out to visit the National Institution for the Education of Young Women. Napoleon inspected the school as gravely and minutely as though it were a military camp or fortress and was pleased with all he saw. He disliked intensely intellectual women—he had never been very fond of his bluestocking sister Elisa—but he and Madame Campan, a plain, heavy-featured woman in a plain black dress, and no nonsense about her, saw eye to eye on essentials.

"What is wrong with female education in France?" Napoleon asked. "What should be done?"

"Girls should be trained to be good mothers," Madame Campan said. Had she perhaps heard the retort that Napoleon had made recently to Madame de Staël, the Queen of Bluestockings, when he told her that the greatest woman in the world was the woman who had borne the most children?

The day of the General's visit was warm. There was a lunch

basket in the carriage, and Madame Campan gave permission for Hortense, Caroline and Émilie to picnic with their relatives in the forest of Saint-Germain. Napoleon had brought Eugène with him and also one of his other officers, General Chamans de Lavalette, a clever man, a good soldier, but unprepossessing, with a balding head and a roll of fat about his thick waist. After lunch had been eaten under the great trees, the others strayed away and Lavalette found himself alone with Émilie.

He had been told by his General that here was a *parti* for him, a match, but Émilie seemed so wistful, a shy Cinderella, with downcast eyes, that he stammered out his proposal and added, "If the arrangement is distasteful to you, please say so. It won't be hard for me to find a pretext for a break. I will go away; you won't be troubled further, and I will keep your secret."

Émilie was holding a little bunch of flowers. She handed them to Lavalette. Though she said nothing, he took her absent-minded gesture for assent.

The wedding was celebrated very quietly a week later at Grandfather Beauharnais' house in Paris. Hortense was present. Émilie was a pale and listless bride. After the ceremony the girls were alone for a few moments, and Émilie's composure cracked. She wept in Hortense's arms. This had all happened so suddenly. She had no time to think. General Lavalette would be very kind to her, she was sure, but the only man she could ever love was Louis Bonaparte.

Hortense was appalled. If only Émilie had spoken earlier! She, Hortense, would have appealed to her mother, her kind, good mother, who would never have allowed Émilie to be married against her will. The swiftness, the inevitability, with which Émilie's fate had been settled to suit Napoleon's purposes made Hortense think of her own marriage, which might take place in the not too distant future. How terrible it would be to find herself married to a man she did not love!

V

TROJAN RETURN

NEITHER Joséphine nor Napoleon saw Émilie de Beauharnais married. They had already left for Provence. On May 19, 1798, the Egyptian Expeditionary Force sailed from Toulon. Joséphine watched the fleet fade into the blue of the Mediterranean. She had promised to join her husband within two months. This time she intended to keep her word, but while waiting to hear further from Napoleon, she went to Plombières, a spa in the Vosges mountains, the waters of which were supposed to have a rejuvenating effect upon the female genital organs.

When she returned to Paris, later in the summer, she learned that a voyage to Egypt was no longer feasible. The French army had captured the island of Malta on its way to Alexandria. Alexandria and Cairo had been taken, Syria invaded less successfully. Plague had broken out among the troops. Meanwhile, the French fleet was defeated by Lord Nelson at Abukir, at the mouth of the Nile. After August 1st, it would have been a major undertaking to send reinforcements to Egypt, and even communication was difficult and dangerous.

But the French public in general knew little of this. Only the most rosy reports found their way home. Joséphine took up her life where she had left it. She went about in society; she saw much of Barras and much also of Louis Hippolyte Charles, the young lieutenant who had been one of her party when she journeyed to Italy in 1797. Charles was no longer a lieutenant; he was now connected with a firm that sold supplies to the army, and Joséphine did all that she could to throw business in his way.

She was delighted with, she was bewitched by Hippolyte Charles! He was nine years younger than she, a droll little jackanapes of a playboy, who was famous for his puns, his absurd jokes, and his gymnastics. He could walk on his hands, he could imitate a number of different dialects, and he sometimes came to call on Joséphine in disguise. Now he was a roaring, boastful Gascon; now he was a creole lady, mincing along in a skirt and wearing a turban. Joséphine laughed until she cried, until she had to cover her mouth with her handkerchief to hide her unsightly smile.

She did not know that Hippolyte Charles was being spoken of in Egypt—though she might have guessed. Napoleon's jealousy was first aroused in Italy, when she delayed so long in coming. Soon after her arrival, he sent Lieutenant Charles away from Milan and ultimately dismissed him from the army. Was it Pauline who had hinted that Charles was her sister-in-law's lover? Or was it General Leclerc, Pauline's husband, who had gone with Napoleon to Egypt? There were other officers also, allies of the Bonaparte clan, who were now closely in contact with Joséphine's husband.

At the end of July two letters concerning her were being written on the farther shore of the Mediterranean. Napoleon was telling his brother Joseph, in whose hands he had left all of his business affairs, that he might be home in two months, that he wanted Joseph to buy him a house in the country near Paris or in Burgundy, to which he could retire. He was sick of glory, he was sick of the entire human race, and, at twenty-nine, felt that life had nothing more to offer. Joséphine was not mentioned by name, but Napoleon spoke darkly of "a great domestic sorrow" and of "a veil that had been rent asunder."

At the same time Eugène de Beauharnais was writing to his

mother. Eugène had matured greatly during the past two years, keeping modestly in the background and serving his stepfather well. At Giza, where Eugène was writing to Joséphine on July 27, 1798, he had overheard fragments of a conversation between Napoleon and three of his generals, the gist of which was that Charles had traveled with Joséphine on her way back to France from Italy and that he was with her now. She had been seen at the opera with him recently in an inconspicuous upper box; he had also given her a little dog to replace Fortuné, who had died an untimely death at Mombello.

"That is all that I was able to gather in the few broken words that I heard. . . . You must know, *maman*, that I don't believe any of it, but what is certain is that the General is deeply stirred. He has been doubly kind to me, however. He seems to want to say by his actions that children are not responsible for their mother's deeds. Your son likes to believe that all of this is just gossip manufactured by your enemies; he loves you nonetheless and longs to embrace you."

Neither of these letters reached their destination. The ships that carried them were taken by the British, and Joséphine continued on her way unwarned.

As the months slipped by, she and others began to think that this might be a second Trojan War, that Napoleon might not be seen again in France for years. As far as the Directory was concerned, it was glad to be rid of him and his popularity, but soon after his departure there was need for his military magic. In the autumn of 1798, a new anti-French coalition was formed, including England, Austria, Russia, Portugal, Naples, and Turkey. Fighting broke out again along the Rhine and in Italy.

There were domestic difficulties as well, a growing hostility between the executive and the legislative branches of the government, as represented by the Assembly of Ancients and the Assembly of the Five Hundred. Price controls had been removed, and the country as a whole was being ruined by inflation. The exchequer was forever empty, since no one who had a friend at the Luxembourg bothered to pay taxes. This was an era of shameless graft and grab, the deputies in the Assembly acting openly as agents for business firms, such as that of the *Compagnie Bodin,* the firm to which Joséphine's friend, Hippolyte Charles, belonged.

For Charles's sake and for her own, Joséphine kept in close touch with the Directors. She pursued Barras with requests, and finding him a trifle cool to her demands cultivated his colleagues. These men represented power, and if Napoleon should die in Egypt— that possibility must be considered—Joséphine would need powerful protection from her enemies, the Bonapartes. Except for Caroline and Jérôme at Saint-Germain, she saw little of the family. Madame Mère, who had set up joint housekeeping with her brother Abbé Fesch, would sometimes receive her, but when Joséphine asked the others to dinner they always refused. Joséphine had all the less reason to love her in-laws, because she was dependent upon them financially.

Before leaving, Napoleon had arranged with Joseph for his wife to be paid a generous allowance, but a generous allowance was all too little for a woman who had a compulsive urge to buy anything that tickled her fancy, and who had never really learned to count. Joséphine was still being pursued for debts that antedated her marriage. It was hard for her even to find the ready money for Hortense's school expenses.

What was more, she wanted to buy a house of her own in the country. Joseph and Lucien Bonaparte, dipping into the family fund, had bought houses in Paris and magnificent estates near the city. The place that Joséphine had set her heart upon was on a much more modest scale. It was less than ten miles from Paris, on a lonely highroad that led toward Saint-Germain. The early seventeenth-century house was in poor repair, but Joséphine could see that it had infinite possibilities for enlargement and remodeling; in its grounds she could create a beautiful flower garden.

In February of 1799, Joséphine borrowed enough money from a banker to make the first down payment on the purchase of La Malmaison. In April she moved in. That spring and summer Hortense came occasionally from Saint-Germain to spend a day with her mother, but when Hortense was absent, there was a much more constant visitor, one who would always disappear if other guests arrived unexpectedly. Neighbors would sometimes see the flutter of a woman's white dress, as Joséphine walked in the evening through the shrubbery, arm in arm with Hippolyte Charles.

Absorbed in her new possession and her new infatuation, Joséphine paid little heed to the crisis that was developing in France. Not since the fall of the monarchy had the Republic been so threatened. There was a royalist revolt in Brittany, there was stalemate on the Rhine, and all of Italy had been lost to the French. Napoleon, who had received no dispatches from Paris since March, learned of his country's plight from reading English newspapers. He handed over his command in Egypt to General Jean Baptiste Kléber, and set out for France.

He escaped the English cruisers that were patroling the Mediterranean. After a long, roundabout voyage, he landed on October 11th at Fréjus, where he was received with rapture as one who had risen from the dead. On his way north, he was accompanied as far as Aix by a torch-light procession that symbolized the return of a hero who was bringing light to a dark land.

Josephine was back in town and was dining with one of the Directors at the Luxembourg when the news reached Paris. She left immediately for the house in the rue de la Victoire and then set off at once to meet her husband. She knew that her brothers-in-law would also be on the road. It was absolutely necessary that she should reach Napoleon before his mind had been poisoned against her. She made a detour to Saint-Germain to pick up Hortense, who might be useful as a buffer between her and Napoleon's wrath.

回

There were two routes that one could take south. Joséphine chose the route that led through Burgundy. She and Hortense traveled fast to Lyons. There they learned that the race had been lost, that they should have gone the other way. Napoleon had already passed through the city. His brothers had met him and had

been with him in Paris for three days, when Joséphine's carriage
once more rolled down the rue de la Victoire.

It was late at night, but lights still burned in Joséphine's house.
She hurried in and ran upstairs to her bedroom. She found it
empty. The door of Napoleon's study across the way was locked.
She knocked, at first gently, then more loudly, calling to her husband, begging him to let her in. There was no answer. She began
to sob—still no answer. For a very long time, there was no sound
in the house but a woman's hysterical weeping.

At last, after an hour or more, Joséphine had worn herself out
and was ready to give up, but her lady's maid, who had followed
her up the stairs, and who, perhaps, had had experience of such a
situation before, told her that she must persist; it was now or
never. Joséphine must send for her son and daughter to see if they
could coax the General out of his fortress.

Hortense and Eugène were summoned. Eugène knew the whole
story, but Hortense, who had been told nothing and was bewildered
by this fantastic end of their swift flight to Lyons and back, could
only guess the reason for her mother's despair. It was still impossible for her to think that her mother could do anything that was
wrong. She herself began to cry, as she beat on the door and begged
her stepfather not to torment them all so cruelly.

The door opened. Years later, Napoleon was to say that it was
the thought of Hortense and Eugène that reconciled him to the wife
whom he had intended to divorce even before he took ship to
France, "but what could I do? . . . I was not given a heart for nothing! . . . Were they to be the victims of their mother's evil conduct?"

At the time, however, he said nothing. As soon as the door was
ajar, Joséphine, who had started to go downstairs again, slow and
heavy footed with defeat, turned back. Another moment and she
had slipped agilely across the threshold; she had flung her arms
about her husband's neck and pressed her mouth to his. Once more
the door was closed.

When Lucien Bonaparte called, early the following morning, to

see his brother on business, he was ushered up to the room where
Napoleon and Joséphine were still in bed together. This was
enough to let the Bonapartes know that their well-planned, well-
fought campaign to oust Joséphine had failed. Their vendetta with
her was not yet over.

But for the moment it could be laid aside; there were other
battles to be won. Joseph and Lucien were often closeted with Napoleon during the next three weeks. He conferred also with leaders
of the army and leaders of the state, the state that was tottering
toward its end. If France was to be saved—and Napoleon felt that
it was written in his stars for him to save it—a new order must be
instituted. He preferred that it should have a show of legitimacy.

Two of the five Directors were willing to coöperate by resigning
and calling for a new constitution. Barras, surly at the thought of
being ridden down by the man whom he had helped into the saddle,
delayed for some time and then followed suit. A guard was set over
the remaining executives to see that they did nothing desperate.

There yet remained the two assemblies to be dealt with, the Assembly of Ancients and the Assembly of the Five Hundred, both of
which were temporarily in session at the Palace of Saint-Cloud outside of Paris. Here, Lucien could play an important role, for he was
President of the Five Hundred.

On the 9th of November, the 18th Brumaire, the Year VII of
the Republic, Napoleon rode out on horseback to Saint-Cloud. He
found that a company of grenadiers had been stationed in the
courtyard. His first visit was to the Ancients. Nervous at finding
himself facing a parliamentary group, he harangued them as he
might have harangued his troops. He had meant to conclude his
address with an oratorical flourish, saying that they should put
their trust in him because he came to them "accompanied by the
God of War and the God of Fortune." Instead his tongue slipped,
and he found himself saying that he *was* the God of War, he *was*
the God of Fortune. There was no applause. His speech was received with groans and murmurs throughout.

Napoleon went next to the glass-roofed orangery of the palace, where were seated the Five Hundred, costumed in flowing cloaks that suggested Roman togas. As he entered, with a bodyguard of four, there was instant hubbub and shouts of "Dictator—down with the dictator! Outlaw—outlaw!"

This was the cry that had brought Robespierre tumbling down to his death in the Convention. The one thing that Napoleon feared and hated was disorder. He tried to speak, stammered, and, as several of the deputies rushed at him in their flapping gowns, his companions closed about him and all but dragged him from the room.

It was Lucien who was man of the hour. Lucien refused violently to put the motion of outlawry to the vote. He resigned as chairman, and tearing off his toga rushed from the council chamber. In the courtyard, he leaped on the back of a horse, and thus raised above the crowd roared at the troops to take action against the "brigands" within, "the traitors who were in the pay of England." Brandishing a sword, Lucien vowed that he would stab his brother to the heart, if Napoleon infringed in any way the liberties of France.

An order was given: "Grenadiers—advance! Drummers— sound the charge! Long live the Republic! Long live Bonaparte!"

With fixed bayonets, to the deafening clatter of the drums, the soldiers, who were supposed to guard the Assembly, tramped into the orangery. The Five Hundred rose as a man and fled, flitting off among the orange trees, some of them dropping their togas behind them. A coup d'etat had after all been necessary to bring Napoleon to supreme command in the nation.

Late that same night, a quartet of husky grenadiers was thundering at the door of the Hôtel de Rohan in Saint-Germain, and, much to the annoyance of Madame Campan, waking everyone, teachers and pupils, to hear the news. The soldiers had been sent by General Joachim Murat, the young man who was in love with Caroline Bonaparte, whom she wanted to marry and who wanted to marry her. That afternoon, Murat had given the order to advance and had led the bloodless march of the troops at Saint-Cloud.

VI

THE MARRIAGE MARKET

Six weeks after the coup d'état of Brumaire, yet another constitution had been written and was in force. General Bonaparte had become the First Consul of the French Republic, more truly an uncrowned king of France than Barras had ever been. It was now time for his sister and stepdaughter to leave the National Institution for the Education of Young Women and to live under his jurisdiction. Madame Campan was not sorry, perhaps, to part with Caroline, but she was sad at the thought of losing her dear Hortense, who had been with her almost constantly, winter and summer, for the past four years. Hortense would be seventeen her next birthday. At that age her mother, Joséphine, was married and well on the way to motherhood.

"Work hard," Madame Campan always said, in bidding goodbye to her pupils. "Don't think that your education is over now. If you want to be an accomplished woman, you must study for the rest of your days."

Hortense had become so accustomed to school life that she found it hard to adapt herself to the routine of the Luxembourg Palace, which was to be her home for the next few months. She tried to devote her mornings to music and painting, her favorite

subjects at Saint-Germain, and was at work on a portrait of Eugène and one, for Madame Campan, of Roustan, a Mameluke
whom Bonaparte had brought home with him from Egypt to be
his personal bodyguard. Hortense was constantly being interrupted, however, by calls to come down to her mother's sitting
room.

Joséphine's salon was crowded nowadays with members of the
old nobility, who looked upon her as their natural protector. They
all had friends in exile who were anxious to return to France. Many
of those whom Joséphine helped claimed relationship. Hortense
was amazed by the number of cousins of whom she had never
heard, and whom she now met for the first time. But the visitors her
mother really wanted her to meet were all of them young men.
Some of them had ringing names, famous in the history of France,
but Hortense, in spite of her royalist sympathies, fancied none of
them in particular. There was safety as yet, she found, in numbers.
At a great ball given by one of the nobility, one of the few who
could afford such luxuries, Hortense danced until dawn with five
partners, all of whom, she had been told by her mother, would have
liked to be her partner for life.

Hortense had never really abandoned the scheme she had once
solemnly discussed with her school chum, Adèle Auguié, of uniting
love with marriage. A happy ending to Caroline's romance with
Joachim Murat gave her encouragement. For various reasons Napoleon was dissatisfied with the match, but at a family meeting,
held on January 18, 1800, to discuss the matter—all Bonapartes
present—Joséphine championed Murat so strongly that Napoleon
gave his consent and scrawled his name at the bottom of the marriage contract. He did not choose, however, to be present at the
ceremony that took place before a magistrate two days later at
Joseph's country house at Mortefontaine. He complained to
Madame Campan that any plans he might have made for Caroline
and his other sisters had all been spoiled by "silly little love affairs."

"I hope at least this one," he said, indicating Hortense by a nod, "will let herself be married properly."

In February, the First Consul and his family left the Luxembourg and went to live on an even larger scale in the Tuileries, which had been renamed "The Palace of the Government." There everything was subject to the great volume of business that passed through Napoleon's hands. He had all the dire work of the Directory to undo. He aimed to purify government, to restore prosperity, to draw up a code of laws, to devise an efficient administrative system, and to institute a Legion of Honor to reward the distinguished citizens of France, all of this while preparing his armies to take the field against the coalition.

Napoleon's capacity for work was limitless. In the morning his secretary, Monsieur Bourrienne, came to his bedside with dispatches that might have arrived during the night. While Napoleon steamed in his bathtub, the secretary read him the newspapers and made notes for the day's correspondence. This process was continued while the Consul was being shaved by his valet, sometimes jerking his head about so violently, as he talked, that his cheek was nicked by the razor. Meals were eaten hastily and often in complete silence. Lights burned in Napoleon's study, on an upper floor of the palace, until far into the night.

This grueling regime was often punctuated by playful week ends at La Malmaison. Napoleon had fallen in love with the little estate that Joséphine had bought. He amused himself by calculating, to the last handful of grain and the last hen's egg, the income he could hope to receive from the farm, but he nevertheless spent lavish sums to transform it into a miniature park and palace. The stables and barns attached to the house were torn down and rebuilt at a distance. A wing was added here, a second story there. Conservatories and greenhouses were built, where Joséphine could grow under glass the exotic flowers that she loved, while an enchanting garden in the informal English style began to take shape.

Artists, scientific men, and even members of the theatrical profession were entertained at La Malmaison. Over week ends the house was crowded with young people. Napoleon brought members of his military staff; Hortense invited her school friends, in particular Adèle Auguié and Adèle's two sisters, Antoinette and Eglé. There were horses to ride; and a favorite outdoor sport in which all, including the master, participated was a game of Prisoner's Base. Napoleon was a very poor runner and was quite apt to fall down. Hortense was so fleet-footed that she was nick-named Atalanta, and she was always one of the first to be chosen when it came to taking sides.

Play acting was another diversion in which she shone. Her step-father refused to appear behind the footlights, but he was an enthusiastic member of the audience, quick to laugh and applaud, quick to criticize. He provided all the costumes, gave beautifully bound copies of the plays to each of the cast, and had one of the best actors from the Comédie Française come down to coach rehearsals. The director would cry, "Heat it up, heat it up," if he thought the action was too languid. Hortense played the lead as Rosine in *The Barber of Seville*, but she was versatile enough to play the character parts of old women as well.

Hortense was blissfully happy at La Malmaison; a return to Paris was a return to prison. There, there were too many restrictions and too little to do, too much talk of marriage and too little opportunity for intimacy with anyone, male or female. Hortense would have liked to go back to school, and actually got permission to spend a week at Saint-Germain, hoping that she would be allowed to stay at least until the end of the term. She was aware, however, that childhood was at an end and that the heavy hand of authority hung over her. Napoleon, who in the country was a gay companion, was often a despot and a drill sergeant in the Tuileries.

"Is that dress muslin?" he would ask. If the answer was yes, he would rip the dress to pieces with his own hands, for he was trying to encourage a revival of the silk trade at Lyon and had forbidden anything but silk or satin to his womenfolk.

Once, Hortense met him in a corridor. Napoleon was frowning. "You are studying English?" he asked.

Hortense had to admit that she was. If she couldn't go back to school, she could at least try Madame Campan's formula for becoming "an accomplished woman."

"Dismiss your teacher," Napoleon said curtly.

"But he seems very good to me," Hortense protested.

"I tell you to dismiss him. He's a spy."

"Oh, but that can't be true!"

"Do as I say. You are nothing but a child and do not understand these things."

On another occasion, when Hortense was talking confidentially to Eugène about marriage, the kind of marriage that she longed for, her brother gave her a warning that she hardly needed.

"Hortense, my dear," Eugène said, "don't fool yourself with false illusions. The higher we rise, the less freedom we have to do as we like. I can see that you will have to marry as the First Consul wishes, perhaps to suit his political plans. Forget your dreams of an impossible bliss."

This seemed such a shrewd prediction and such sound advice that Hortense was depressed for days. She did not guess that a husband would soon be selected for her, not by her stepfather, but by her mother.

॥

Since that night in October of 1799 when she came home to the rue de la Victoire and found a door locked against her, Joséphine had walked very warily. There had been no reproaches; Napoleon had even paid most of her debts—and might have paid them all, if Joséphine could have brought herself to own up to more than half of the amount that was actually due. She was glad that the past could be buried so easily. It made her tremble to think how close she had come to catastrophe.

As soon as Hippolyte Charles was banished from her life, along with Barras, Madame Tallien, and the rest of the Directory crew, Joséphine gracefully reassumed her role of the devoted homemaker who lives only to make her husband happy. She could be of real service to Napoleon now as a hostess, saying gracious and soothing things, not only to visiting aristocrats, but to ministers of state, foreign ministers, and to many humble folk as well: the bores, the cranks, the spongers, whom Napoleon was too busy to see or too impatient to handle gently. He, though less demanding physically, was still her lover. He would sometimes steal a moment from his work and would run downstairs to her dressing room to discover what dress she had chosen for the day, or to consider as seriously, as though it were a matter of prime importance, the way in which her hair was being arranged.

Women, Napoleon thought, should devote all their energies to making themselves beautiful, or else to knitting or embroidery; they should keep their pretty fingers out of politics. Nonchalant though she appeared, Joséphine nevertheless kept an anxious eye upon events as they developed. Where was all of this grandeur and high authority to end? The move to the Tuileries had hardly taken place, when a letter came from the Comte de Provence, the elder of Louis XVI's two brothers and his legal heir, suggesting that Bonaparte should restore a Bourbon to the throne and be richly rewarded for his services. This would have satisfied Joséphine completely. She could count at least on being a duchess or the wife of a Constable of France. The letter, however, lay unanswered for many months. When at last Louis XVIII, as he now styled himself, was told that he could only hope to enter France over "a hundred thousand corpses" Napoleon's position had strengthened immeasurably.

In March of 1800, the First Consul ordered his secretary to unroll a big map of Italy and hovered above it, puncturing it here and there with pins, some black, some red. In May, he led his army through the Saint Bernard Pass in the Alps, to fall unexpectedly upon the Austrians and cut off their lines of communication. The decisive battle of the campaign was fought at Marengo, and might have been a defeat except for a daring cavalry charge, led by General François Kellermann. Napoleon, by the skillful use of flattery, plus a few minor concessions, persuaded the Russian

Emperor Paul to withdraw from the Coalition, which collapsed after yet another victory, that of Hohenlinden in Bavaria. Negotiations for peace—there had been no lasting peace for France in the past ten years—were begun. The nation went wild with enthusiasm and with love for General Bonaparte. There were great popular demonstrations after his return from Italy, and later, in December, after Napoleon had had a narrow escape from assassination.

On the evening of December 24, 1800, there was to be a performance of Haydn's oratorio, *The Creation*, at the Opera House. Joséphine was anxious to go, and persuaded Napoleon to take the evening from his work for a little relaxation. He was in the first carriage to leave the Tuileries. It had just passed through the rue Saint Nicaise when a keg of gunpowder exploded in its rear, wrecking the surrounding buildings and killing more than a dozen people.

The second carriage, in which Joséphine, Hortense, and Caroline Murat were riding, would have been caught by the blast, full force, if there hadn't been a delay in starting from the palace. At the last moment, Joséphine's escort criticized the shawl that she was wearing, and she went back to change it. The carriage was near enough to the explosion, however, to be lifted for a moment from the ground. Its windows shattered; Hortense's hand was cut by a flying fragment of glass. Joséphine was hysterical, as the frightened horses wheeled about and dashed back to the Tuileries. Caroline Murat, who was pregnant and whose first baby was born a few weeks later, behaved with the greatest coolness, as did also Napoleon, when he discovered that all of his party were unhurt.

"What is the matter with you? What happened? That? Why that was only an accident!" he said to Joséphine, as, still white and trembling, she arrived at the Opera House. But to one of his aides Napoleon said grimly, as he entered his box, "Those rascals were trying to blow me sky high—go get me a libretto of the concert."

Napoleon was certain that this attempt upon his life was the work of ultra-republicans, and arbitrarily ordered one hundred and thirty Jacobins to be deported to French Guiana. Six weeks later, his Minister of Police, Joseph Fouché, himself an ex-Jacobin, brought positive proof that the conspirators were royalist fanatics. This was disconcerting news for Joséphine, who had so many royalist connections and who was forever being approached in connection with the movement to restore the Bourbons. The excitement over the gunpowder plot brought into the open a question that deeply concerned her, the question of who would succeed Bonaparte in case of his death, or at the end of his term of office, which was presently extended to a ten-year period.

With his Corsican background, it was to be expected that Napoleon would designate one of his brothers. But which of the three would he choose—Joseph, Lucien, or Louis? (Jérôme was still too young to be considered seriously.) The one whom Joséphine feared the most was Lucien, the most fiery, the most deeply concerned with politics. Though only twenty-five, Lucien had been appointed Minister of the Interior, a reward for the stout assist he had given to the coup d'état at Saint-Cloud. At the time of the assassination attempt, however, Lucien was out of office and had been sent as Ambassador to Spain. He had distributed through his department a pamphlet entitled *A Parallel between Caesar, Cromwell and Bonaparte* that dealt directly with the succession issue. Napoleon, thinking that the time was not yet ripe for such plain speaking, was enraged. Lucien's embassy to Spain was, in effect, a trip to Coventry.

With Lucien out of the running—and Joséphine was thankful for that—there remained only two candidates. Joseph, the oldest of the Bonapartes, had been heaped with honors, was a Councilor of State, and was to be Napoleon's representative at the peace treaties with Austria and England; but Joseph was an indolent man, who preferred entertaining writers and artists to working long hours at his desk. He, also, had had no military experience. Louis, on the other hand, had this qualification: He had recently been promoted to be a colonel in command of a regiment of dragoons. What was more, Louis was Napoleon's favorite, the boy whom he had brought from Corsica to France to educate, who, almost a son to Napoleon, had shared his years of poverty and insecurity.

From Joséphine's point of view, Louis seemed far less obnoxious than his brothers, though she knew him far less well. He had always been courteous; he had shown her no overt hostility; the worst that she could find to say of him was that he had tended to ignore her. If Louis should ever come to be the ruler of France, Joséphine wanted him to give her special consideration. In any case, she wanted him as an ally, not in the unpredictable future, but now in the family squabbles that seemed so inevitable in the Bonaparte clan.

So why not Louis for a son-in-law?

From the moment when Hortense reached puberty, Joséphine had pondered how she could marry her daughter with the greatest advantage to Hortense and to herself. When Napoleon was in Egypt, perhaps never to return, she had toyed with the idea of a match with a Director's son; at that time there were two to choose from. After the coup d'état of Brumaire, a noble alliance seemed to be the safest course. But now, everything pointed to a Bonaparte, the only Bonaparte who was available.

And there was yet another angle to this question of a successor. When Joséphine was a young girl and was going to France to be married to Alexandre de Beauharnais, a Negro fortuneteller in Martinique told her that she would be married twice, and the second time she would be a queen—"and more than queen." Joséphine once came into Napoleon's study, and, perching herself on his knee, putting her arms about his neck to stroke his hair, whispered in his ear, "Please, Bonaparte, don't make yourself a king. It's that wicked Lucien who is egging you on. Don't listen to him, please!"

Little though she wanted her husband to establish a new dynasty in France, it was already being said that this was his intention, in which case he would want a son of his loins to follow after him. In the year that followed the gunpowder explosion in the rue Saint Nicaise, Joséphine, who had reached the menopause, was under a doctor's care, and made a second visit to the fertilizing waters of Plombières. At the same time, she worked steadily and subtly to bring about a marriage between Hortense and Louis Bonaparte. From the first she saw that this might take a good deal of skilled diplomacy.

VII

THE SACRIFICE

NAPOLEON'S sense of humor was aggressive. He liked to tease, and when he had scored his point, he would pinch the ears of his victim. He pinched the ears of his valet and also the ears of his generals. He sometimes pinched Hortense's ears until she was ready to scream.

One evening, in the spring of 1801, he entered the salon where she and others were waiting for his arrival and for dinner to be announced; he said in a low, conspiratorial voice to Hortense, "We have just been to your bedroom, your mother and I. We have ransacked everything and have read all your letters. How wonderful it must be to get so many beautiful declarations of love!"

This was a threadbare joke—Napoleon had perpetrated it more than once—but instead of Hortense laughing, or making the sort of spirited counterattack that she knew would amuse her stepfather, she said nothing. The color in her cheeks had deepened. A moment later she left the room.

Hortense ran down to the small suite she occupied on the ground floor of the palace, that consisted only of a bedroom and what had once been a tiny oratory, where she stored her painting material. There was no sign of anything having been disturbed. She opened her desk and found in it a letter she had received only the day before. Its seal had not yet been broken.

The day before, having mislaid a book, Hortense went to look for it in one of the large reception rooms. She found there one of her stepfather's young staff officers, Colonel Duroc. Duroc helped her to hunt for her book, found it with surprising ease, and presented it to her. He told her that he had come to say good-bye. He was about to leave for Berlin, on his way to Russia. The First Consul was sending him to congratulate a new Czar, Alexander I, on his accession to the throne, Alexander's father, Paul, whom Napoleon had been so successful in detaching from the Coalition, having died suddenly and mysteriously in March. When she was back in her room, Hortense opened her book and found in it a letter addressed to her in Duroc's handwriting.

A letter from man to maiden, delivered surreptitiously—tossed in at a window, hidden in a bunch of flowers or in a book—this was a romantic situation often treated in the novels that Hortense had read. It was the subject of many a pretty picture she had seen. She knew that she should receive no communication of any kind from a suitor without her parents' permission, and did not question their right to rummage in her desk, but how she longed to open that letter! It took a great deal of determination to resist her curiosity, for she had come to be very much interested in Colonel Duroc, who had often been a week-end guest at La Malmaison.

There, where everything was so relaxed and so informal, Napoleon, after dinner, would give his arm to Joséphine, and they would go off for a long walk about the estate. Hortense would often be left alone to entertain a group of young men, some of them perhaps a little uncouth, who were veterans of Napoleon's campaigns in Italy or Egypt. They were always on their very best behavior with her; she was the daughter of their general, before whom they stood, quite literally, in awe.

Hortense, who had never suffered seriously from bashfulness and who had all of her mother's social techniques at her fingertips, put the young warriors at their ease by encouraging them to talk about their adventures in foreign lands. They came to confide in her and to ask her advice, as though she were much older and wiser than they. Several of them asked her to find them wives among her school friends. One youth insisted that she should inspect the girl selected for him by his family before he found himself entangled in an engagement.

Only Colonel Duroc stood somewhat apart from the circle surrounding Hortense. She liked him all the better for that! He seemed more mature than the others, more purposeful. Behind his dignified reserve she sensed his watchfulness, his admiration. She admired him also. Here was somebody, she thought, whom she might really come to love.

Suddenly the whole problem of marriage seemed to Hortense to have been simplified. She might attain what Eugène had called "an impossible bliss," since Napoleon, who had married Pauline to General Leclerc and Caroline to General Murat, might not object to mating her with yet another of his officers. She knew that he thought very highly of Duroc. The fact that Duroc was being sent to Moscow was proof of that.

Hortense allowed herself to dream pleasant dreams and to put off deciding what she should do with her billet-doux, until Napoleon's heavy-footed witticism startled her and sent her flying to her bedroom. Having satisfied herself that Duroc's letter was still there and still unopened, Hortense returned to the salon.

Napoleon came quickly to her side. "Then it is true?" he asked in surprise. "You *do* have secrets? You ran away so quickly!"

Hortense was glad that she did not have to answer; at that moment the great doors of the salon were thrown open, and the march to the dining room began.

Later, when she was going to bed, Hortense was visited by Joséphine. Hortense produced the letter and told her mother exactly what had happened. There was a painful scene. All Hortense's hopes were washed away in the gentle flow of Joséphine's tears. Joséphine would not hear of Duroc as a suitor for her daughter. She had nothing to say against him, except that he was not well

born and that he had not yet distinguished himself in any way.
Hortense could expect a much, much better alliance than this.

"I could never get used to hearing you called Madame Duroc,"
Joséphine said between her sobs. "Are you really in love with
him? I would be heartbroken if you were!"

The letter was confiscated and Hortense was assured that no one
would read it now. It would be sent back, just as it was, intact,
to its author in Berlin.

In the weeks that followed, Hortense found a little cold comfort in telling herself that she was not completely heartbroken.
Colonel Duroc might not have lived up to all of her expectations;
perhaps this had been only an *amourette*, "a silly little love affair,"
to quote her stepfather's phrase. Hortense realized, however, that
things could not be allowed to drift indefinitely. Soon a serious
offer would be made that must be seriously considered.

In July, she went with her mother to Plombières for a month.
Hortense knew—everyone in the palace knew—the importance to
Joséphine of this cure. There were some who said that Napoleon
was the one who was sterile, but there were many others who
urged him to divorce Joséphine and to take a younger wife, who
would be more likely to give him a child. While Hortense and her
mother were taking the waters, an agreement, long in the making,
was signed with the Vatican, the Concordat of 1801, that reëstab-
lished officially the Catholic religion in France; thus far, under
the Republic, it had been allowed to exist, if at all, only on suf-
ferance. Since Joséphine had been married by a mayor of Paris
and not by a priest, she was, in the eyes of the church, only a
concubine.

What gave Joséphine an even greater feeling of insecurity was
that Lucien—that wicked Lucien—when he returned from Spain,
reported that a Spanish infanta might be available as a wife for
the First Consul. Lucien infuriated Joséphine by blandly suggesting, just before she left for Plombières, that, if the waters took
effect, she should have a baby by her husband, and if that was

impossible by another man. Then she and Napoleon could adopt it and thus settle the question of succession.

Was it Lucien's insult that put into Joséphine's mouth the argument that she used so effectively after her return from the mountains? She told Napoleon over and over that they must face the fact of their childlessness. They should adopt an heir; not a grown man, whom Napoleon might outlive, but an infant; not a bastard, but a Bonaparte, the son that Hortense would surely bear if she married Louis.

Joséphine realized that this was not quite the line to take with the prospective father, who might have ambitions of his own. With him, she must rely more on Hortense's charms and on Louis' seeing how advantageous it would be to do as she and Napoleon wished. Thus far she had not been able to work upon Louis directly. For the past six months he had been traveling in Germany and had been with his regiment at Bordeaux or in Spain. When Joséphine returned in August to La Malmaison, however, she found him there, and far less difficult to win over than she had feared. He would have to stand firm, she knew, against a great deal of adverse pressure from his family.

When it came to telling Hortense what lay in store for her, Joséphine's heart failed her. She preferred to have another speak the first word, just as once she had preferred to have Madame Campan tell Hortense of her own marriage to General Bonaparte.

In the complexity of palace politics, Monsieur Bourrienne, Napoleon's secretary, was one of Joséphine's allies. He was a friend also of Hortense, a fellow actor in the Malmaison troupe. Though he was married, over thirty, and thus in Hortense's eyes "of a certain age," he had once made an attempt, that was firmly frustrated, to make love to her. She was surprised, therefore, and a little on her guard when Bourrienne asked for a private interview and told her that she would soon receive an offer of marriage from Louis Bonaparte. Bourrienne said that it was her duty to accept, a duty not only to her parents, and especially to her mother, but a duty to her country.

Louis Bonaparte! Hortense had never thought of Louis except
as a member of the Clan, less flamboyant and more mannerly than
the rest, and less often seen, since, even when in Paris, Louis kept
much to himself. Though he occasionally came to La Malmaison
for theatricals, Hortense had rarely come in contact with him
since the days when he used to visit Caroline at Saint-Germain—
and then he was in love with her cousin, Émilie de Beauharnais.
After Napoleon became First Consul, Émilie asked him for permission to get a divorce from her husband, so that she might
marry Louis. The permission was, of course, refused. Hortense
had heard that Louis, when consulted, said that he was no longer
interested in Émilie, because she had recently had an attack of
smallpox that disfigured her. This, as well as the fact that Hortense found Louis neither sympathetic nor attractive, had turned
her against him.

In the first moment of her bewilderment and recoil, Hortense
felt that she must get help from someone, but from whom? Her
mother? Bourrienne had emphasized that he was speaking as Joséphine wished. From Eugène? Eugène was far away on military
duty. It never occurred to Hortense that she might turn to Napoleon for support; his word represented for her inflexible law.

Hortense told Bourrienne that she could not give an answer
now. She must have at least a week to consider. During that week,
and later still, she knew no peace. The battle joined, Joséphine
fought hard for victory. Hortense's room at the Tuileries was
next to hers. She was forever at her daughter's side with her gentle
voice, her caresses, and her tears. What she said once she said
many times: "You know, my darling, that all the Bonapartes hate
me. They want to separate me from your stepfather. They want
him to divorce me. And you, only you, can save me. The day when
you become Madame Louis, they will no longer dare to do anything against me."

Madame Campan, alerted by Joséphine, helped to wear down
Hortense's resistance. Ever since parting, teacher and pupil had
carried on a constant correspondence. Madame Campan now wrote

"her dear angel" a letter that was a defense of the French marriage system, indeed of the whole philosophy that had dominated the eighteenth century, the philosophy that sees reason, and only reason, as the guide to life. Young people were too often swayed by emotion, Madame Campan said, to choose wisely. In marriage, love was a passing illusion. When it was gone, there was nothing left—no affection, no community of interest—to take its place. Madame Campan confessed that she herself had once been deeply in love with a man of whom her relatives did not approve. She listened to their advice, dismissed her suitor, and married as they saw fit. No two people could have been happier together than she and her husband. Madame Campan came to see Hortense and to repeat her arguments in person.

In September, there was a ball at La Malmaison, and Louis, who had been mercifully absent during Hortense's ordeal, was present. In the course of the evening, prompted by Joséphine, he asked Hortense to be his wife.

The engagement was announced in October. There were congratulations for the fiancée and, more appropriately, for the fiancée's mother. Hortense's friends, the young officers, told her how glad they were that she was marrying a soldier and a Frenchman. Now they could be sure that she would stay in France. Napoleon was strangely silent, though a few days after the ball he said casually to Hortense, "So Louis is courting you . . . That ought to be just the thing for you, as well as for your mother. I give my consent to the match."

Hortense saw a great deal of Louis during their three month's engagement. They were never alone, however, and had no chance to become better acquainted. She felt that he, too, was living under strain. He told her once that he was afraid that she wouldn't like the quiet of home life, after so much gaiety. She tried to reassure him on that point, but his reply puzzled her, and showed her that they had been talking at cross purposes.

"If popularity hasn't spoiled you," Louis said, "you must be an angel. There can be no middle ground. Either you are all good or all bad."

That same day he slipped into her hand a bulky manuscript, a twenty-page letter that gave a history of his entire love life. There was much in it about his devotion to a woman whom he named only as Sophie, but Émilie de Beauharnais was not even mentioned. Louis asked Hortense for a similar letter in reply, but she, offended by this suggestion that she had had many love affairs, told him coldly that she had nothing to confess.

Before the ball at La Malmaison, Hortense had shed many tears, but now she managed to be calm and was fortified by a sense of virtue. It was Joséphine who wept when Napoleon asked her to name the day for her daughter's wedding. It must take place before he, Napoleon, had to leave for a meeting in Lyon, to settle the affairs of the Cisalpine Republic that had been formed during the first Italian campaign.

On January 3, 1802, the marriage contract was signed. The following day, her wedding day, Hortense was surprised by a visit from her nurse, Madame Rousseau, the foster mother with whom she had spent the first two years of her life. The stout old peasant woman had come from her native village to marvel at the splendors that surrounded her nursling, thinking, no doubt, when Hortense shed a few tears, that this was only girlish shyness at the thought of going to bed so soon with a man. Hortense spent the day in saying good-bye to the servants and distributing most of her jewelry among them. She would have richer jewels now! Napoleon had given her a magnificent set of diamonds.

An elaborate, flower-embroidered wedding gown had been provided by Joséphine, but at the last moment Hortense could not bear to put it on. She didn't want to make herself resplendent; she would wear a plain white dress, a small string of pearls her only ornament. In the evening, the marriage was performed by the Mayor of Paris before all of the Bonaparte family, except Pauline. She had left a few weeks earlier with her husband, General Leclerc, on an expedition to reconquer the rich colony of Santo

Domingo, where a Negro republic had been established by Toussaint L'Ouverture. Eugène was also absent, in Italy. Hortense was glad that he was not there; his silent sympathy would have been a threat to her self control.

At eleven o'clock, the whole party drove to the house in the rue de la Victoire, Joséphine's house, which had been given to Louis and Hortense as a wedding gift. There, the religious ceremony was performed by Cardinal Giovanni Caprara, the papal legate who had come to Paris in connection with the signing of the Concordat. Caroline and Joachim Murat, whose marriage two years earlier had not as yet been blessed by the Church, shared in the Nuptial Mass. Hortense thought how radiant this moment must be for Caroline; she and Joachim were lovers!

In the room that adjoined the salon, the *corbeille de noces*, the traditional Gallic offering of trousseau and jewels from groom to bride, was displayed, spread out, all a-glitter, to be examined and admired. In spite of her fondness for jewelry, Hortense's interest in it was only feigned, so as not to hurt Louis' feelings.

The moment to say good-bye had come. All of the Bonapartes crowded about Hortense. She knew that they all, Madame Bonaparte and Lucien in particular, had opposed the marriage, but the ritual kiss to the member of the Clan could not be shirked. "You will be happy," they cried—it was almost a chorus—"Louis is so good, so gentle!"

Then the door closed upon the wedding guests, and Hortense and Louis, two strangers with everything as yet to learn of one another, were left alone.

PART

II

(January 4, 1802–June 15, 1806)

回口回口回口回口回口回

㺍㺍㺍㺍㺍㺍㺍㺍㺍㺍㺍㺍

VIII

HONEYMOON

EVEN to those who knew him best, Louis Bonaparte was something of an enigma. Napoleon had once said that Louis was the most promising member of his family. That was when the two brothers were living together in the garrison town of Auxonne, Louis, a boy of twelve, fresh from Corsica, Napoleon, a shaveling lieutenant of twenty-one. They shared a garret room, where Louis slept on a mattress laid on the floor. To pare down expenses, Napoleon learned how to cook their food himself and how to patch and darn their clothes.

During the day, while Napoleon was out, Louis was supposed to spend most of his time studying. In the evening, he was tutored in mathematics. If he had failed to do his homework satisfactorily, Napoleon would lock the door of the garret when he left the following morning. Once, when he came home at night and discovered Louis reading a novel, he threw the book out of the window and sent the boy to the guardhouse to sleep on a board and dine on bread and water for forty-eight hours.

Only a strict discipline could make a good soldier, and Louis, who showed a doglike devotion to his severe but prideful elder brother, passed successfully into military school. Later, he fought well and bravely during the first Italian campaign. That year of 1796, however, marked a turning point in Louis' life and a change in his disposition. From having been cheerful and alert, he became morose and gloomy. Though he accepted, as a matter of course, the military promotions that came his way, he seemed to lose all interest in his profession.

Except for attending lectures on science and art while he was in Paris and writing poetry, Louis' chief occupation was his health —or rather lack of health. Though never completely incapacitated, he suffered from vague, multiple complaints, which were sometimes diagnosed as rheumatism and sometimes as muscular atrophy. Each doctor consulted—and Louis consulted many— found a different underlying cause. His symptoms might be due to a slight congenital curvature of the spine, to an overdose of mercury that had been used to cure a syphilis infection contracted at Milan, or else to a head injury, the result of a fall from his horse.

Napoleon, who had little faith in the medical profession, laid Louis' illnesses and his dismal ways to his having read too deeply in the works of Jean Jacques Rousseau, the author whose works had been hurled through the window at Auxonne.

A modern psychiatrist might probe deeper still. Louis had tried to give an honest account of his emotional experiences to Hortense in the long letter that he put into her hand before their marriage, but his self knowledge was then—and would always be—incomplete. Certainly his heart line had followed an unusual course. Louis wrote and published a novel, *Marie, or the Pains of Love*, after his frustrated affair with Émilie de Beauharnais, but even while he was working on it, he was absorbed by a passion for a woman to whom he had never spoken, whose name he did not even know, a young girl whom he saw frequently, walking in the garden of the Tuileries. Was she perhaps the Sophie whom Louis mentioned in his prenuptial confession to his fiancée?

His closest male friendships were not with his military colleagues, but with obscure young men with whom he discussed literary matters and exchanged confidences, demanding their complete loyalty and jealously directing their lives in every particular. Joséphine had perhaps unwittingly put her finger on the mainspring of Louis' character, when she once said that Louis loved Napoleon "as a lover loves his mistress."

Unaware of his deviation from the norm, Louis thought that he could find happiness in marriage. Before the ball at La Malmaison, he consulted Lucien more than once, and when Lucien told him emphatically that he was a fool to marry the daughter of Joséphine, Louis blurted out that he was in love with the girl.

"In love!" Lucien exclaimed impatiently. "Then why the devil did you come to ask my advice? Forget everything that I have said. Marry her, and God help you!"

Hortense, on the other hand, though she sensed Louis' strangeness, thought that at least she could live with him a tranquil life of mutual forebearance. She soon discovered how easily her husband was thrown off balance by what seemed to her the merest trifles.

The day after the wedding, she and Louis went to dine at the Tuileries. Joséphine was still tearful, but Napoleon was in good spirits and made some earthy comments on the married state to Hortense, who sat beside him. His mood changed abruptly when Louis asked Joséphine for a list of the Beauharnais relatives, as he intended to send out announcements of the marriage in her name and in that of his mother.

"What are you meddling with now?" Napoleon asked indignantly. It was he who should send out the announcements, he said. and since this was a marriage of more than private significance, the notices should go to all high state officials and to the ambassadors of foreign countries. "The stupid things you do," Napoleon fumed "fall back on me. You have no business trying to be independent. I won't allow it!"

Hortense felt sorry for her husband's being scolded like a child in her presence, but she felt that there was nothing she could say to help him, and that Louis was unduly upset. On the way home, he said over and over that though Napoleon might be head of state, he was not the head of the Bonaparte family.

A few days later, he vented his irritation on her. Hortense, almost naked, was trying on a corset with the help of her maid, when Louis suddenly entered her dressing room. She instinctively threw a shawl over her bare shoulders. After the maid had left the room, Louis blazed out at her. "Don't you know, madame," he said, "that a married woman should never be prudish with her husband? Don't you care for what the servants think? Now they will go around saying that you do not love me and were forced to marry me."

Three days after the wedding Napoleon and Joséphine left for Lyon, and La Malmaison was put at the disposal of the bride and groom. While they were there, Madame Campan gave a little party for them at Saint-Germain. There was a magic lantern show of drawings that Monsieur Isabey, the art instructor, had made to illustrate Hortense's career at the school. Some of the girls recited couplets that had been written for each of the pictures. Hortense was touched and charmed, but Louis was not amused, and said later that he felt like a fool and would never go again to Saint-Germain. Hortense, though offended, passed over this remark in silence. She was quite unprepared for their next and more serious misunderstanding.

She had invited Adèle Auguié to visit her, and Louis had also invited a young officer in his regiment. The weather was very cold. By day, there were long, exhilarating walks through the snowy woods. The evenings were spent in front of a blazing fire. One evening Louis read aloud to them. The young officer was sitting at a table on which some puzzles were spread out, and seemed to be completely baffled as he tried to do them, one by one. Hortense and Adèle exchanged glances over his bent head and giggled. Louis looked up from his book, and they sobered instantly, but, as the stupid young man, quite unaware that they were laughing at him, struggled mightily to remove the hoop from the ring puzzle, they laughed again.

Louis flung down his book and left the room. When Hortense went to look for him and to apologize for having interrupted his reading, she found that he was trembling with rage. "What do you take me for?" he cried. "Do you think I like being made the butt of your jokes? Let me tell you, only immoral women laugh at their husbands and show no consideration for them. If you humiliate me again in this way, I will leave you!"

Hortense burst into tears, and Louis, who had been absurdly angry, became absurdly tender and took her in his arms. For the moment they were reconciled, but Hortense felt how bleak was the outlook for the future. She could never be at ease with Louis, because she could never foresee what would annoy him. Perhaps she really had been spoiled by her popularity. She was too impulsive, too thoughtless. Could she ever learn to weigh every word, every action?

When Napoleon and Joséphine returned at the end of January, Hortense was closely questioned about her marriage by her mother. She insisted stoically, though untruthfully, that all was well. Whenever she went to the Tuileries, she felt that her parents' eyes were boring into her to detect the first signs of pregnancy. She did not need to keep them long in suspense. When she told them that she was going to have a child, they were equally delighted. No girls, Napoleon said, he insisted on a boy; and when Louis went away to the country, leaving Hortense alone for several days, his brother upbraided him for neglecting a wife who gave him "the joy of future fatherhood." Hortense herself did not care whether her baby was male or female. A child, whether son or daughter, she felt, would become the emotional center of her life. She would fulfill herself in motherhood, if not in marriage.

The fact that she was pregnant, however, brought her into fresh conflict with her husband. Louis wanted to take a cure for his rheumatism at a health resort in the Pyrénées. Napoleon opposed the scheme. "They will say that I married my stepdaughter to an invalid, or a hypochondriac," he said. Joséphine, when she heard that Louis wanted to take Hortense with him, protested that a long, jolting journey might bring on a miscarriage. Hortense's doctor was consulted, and he advised against the trip.

But still Louis persisted. It became a fixed idea with him that Hortense should say that she would dare anything to go with him. He wanted her complete submission. It maddened him to think that it was Joséphine who was thwarting him. Louis had tried to detach Hortense from her mother by telling her all that he knew of Joséphine's misdoings in detail, all that Hortense may have suspected, but to which she had resolutely closed her mind.

"You are now a Bonaparte," Louis said. "*Our* interests should be *your* interests; those of your own relatives no longer count."

He could not have taken a surer method of steeling Hortense's resistance. She had allowed herself to be married to this man only in order to protect her mother!

Louis' behavior became more and more bizarre. He shed tears. He woke Hortense sometimes in the middle of the night, to see if he could catch her off her guard, but she stubbornly refused to say that she would gladly follow him to the ends of the earth.

"Let me be neutral," she said sullenly. "I'll do what you want, when you have made up your mind."

But she warned him that if there was a miscarriage, he would be responsible, and Louis did not quite dare to carry her off by force. Besides, this would not have fully satisfied his desire to dominate, to be obeyed. On the 1st of March, he left to spend a short time at Joigny with his regiment, and from there to go for a much longer stay at Barèges in the Pyrénées. When Hortense heard the sound of the wheels of his carriage, as it drove out of the courtyard, she felt a great sense of relief and also of defeat. How miserably she had failed to achieve any of her foolishly romantic notions! In her innocence, she had once told Adèle that, if the man she married had any faults, she would reform him. It would be impossible to reform Louis. Hortense not only disliked

—she feared—him. Now, for a short time at least, she would be free from the shadow of his presence.

◫

All during the year 1802, the first year of Hortense's marriage, Paris was on parade. France was prosperous. Napoleon's financial policy of stimulating trade, of stamping out corruption in the collection of taxes, as well as the establishment of a sound banking system, had had its effect.

France was at peace. In March, the treaty with Great Britain was signed, which recognized the favorable provisions of the treaty made earlier with Austria. Joséphine was able now to import openly cashmere shawls from England and English flowers for the gardens of La Malmaison. There was a great influx of outlanders, mostly British, to the capital. This was a novelty for the French, who for years had been cut off from the rest of the world by war and revolution. Crowds gathered on the Carrousel to see the military reviews, but also to see the foreign ambassadors as they rode by in their carriages.

Since the signing of the Concordat, a notice had appeared occasionally in the *Moniteur*, saying that the First Consul had attended Mass at the Tuileries, which meant that an altar had been set up in Napoleon's study and the rite performed while he continued to work at his desk. He showed greater piety when, on Easter Sunday, the first Mass was celebrated at Notre Dame. There was a mile-long procession of dignitaries and of the military, Napoleon and Joséphine riding in a coach drawn by eight beautifully matched Arabian horses. Some of the ex-revolutionists, who still made up the bulk of Napoleon's armies, his "old mustaches" as he called them, grumbled at having to go to church and threatened to hiss the performance if they didn't like it, but orders of the day were orders of the day. Not the faintest hiss was heard. The nave of the cathedral was a mosaic of brilliant, multicolored flags and uniforms. Cannon thundered at the elevation of the Host.

All of these shows of magnificence were part of Napoleon's program of impressing Europe with the might and solidity of his regime. He was contemplating a further step that would give it even greater stability, his election to the consulship for life. There was no need for further personal power; Napoleon's fellow consuls were figureheads; he controlled the army and the press; his administrative system was strongly centralized. But he wanted the world to know that his policies would endure, and, since France was still, in name, a republic, he wanted the will of the people to be manifest. Some small remains of independence still existed in the Triumvirate, in the Council of State, and in the Senate. Lucien Bonaparte, who had been out of favor since his appointment as Ambassador to Spain, was again put to work as persuader and exhorter. In May, a national plebiscite was held, the result of which was more than three million votes in favor of lifetime reign and a mere eight thousand opposed.

The vote had also given Napoleon the privilege, enjoyed by the Caesars of the ancient Roman Empire, of choosing his successor. Whenever there was a state function in Paris—the laying of a cornerstone, the dedication of a monument, or the opening of the art show at the Louvre, where the Venus de' Medici and other looted masterpieces were displayed—the First Consul appeared accompanied by two ladies: his wife, Madame Bonaparte, and her daughter, Madame Louis. As it became more and more evident that Madame Louis was with child, a rumor began to go the rounds. Where it had started nobody knew—perhaps in the faubourg Saint Germain, the neighborhood of Paris most thickly populated by disgruntled royalists. The English visitors took the story home across the Channel, where it found its way into print. It was reported there, it was whispered in France, that the father of Madame Louis' baby was not her husband, but Napoleon.

IX

NAPOLÉON CHARLES

AFTER Louis' departure, Hortense spent most of her time at the Tuileries, where the servants, forgetful that she had ever left, continued to call her Mademoiselle Hortense. When summer came, she went to La Malmaison, Joséphine was soon away to Plombières for yet another cure, and Hortense took over her mother's functions of homemaker and hostess, presiding at her stepfather's table, chatting with him when he was talkative, respecting his silence when, as often happened, he was deep in thought. In the evenings, she played chess with him, a game which Napoleon had never taken seriously enough to master.

Hortense got little help from the other female guests in keeping him amused. They were, for the most part, wives of the junior officers who had asked Hortense's help in arranging their marriages. Most of them were Saint-Germain girls; most of them were also pregnant. In the mornings, they would congregate in Hortense's boudoir to chatter happily while they embroidered babies' caps, but in Napoleon's presence they were tongue-tied, fearful of his piercing glance and his abrupt and disconcerting questions.

Napoleon had made use of Hortense's talent as a matchmaker in finding a wife for his trusted servant and henchman, Colonel

Duroc. Hortense brought forward one of Madame Campan's foreign students, a richly dowered Spanish girl, the daughter of a banker. At one of Hortense's interviews with Duroc, he let slip for an instant the mask of cold reserve he habitually wore. "I am grateful," he said, "for all the good that is coming to me—but it is not you."

Thereafter, he avoided her as much as possible. In the new position to which he had been appointed, that of Governor of the Palace, he must be discreet and impersonal. His fiancée was not in the least worried to learn that there had once been the beginning of an affair between Duroc and Hortense. "If he loved her, that shows that he had good taste," she said. "If she loved him in return, he must have deserved it."

The Duroc marriage took place on August 2, 1802, the same day that a delegation from the Senate came to announce formally to Napoleon that he was Consul for life. On the 15th of the same month, Napoleon's thirty-third birthday was celebrated elaborately at La Malmaison. A large audience came from Paris for a one-act play, followed by a cotillion.

Hortense had arranged and rehearsed the entertainment and played a small part in the comedy, but she had given up all idea of dancing herself. She was beginning to be heavy and unwieldy and she thought that her stepfather would be displeased, for he did not like the sight of pregnant women; one of the things that he admired most in Joséphine and in her daughter was their slimness and their light, graceful movements. While she was sitting out the first number, Napoleon, who never danced himself, urged her to find a partner for the following set. She demurred, but when he insisted, she allowed herself to be led out on the floor and went through the routine of a lively gavotte.

The next day there was an account in the *Journal de Paris* of the party at La Malmaison, mentioning the fact that Madame Louis Bonaparte had danced, though seven months pregnant; some sentimental verses on the subject followed. Hortense, whose dislike of publicity and rhymed flattery was of long standing, complained to Monsieur Bourrienne.

Bourrienne shrugged his shoulders. He told her that the verses had probably been written to order in advance and that there was a good reason for them. "You don't read all the malicious things that appear in the English newspapers," he said.

When she asked him to explain, he refused to say anything further, for the paragraph in the *Journal de Paris* had indeed been a reply to a statement published in England that Hortense had already given birth to a child, thus proving that she was pregnant before her marriage.

Hortense wondered if Napoleon's publicity agents were making use of media other than the Paris newspapers, when she learned from her childhood nurse, Madame Rousseau, of an item in a country almanac, fortelling the birth in October of a child who was destined to rule over "the greatest country in Europe." The old woman believed implicitly in the genuineness of the prophecy, but Hortense was sceptical.

In September, she moved into a new house Napoleon had bought for her in the rue de la Victoire. The excuse she gave for wanting a change was that Joséphine's house was too small; actually it was overcrowded with unhappy memories. Hortense was installed in her new home when Louis returned from Barèges.

Neither Louis' health nor his spirits had been improved by his prolonged cure. He may not have read the English newspapers, but he had been kept abreast of the gossip of Paris by Caroline Murat and by Lucien. Louis paled when Hortense told him casually that her obstetrician, Jean Louis Baudelocque, said that she could expect to be delivered the first week in October, or possibly a little earlier, a few days short of the nine months period.

"If it is earlier," Louis said, "I would never set eyes on you again."

"But you don't suspect me of having deceived you!" Hortense wailed.

"I know the truth, but what would people say?"

Nervous and exasperated, Hortense was much relieved when the first week of October had gone by and she was still on her feet and still able to appear in public. She visited an industrial exhibit and attended a big reception at the Tuileries on October 9th. Eugène was with her the following day when her first labor pains began; he hurried off to the palace to fetch Joséphine. Louis, whose behavior was, as always, unpredictable, became suddenly tender and solicitous. He insisted on staying with his wife; he would not leave her for an instant and, as the birth proceeded, he seemed to share in Hortense's suffering.

At nine o'clock in the evening, the baby was born—a boy. He was even more beautiful, Hortense thought, than a drawing of an infant by Greuze that she had been copying during the past few days. One of the nurses said, "Here is our dauphin," as she brought the baby to the bed. Louis scowled at the woman and told her to hold her tongue, but he, too, was loud in admiration of his son. For the first time since their marriage, Hortense's heart warmed toward her husband.

For a few weeks, she luxuriated in being pampered and praised by everyone for having produced the first male Bonaparte of the new generation; Caroline and Pauline had boys, but Joseph and Lucien only girls. Napoleon was one of the first of Hortense's bedside visitors, and announced that the baby should be named Napoléon Charles, Napoleon for himself, Charles for the child's paternal grandfather.

Louis, unprompted, arranged a celebration on the name day of Hortense's patron saint in November, and made a magificent donation to Hortense's already overflowing jewel box. After the fête, Madame Campan, who had suspected that her angel's marriage was not completely satisfactory, wrote that she hoped Hortense was meeting her husband more than halfway in affection.

There was no need for this word of advice, the advice, Madame Campan said, not of a schoolteacher but of a mother. Hortense's only quarrel with Louis was that she couldn't have sole possession of the baby. Louis, who had retired to a separate bedroom for a rest

cure that the doctor had ordered, was continually wanting Napoléon Charles to be brought to him. But this was a weakness that
Hortense could understand and could easily forgive. For the
time being, all the bitter things that had been said and thought
by husband and by wife were forgotten.

回

But of all those who stood on tiptoe about the crib of Napoléon
Charles, only Joséphine was not altogether satisfied. Though everything had gone very much as she had planned, she was still uneasy,
she was still unsure of her position, though her position was that
of queen in all but name. In the autumn and winter of 1802, Joséphine made two triumphal journeys with her husband through the
provinces of France, greeted everywhere by bowing, obsequious
officials and—more significantly—by cheering crowds. In certain
towns, the horses were taken out of the carriage in which the First
Consul and his wife were riding and they were dragged through
the streets by the townspeople.

At this time, the palace of Saint-Cloud was presented to Napoleon by the nation for a summer residence. La Malmaison was no
longer large enough for his official household. Joséphine had a full
complement of ladies in waiting, Napoleon having taken care that
all the ladies appointed should be highly respectable. His court,
he felt, should set a moral standard for society, a society in which
the male predominated and women played a purely decorative and
subordinate role. If there was any impropriety or philandering,
it should be very well concealed.

This was a rule that Napoleon had set for himself, for he was
no longer, as in the first few years of his marriage, so much in
love with his wife as to be oblivious to every other woman in the
world. While he was in Egypt and thought that Joséphine was unfaithful, Napoleon had, as mistress, the wife of an officer, who
had smuggled herself on board ship in men's clothing. After his
return to France, however, and his reconciliation with Joséphine,
he refused to see his Egyptian inamorata, who had followed him

to Paris. Only gradually did he drift into the habit of temporary, fleeting relations with women who were always glad to offer him their services and who were always well rewarded. They might be singers at the opera, they might be actresses, or merely indiscreet young ladies who held some very minor position at the court.

In a remote corner of the Tuileries, there was a small room for which a fresh bouquet of flowers was supplied every day and which had a private entrance to the street. Sometimes, when Napoleon was at work, his valet would come to whisper in his ear that a lady was waiting for him in the secret room. "Let her wait," was often the response. If the valet came a second time and Napoleon was still engrossed, he would say, "Tell her that she can go home now."

But often, usually late in the evening, Napoleon went to the secret room. And Joséphine was nearly always aware of the visit. The increasing ceremony of their life—they no longer shared a bedroom, but, like king and queen, had separate apartments of their own—facilitated Napoleon's nighttime adventures; but Joséphine kept a close watch on his movements and on those of his valet, Louis Constant, and of his personal bodyguard, Roustan, the Mameluke whom he had brought home with him from Egypt.

Napoleon could not understand the torments of jealousy that Joséphine was suffering. He was not an ordinary man, he felt, and the ordinary rules of conduct did not apply to him. What was adultery, he asked contemptuously? It was nothing; it was fifteen minutes on a sofa. He was not the sort to throw the world away for love, and had no intention of setting up a mistress on a throne of her own. Napoleon had a great fear of petticoat government, an echo, perhaps, of his childhood, in which a matriarch had reigned supreme. He often pointed out the disastrous influence that the female favorites of kings had had upon the destinies of France.

Joséphine's insistence on her rights as wife was a desperate attempt to maintain her status and to avoid divorce; the word was never mentioned by Napoleon, but the idea, the possibility, was there—a constant threat. Since she had never been very good at keeping a secret, Joséphine complained of her husband's infidelities to Hortense, to her ladies in waiting, to anyone in whom she felt she could confide. When she complained to Napoleon himself, his hot, Corsican temper flared. He sometimes told her brutally that he was determined to do as he pleased, and that she must put up with all of his whims. The end was always the same: Joséphine in tears and Napoleon mollified and trying to console her; tears, he thought, were very becoming to a woman.

Though Joséphine was happy to be the grandmother of Hortense's son, even the advent of Napoléon Charles had been embittered by the whispering campaign that preceded his birth. Joséphine's ears were attuned to every whisper. She was sure that the Bonaparte family had done all that they could to foist on her the monstrous role of procuress to her daughter's seduction. Louis may not have believed that this was so, but he found it convenient, at times, to pretend that it was, and his real, unfeigned love for his son made him hypersensitive and overpossessive.

When his rest cure was over, Louis wanted to leave Paris for the winter and to go to Italy with his family. Napoleon was pleased with the idea, and said that the trip should be a state visit, such as he and Joséphine had made to various parts of France. An Italian lady in waiting was appointed to accompany Hortense, arrangements were made for her reception in various cities, and presents were bought for distribution along the way. But it would be impossible to take Napoléon Charles on such a journey. Neither Hortense nor Louis wanted to leave their child. Louis became ill at the very idea of his son's spending the winter with his mother-in-law. To avoid doing as his brother had planned, he soon went off alone to the medical center at Montpellier, for an indefinite stay.

Once more abandoned, Hortense's life was again centered on the Tuileries. She went there nearly every day, taking the baby with her. Napoleon was fond of all children, but he was more than fond of Napoléon Charles. He liked to hold the baby in his lap at the dinner table, and, to Hortense's horror, would give him a sip from his wine glass or from his cup of black coffee. Then he would put the little thing down on its back in the middle of the table and laugh to see it kick the plates and glasses to the floor. Napoléon Charles cried sometimes when Napoleon kissed him violently and pinched his cheeks, but he soon came to know his uncle and would put out his arms to him.

One day Napoleon was holding Hortense's son on his knee when Caroline Murat was present with her son, Achille, who was three years old. "Did you know, baby," Napoleon said to Napoléon Charles, "that you run the risk of being a king some day?"

Caroline flushed with anger. "And Achille?" she cried.

"Oh, Achille will make a good soldier," Napoleon said indifferently. Teasing Caroline, he continued his conversation with the baby. "Take my advice, you poor little thing," he said. "If you want to live, never accept anything to eat from one of your cousins."

These were merely pinpricks, but they did not make for family unity or lessen the hatred that the Bonapartes felt for Joséphine and for her daughter.

Hortense and Napoléon Charles happened to be at the palace on a day that was fateful for France and for all of Europe. It was March 13, 1803, the day of the week when the regular reception for foreign ambassadors, and in particular for their wives, was held at the Tuileries. It was customary for the household to gather in Joséphine's salon and to wait for Napoleon's arrival, before going into the larger reception room where the foreigners were assembled.

Napoleon came down from his study. He was preoccupied and grim. He spoke to no one and began to pace up and down the room, hands behind back, his meager body thrust forward. As he passed the nurse who was holding Napoléon Charles, the baby gurgled and stretched out his hands. Napoleon took the child in his arms and continued his uneasy walk. He walked so long and seemed so heedless of all that surrounded him, that Hortense was afraid he might have forgotten that he was holding her son and might let him drop.

After almost half an hour of pacing, Napoleon handed the baby back to the nurse and gave the signal for the doors to be opened. Down a vista of corridor a room was revealed that was crowded with the foreign representatives and their ladies, the men glittering with decorations, the women elegant and bejeweled.

As soon as she entered the room, Joséphine began to move down the long line of visitors, saying, as always, something gracious and appropriate to each of her guests. She had a prodigious memory for names and personalities. Hortense prepared to follow and imitate her. But Napoleon had marched ahead of them to the farther end of the room, where the English Ambassador, Lord Whitworth, was standing. Looking fiercely up at the tall, bland Englishman, Napoleon launched into a violent denunciation of the British failure to live up to certain articles of the peace treaty, which had been signed a year earlier at Amiens. Lord Whitworth tried to put in a pacific word now and then, but Napoleon gave him no chance to speak. The peace of Europe was at stake, he said. If there was war, it would be a war of vengeance, and victory would go to those who had fulfilled their international obligations.

The deep, resonant voice carried to the farthest corner of the salon, though Joséphine tried to cover it by her gentle, inconsequential talk. A few minutes later, Napoleon left the room.

When he was once more alone with Joséphine and Hortense, Napoleon looked from one to the other with amusement and surprise. His anger had evaporated. "Well, what is the matter now?" he asked with a grin.

"But you made everybody tremble!" Joséphine protested. "You seemed so terrible. What will all those ladies think, who don't know you and who were looking forward so to meeting you? Instead of being kind and pleasant, you had to talk politics. It was no time to be doing that!"

Napoleon laughingly admitted that she was right, and that he had made a mistake even to come downstairs that day. Talleyrand, his Minister of Foreign Affairs, had been telling him things that put him in a black mood. "I was angry, and then I come into the room, and I see that great cart horse of an Ambassador standing there before me!"

Napoleon's tantrum had only precipitated, it did not cause, the break that was inevitable between the two most powerful nations of the Western World. The old rivalry for colonies had not been forgotten. France's predominance on the Continent and the flourishing state of her industries were a menace to the Nation of Shopkeepers.

No sooner had the word war been spoken, than it echoed far beyond the walls of the Tuileries. As spring came on in Paris, every day a crowd would gather before the English embassy to see if there was any sign of its being vacated. In May, Lord Whitworth asked for his passport, for he had been recalled to London. A state of war again existed between England and France.

X

"PRINCESS LOUIS"

HORTENSE and Louis had parted, before the incident at the Tuileries and on fairly good terms. At least, neither of them had wanted to make the tour of Italy, and Louis did not ask his wife to go with him to Montpellier. It was her duty, he said, to stay at home with their child.

Louis' letters were at first affectionate, though they sometimes contained warnings and recommendations that Hortense could not fully understand. She had been puzzled by a solemn promise that he exacted of her before leaving, the promise being that whenever she went to Saint-Cloud that summer, she should only go for the day and should never spend the night. Hortense thought that her mother's feelings would be hurt if she didn't have a good excuse for refusing invitations, and so she filled her morning hours with lessons in painting and in music. In the afternoon, she would drive out to the palace with Napoléon Charles. Even if the weather was bad and her mother urged her to stay, she always said that she had to be back in Paris for her early morning appointments.

One day in May, when Hortense was at Saint-Cloud, Napoleon took her, Joséphine, and Caroline for a drive in a carriage, to which was harnessed a six-horse team. He had never before driven

83

more than a single pair. The horses were young and lively, and Napoleon was not able to negotiate a sharp turn in coming out of the courtyard. The carriage crashed into the gate post. The horses stopped short, but Napoleon was thrown far from the driver's seat and landed on his face. Blood trickled from his nose and mouth; for a few moments he was unconscious. When he came to himself, he made light of the accident, but Joséphine was very much frightened and was so upset that, when evening came, she begged Hortense not to leave her.

When Hortense made her usual excuse, Joséphine wept. "My daughter no longer loves me," she said.

"I will tell you how it is," Napoleon put in from the sofa on which he was lying. "It is very simple: Hortense enjoys herself in Paris. We are old, and she is bored when she is with us."

Hortense could not bear this to be said, even in fun, and blurted out that the real reason why she could never stay overnight at Saint-Cloud was because her husband had forbidden it.

"What's that?" Napoleon asked, suddenly sitting up. "Your husband has forbidden you? Why? Is he getting his information from the English scandal sheets? Write to him that he cannot separate a daughter from her mother. . . . A wife who is as well behaved as you has a right to speak her mind once in a while and not to submit to such ridiculous restrictions."

Hortense saw how greatly she had blundered. Now Napoleon would blast Louis with his anger, and her mother would be certain to tell all of her ladies in waiting. Soon, all the world would know the secret discords of Hortense's marriage that she had kept from everyone except her friend, Adèle Auguié.

Hortense realized, from the change in tone of Louis' letters, that someone had told him promptly of her faux pas. When, early in September, he came back from Montpellier, he was very cold and distant. He kept to his own room and talked of a separation. But he was annoyed when Hortense readily agreed, and he soon had changed his mind. Louis had been upgraded—much against his will, he said—from colonel to brigadier general, and his brigade was based at Compiègne, to the northeast of Paris. Since he was in better physical condition, he consented to spend the winter there, taking Hortense with him and, of course, Napoléon Charles, who was now a year old.

Hortense found herself the great lady of the garrison town, and enjoyed entertaining all the local people, as well as the military, until Louis, unsocial and suspicious of her success as a hostess, put a stop to it. In February, she discovered that she was again pregnant. Louis was pleased, but, as usual, took an eccentric way of showing his satisfaction. "I only ask one thing of you," he said solemnly, "and that is that this child should look like me."

"And how am I to manage that?" Hortense asked, rather acidly.

"If you love me, if you think of me continually, there will be a resemblance," Louis said. "And then I will adore you and will be the happiest man in all the world."

Shortly thereafter, the stay at Compiègne came to an abrupt end and the Bonapartes were recalled to Paris, where a serious situation had developed. As they approached the city, it looked as if it were in a state of siege. There were guards placed at close intervals about the walls and at the gates, where no one was allowed to pass in or out without being questioned. Everyone was talking about the great conspiracy that had recently been uncovered, to kidnap and kill the First Consul.

Dozens, perhaps hundreds, of people were involved in the plot, and a number of arrests had already been made, the most sensational being that of General Jean Moreau, the victor of Hohenlinden and Napoleon's only rival for popularity in the army. The leader of the plot, also in prison and soon to be brought to trial, was Georges Cadoudal, a Breton peasant. He had been a guerrilla fighter and member of the underground royalist movement, the Chouans, that dated back to the days of the Terror.

It was Joseph Fouché, himself a relic of the Terror and Napoleon's Minister of Police at the time of the gunpowder explosion in the rue Saint Nicaise, who unearthed the conspiracy. Napoleon

disliked Fouché, as he disliked all former Jacobins, and had retired him to the Senate, thinking that he would be less powerful
there than at the head of the police force. Fouché, however, had
kept in touch with the large body of spies and undercover agents
who had served him so well while he was in office. From them, he
learned that palace servants and even members of the First Consul's bodyguard had been corrupted. "There are daggers in the
very air you breathe," Fouché told Napoleon.

The daggers were royalist daggers—no doubt of that, though
English money was behind all anti-Napoleon activities. Now that
England and France were at war, the British government gave
open aid and comfort to the Bourbon princes, Louis XVIII and his
brother, the Comte d' Artois. If any counter move was to be made
to put the fear of death into conspirators, high and low, it should
be aimed at the house of Bourbon.

Joachim Murat, Caroline's husband, had been appointed the
military Governor of Paris. The Murats lived near the rue de la
Victoire, and after returning from Compiègne, Hortense and Louis
went frequently to visit them. One evening—it was the 20th of
March, 1804—Caroline told Hortense that she had learned from
her husband that the Duc d'Enghien had been arrested; he had
been taken to the fortress of Vincennes, just outside the walls of
Paris, where he would be judged that evening by a military court.

The Duc d'Enghien was a Bourbon, of the Condé branch of the
family. His arrest and speedy trial seemed ominous. Hortense was
worried, and early the next morning went to La Malmaison to see
her mother. She found Joséphine in despair. Joséphine had
learned from Napoleon that the young Bourbon prince, against
whom there was only the flimsiest evidence of conspiracy, had
been shot that morning at daybreak. Napoleon himself seemed
shaken when he told the news, but, seeing Joséphine's look of horror, he cried out passionately, "Do you want me to be assassin-
ated?"

"This is the first great mistake that Napoleon has made," Joséphine lamented. She could not believe that her husband had given unprompted the order for the Duke's execution. "Who could have given him such advice?" she asked, over and over, while Hortense sat stunned and silent beside her.

Later Monsieur Bourrienne gave Joséphine and Hortense the story of what had happened at Vincennes, just as he had had it from the commandant of the fortress. When arrested, the Duke was not on French soil, but dangerously near it, at Ettenheim in the principality of Baden. There he came often from across the Rhine, to see a woman with whom he was in love, and it was these frequent visits that first attracted the attention of the police. The prisoner was taken to Strasbourg and then to Vincennes. When he arrived at the fortress, he was cold and hungry after his long journey, and only wanted to warm himself and to be given a hearty meal. He had no idea of why he had been arrested and was not particularly alarmed.

The Duke had gone to bed and was sound asleep, when roused to be taken before the officers who examined him. To them, he admitted frankly that he was living on a pension paid him by the British government, though he denied acquaintance with any of the accused who were now under arrest in Paris.

D'Enghien was again asleep when the guard came at six o'clock in the morning to take him to the place of execution in the empty moat of the fortress. Still he did not seem to realize his danger. As he was led down the steep, winding stairs, a cold wind blew up from below. "They're not going to put me into a dungeon, are they?" he asked.

And then he saw the firing squad and the troops drawn up along the rim of the moat, the grave already dug. Before he died, D'Enghien asked for a pair of scissors and cut off a lock of his hair to be sent to his sweetheart. There was yet another detail, very moving, no doubt, to Joséphine, who was so fond of dogs: the Duke had a spaniel that followed him to the moat, and after the body had been hastily buried without a coffin, the dead man's pet refused to leave his grave.

Though at the time it suited Napoleon to leave the circumstances surrounding the death of the Duc d'Enghien vague, he took full responsibility for it later. It was necessary, Napoleon said, to put a stop to the constant threats to his life. The Bourbons had declared a secret war upon him; but one could hardly call it secret when one of their number, the Comte d'Artois, openly boasted that he had sixty would-be First Consul killers in his pay in Paris alone. It was a case of blood for blood, of life for life.

Except in the royalist faubourg Saint Germain, there was little outcry, though some of the sober citizens of Paris may have wondered if the Terror was not coming back to their city. When Napoleon entered his box at the opera, a few days later, he received his usual ovation. Interest in the death at Vincennes was swallowed up by the still greater interest taken in the conspiracy trials. When a large number of the accused were condemned to death, Napoleon was inclined to mercy, and, at the request of Joséphine and Hortense, pardoned some of those who had taken only a minor part.

The execution of D'Enghien had the effect, that Napoleon had foreseen, of rallying to him the men of the Revolution, such men as Fouché, with whom the fear still lingered that Napoleon might even yet restore the Bourbons to the throne. He, Napoleon, was preparing to mount the throne himself, and the title he had chosen was that of Emperor of the French, since an emperor could conceivably rule over a republic, while a king could only rule a kingdom. Speeches were being made; debates—so-called—were being held in the various governmental bodies. Again, the result of a nationwide vote would be overwhelmingly in favor of the establishment of the empire.

On April 7, 1804, while the preliminaries to the plebiscite were still going on, Napoleon and Joséphine came in state to call at the house in the rue de la Victoire. This was a very rare occurrence. Louis was not at home. Napoleon seemed annoyed by his absence and went out to walk alone in the garden. Meanwhile, Joséphine was whispering to Hortense in the salon that they had come to make a formal offer to adopt Napoléon Charles.

After all the hints, after all the partiality shown, this was no great surprise to Hortense, nor to Louis, who came in just as the visitors were getting into their carriage to go home. That evening, Hortense learned from Caroline that the whole Bonaparte Clan knew of the offer and would fight it individually and collectively.

"What—your children to be princes and heirs to the throne of France," Caroline shrilled, "and my children, their cousins, to be nobodies! I will never put up with an injustice of that sort! I will bring my children up to know their rights and to fight for them!"

There was a tempestuous interview at the Tuileries between Napoleon, Joseph, Lucien, and Louis. Louis refused to give up his son, and his brothers, who had in mind advancing their own claims to consideration, upheld him. Sooner than consent, Louis said, he would leave France and take Napoléon Charles with him. He and all the family saw no other solution to the succession issue than the one that they had been urging for years: that Napoleon should divorce Joséphine and take another wife.

A few days later, Napoleon discussed the matter soberly with Hortense, and for the first time spoke to her as adult to adult; hitherto he had always been either the strict or the facetious parent. Was Hortense for or against the adoption scheme? She said that she did not want to take a stand one way or the other. She was fearful—and she could see that Louis was also fearful—of exposing their child to the hatred of its near relatives.

Napoleon could not deny that there was hatred. He was silent for a few moments and then said, "I will pass a law that will at least make me master in my own family!"

He spoke with feeling. It was exasperating to him that, now that he was about to reach the climax of his public career, his family was so uncoöperative and so obstreperous. During the past year, his authority had been flouted on three separate occasions.

Pauline, the impish, the beautiful Pauline, to whom Napoleon was more inclined to be indulgent than to either Elisa or to Caroline, was the first offender. Just before Hortense's and Louis' wedding, Pauline went with her husband, General Leclerc, on an expedition to regain Santo Domingo. The insurrection was quelled and Toussaint L'Ouverture, the great Negro leader, was tricked into submission and sent to die in France, but yellow fever took a terrible revenge on the conquerors. After a few weeks of horror in the French camps, where doctors and medicines were in short supply, only a handful of the invading force was still alive.

Pauline came back to France in January of 1803, a widow, bringing with her, her husband's body in a lead coffin. She had been surprisingly heroic, for a spoiled child who had a fantastic taste for luxury, as well as some of her brother Louis' penchant for chronic invalidism. Napoleon greeted her tenderly and put her in Joseph's charge. All in good time, he intended to find Pauline another husband. She had loved Leclerc, but, being Pauline, she could not be expected to mourn him very long.

After only a few months of wearing ugly black clothes and sitting at home while all the world, it seemed, was going to balls, Pauline was so bored that she was ready, she said, to commit suicide. A young Italian prince, of the very ancient and very affluent Borghese family, appeared in Paris. He was introduced to the Widow Leclerc, and there was on either hand an immediate attraction. Even in her widow's weeds Pauline was intoxicating. The Prince, though not very bright intellectually, was handsome, and Pauline was enchanted with the idea of becoming a princess, thus taking social precedence over her sisters and—better still—over her despised sister-in-law, Joséphine.

Napoleon had no objection to Pauline's marrying Camillio Borghese, if the conventions were observed. According to the Napoleonic Code, it was illegal for a widow to remarry until ten months after her husband's death; in August, 1803, only eight months after General Leclerc succumbed to yellow fever and even less since his state funeral in the Pantheon, Pauline was secretly married to Borghese by a priest. Napoleon did not know that the couple had been living together, more or less openly, until he gave a betrothal dinner in October. The best that could be done then was to see that there was a legal marriage as soon as the period of mourning was up. That autumn, Pauline left for Rome, where Napoleon hoped that his mother, who had gone to live with Uncle Fesch, now a cardinal and legate to the Vatican, would keep an eye on her.

Pauline's marriage was an annoyance and a flouting of Napoleon's attempt to restore a stricter decorum in marital affairs, but a thousand times worse was the behavior of Lucien—Lucien, who had always been inclined to rebellion and, even as a boy, had complained of "Nabulione's" dictatorial ways. When only nineteen and while the Bonapartes were still struggling to maintain themselves as refugees in southern France, Lucien married the daughter of an innkeeper, a girl who could neither read nor write. She endeared herself to her mother-in-law, Letizia, however, and to the family in general. Lucien loved her and was a devoted husband until her death in 1800.

For the next two years he had many passing affairs with women, until he fell seriously in love with a beautiful, dark-eyed lady, Alexandrine Jouberthou, who was separated from her husband. Lucien installed her in his country house at Plessis, and before her husband died conveniently in June, 1803, she had borne Lucien a son. They were married by a priest the following day and by a magistrate in October.

Lucien chose the moment to announce his marriage to the family when Napoleon was absent at Boulogne, where he was massing his army for an attack on England. Lucien brought his bride to call on all the Bonapartes, including Hortense and Louis, and the calls were returned. When the First Consul came back to Paris, there were harsh words for all, and Hortense was scolded for her very minor part in the affair. Never had she seen Napoleon so angry with her. As usual when aroused, he paced back and forth in the room—a lion behind bars—and seemed to be speaking, not so much to her, as to the world at large.

"I try to reëstablish morals," he cried, "and then they bring a woman of that sort into my family! I want you to know I am head of a nation to which I am responsible not only for my actions, but for the moral example that I set. . . . The French people are a moral people; their chiefs should be moral also. . . . Those who are not with me are against me. I have certain duties to perform, and I will be inexorable!"

Just before he stamped out of the room, without glancing again at Hortense and Caroline, who was also present, he said, "I am only sorry that I am not a bastard. I ought to be a bastard, for no one understands me!"

Napoleon had had other matrimonial plans for Lucien. He had been surprised, when in June, his brother refused to be named Ambassador to Florence where a Bourbon princess, the Queen of Etruria, had recently been widowed. A royal wedding might still be possible. Using Joseph as intermediary, Napoleon made every effort to get Lucien to annul his marriage and to reduce Madame Jouberthou again to the status of mistress. Soon after the offer to adopt Napoléon Charles, the two brothers had their final encounter.

Napoleon suggested that Lucien should be given the right to the succession, with the exclusion of his children.

Lucien shouted his defiance, "My wife, my son, and I are one!"

He faced his brother with Roman fury, as though he were draped in the toga he had once worn as President of the Assembly of the Five Hundred. He rejected the entire scheme of empire. "You want to kill the Republic," he thundered. "Very well—raise yourself still higher by stepping on its corpse. But listen to me, a faithful son of the Revolution; this empire of yours can only be maintained by force. One day it will fall by force. You will be smashed to pieces—like this."

Lucien snatched his watch out of his pocket, hurled it on the floor, and stamped upon it. With hate in his heart, he soon departed with his family for Rome, where he knew that he would have the support of his mother. Letizia had said that Napoleon himself had married without family consent and that Lucien should have the same privilege.

As if the rebellion of Pauline and Lucien was not enough, Napoleon learned that on Christmas Eve, 1803, Jérôme Bonaparte, the baby of the family, who had been pushed into a naval career, had, while on a visit to the United States, married an American girl, Elizabeth Patterson of Baltimore.

The schisms in the Bonaparte Clan were taken into account when the Senate came to define the future emperor's domestic prerogatives. Succession to the imperium was to go by primogeniture in the male line, but only Joseph, Louis, and their children could qualify, and the Emperor was given the power to adopt his brothers' sons or grandsons when they had reached the age of eighteen. There could be no marriage in the imperial family without the Emperor's consent.

On May 18, 1804, yet another delegation from the Senate came to Saint-Cloud to announce the inauguration of the Empire. Napoleon was told that he should complete his glory by "making it eternal." For the first time he was addressed as "sire." The ceremony was followed by a state banquet. Duroc, the Palace Governor, announced the titles of those who stood close to the throne. He spoke of Prince and Princess Joseph and of Prince and Princess Louis, but, though Elisa Bacciocchi and Caroline Murat were present, there was no mention made of Princess Félix or Princess Joachim. There was too much protocol, too many observers for either of the ladies to speak her mind, but Elisa was pale and haughty, Caroline's pretty face was crimson and distorted. She tried to fight back her tears by taking repeated sips of water.

There were repercussions the following day at a private family gathering. Caroline, the tears now rolling down her cheeks, wanted to know why she and her sisters should remain obscure, "while strangers were being loaded down with honors."

"To hear you talk," Napoleon said ironically, "one would think that I was robbing you of the heritage of our father, the late king."

Caroline screamed and fell to the floor in a faint. When she was revived, Napoleon relented and promised her that she and Elisa should receive the titles that meant so much to them.

XI

THE LAUGHING CAVALIER

Now that she was a princess, Hortense had the privilege of speaking of any royal personnage in Europe as "my cousin." Ambassadors came to pay her visits of state, to present her their compliments and congratulations. She soon had a household of her own, that consisted of six ladies in waiting, a chamberlain, three chaplains, two equerries, a secretary, a doctor, a surgeon, a pharmacist, and a librarian. All these appointments were made by the Emperor, though Hortense saw to it that one of her chaplains should be Abbé Bertrand, who had been the teacher of the graduating class at Saint-Germain, and that Adèle Auguié should be one of her ladies.

The house in the rue de la Victoire was much too small now. Louis had been named Constable of France and would have to entertain on a large scale. Without consulting Hortense, he bought a mansion in the rue Cerutti, the street in which the Murats lived. The house was vast and sunless, with an enormous courtyard and a garden in its rear, filled with hideous statues, a lake, a rustic waterfall and bridge, a thatched cottage, and a Temple of the Four Seasons.

Hortense would have been glad to exchange all this grandeur

for a little domestic peace and quiet. Her relations with Louis had again deteriorated. He blamed her for having remained neutral in the matter of Napoléon Charles's adoption. In this maneuver, he saw the diabolic hand of Joséphine—"your unprincipled mother," as he named her to Hortense. He tried to prevent Hortense from going to see Joséphine alone at the Tuileries, and from having anything to do with her other relatives. Two young male Tascher cousins had turned up from Martinique and would have been glad of Hortense's help and hospitality, but Louis forbade them his house. When the older of the two youths called once at seven o'clock in the morning on family business, Louis threatened to run him through with his sword if he called again at such an hour.

Louis had always been irritated by Hortense's popularity. From the first, the Paris public had taken her to its heart as the young lady of the Tuileries. Unlike Napoleon's sisters, whose speech and looks were slightly foreign, she was unmistakably French. In the ballroom, the best dancer in Madame Campan's school was much in demand. At this time dancing was more than a diversion; it was a cult. New steps, the waltz and polka, were becoming popular; and the set dances, that were always carefully rehearsed, were almost miniature ballets. People sometimes mounted chairs to see more plainly, when Hortense led one of these performances.

One evening, as the music died away and Hortense was leaving the dance floor, a young man applauded her vigorously. Hortense thought that this was going a little bit too far. She knew the young man slightly. His name was Charles de Flahaut. He had been a sublieutenant in Louis' regiment of dragoons, with whom Louis was on very friendly terms—a tall, boyish, pink-cheeked fellow, who was always laughing. Hortense also knew the young man's mother. She was one of the many aristocrats who had fled during the Terror and whom Joséphine had helped to return to France in 1799. Recently, Madame de Flahaut had married the Portuguese Ambassador, Marquês José Maria de Souza Botelho. She, too, was present at the ball. Hortense spoke in passing to Madame de

Souza and said, with a pout that she danced for her own pleasure and not to be claqued as if she were a ballerina from the opera.

The next day, Madame de Souza, a plump, still pretty woman, in her early forties, came to call with her son to beg Hortense's pardon. Thereafter, whenever young Charles, the laughing cavalier, came to see Louis, he also asked the servant if Madame was at home and if he could pay her his respects. These visits were usually in the morning, and if Hortense, as often happened, was taking a singing lesson, she would ask De Flahaut to come up to her sitting room. She had discovered that they had the same vocal teacher. For an hour they would sing duets, De Flahaut having a pleasing tenor voice.

Sometimes, however, when she was otherwise occupied, Hortense would refuse to see her visitor. One day, when the servant came to announce him, she said rather sharply, "Tell him that I am not at home today."

Charles was directly behind the man; he had overheard what she said. Hortense had a fleeting glimpse of him in the doorway and saw the smile vanish from his cheerful face. He was like a child who has been playing happily and has been suddenly told that he must go home. Hortense was sorry to have hurt his feelings and stepped forward to beg his pardon, but he had already disappeared.

After that De Flahaut's calls ceased. He was now aide-de-camp to Joachim Murat, and Hortense did not see him again until she met him one evening at Caroline's house. Wanting to make amends, Hortense politely reproached De Flahaut for having neglected her.

"I still come," he said, in an aggrieved tone, "but you are never there."

Hortense thought that this might be an exaggeration. The doorman at the house in the rue Cerutti kept a list of all those who called, and Hortense, consulting this visitors' book, saw that De Flahaut's name appeared frequently. She learned from the doorman that Louis had told him never to let this young man in.

This was another of Louis' vagaries. Of late, he had become doubly suspicious. Louis prowled the house in the rue Cerutti and was forever shutting doors or opening them suddenly, as if he expected to find someone hiding in the next room. Once, Hortense's maid complained that she had been locked into her bedroom, and a manservant was dismissed merely because he was found loitering in the hall outside of Hortense's boudoir, as if he had been posted there as a sentinel. Louis, Hortense learned, actually paid spies to shadow the men with whom she danced most frequently, but why, she wondered, was he so jealous of De Flahaut, of whom she had seen so little, who had been his protégé rather than hers?

She felt that she had been put in a false position and wanted to clear herself, but for some time there was no opportunity. Again De Flahaut had dropped out of sight. And then, one evening, he was suddenly there, standing behind her chair at a supper party. In the same injured tone he had used earlier, he asked her why he was always turned away from her door when he saw others going in and out.

Hortense was embarrassed. "But it is not my fault," she cried, and added impulsively, "please, don't ever come again!"

She could have bitten her tongue for having spoken so emotionally, for she still tried to keep her troubles with Louis to herself. In public esteem, she and her husband were considered an ideal couple, devoted to their children and devoted to one another.

De Flahaut seemed much exhilarated to learn that it was not she who had given the doorman his orders. His joyous smile had returned. For a moment, however, he was very serious, as he said in a low, sympathetic voice, "You will never see me at your house again. I couldn't bear to think that it was I who was making you unhappy."

Hitherto, Hortense had thought that De Flahaut was just another frivolous young man, of whom she knew so many, the sort who would pay her compliments or try to flirt with her as a way of getting on in the world, since she was now a person of some importance. He was neither heartless, nor self-seeking, and he was sensitive enough to understand her unfortunate situation and to consider her feelings rather than his own. She had undervalued him.

She had undervalued also the effect upon her of his gaiety, his good looks, and his tenor voice. Hortense loved Napoléon Charles and was prepared to love her unborn baby, but she couldn't find complete compensation in her children for the dreary, vexatious life she led with Louis. During the next few days, she found herself thinking constantly of that brief interchange with De Flahaut at the supper table.

The next time that she saw him, she was even more strongly drawn to him, though the circumstances were unusual. They met, or rather they were both present, at a lunch party that Eugène de Beauharnais gave at a little country house that he had bought near La Malmaison. Here, Eugène led a jolly bachelor existence, on the rare occasions when he was on leave from the army. There were many guests, and Hortense had no chance to speak to De Flahaut. He was giving all his attention to a pretty young Polish countess, who had been for some time in Paris and who was about to go home to Poland. It was obvious that they were much in love with one another. The Polish girl was in tears; there were tears also in De Flahaut's eyes.

As she watched the pair from a distance, Hortense carried on an unspoken, one-sided conversation with herself, in the best Madame Campan tradition of trying to find a good and sufficient reason for everything she did or thought. "He can love someone, he is unhappy now, and that interests me very much," she said to herself. "I misjudged him when I thought him insincere. He has shown that he would like to be my friend, and I will be his."

The illogical conclusion, toward which Hortense was working, was that because De Flahaut was in love with another woman and could shed tears at the thought of being separated from her, his friendship would not be dangerous. She would soon discover how mistaken she and Madame Campan could be.

▣

In the course of a short life, Charles de Flahaut had seen a good deal of the world and its ways, and he was not as unambitious as Hortense imagined.

Four years earlier, in February, 1800, the following letter was received by Napoleon, who had just become First Consul:

General, I am only sixteen years old, but I am big and strong for my age. I know three languages so well that in three different countries it would be hard to say whether I was English, German, or French. Though I am too young to be a soldier, I ask you to let me be your aide-de-camp. You may be sure that I will either be dead at the end of my first campaign, or I will have justified your choice.

That you may see just how serious I am, I would like to tell you of something that has had an effect upon my entire life. My father was condemned to death during the Terror. After sentence was passed upon him, my mother was able to persuade his jailer to let him escape from prison. The next day, my father learned that the man who had helped him had been arrested and would be executed because of the escape. He left his place of refuge and gave himself up to the Commune, saying that he didn't want an innocent man to suffer for him. Two hours later he was dead. Don't you think, General, that with this example forever in mind, I might prove to be faithful to honor and to you?

Greeting and respects,
Charles de Flahaut

This excellent letter was true in outline, but not in every detail. Charles was not sixteen when he asked to be Napoleon's aide-de-camp; he was several months short of fifteen and almost exactly two years younger than Hortense. It was true that in October, 1793, a Comte Flahaut de la Billarderie died an heroic death, as outlined, at Arras, but though Charles bore his name, the count was not Charles's father.

Charles's mother, Adélaide Filleul, a clever girl without a sou for dowry, was married at nineteen to a man who was more than twenty years older than she. He also was poor. The couple were almost completely dependent on the patronage of the Comte d'Artois, De Flahaut, Senior, having a sinecure appointment as Director of the Jardin des Plantes. They lived in the Louvre, a portion of which was then used as an apartment house, stove and water pipes marring the symmetry of the evil-smelling palace corridors, dark corners of which were sometimes used as comfort stations by the public.

When Charles was a small boy, a constant visitor to the De Flahaut home was Charles Maurice de Talleyrand-Périgord, the Bishop of Autun, a member of one of the most ancient families of France. Brilliant, witty, and ironic, the Bishop never visited his diocese and did not believe in any of the dogmas of the church. He had a pale, impassive face—half-cat, half-woman—and was so lame, from an injury he had received in childhood, that he walked as though a ball and chain were attached to one of his ankles.

There was yet another lame man who was a frequent visitor. Mr. Gouverneur Morris, later the American Minister to France, had a wooden leg, as well as a conviction that he was irresistible to women. He, also, was on very intimate terms with Madame de Flahaut, though she had confessed to him that she was united by a "marriage of the heart" to Talleyrand and that Charles was Talleyrand's son. Charles himself was unaware of this relationship, and was much devoted to the kindly, indulgent old man whom he called "Papa."

The fall of the monarchy on August 10, 1792, brought an end to this odd, multilateral ménage. All sources of income suddenly dried up. The Comte de Flahaut went to hide in La Boulonnais, his native province, and his wife, after having rescued him once from prison and thinking that he was safe, fled to England with

Charles. There they found Talleyrand. He was no longer Bishop of Autun; he had resigned his see and had been excommunicated by the Pope. His great talents for diplomacy had been put at the service of the Constituent Assembly. Talleyrand was in England on a diplomatic mission at the time of the August crash.

For a short time he and the De Flahauts made common cause, but a break between Great Britain and France was imminent. Talleyrand, who had tried to prevent the break even after the Jacobins took over, was no longer persona grata in England. He left for America in January, 1793, Adélaide de Flahaut was left to manage as best she could. She had asked Talleyrand for money, but he had told her that he had none to spare.

In an amazingly short time, the resourceful little lady had re-worked for publication a novel written earlier, *Adèle de Sénanges*, that was largely autobiographical. It was a great success, its sale netting the author forty thousand francs. Though she had made excellent connections in England and the list of subscribers to her book was studded with noble names, Madame de Flahaut realized that she and Charles could live more economically on the Continent. Mother and son made their way to Switzerland and from thence to Hamburg, where there was a large colony of émigrés. Money had by this time run out, and Adélaide turned to millinery for support, making hats and ladies' evening turbans by day and enjoying the shabby-genteel society of her compatriots by night.

Meanwhile, the Terror had come to an end. Early in 1796, Talleyrand appeared in Hamburg and spent several months there. He had friends in France who gave him the signal when it would be safe and profitable to return. Within a year, he was back in Paris and was appointed Minister for Foreign Affairs by Barras.

It was now time for the De Flahauts to try their luck at repatriation. Charles's mother followed the usual procedure of going home first and then trying, through some influential person, to get her name erased from the list of proscribed emigrants. In this she was helped, not by Talleyrand, but by Joséphine. A small job was found for Charles in the Naval Ministry, but he could hardly wait to get into the army. His letter to the First Consul opened the door. Charles was not appointed aide-de-camp, but he was admitted to the Volunteer Hussars that made up General Bonaparte's guard of honor. The uniform of the corps was bright yellow, and the guardsmen were popularly known as "the Canaries."

Soon, however, an even better way to advancement opened before him. Madame de Flahaut cultivated the society of the elder Bonapartes, all of whom had literary tastes. Joseph, Lucien, and Elisa had all published novels, and the latest to appear in print was Louis, who, still unmarried, had just written his *Marie, or the Pains of Love*. Louis had the idea of writing a play that might be acted by the Malmaison troupe, and asked Madame de Flahaut to read and criticize it. At her suggestion, he arranged for Charles to be transferred from the Canaries to his own regiment, the Fifth Dragoons.

"You must be very attentive to him in every way," Adélaide told her son. "You must let him see how pleasant it would be to have a well brought up boy like you for a friend."

Charles, who believed in doing nothing by halves, offered Louis his most prized possession, a fine Normandy mare. The gift was declined, Louis saying that it was more important for a dragoon to have a good horse than for a colonel. He made a special pet of Charles, however, so much so that at least one observer noted that "he didn't seem happy when the boy was out of his sight." When Louis went to Germany not long before his marriage to Hortense, Charles went with him; and when the Fifth Dragoons were ordered to Spain, double reports came back to Adélaide of how well her son was getting on.

"The Colonel continues to show me kindness. I am dining with him today," Charles wrote. "He occasionally puts me under arrest, but it is all done in a very friendly way."

Adélaide was also assured by Louis that Charles was not being mollycoddled. "I scold him, I punish him when he misbehaves, just like all the rest. I was treated thus at his age. Ours is a hard profession for a boy who has been overindulged. . . . As for money, you are sending him too much."

Even after Charles was transferred to Murat's command, Louis continued to take a tender interest in him and expected to hear from him regularly. Once, when Charles wrote to him to apologize for not having been a better correspondent, Louis replied, "I was not offended by your silence, my dear De Flahaut; that seemed to me mere thoughtlessness. But what really hurt me was your writing that you couldn't think what to say to me, or how to begin."

This friendship was much to Louis' taste, reproducing as it did the situation that had once existed between Napoleon and himself, only now Louis was the masterful elder brother, Charles was his obedient junior. The friendship came to an abrupt end when the visits to Hortense were discovered. Did Louis cross-examine his doorman, or did the sound of a boyish tenor voice drift down from Hortense's sitting room?

Louis' precautions, however, had come too late. It was Charles's enterprising mother who had first taken him to call on Hortense, but Charles needed no prompting to continue his visits. It was as natural for him to follow an attractive woman as it was to smile or laugh, and if the woman happened to be a princess, so much the better for Charles. He was exuberantly heterosexual, and had none of Louis' painful conflict of emotions with which to contend. Having been closely associated with Louis, De Flahaut could pity the woman who was tied to such a husband.

In August, 1804, Hortense was given a brief respite from Louis' supervision. He had to go to Turin to preside over a meeting of the Electoral College of the Po District, and on the way would stop at Plombières to see if the waters there could do anything for his rheumatism. Napoleon and Joséphine were also away from Paris, on a trip to Boulogne and Belgium.

On summer afternoons, Hortense would drive in the Bois de Boulogne with Napoléon Charles and his governess, Madame de Boubers. They would see a rider approaching on a handsome gray horse, and Hortense's pulse would quicken. De Flahaut knew to the minute when she took her drive. Sometimes he rode beside her. Sometimes the carriage would halt, the rider would dismount, and he and Hortense would walk together on one of the forest paths.

They sometimes talked of the Polish girl with whom Hortense had seen De Flahaut at Eugène's lunch party. If Charles spoke kindly of her, he rose in Hortense's estimation; if he dismissed the subject with a shrug, she would say to herself that he was just another heartless flirt. He assured her that the feeling he had for her, Hortense, had antedated the other affair and had not been affected by it. To this Hortense said nothing, but turned away her head so that he couldn't see how pleased she was.

They met often in other spots than in the Bois de Boulogne, most often at Caroline's house. The Murats had a beautiful estate at Neuilly, where there was a large lake with an island in its center. There were boating parties in the afternoon and dancing in the evening. Caroline, the eagle-eyed, soon saw how it was between De Flahaut and her sister-in-law. She noticed that when Hortense asked the young man to dance, he was quick to oblige, even if he had just excused himself to his hostess.

Caroline could see nothing that belonged to her schoolgirl rival without wanting to snatch it. She had come to feel that De Flahaut was her possession. She twitted him on his devotion. She told him seriously, as friend to friend, that he was wasting his time. Hortense might seem to be a sweet, amiable creature, but she was in reality frigid, and it tickled her vanity to have a hopeless suitor dangling after her. It would be a kindness, moreover, to break with Hortense, since Louis was so jealous that any masculine attention would only make his wife's lot the worse.

These remarks were reported to Hortense by De Flahaut, and she wondered if Caroline's campaign was not having its effect, when she drove out several days into the Bois without meeting him. When they met in company, she thought that he was trying to avoid her. She was surprised at first, then hurt, then deeply troubled at her own unhappiness. She told herself, and told her friend, Adèle Auguié, whom she let into her secret, that she must get rid of this constant preoccupation with a man who seemed to care so little for her.

For several weeks, Hortense avoided the gatherings at Caroline's house, but one evening, when she felt easier in mind, she had a sudden impulse to drive out alone to Neuilly. It was a moonlit night. The château was empty except for the servants, who told her that no guests were expected and that Madame la Princesse was on the island in the lake. Hortense walked down toward the water and seated herself on a bench to wait. Presently she saw two people coming up the path, De Flahaut and Caroline, arm in arm.

At sight of them together, Hortense felt as though all the blood in her body had rushed to her heart. Caroline, for once, seemed embarrassed. Only De Flahaut was unconcerned. He tried to speak to Hortense, but she could barely answer him. She hastily took her leave.

When she reached home it was very late, but she could not force herself to go to bed. She sank down on a chair that faced a mirror in her bedroom. There was no use pretending any longer that she could be merely De Flahaut's friend. She loved him. All she wanted now was to escape from the anguish of seeing him with another woman, whether Caroline or his Polish countess. If Louis were here, Hortense said to herself, I would tell him everything and would beg him to take me away from Paris.

She saw in the mirror that the door behind her was opening softly. A man slipped into the room. Hortense screamed—Louis, Louis, whom she had thought a thousand miles away!

"Oh, how you frightened me!" she panted.

"Why are you up so late?" Louis asked suspiciously.

As he told her that he had traveled day and night from Turin, that he had left his carriage on the boulevard and come on foot to the rue Cerutti so that he could let himself into the house without arousing anyone, all thought of confiding in Louis faded. He has come to spy upon me, Hortense said to herself. He doesn't care what might happen to me or to my baby. He might have frightened me into a miscarriage.

All that she said was that she wanted to go away to the country and stay there until it was time for their child to be born.

XII

IMPERIAL OVERTURE

EARLIER in the summer, Louis had bought two neighboring estates at Saint-Leu, one of which had belonged to the Duc d'Orléans. During the past few months the older of the two châteaux had been pulled down, and the surrounding parks had been thrown into one. Hortense shared her mother's fondness for flowers and landscape gardening. She found much at Saint-Leu to distract her and to strengthen her determination to see no more of Charles de Flahaut, though just before leaving Paris she received a letter from Madame de Souza, saying that Charles was distressed that she was going to the country; he only needed a word from her to devote his entire life to her service.

Hortense spent a month at Saint-Leu. When she returned to the rue Cerutti, she found that Louis had made a number of alterations during her absence. The walls around the garden had been raised by several feet; a sentry box had been placed just under Hortense's bedroom window, while the bedroom itself had been made as inaccessible as possible; all of its doors but one leading into the salon had been walled up.

Hortense's term of pregnancy was close at hand, and this time a princess would be brought to bed. Largesse was to be distributed to two hundred needy maternity cases, and Louis had built a hospital at Saint-Leu in honor of the event.

On October 11, 1804, the Archchancellor of the Empire and other dignitaries were waiting in the salon next to Hortense's bedroom to certify the birth. Louis was again solicitous and harrowed by Hortense's pain, but soon after the baby, a second boy, was born, he became his usual somber and suspicious self. The night nurse told Hortense that she heard someone come to the door several times during the night to listen; she wondered who it could be. Hortense did not enlighten her. A few days later, the woman was dismissed and Louis' bed was moved into the room. "What a good, kind husband to want to take care of his wife himself," the nurse said.

But with Louis in constant attendance, Hortense's convalescence was slow. She was roused when he came late to bed at night and when his valet came to call him early in the morning. Both husband and wife were more than usually irritable. Once, just before Hortense's dinner was brought in to her, there was a sharp dispute over Napoléon Charles's dining every day with his father and being allowed to eat anything he liked. Hortense found she could swallow nothing that was set before her. For weeks she was nauseated by the sight of food, lived on sips of wine and morsels of dry bread, and grew thin and pale.

Napoleon commented on how ill she looked. He had returned to Paris, from a tour of Belgium and the Rhineland, the day after the baby was born. Shortly thereafter the birth was registered formally in his presence. Louis wanted the child to be named for himself and had written "Louis" on the register. Napoleon crossed this out and wrote above it "Napoléon Louis." Hortense had to listen to prolonged complaints of this arbitrary act, quite as if she herself were to blame.

Immediately after Napoleon's return, a family meeting was held to decide the details of the coronation; they had been under discussion for many months. Thirty years had gone by since a ruler was crowned. Old records were consulted and elderly people

—Madame Campan was one—were asked to ransack their memories. Napoleon was determined that his crowning should be more colorful, more magnificent, more stupendous than anything that had been seen in France.

As yet, one question remained unanswered. What part in the drama would be assigned to Joséphine? Would she be leading lady or merely a spectator?

The Bonapartes, of course, were violently opposed to her being crowned. Napoleon himself had not made up his mind. Joséphine had just traveled with him along the Rhine, and had shared with him the groveling homage of German princelings. At Aix-la-Chapelle, the presumed birthplace of Charlemagne, Joséphine was given a talisman taken from the tomb of the predecessor with whom Napoleon was most frequently compared, the great emperor, a legendary as well as an historical figure, under whom almost all of Europe had been united. After having been recognized so often as her husband's consort, it would seem illogical to exclude Joséphine now.

It would also be very cruel. Joséphine had set her heart on being crowned. She wanted the old prophecy of "queen and more than queen" to be fulfilled, and she was obsessed with the fear that even at this eleventh hour she might be displaced. Joséphine had resented her husband's affairs with actresses and singers, but such women were not serious rivals to her position. During the autumn of 1804, she was dismayed by the interest that Napoleon was taking in one of the ladies of his court. Whenever the lady was present, he was as charming as only he could be when in good humor; when the lady was absent, he was fretful.

One morning at Saint-Cloud, when Joséphine's salon was full of visitors, she saw the lady in question slip quietly from the room. Joséphine scented an assignation. She found a pretext for leaving her guests and hurried to Napoleon's study. The room was empty. She climbed a narrow staircase to a suite of apartments directly above, which had just been prettily decorated at Napoleon's command. Joséphine heard voices, unmistakably familiar voices behind a closed door. She knocked and called out loudly and angrily to be let in.

When the door was opened, the lady pushed by Joséphine and fled down the stairs. Joséphine also fled before the hurricane of Napoleon's anger. He pursued her to her bedroom where he flung himself back and forth, kicking aside and breaking the furniture. This time, he shouted, she had gone too far. He would not put up with her spying and nagging a moment longer. He would no longer consider her feelings in the shaping of his policies. She must leave Saint-Cloud at once. He would send for Eugène to take her away.

Hortense, who was still an invalid, was visited both by Eugène and by one of Joséphine's ladies in waiting, Madame de Rémusat, who asked her to intervene. Hortense sadly shook her head. Absorbed as she was in her own problems, her mother's seemed small by comparison. Wouldn't it be better, she said, to exchange a crown for a quiet life? Besides, it would be useless for a third party to step in between the two contestants. Joséphine's tears— Hortense knew the power of Joséphine's tears—would do more than anything else to placate Napoleon.

Hortense was right. By the time Eugène reached Saint-Cloud, Napoleon's anger had begun to subside. He spoke of some sort of compensation to mother and son, to soften the separation, and this Eugène proudly and categorically refused. A few days later, husband and wife were reconciled. Napoleon wept as he said, "I haven't the courage to send you away." He added, with a note of pleading in his voice, that he wished Joséphine herself would make the first move toward a divorce, so that he would be free to contract another marriage.

But Joséphine had no intention of doing anything of the sort. She continued to weep and to be meekly submissive. As so often before, she wept her way to victory. One evening in November, Napoleon told her that the Pope, who had been invited by Cardinal Fesch to be present at the coronation, would soon arrive at

Fontainebleau. Joséphine must order at once the costume in which she would be crowned.

There were mighty preparations in the final weeks before the event, which had been twice deferred and which had been set for December 2nd. There were bitter family disputes as to protocol and position in the cortege, the Bonaparte sisters waging—and losing—a war to prevent their being cast as trainbearers to the Empress.

Napoleon, who had told them that they could do as he wished or not set foot in Notre Dame, was digusted by their venom. At this time, his heart was turned away from his blood relatives to his adopted family. Just before the coronation he had a long, uninhibited conversation with a friend of Joseph, Comte Pierre Rœderer, in which he contrasted the Bonapartes with the Beauharnais brother and sister, and in which he particularly mentioned Napoléon Charles.

Napoléon Charles, who all the autumn had been a constant visitor at Saint-Cloud, had learned to talk. His version of his own name was "Nonon" and Napoleon was "l'oncle Bibiche" This was because his uncle would carry him down on his back to the deer park to feed the deer (les biches) with tobacco. As, hand in hand, the two Napoleons walked past the guard of honor, the little boy would shout, "Vive 'Nonon,' le soldat!"

How different this delightful child was from the daughters of Joseph, who rarely came to see their uncle! "They don't know even yet that I am emperor," Napoleon said to Rœderer, "and they think that I am in the habit of beating their mother."

His brothers and sisters, Napoleon continued, who were so greedy, had done nothing for the state, the state that had given him and them so much. Eugène de Beauharnais, on the other hand, had served his country on the battlefield and had asked for nothing in return. His modest bachelor hall near La Malmaison was very different from the fairy palaces of Mortefontaine, Neuilly, and Saint-Leu. When they were on maneuvers, Eugène kept close watch on his step-father. If there was an unexplained cannon shot, he would hurry off to see what had gone wrong; if there was a ditch to be crossed, he was there with outstretched hand.

And Hortense—"I love Hortense," Napoleon said, "yes, I love her. . . . If I were at a council meeting and Hortense asked to speak to me, I would go out to see her. If Madame Murat asked to see me, I would stay where I was. With her, I must always be on my guard and armed to the teeth. . . . They"—by they, Napoleon meant the Bonapartes—"say that my wife is a hypocrite and that her children's attentions to me are due entirely to self-interest. Well, I like it that way! They treat me like a good old uncle. . . . I am getting old; I'm thirty-six, and I would like to take my ease."

On November 25, 1804, Pope Pius VII arrived at Fontainebleau, and his presence in France caused great excitement. Even non-believers were curious to see the saintly old man and his suite of Italian cardinals. He and Joséphine had corresponded in the past; she had sent him vestments of priceless lace. On the 26th, Joséphine had a private audience with the Pontiff, and confessed to him that for the past eight years she and her husband had been living in sin; they had not been married by a priest. Pius was distressed to hear this, and promised to take up the matter himself with Napoleon.

It was no time for the unanointed Emperor of the French to argue with the Pope! The Holy Father might return to Rome at once, and all of Europe would know the reason; all of Europe would laugh. A few days later an altar was set up in Napoleon's study, and he and Joséphine were married by Cardinal Fesch, with only two of Napoleon's aides to witness the ceremony.

This was Joséphine's supreme moment; for once she had forced her indomitable husband to do something against his will. The coronation itself was the lesser, though the more spectacular, achievement, a circus pageant in which all the gilt was gold and all the jewels genuine. As Joséphine moved forward gracefully to the steps of the dais in Notre Dame and knelt before Napoleon to be crowned, there was a murmur of admiration. She was dressed in a white grown, thickly embroidered with golden bees, the imperial symbol that was to replace the fleur-de-lis of the Bourbons; her hair was arranged in soft curls all over her head, the coiffeur of a Roman empress; though she was in her forty-second year, she did not look a day over twenty-five.

As she rose to retire, Joséphine halted for a moment, unable to move under the ponderous weight of her ermine robe, which the Bonaparte sisters had left lying on the floor. A low, angry word from Napoleon quelled this final act of rebellion.

Napoleon himself seemed almost crushed by his gold-encrusted garments. His pale face, which had the beauty of an antique medallion, was stern and sad. Just before entering the cathedral, he had turned to Joseph and said exultingly, "If our father could only see us now!"

But he knew only too well that there were three of Bonaparte flesh and blood who had failed him. Jérôme was still in America with his bride. Letizia, the mother of them all, was in Italy with Lucien. Letizia had made a brief trip to Paris during the summer, in a vain attempt to make peace between her warring sons. At the last, she had elected to stay with the child who was in disgrace, but her absence seemed so inappropriate that Napoleon had ordered David, the artist who would record the scene in the cathedral for posterity, to paint Madame Mère into his picture.

In his gigantic dream of empire, Napoleon's faith in family loyalty, though battered, was still intact. Some six weeks after the coronation, he sent for Hortense and Louis to come to the Tuileries. He told them that it was absolutely necessary for him to adopt Napoléon Charles and to name him King of Italy, with the title of Napoleon II. Until the child was of age, his father would be regent.

At this point Louis began to protest. Never, never would he consent for his son to be set above him.

Napoleon's anger was rising, but he managed to control himself. He explained that the boy would remain in France until he had reached his majority, that he would have a French as well

as an Italian education, and that this was the best way to keep
Lombardy under the control of France and at the same time
avoid a war with Austria.

Louis was obstinate, and Napoleon became emotional. How
cruel it was, he lamented, to have a family that refused to help
him in his work! Every day of his life he was made to feel how
unlucky he was to have no son. He wished he could get along
without asking his brother to do anything more for him. But Louis
could not be budged. He and Hortense, who had said nothing at
all during this altercation, were dismissed.

Perhaps Napoleon had expected that Louis, who was so touchy
on the subject of Napoléon Charles, would refuse. Louis was a
last resort. Napoleon had already offered the Italian throne to
Joseph, with the proviso that Joseph would give up all claim to
the French succession. He had even sounded out Lucien on a
proposition to abandon his wife and to accept the regency. When,
in March, an Italian delegation, fully cognizant of Napoleon's
wishes, came to Paris to offer him the crown, the Emperor accepted it for himself, and left with Joséphine for another series
of elaborate and exhausting ceremonies at Milan.

Before his departure, however, Napoleon attended to two pieces
of family business on an imperial scale. Napoléon Charles's baby
brother was christened by the Pope in the blue salon at Saint-
Cloud, with full imperial pomp. Four Marshals of France held
up the four corners of the ermine robe in which the child was
wrapped. Letizia was the offical godmother, but Hortense herself, held the baby at the font, and was chiefly concerned because
Napoléon Louis wailed loudly throughout the ceremony. That
evening, the park of the palace was illuminated and the public was
invited in to see the fireworks. There was a special performance,
open to all, in the Saint-Cloud theater of Racine's tragedy of
Athalie.

At the same time, Napoleon announced to the Senate that the
little principality of Piombino, the Italian state nearest to the
islands of Corsica and Elba, was to be handed over to his sister,

Elisa Bacciochi, and her husband, to be held as a fief of the French crown. Piombino had only 1,300 inhabitants—later Lucca was added to it—but the gift of this tidbit kingdom to Elisa scorched the hearts of Pauline Borghese and Caroline Murat. Hortense and Louis happened to call on both of the sisters on the day when the announcement was made. Caroline chose to be sarcastic. "So now Elisa is a reigning sovereign," she said with a sniff. "She will have an army consisting of four men and a corporal. Won't that be splendid!"

Pauline was more outspoken. "My brother is only fond of Elisa and forgets all the rest of us," she said, from the chaise longue on which she was lying. "Caroline, who has children and a distinguished husband, deserves better treatment. As far as I am concerned, I ask for nothing, for I am such an invalid, but it isn't fair to Caroline!"

Hortense tried to console her by saying that Napoleon had the same feeling for all of his sisters. He had begun with Elisa merely because she was the eldest.

"You're a fine one to talk," Pauline cried. "You, who get everything that you ask for!"

It was on the tip of Hortense's tongue to retort that she had never asked for a principality, and that the things she wanted most were not within the Emperor's power to give. She managed, however, to pass over Pauline's jibe in silence.

XIII

THE EAGLE STRIKES

IT WAS inevitable that during the series of balls, receptions, and military events that followed the coronation, Hortense should sometimes see Charles de Flahaut. She took care to see him only in the distance. Once, when he rode up to her carriage to speak to her, she leaned forward and told the coachman to drive on.

This resulted in yet another visit from Madame de Souza. Charles's mother, who had fostered her son's courtship so actively, said that Charles was desolated because the Princess would not even speak to him. How had he offended her?

Hortense protested feebly that no offense had been taken; she had not meant to be rude. She saw that she could not avoid De Flahaut forever, and must meet him without embarrassment. At the next ball she spoke a few words to him, hoping that they sounded casual, though she was aware how awkward and breathless they were. The following evening she asked him to waltz with her.

As they slowly circled the room, De Flahaut whispered in her ear how unhappy she had made him by her coquetry.

"I coquettish!" Hortense exclaimed indignantly.

"Yes. Once you were kind to me and I asked for nothing more.

You made me very happy, and then suddenly it seemed as if you hated me."

What he said was true perhaps, but Hortense could not bear to be so misjudged. She felt tears pricking at her eyelids and rolling down her cheeks. She remembered, too late, that she was in a public place and was being watched. What would people say if they saw that she was crying?

De Flahaut looked down at her. "Then you *did* have some feeling for me," he said. "Why didn't you tell me? You could have saved me much sorrow, and things wouldn't be as they are now. I am still in love with you, but I have pledged myself to another woman."

Another woman—who but Caroline? Caroline had boasted recently to Hortense of a deliciously secret love affair. Hortense felt, as she had felt that night at Neuilly, that she must escape from De Flahaut. She must declare her independence. His power to hurt her was too great.

"No, no," she said in a low, vehement voice. "I don't love you. I may have thought so once, but that is all over now. You must believe what I say!"

The music was fading. The dance was coming to an end.

"Won't you at least be my friend?" De Flahaut pleaded. "That at least would be some consolation."

"Yes, I will be your friend," Hortense murmured, though she knew how hopeless it was for her to speak of friendship.

She and De Flahaut had no further opportunity for private talk that evening, and Hortense was glad when the festive season was over and she could go with Louis to Saint-Leu.

All of Hortense's household were young and gay, and they were looking forward to a summer to be passed in a beautiful and luxurious country house. They soon discovered how dull Saint-Leu could be, and how severe its master. Saint-Leu was run like a fortress. One of Louis' aides was in charge of the night patrol and

was constantly being scolded for inefficiency. Louis even criti-
cised the ladies in waiting for wandering about the grounds in
the daytime; and once, when they pushed open a door in the wall
that surrounded the park and made an excursion into the open
forest beyond, he was very angry and had the exit filled in with
masonry.

There were few visitors, and none of them were men, except
those who came on business. When the ladies went to Paris, Louis
set a spy to shadow their movements. They found also that, while
they were gone, their desks had been opened and that someone
had been reading their correspondence. Hitherto, they had tended
to think that Hortense was unduly cold toward her husband, but
now they began to be sorry for her. One day, she caught her *valet
de chambre* going through her papers, and the man confessed that
Louis had promised to pay him well if he could find some damaging
document.

Hortense tried to ignore Louis' espionage as much as possible,
and spent her time with her children or else in copying an oil
painting of herself by Gérard, though the smell of the paint induced nausea and she was still much troubled by her nervous indigestion. In June, she received some news that greatly depressed
her. Eugène, who had preceded Napoleon and Joséphine to Milan,
had been named Viceroy of Italy. Napoleon had decided on this
step before leaving France, and had paved the way for it by a
letter published in the *Moniteur*, praising Eugène's services and
unselfish devotion to the Emperor. This was a great honor for a
young man of twenty-four, but it meant that Hortense would rarely
see Eugène in the future. Louis' lack of sympathy on the subject
was hard to bear.

In spite of the constant irritation that he caused her, Hortense
realized that some of her husband's oddities were due to his poor
health. His rheumatism had become worse during the past year;
he had almost lost the use of his right hand. His doctors suggested
that he might benefit from mud baths at Saint-Amand, a health

resort in northern France. Hortense sent the baby to stay with her mother, who had just returned from Italy, and in July left with Louis when he went to take his cure.

Saint-Amand was a dreary spot; in spite of its medicinal mud, Hortense could not help feeling that it was unhealthy. After a month of boredom, there came the hope of something better, an invitation from Napoleon for her to come to visit him at Boulogne for a week and to bring Napoléon Charles with her. "Arrange this with Louis. . . . I will be glad to see you. You will never know how fond I am of you, or how much I care for you."

Hortense was very anxious to see the great encampment at Boulogne, where, for the past two years, Napoleon had been massing his troops for an invasion of Great Britain. She was kept in suspense for several days, before Louis gave her permission to leave him. When she set off, it was with a sense of renewed health, of adventure, and of escape.

The camps which fringed Boulogne were set close to the sea, vast towns of wooden buildings laid out in streets and squares, each barrack having its flower garden and its cage of singing birds. The harbors were filled with a flotilla of flat-bottomed praams, for the crossing of the channel. On a clear day, one could see the shores of England and the watchdog fleet of British ships, hovering in the blue between.

Hortense was warmly welcomed by Napoleon, and was lodged in a small country house, Pont des Bricques, that was so crowded that two or three must share a room. An imperial equerry was detailed to accompany the Princess on her visits to the various regiments. As she drove up in her carriage, surrounded by its mounted escort, she would see the men hurrying out of their barracks to fall into line for a parade. She was greeted by military music, and was loudly cheered when she asked that all those under disciplinary arrest should be released in her honor.

Hortense had witnessed many military reviews in Paris, but had never come as close as this to the soldier in the ranks. He looked so fiercely efficient on parade, that it was surprising to see how naïve and boyish he could be when at liberty. Hortense watched from the window of the house, as one of Napoleon's gigantic bodyguards played the violin and gave a dancing lesson to his fellows, who were putting their hearts and souls into learning the steps that Hortense had learned in childhood, leaping about and shuffling their great feet in *jetés* and *entrechats*. She was given lunch at one of the camps, out-of-doors under a tent, and some soldiers, very shy, very much embarrassed, came to sing her a song about the invasion of Britain, the refrain of each verse being that "to cross the ditch, one doesn't need to drink dry the sea."

One day, when Hortense and Napoléon Charles were walking about one of the camps with the Emperor, they found themselves in the midst of a skirmish. The English ships had pressed in close to shore and fired a few cannon shot. Napoleon at once reverted to his favorite role of artillery captain, shouting orders, running up and down the line of guns, in constant risk of being struck by a ball or by one of the lanyards as they backfired. He was very much pleased, because Napoléon Charles was not frightened during the brief barrage. "Nonon" clapped his hands at each explosion.

"Now everybody fire!" he shouted. "*Mon Dieu*, how I wish 'Tété'"—his name for his Uncle Eugène—"could see this! How beautiful war is!"

Adèle Auguié had come to the encampment with Hortense, and her sister Eglé, now the wife of General Michel Ney, gave a fête in Hortense's honor at Montreuil, just outside of Boulogne. There was a military parade in the afternoon, and a ball in the evening. Suddenly the music stopped. An excited announcement was made, that the attack on England was about to begin and that the Emperor had already embarked.

In an instant the ballroom was empty. The young officers left their partners in the lurch, as they scrambled to get some sort of conveyance back to Boulogne. Hortense was whisked away to Pont desBricques by her equerry, who all the way groaned at the thought of being too late "to cross the ditch." It seemed as if within a few hours, as soon as it was light, Hortense would witness a great naval battle from the watchtower of the camp.

She and the others soon learned that this had been a false alarm, though Napoleon had spent the greater part of the night in embarking his troops and timing the manuever. He was only waiting to hear by semaphore telegraph that the French fleet was in the Channel.

All too soon, the week's liberty that Hortense had been granted by Louis was up. Napoleon urged her to stay a day or two longer and was gruff when she demurred. "If you would rather displease me than your husband, very well," he said. When she yielded, he told her that she was much too afraid of Louis; Louis was unreasonable because she gave in to him.

Hortense, on her way back to Saint-Amand, passed through Dunkerque and Calais, where she saw more military activity. She had been lifted out of a long period of depression by her visit. She had even seen Charles de Flahaut several times at Boulogne, without disturbance to her equilibrium. He had ridden beside her carriage and they had sung duets together, though they had had no chance for the private conversation that De Flahaut seemed to want.

It was a chilly return to reality to find herself once more with Louis. He was sulky because she had overstayed her leave, and cool to her enthusiasm for the army and her interest in its movements.

Every day at Saint-Amand they expected to hear that the invasion of England had taken place. Then troops began to pass rapidly through the town, moving by forced marches away from the Channel and toward the Rhine. Napoleon had made one of his thunderbolt decisions. He realized that his fleet was no match for the British. He knew nothing himself of naval operations, and had never found an admiral whose genius for war on the sea was equal to his upon the land. Someday he would settle his account with

England. In the meantime, he would make himself master of the Continent.

回

After his crowning in Italy, a new anti-French coalition had been formed between England, Austria, Sweden, and Russia. As always, Napoleon was determined to strike hard and to strike swiftly. While his armies were being pushed eastward at as rapid a pace as human flesh—and horseflesh—could withstand, he directed their movements from Paris and made final preparations. In his schedule, night and day were ignored; Napoleon would work until exhausted, sleep a few hours, then work again.

He found a moment, however, to dash off a note to Hortense, saying that he hoped to see her before his departure. She and Louis returned to the capital to get his instructions. Napoleon was leaving Joseph to be his political figurehead. Joachim Murat, his most dashing cavalry commander, would go with him, and Louis would take Murat's place as military Governor of Paris.

Louis accepted the post with reluctance and lamentation. He told Hortense that he suspected his brother was trying to use him as a scapegoat. Suppose some crisis should arise, as at the time of the Duc d'Enghien affair, and he should have to act severely. His being left at home, also, was an announcement to the world that he was just an invalid.

One September morning Paris awoke to find that the Emperor was gone. Napoleon, to save delay, always left for a journey in dead of night. Joséphine, who had been at Plombières for her annual cure while her husband was at Boulogne, left also, with most of her household and an overladen baggage train. She went to Strasbourg, where she would be as close to the theater of war as possible. This would be a welcome change for her, from the stately monotony of her life at Saint-Cloud.

Hortense was much alone that autumn and winter. In November, Louis was ordered to lead an army into the Netherlands to discourage Prussia from joining in the fight. The outbreak of war had brought on a financial crisis, and, after a period of great prosperity, there was unemployment and poverty. Hortense busied herself not only with music and painting, but also with charitable organizations: an old peoples' home, a mothers' aid. Her only charities thus far had been privately administered by Madame Campan, and took the form of scholarships for girls at Saint-Germain.

In distributing her largesse, Hortense preferred the personal touch. She took her children often to the Bois and struck up a friendship there with an old woman who sold cakes and gingerbread. Hortense would give the boys a louis to present to the cake-seller when they left.

But no handsome gray horse and rider came cantering down the bridle paths under the bare-branched trees. De Flahaut was far away. He was one of Murat's cavaliers. The cavalry was perhaps the most dangerous branch of the service; the saying was that Death rode pillion behind every saddle.

Hortense searched the military bulletins, fearing that she might find De Flahaut's name among the dead. In October, the great Austrian stronghold of Ulm was taken, and Charles was cited for bravery. On November 1st, he was wounded at Lambach. Hortense was glad that she was alone when she read the news item. She kept a watch on Caroline. If Caroline was gay, Hortense held it against her. If Caroline seemed depressed, Hortense was sorry for her and was almost ready to forgive her for the unhappy moments that she had suffered herself.

Meanwhile, Joséphine was sending from Strasbourg copies of Napoleon's brief, but spirited, letters. The financial situation eased under the constant flow of good news from the front.

On November 12th, the French army entered Vienna, from which the Austrian Emperor had fled. Protected by Murat's cavalry, the troops were given a chance for rest, and time for reinforcements to arrive. Napoleon had selected December 2nd, the first anniversary of his coronation, for the day of battle. He moved eastward into Moravia to meet the combined Austrian and Russian armies, and on December 1, 1805, was encamped near the town of Austerlitz. That night he again demonstrated his skill as mass magician. He issued a stirring bulletin to his troops that outlined his strategy: "Our position is strong; while they march to turn our right, they will expose their own flank." He promised victory, but promised also that if victory was in doubt, he would expose himself to enemy fire in the front rank.

At nine o'clock in the evening, Napoleon made a round of the bivouacs alone and on foot. Everywhere he was recognized. The soldiers stuck wads of straw from their bedding on poles, lighted them at their campfires, and waved them wildly as they cheered. One old Mustache shouted to Napoleon to "keep out of the fight . . . We will bring you the standards, we will bring you the guns of the Russians for your anniversary."

Enemy scouts, seeing the flickering torches, thought that this was a sign that something had gone wrong and that the French were retreating. This was only the first of a series of miscalculations. The following day, the Russo-Austrian army of almost a hundred thousand men was totally defeated in less than four hours. The French were so rich in reserves that the infantry of the guard was not even sent into action, and the men wept with rage when they saw how the fight was going. Napoleon had been in thirty battles and had never known defeat, but Austerlitz was his greatest, his classic victory. It compensated for the destruction of a large part of the French fleet at Trafalgar in October, an action that was glossed over in the account given to the public.

Napoleon had the idea of sending for Napoléon Charles, so that the boy could share in his triumph and be exhibited to the army. He wrote to Louis on the subject—Louis, who was still in Holland. Hortense was not sorry to learn that Louis had refused to send their child on the long, winter journey into Austria, though it was plain that Napoléon Charles still figured in the Emperor's plans for the future. Napoleon wrote to Hortense that he hoped her son would grow up to be worthy of the great responsibilities that were in store for him.

XIV

QUEEN HORTENSE

NAPOLEON had received help in his campaign from various South German principalities; at Austerlitz, Bavarians had fought beside the French. In the Treaty of Pressburg, that followed the victory, the dissolution of the Holy Roman Empire was foreshadowed. Austria was forced not only to recognize Napoleon's arrangements in Italy, but those in Germany as well. The Electors of Bavaria and Württemberg were to be recognized as independent sovereigns; and the grand duchies of Baden, Nassau, Hesse-Darmstadt, Berg, and Clèves were to be united under French protection in a Confederation of the Rhine.

Napoleon lost no time in making personal ties with these political entities. He turned his attention first to Bavaria, where an unmarried daughter of the House of Wittelsbach was engaged to the Grand Duke of Baden. Word was sent to Joséphine to hurry from Strasbourg to Munich, to break this engagement and to make a new one, with Eugène de Beauharnais as fiancé.

Joséphine's heart was in her task. This would be a glorious match for Eugène, for the Bavarian royal family could trace its descent from Charlemagne. At first, however, Joséphine made little headway. General Duroc was sent from Vienna to lend her a helping hand, and eventually Napoleon himself came to Munich.

He arrived on the last day of December, 1805. He found that the Bavarian King was urging his daughter to accept; the real trouble was with the Princess herself and with her stepmother, the Queen, who was a sister of the Grand Duke of Baden.

Napoleon all but made love to the Queen; Joséphine might have been jealous of this affair, except for its political implications. He also turned his full powers, to fascinate and to subdue, on the Princess Amalie Augusta, who, though only in her teens, could drive a sharp bargain. She said that she would submit to what she called "her sad fate," if Eugène was crowned King of Italy. Napoleon boggled at this proviso, but promised to confirm Eugène as viceroy for life and to adopt him as his son, with the title of Prince Eugène Napoléon of France. Napoleon himself would provide Augusta with a large dowry.

The young lady quickly canceled her attachment to her step-uncle-in-law and came to terms. The preparations for the marriage, that was to take place on January 14th, were hurried. All of the Bonaparte family were told to send expensive wedding presents, costing no less than twenty thousand francs apiece, but there was no time to send to Paris for Augusta's trousseau. Joséphine had to strip her own wardrobe and sacrifice some of her fabulous collection of shawls for Eugène's *corbeille*.

Eugène came obediently from Italy, not knowing at first why he had been summoned. En route he received a picture of his bride, painted on a teacup. In the covering letter, Napoleon said that Augusta was very much prettier than her portrait—as indeed she was. Because she was known to dislike hairy men, Eugène nobly consented to shave off his military mustache. When he was introduced to his future wife and to her parents by the Emperor, it suited Napoleon's whim to play the proud father, who tries to hide his pride under a bluff and hearty manner. "I want to present to you my great booby of a son," he said.

Hortense was unable to see Eugène married—a cruel disappointment; Louis would not let her go to Munich. She and some of Eugène's friends met at his house in Paris on the wedding day, to

drink his health and wreathe his picture with laurel. Hortense had
an account of the wedding later from Caroline Murat, who had
gone to join her husband in Munich after Austerlitz. The Murats
had attended the ceremony under duress, for Joachim was as
jealous of Eugène as Caroline was of Hortense. When he heard
that the upstart Beauharnais was to be a Prince of France, Murat
wrathfully broke his sword across his knee. He himself, the son of
an innkeeper, was soon to be Grand Duke of Berg and Clèves, but
to a bold Gascon that seemed a shabby recompense for the brilliant
campaign that he had just fought in Austria.

On his way home from Munich, Napoleon stopped in Baden to
smooth down any feathers that might have been ruffled by his
high-handed doings in Bavaria, and to offer the jilted bridegroom
another bride. The nearest female relative Napoleon could produce for the Grand Duke was Stéphanie de Beauharnais, a cousin
in the fifth degree of Hortense. She was a half-orphan, who, like
Émilie de Beauharnais, had been more or less abandoned by her
family, rescued by Napoleon and Joséphine, and sent to Madame
Campan's school. Pert, flirtatious—she was even flirtatious with
the Emperor—and not yet seventeen, Stéphanie had been kept in
the background hitherto, though Joséphine and Hortense had been
kind to her and invited her often to La Malmaison and Saint-Leu.
Soon after Napoleon's return to Paris, Stéphanie was adopted by
imperial decree, and was married in April to the Grand Duke of
Baden with great pomp: a dowry of a million and a half francs,
trousseau and diamonds to match, a blaze of fireworks in the
Place de la Concorde.

Napoleon's conception of the Great Empire was becoming a
reality. In January, he had sent Joseph, at the head of a French
army, to push off the throne of Naples a feckless Bourbon king,
who had allied himself with England. In Piombino and Lucca,
while Prince Félix Bacciochi played the violin and rode horseback, Princess Elisa was proving an able administrator: draining
swamps, building roads, encouraging the arts, and imposing on her

tiny court as elaborate a ceremonial as was in force at the Tuileries.

Pauline was given the Duchy of Guastalla in Italy, but was so little impressed by the gift that she was ready to sell it to the highest bidder. Bored by Prince Borghese, Pauline was chiefly interested in living a luxurious and amorous life in Paris while her husband was kept busy in the army. Jérôme, who closely resembled Pauline in temperament, was also being groomed for kingship. He had come to Europe with his American wife while Napoleon and Joséphine were being crowned in Italy, but Napoleon refused to see him until "Miss Patterson," as he persisted in calling her, was sent back to America with the son she had borne Jérôme. Though, much to Napoleon's indignation, the Pope refused to dissolve Jérôme's marriage, a bride had already been selected for him, Catherine, the daughter of the King of Würtemberg. Jérôme's kingdom of Westphalia would be part of the new German federation, which would be further strengthened by the donation of certain ecclesiastical holdings in the Rhineland to Uncle Cardinal Fesch.

With the Corsican clan thus spreading over all of Europe, it was now the turn of Louis and Hortense to take their places. Napoleon had sent Louis into Holland in the autumn, less for military glory than to make a good impression in the country. Holland, a commercial country, loomed large in Napoleon's imperial plans. He was building his empire to break, by a blockade of English goods, the strangle hold England had on the economic life of the Continent.

For the past twelve years, the fortunes of the Netherlands had been closely bound to France. In the winter of 1794, Holland was overrun by a French revolutionary army, and the Stadholder, William V of Orange, fled to England. A Batavian Republic was established with local patriot support, but firmly tied to France. As a result, during the war years, Dutch commerce was destroyed and Dutch colonies were seized by the British. When Napoleon's peace treaty with England was signed at Amiens in 1802, Holland got back the Cape of Good Hope and her West Indian possessions,

but they were promptly snatched away from her when war broke
out again. Two events had recently taken place that gave Napoleon
an excuse to intervene: The Stadholder had died in exile, and the
present head of state, the Grand Pensioner Schimmelpennick, was
threatened with blindness.

A delegation of four prominent Dutchmen—one of them an admiral, one a minister of finance—came to Paris to ask Napoleon to
suggest someone, acceptable to him, who could take the Grand
Pensioner's place. The quartet never reached the Tuileries. Napoleon refused to grant an audience until consent had been given
to an hereditary monarchy.

Early in May, Louis announced to Hortense that he had been
offered the throne of Holland.

"I certainly hope that you won't accept it," she cried.

She expected that Louis, with his pronounced tendency to say
no to everything that his brother proposed, would decline the
offer. He seemed unenthusiastic, and Hortense found an unexpected ally in Caroline, who was presently knocking at the door
of the house in the rue Cerutti. Caroline had been so little gratified
to find herself Duchess of Berg and Clèves, that she refused to
visit her principality with Murat.

"I only went to the marriage of Prince Eugène in Munich,"
Caroline said, "because the Emperor promised me the Dutch
crown. I don't want to remind him of his promise without your
consent. Will it be all right if I do so?"

Both Louis and Hortense assured Caroline that they would be
very happy if she got what she wanted, but they soon learned that
she had been unsuccessful.

Hortense was dismayed to see that Louis was not really sorry
for Caroline's discomforture and that he was going, for once, to
fall in with Napoleon's plans. Was it the thought of partial independence that attracted him? Did he think also that in a foreign
country, where his wife was separated from her mother and her
stepfather, he could play the domestic tyrant to his heart's content?

Hortense realized now how much she had counted in the past on Napoleon's holding Louis in check. In Holland she would be at her husband's mercy; there would be no court of last appeal. For a moment, she thought that she would go to the Emperor, fall at his feet, tell him, as she had never told him before, how unhappy she was, and beg him to let her stay in France. But then she thought of her children, now heirs to a throne; they would have to go to Holland in any case, and she could not bear to be separated from them. She remembered a folk tale that she had heard when she was a little girl, that had made a deep impression on her. It was about a high-born lady, who left her cruel husband, and some years later came back in disguise to be her children's nurse, putting up with a hard life and many cruelties so that she could be near them. Hortense would have to make a similar sacrifice for the sake of Napoléon Charles and Napoléon Louis.

When the news of Louis' accession was announced, the court happened to be in ten days mourning for the death of a Spanish princess, and everyone was wearing black. This fitted Hortense's mood exactly, though it was taken for granted that she was overjoyed, and there were official visits of congratulation from every embassy in Paris. Napoleon noticed Hortense's depression and took her to task. He, who was so ambitious himself, could not understand her attitude.

"Why don't you rise to the situation?" he exclaimed. "Go, reign, and make your people happy. That ought to be some satisfaction to you! I have done something for you that is unknown in any other country. According to the constitution, you will have regency rights, and that's a very flattering distinction. Show yourself worthy of it."

"Oh, sire," Hortense said, "it's no use trying to make me over. I will always be a bourgeois at heart, if that is what you call being passionately fond of my own country, my own friends, my own family."

On June 3rd, Talleyrand, the Minister of Foreign Affairs, came to Saint-Leu to read the constitution to the King and Queen. Need-

less to say, it gave every opportunity for supervision by France.
Two days later, Louis and Hortense went to the Tuileries for the
formal proclamation. They took Napoléon Charles with them.
While they were waiting in an anteroom, during a pause in the
ceremony, Napoleon chatted with his namesake. "Nonon's" education had begun. Though he couldn't read, he was being taught
to recite poems by heart.

"What have you been learning today?" the Emperor asked.

"A fable, Uncle."

"I would like to hear it."

Napoléon Charles drew himself up and began to recite in a
childish singsong:

The Frogs Who Asked for a King

The frogs, sick to death
Of being democratic,
Made such a croaking, such a racket,
That Jupiter . . .

"Nonon's" recitation piece was La Fontaine's version of the
fable of King Stork and King Log, and it was so apt to the present
situation—Napoleon as Jupiter, the delegation from Holland as
the frogs, who might, or might not, like the king who would soon
descend upon them from on high—that the corners of Napoleon's
mouth began to twitch. The end of the fable was unheard. Napoléon Charles's small voice was buried under an avalanche of
Olympian laughter.

There was no laughter during the rest of the day's proceedings.
When the doors were opened into the audience hall, where a
large company was assembled, Louis entered first, the major-
domo giving forth in booming tones, "His Majesty, the King of
Holland." There was a speech from the imperial throne and one
in reply from Louis. Napoleon pointed out that Louis was still
a Constable of France and owed allegiance to the empire; he must

never forget that he was a Frenchman. Louis urged the Emperor to keep the peace in Europe, and promised that he would serve his newly acquired subjects well.

Immediately after the ceremony, the Dutch delegation left for home, and royalty began to pack. There were many ambitious men who wanted to find places for themselves in the new court, but Louis was wary in making any promises. He told Hortense frankly that he did not want any "attractive" men in his household.

Hortense, in the past, had been constantly asked to present petitions to the Emperor, sometimes for mercy, sometimes for a post. She had made her requests either through her mother, or in her own person, with fear and trembling. She took the opportunity now of clearing her docket and getting a favorable answer from Napoleon, who was in a mood to grant her anything.

There was one piece of unfinished business that she was sorry to leave behind; she had been trying for years to find a good husband for Adèle Auguié, who, a year younger than Hortense, was twenty-two, and should have been married long ago. Hortense had considered many candidates, but none of them seemed worthy of her dearest friend, who, though often courted, seemed willing to remain an old maid and to devote her life to Hortense. Even Louis, who disliked most women, could find nothing harsh to say of Mademoiselle Auguié. Hortense made arrangements for Adèle to join her soon at the Hague. Perhaps the perfect match could be made there.

Departure from Saint-Leu was set for mid-June. The day before, Hortense went to Saint-Cloud to say good-bye to her mother, Napoleon cutting short a farewell that threatened to become overemotional. Hortense also stopped at her house in Paris for various errands. The courtyard was full of people, carriages, and baggage vans, as the first convoy for Holland was about to start. The big, gloomy house was empty, except for a single servant. Hortense and one of her ladies were waiting indoors for the carriage that was to take them to Saint-Leu, when she was told that someone wanted to see her and would like to speak to her alone. Hortense's companion retired, and a man, muffled to the eyes, entered the room.

Hortense gave a little shriek of surprise as she recognized Charles de Flahaut. She had not seen him since his return from the wars and his promotion to a captaincy.

"Be careful," he whispered, "someone might come in and you would be compromised."

"I don't care what people think," Hortense cried, "so long as I do no harm."

She would not let him come near her, for she did not trust herself. She told him that she loved him, but that she refused to be his mistress. She would keep that weapon from her husband, small though the consolation was. They might never meet again, she said, and she hoped he would be happy. Before he could say anything further, she had left the room.

The following night, Hortense and Louis set out for their kingdom. Hortense held the sleeping Napoléon Charles on her lap; Napoléon Louis slumbered in his nurse's arms. Hortense sensed that her husband, beside her in the dark carriage, was as depressed at leaving France as she, and that he faced the future with some of her foreboding. But she could find nothing to say to him. He, too, was silent. It was impossible for either of them to share this moment with the other.

PART

III

(June 15, 1806–July 8, 1810)

꙰꙰꙰꙰꙰꙰꙰꙰꙰꙰

XV

THE KINGDOM OF FROGS

IN the French towns through which the King and Queen of Holland passed, they were given royal honors. There were dull and pompous speeches to which one was forced to listen with a royal smile; there were royal replies to be made. Hortense had to admit that Louis acquitted himself well in this respect. He had dignity and a good command of rhetoric. When the border was reached, the escort that had come with them thus far turned back, and Hortense saw it go with a pang of incipient homesickness. Ahead lay exile and all that was strange and unfamiliar.

She had thought of Holland as a soggy, subaqueous region, shrouded in mist, but her first impression of its green fields and the trees that lined its canals was pleasing. On June 18th, the King and Queen reached the Hus ten Bosch, the House in the Woods, just outside of the Hague, where they waited for a few days until the city was ready to receive them. On the day of their entry, there was a great turnout in the streets and a great reception at the picturesque old palace, the Binnenhof. It was Hortense's first duty as Queen, one that she enjoyed, to preside at a ball, and respond to the deep curtseys of four hundred Dutch ladies who were presented to her. With Joséphine in mind, she made a point of rewarding each bow with a smile and few gracious words.

A week later, she and Louis visited Rotterdam for the launching of a vessel. Holland's largest seaport had suffered cruelly from the stoppage of trade, and its inhabitants apparently thought that any change would be for the better. The horses were unhitched from the royal coach, man power was substituted, and Hortense found herself being swept through the narrow, canyoned streets on a torrent of upturned faces. She found it hard to enter into the spirit of the occasion. Every moment she was afraid that she might see someone fall and go down under the wheels of the carriage. She was reminded of the stories that Madame Campan used to tell to her pupils of the enthusiastic receptions that were given to Marie Antoinette when she first came to France. Hortense wondered morbidly if these people, who were capering and shouting about her now, would be glad someday to see her ride to her death.

Louis busied himself by becoming acquainted with his new duties and began to take lessons in Dutch. Though Hortense was obviously an asset in the creation of good-will, he made it plain that he wanted her to remain in the background. Admiral Carel Ver-Huell, the interregnum chief of state, had put the names of the King and Queen into the prayers to be recited in churches, but Louis told him that in future only the King should be brought to the attention of the Deity.

Hortense was to present some banners to the royal guard, and sent to Paris to get ribbons embroiderd with her name to be fastened to the standards. Louis would not allow their use. "It would seem as if it were you who were giving them these things," he said. Since he found it tiring to stand at receptions for any length of time, he forbade Hortense to move about among the crowd and speak to her guests. She must merely bow to the assembly and then retire to her chair or throne.

Louis had brought three physicians with him from France, for he feared the effect of the damp Dutch climate on his rheumatism. He had hardly arrived and shown himself to his subjects, when he wanted to go to Wiesbaden for a cure. He and Hortense left the

Hague on July 26th. After only a few weeks at the spa, Louis
decided that he would get better results from the hot sulphur baths
at Aix-la-Chapelle. He went there as quickly as possible by land,
but allowed Hortense to follow him up the Rhine as far as
Cologne in the private yacht of the Prince of Nassau. Adèle
Auguié and Adèle's father, who had come from Paris to meet
Hortense, were to be her only adult companions.

The river voyage was a delicious interlude. By day, Hortense
sat in the shadow of a sail and admired medieval castles and the
sort of sketchbook scenery she had been copying all her life.
She discovered a new talent; she composed romantic ballads and
sang them to the accompaniment of her guitar. At Cologne, she
had to be a queen again. She rode in a coach of state that smelled
of mildew, and in the evening attended a ball given for Murat,
Grand Duke of Berg and Clèves, who was on his way to visit
his estates, unaccompanied by Caroline.

There was a good reason, it seemed, for Murat's presence in
this part of the world. While Hortense and Louis were at Aix,
the Grand Army was on the move. Prussia, which had joined the
Coalition before the close of the Austerlitz campaign, had declared
war on France. The Prussian King, Frederick William III, was
timid; but his beautiful, spirited wife, Queen Louise, was ven-
turesome. She was rash enough to think that the ghost of Frederick the Great would be a match for a live Napoleon.

In September, Louis was told by Napoleon what was expected
of him in the coming campaign. He was to return to Holland,
collect a year's taxes in advance, and lead a combined French and
Dutch army against the fortress of Wesel on the Lower Rhine.
Louis hesitated, told Napoleon that he was not sure that he was
strong enough physically for a winter expedition, but, as usual,
obeyed. Since there was a possibility of an English attack on the
coast, Hortense was to go to Mainz, where Joséphine had come to
sit out the war, just as a year earlier she had gone to Strasbourg.

To go to Mainz was almost as good as to go home to Paris.
Hortense was not only reunited with her mother and her cousin

Stéphanie, the Grand Duchess of Baden, but with a whole covey of her school friends, wives of officers who had gone into Prussia. Madame Campan's girls were constantly together. Their chief concern was for news from the army. They were forever listening for the bugle flourish of a courier as he came galloping into the town. Napoleon had so conditioned them to victory that they did not expect to hear of a defeat. They feared only personal loss. Hortense was again anxious for Charles de Flahaut. She had caught a glimpse, but only a glimpse, of him as he passed through Aix earlier in the summer.

The Prussian campaign proved, at first, to be as swift and lethal as all of Napoleon's military undertakings. On October 14th, the Prussian army was shattered at Jena and Auerstedt; less than a fortnight later the French took possession of Berlin. Droves of prisoners began to pass through Mainz. They plodded directly under Hortense's windows, and looked so miserable, that she sent out a servant to distribute money among them.

Mainz was crowded, not only with the French officers, but with German royalty who came to pay court to Joséphine.

Talleyrand, now, by Napoleon's gift, Prince of Benevento, arrived from Paris on his way to Berlin. Hortense had known Charles de Flahaut's unofficial father for years. She had often seen him limp into the salon at La Malmaison and, resting his hand on the back of a chair to balance the weight of his crippled foot, look about him with a supercilious smile. He had rarely spoken more than a word to Hortense, but now he sought her out and made himself agreeable. Flattered, she tried to analyze his charm. The technique of his wit, she noted, was to let others talk—often foolishly—and then interpose a single perfect word or comment that summed up the entire situation. The secret of his power over others lay not in character, but in intellect, and was all the greater because he so rarely gave himself away.

Talleyrand introduced to Hortense—was this the reason for his cordiality—a young man, a cousin of De Flahaut, Charles de la Bédoyère, who was anxious to get a commission in a new cavalry unit that was being formed at Mainz. Hortense saw to it that the young man got a sublieutenancy. She would do all that she could for a relative of De Flahaut; in the evening, when Joséphine's salon was full of officers, she singled out De la Bédoyère for special attention.

De la Bédoyère was a handsome youth, self-consciously romantic and melancholy, who posed as a misogynist and misanthrope. He told Hortense that he had entered the army against the wishes of his family, who were old-fashioned royalists. He, too, had little love for the Empire, but his great ambition was to live dangerously.

Hortense and her friends went, for a few days, to Frankfurt, where they were elaborately entertained by the Grand Duke of Nassau. One of the diversions was a masked ball. Hortense walked about the assembly room, arm in arm with one of her ladies in waiting, not venturing to speak to anyone for fear of being recognized. Every one thought that a figure seated in a great armchair was she, though the masquerader was actually a boy, an imperial page in disguise.

After the return to Mainz, De la Bédoyère assured Hortense, with a meaningful smile, that he had recognized one of the ladies at the ball and had had a long conversation with her, which he had transcribed word for word. He handed Hortense his manuscript. She thought that this was a joke of some sort and started to read De la Bédoyère's effusion aloud to her school friends. She was embarrassed to find that she was reading a thinly veiled declaration of love addressed to herself. She took care to tell her admirer, the next time she saw him, that she would be sorry to think that anyone had developed a feeling for her that she could never reciprocate. Her heart was no longer hers to give. She thought, perhaps, that what she said would be reported to De Flahaut by his cousin.

A few days later, the new cavalry corps left to join the Grand Army, and De la Bédoyère took leave of Hortense, trying hard— but not too hard—to hide his anguish.

Hortense hoped that she herself might soon be going to Berlin with her mother, for the signing of a peace treaty, but the visit was deferred. The war was taking a new direction. Prussia had been crushed, but not the Coalition. From Berlin, Napoleon issued decrees declaring a blockade of all Continental ports to English ships. He intended also to strike at Russia. Sending Murat and his cavalry on ahead, he pushed eastward into the snow and mud of a Polish winter. On January 1, 1807, he was in Warsaw.

In Mainz, the jolly New Year's wishes that Hortense received from all sides only brought tears to her eyes. Louis, home from the wars, had written her to come to the Hague. She delayed as long as possible, but knew that in the end she would have to go, feeling a premonition—later remembered—of disaster.

"I wonder what misfortune will come to me this year?" she said gloomily to Adèle.

Adèle, who always tempered her sympathy with common sense, replied, "Don't go looking for trouble. Haven't you had enough already?"

凹

In Holland, the year 1807 had begun with a national calamity. A vessel, heavily freighted with gunpower, exploded in one of the canals of Leiden, causing immense damage and hundreds of casualties. Louis hurried to the scene, took an active part himself in rescue work, and gave large donations to relief funds. Hortense wanted to contribute something herself and, over Louis' veto, gave twenty thousand francs. Louis, who was so generous to charity himself, would not allow his wife to lend her name to charitable organizations or to preside at their meetings, though Hortense felt that this was one of her functions as a queen.

Apparently, there had been pleasant social gatherings at the Binnenhof before Hortense's arrival, but as soon as she appeared, they ceased altogether. Everything bcame dull, formal, and overladen with etiquette. All the Frenchmen with whom Louis had chosen to surround himself were ordered to find lodgings outside the palace, and after six o'clock in the evening, no one was allowed to enter without a written card of permission from the Grand Chamberlain. Louis had selected two ancient, though worthy, gentlemen to be the Queen's equerries. One looked like Don Quixote, and the other like a blend of Sancho Panza with Punch. When Hortense rode horseback, she didn't dare to go faster than a slow trot, for fear that it would be too much for her elderly squires.

She had brought Adèle and Madame Duroc back with her from Mainz, but they soon left for France. Adèle was going home to be married, a suitable match having at last been arranged for her with a Monsieur de Broc, one of the few of Louis' courtiers who was not unappetizing. Hortense felt abandoned, and lived in great isolation. She saw Louis only at mealtimes. He went alone to the theater and sometimes gave concerts in his apartments, to which she was not invited. He was punishing her, perhaps, for having refused to resume marital relations. They had often shared a room, but had not slept in the same bed since the birth of Napoléon Louis, who was now more than two years old.

The children, unfortunately, had begun to notice the discord of their parents. Napoléon Charles was very partial to his mother. Once, when Louis called him to come sit beside him, the boy clung to Hortense and she couldn't persuade him to leave her until she whispered in his ear, "Go, or your father will be angry with me." When he heard someone singing in his father's salon and the applause that followed, Napoléon Charles wanted to know why Hortense didn't show all those people how well she could sing. One day she overheard him say to Napoléon Louis, who was about to trot off to his nurse, "You'd better stay with *maman*. She's been crying; something is hurting her."

The children were a consolation, but Hortense wondered whether, when they were older, they might not be weaned away from her. She often drove with her ladies in waiting down to the sea, and would walk on the dunes, entertaining the fantasy that an English vessel might suddenly appear and take her prisoner. It might be better to be a prisoner in the Tower of London than a prisoner here.

Three months went by. One day in April Louis appeared in Hortense's room, greatly agitated. He held a letter in his hand.

"You have been complaining of me," he cried. "Look what my brother writes me!"

Napoleon had written from Finkenstein on the Austrian border. He had fought a bloody, indecisive battle at Eylau in February and was waiting to meet the Russians again and give them their coup de grâce. He took Louis to task for having been too lenient with his subjects and then passed on to domestic matters. "Your quarrels with the Queen are known to the public. Show in your private life the paternal and soft side of your character, and in your administration the rigor you display at home. You treat your young wife as though she were a regiment. Let her dance as much as she likes; she is just at an age to enjoy it. I have a wife of forty, and from the battlefields I write to her to go to balls; but you expect a young woman in her twenties to live in a cloister, to be like a nurse, forever washing the baby! The trouble is that you have a wife who is too virtuous. If she were a coquette, she would lead you around by the nose. Instead of that, her pride is hurt, and she rebels because you have such a poor opinion of her."

Hortense handed the letter back to Louis, and said that she had complained to no one and that he had seen everything that she wrote to the emperor.

"Then it must be the French ambassador," Louis exclaimed with fury. "I will no longer give him a private audience. He will have to come in with the rest of the diplomatic corps. But what an injustice! To say that I treat you badly! You must write and say that nothing is wrong."

Hortense did write—though it went against the grain. In time, she, too, received a letter of admonition, but far less caustic in tone.

"My daughter . . . I don't need to tell you that your first duty is to please your husband. I know he has done wrong to let you see his jealousy, but that, after all, is proof of his love. . . . Louis is a just man, though he may at times have some strange ideas. You will only find happiness when you sacrifice everything to him, even what may seem your due rights."

The letter concluded with "your very affectionate father, Napoleon."

Louis, resentful, yet alarmed, was determined to bring about a complete reconciliation, physical and spiritual. There was a hidden staircase, communicating between Hortense's room and his, that he used for frequent visits. He told her over and over that he loved her, and asked her to show him some signs of affection, both in public and in private. Her reply was always; "Be good to me and I *will* love you, but not at once."

When, at times, they seemed to be coming closer to an understanding, he told her that all would be well if she would only confess "all the sins she had committed."

Hortense laughed in his face. "If I haven't committed any sins, it hasn't been your fault," she cried. "It is because I want the satisfaction of having nothing on my conscience."

As in the first weeks of their marriage, Louis came often to wake Hortense in the middle of the night. He told her that sorrow had undermined his health, that she was killing him. Tormented though she was, she felt he was even more wretched than she; he was driven by a blind force that neither he nor she could understand. Her resistance to him was equally blind.

When he was not there in person, Louis would write Hortense a letter, repeating all that he had said so often. At last, he appeared before her with a lengthy document in the form of an agreement, that he asked her to sign. It began with a preamble: "We, Louis and Hortense, wishing to end the unhappy state in which we have lived for some time . . ." Eight articles followed. The first was that all past wrongs should be forgiven and forgotten; the second that husband and wife should be all in all to one another and that no relative should be allowed to come between them.

Hortense, as she read, made notes in the margin against each article. "As to Article Two," she wrote, "you haven't made me so happy that you can take the place of my family. It consists of the Emperor, whom I have looked upon as my father, of the Empress, and of my brother. I will always seize the opportunity of being with them as much as possible."

Article Three exacted a promise from Hortense to write to no one, not even to her family, without Louis' permission. Hortense's comment was, "To write to others, yes; to my family, no."

Nor would she consent to Article Four, which had to do with the children and their never being handed over to the Emperor or the Empress. "I shall always want my children to be with me," Hortense wrote. She added, rather out of character, for she seldom used the language of piety, that, "God has made their fate and will have to decide it."

To the final articles, that were concerned with the choice of servants, household arrangements, and a common purse, Hortense gave a grudging assent, though she complained that they showed how little confidence Louis had in her integrity. She concluded with a statement of the reasons why she could not sign the agreement as a whole:

My way of thinking is entirely different from yours. . . . You want to have, immediately, what only time can give and, above all, a frankness and consideration that you have never shown me. Nevertheless, you may be sure that, whatever you do, my good will will follow you, and that the father of my children can never be indifferent to me.

(signed) *Hortense*

XVI

FLIGHT TO THE MOUNTAINS

HORTENSE felt a certain satisfaction in her defiance of Louis. She had often taken a somewhat unhealthy pride in submitting to him and in being a martyr. She would be a martyr no longer. Louis had threatened that if she didn't sign the agreement, he would complain to the Emperor and ask for a separation. For several days after Hortense delivered her ultimatum, he took to his bed. Then it was the turn of Napoléon Charles to fall ill.

At first, it was thought to be merely a case of measles or perhaps of undulant fever. New symptoms developed with a fearful suddenness. One moment the child was well, the next he was gasping for breath and his face had taken on a bluish tinge.

The best doctors available—and there were famous doctors in Holland—were summoned. They could recognize croup and knew that this was only a manifestation, but they could not diagnose the disease. Louis was panic-stricken, and sent to Paris for Dr. Jean Corvisart, the imperial physician. Hortense forced herself to be calm in talking with the doctors, but she felt a layman's rage at their helplessness when the life of her child was at stake.

For two days the attacks continued. Leeches and blistering were tried without effect and, as a last resort, a quack medicine, called

147

"English powder." The effect was miraculous. Napoléon Charles was better; he sat up in bed and asked for a game of cards. But that evening—the 4th of May—he relapsed. Hortense, as she watched beside him, saw with despair how labored his breathing had become. She leaned over to kiss him and he murmured, "*Bon jour, maman*," but did not open his eyes.

Shortly before midnight, Hortense left the sickroom for a few minutes. When she returned, the nurses tried to bar her way into the room. They wanted to prepare her for what she would see, but she pushed them aside. Napoléon Charles was dead. He had turned as if to look for his mother in his final struggle; his pale lips were parted as if he were trying to pronounce her name. Louis had thrown himself down at the foot of the bed and was sobbing.

Hortense shrieked and fell. She didn't lose consciousness, but she seemed to be paralyzed. She could hear one of the attendants who lifted her say, "She's dead"; she could hear Louis, who had taken her in his arms, begging her to live for his sake and to forgive him all the pain that he had caused her, but she could say nothing.

She was carried to her bed and lay there until dawn without moving. Her window stood open. The hours were marked by the mournful cry from the watchmen in the streets that all was well. Religion had never meant very much to Hortense. She had been told that God was just; she could no longer believe that he was good, unless he would let her die and go to a heaven where she would find Napoléon Charles. "I am going to die," she said to herself. Every moment she expected that the great change would come.

The certainty and comfort of death, however, faded with the night. Hortense realized that she was still alive, that she must continue living. Her paralysis had disappeared. She could move about and answer mechanically when spoken to, but only a husk of her former self existed. It was as if she had been anesthetized to all emotion. She was fully aware of her loss, but it no longer seemed

Hortense as a young girl
From a painting by Baron Gerard

Joséphine
From a sketch by David

Napoleon
From a painting by J.A. Gros

Napoleon with his nieces and nephews
From a painting by Ducis

Hortense's château of Saint-Leu

Louis, King of Holland,
and Napoléon Louis

Hortense with Napoleon III
From a marble by Chatrousse

Count Charles de Flahaut
*From an engraving
in the possession of
White's of London*

The Bettmann Archive

Hortense
in later life

The marriage of Napoleon and Marie-Louise
From a painting by Rouget

Louis Napoleon
at Strasbourg,
October 30, 1836
*From a contemporary
engraving*

The château of
Arenenberg,
1815-1836
From an old print

The Duc de Morny
From a lithograph

Napoleon III

to matter. Her baby was brought to her, but she pushed him away. "I can never love anything again," she said.

Louis was alarmed by her state. Two days after their son's death, he and Hortense fled from the palace. The Hus ten Bosch was only a summer residence, and it was still too cold to go there. They took refuge in the castle of a Dutch nobleman. Caroline Murat, the one of the family nearest at hand, arrived, and advised that Hortense should be taken to Laeken, near Brussels, whither Joséphine, Adèle de Broc, and Adèle's sister, Madame Ney, were hurrying to meet her. Hortense greeted them all, friend and foe alike, dry-eyed and with indifference. Even her mother's tears had no effect upon her.

She was a docile invalid. She listened, but only with the margin of her mind, to the books that were read aloud to her, hour after hour. Every day she was taken for a drive by Joséphine, to visit various country houses in the neighborhood, but Hortense, who had always been so gregarious, shrank from speaking to strangers. She and Adèle would go for a walk in the grounds, while Joséphine was being entertained within. During one of these walks, Hortense heard the distant sound of a hunting horn; she felt short of breath, remembered how Napoléon Charles had strangled before her eyes, and began to cry. This was considered a good sign.

Dr. Corvisart, Napoleon's physician, who had come too late to do anything for Napoléon Charles, prescribed travel. Louis had to return to Holland, but before the end of May, Hortense and her party left for Paris. She saw her native land again, unmoved. She remembered nothing of the journey later, except that she thought, as she passed through Saint-Denis, that her son would be buried soon in the abbey tomb of the Kings of France; it had been destroyed during the Revolution and was now being rebuilt. After spending a night at La Malmaison and a day or two at Saint-Cloud, Hortense said good-bye to her mother, as she had said good-bye earlier to Napoléon Louis at Laeken, without a tear. She, with Adèle, three of her ladies, and three equerries, traveled south to the Pyrénées.

Hortense had always loved the mountains, but she found their first halting place, at Bagnères-de-Bigorre, overlooking a fertile valley, too tame and too populous. Peasants in the surrounding villages heard that a queen was visiting the town and came to gape at her. Hortense craved a more remote and savage landscape.

At Cauterets, she stayed for some time. She and her devoted, ever kind Adèle took long drives along the steep, winding roads, with their escort following on horseback. They would often leave the carriage and follow a path that led deep into the mountains. They made some perilous climbs, crossed rushing streams on fallen logs. When she stopped to look back, Hortense often wondered how she had had the courage and the sureness of foot to follow the trail. She was beginning to take a grip on herself and had frequent crying spells that seemed to relieve her. She no longer felt like a disembodied spirit, a head, as she phrased it, without a heart.

Her equerries, however, were worried to see her go off so often alone with Adèle. Hortense was roused from her self-absorption to feel sorry for the elderly gentleman who resembled Don Quixote. In trying to follow her, he had had a number of bad falls. Afraid that he might break his neck in the mountains, she insisted that he should leave her and go back to Holland. Her male bodyguard was thus reduced to two.

All along her route, Hortense had received letters from Louis that touched her by their tenderness. He suddenly appeared at Cauterets and wanted to share her room and bed, but he was considerate enough to see that she was not yet ready to resume the normal life of a married woman. She could only talk to him about Napoléon Charles. After a few days, Louis went to another watering place, from which he continued to write to her affectionately.

Several letters from the Emperor had also reached Hortense during her travels, telling her how deeply he shared her sorrow, but urging her to be brave. He, who had seen more of life than she, said that he could not believe "death was the worst misfortune." He complained of not having heard from Hortense herself. On her way to the Pyrénées, she forced herself to write a few lines to him and also to Eugène. She received a reply from Napoleon dated from Prussia, June 16, 1807:

My daughter:

I have received your letter from Orléans. I am touched by your suffering, but I wish that you were more courageous. To live is to suffer, and a human being who is worthy of honor must alway struggle for mastery of self. I don't like to see you so unjust to little Napoléon Louis and to all who love you. Your mother and I hoped that we had a larger room in your heart!

I had a great victory on June 14th. I am well, and I love you very much. Farewell, my daughter, I embrace you with all my heart.

回

The great victory, that Napoleon merely mentioned in passing, was the Battle of Friedland, in which the Russians were overwhelmed on the seventh anniversary of Marengo. Again, as at Austerlitz, Napoleon had chosen a lucky day. Scornful though he was of superstition in others, he more than half-believed in omens that concerned his own destiny.

On June 25, 1807, he met the Czar Alexander, on a raft moored in the middle of the River Neman at Tilsit. This was Napoleon's first encounter with the impressionable young man who had been educated by a French disciple of Rousseau and who now ruled over the vast, untidy empire of Catherine the Great. Napoleon was drawn strongly to Alexander; Alexander was dazzled by Napoleon's brilliance, and by his apparent generosity to a man whom he had just defeated. They spent many days together, in which they discussed subjects of common interest. All that Napoleon asked of Russia was that she should block her ports to British ships. France and Russia should be allies, he said. Geographically they had a pincers hold upon the continent of Europe. And beyond Europe lay the world. All in good time, the Emperor of the East and the Emperor of the West might join hands to drive the Turk from Constantinople, then march across the plains of Asia to the conquest of India. This was the old dream of world dominance that had once led Napoleon to Egypt.

Other visitors to the raft, and to the meetings held later in the town of Tilsit, were the King and Queen of Prussia. Napoleon flattered the beautiful Queen Louise outrageously, though earlier he had characterized her in letters to Joséphine as a "hateful, intriguing woman." His flattery was intended to conceal the fact that Prussia was to be reduced to a second-rate power. A portion of it was to be joined with Westphalia to create the new kingdom that Napoleon had planned as a wedding gift to Jérôme. Jérôme, chastened and obedient, had received from the French ecclesiastical and civil courts the divorce denied him by the Pope. Once more a bachelor, he was engaged to Catherine, the daughter of the King of Württemberg.

An elaborate royal wedding was planned for August, in Paris. Hortense felt that she still could face neither crowds nor festivity. Cauterets was close to the Spanish border. She wanted to slip across it and take a look at what lay beyond, though in the rules laid down for the imperial family, it was forbidden for any one of them to visit a foreign country without permission. A strict incognito would have to be maintained.

Hortense, Adèle, and a single equerry set out on horseback. At Lourdes, they hired a char-a-banc and a single saddle horse that Hortense chose to ride, saying that the jolting of the carriage gave her a pain in her chest. She would let the carriage go on ahead of her and, when it had disappeared around a bend in the road, exulted in the feeling that she was absolutely alone. Solitude was a luxury she had missed since becoming a queen.

The party picnicked by the roadside. Whenever they came to a picturesque spot, Hortense and Adèle would stop to sketch. The dash across the border was made in an ancient "Gothic" carriage drawn by six mules, but only a hurried view could be taken of San Sebastián and the beautiful seaport of Los Passajes, before it was time to turn back. The equerry, Monsieur de Boucheporn, who was responsible for Hortense's safety, was made very uneasy by stories of travelers who were attacked and killed in broad daylight; he was frantic when Hortense was thrown from her horse, a stallion, during a fight with the horse of a muleteer they met on the road.

Hortense, however, was only exhilarated by her spill and was chagrined when they were safe again in France, and she found that news of her journey had circulated. At Cauterets, she received a letter from Louis, saying that he was waiting for her at Toulouse to return with him to Paris. She begged off for a few days, with the excuse that she wanted to visit the waterfall of Gavarnie on the other side of the mountain from Cauterets.

A party was organized to ride around the mountain on horseback. Hortense forestalled this arrangement by getting up at three o'clock in the morning and slipping away from the town to cross the Vignemale glacier on foot. With her, went Adèle, an artist who was staying at Cauterets, and a guide, who was a hunter of bear and chamois. This was real mountain climbing, in which crevasses were crossed and ropes and crampons used. No woman had ever before attempted the ascent. At six o'clock in the evening, the adventurers arrived at the inn at Gavarnie. The artist went to bed immediately, saying that he would rather be shot than cross the Vignemale again, but Hortense was still so fresh that she took a walk around the village in the evening and made several pencil sketches.

The strength and poise she had regained during her travels deserted her completely, when she turned her back upon the mountains and took the road to Toulouse. Hortense felt repugnance and a physical distaste for her reunion with Louis, but her mother, from whom she heard constantly, urged her to it; for the first time Louis had shown affection to his mother-in-law. Adèle, also, happy in her own marriage, was gently persuasive. From Toulouse, Louis and Hortense traveled slowly north, visiting various historic spots: Montpellier, Nîmes, Avignon and the Fountain of Vaucluse, sacred to the memory of Laura and Petrarch. Louis was in better health and tried to be considerate, but Hortense languished in the summer heat and already was beginning to wonder if her husband's reform were permanent.

On the evening of the 1st of September, 1807, the travelers reached Saint-Cloud. A play was in progress in the palace theater, but Joséphine was told of their arrival and came down to greet them. Napoléon Louis was brought from his crib to be hugged and kissed, and dampened by his mother's tears.

The Emperor appeared. He was about to embrace Hortense, but seeing that she was crying, drew back. "Come, stop being so childish!" he said sharply. "You have wept enough for your son. . . . You are not the only one to have had this sorrow. Mothers should be brave, particularly when they have dear ones and duties to perform. You have a child who needs your care, a kingdom that is waiting for you, and a mother whom you make unhappy. . . . Why did you run away to the mountains? . . . If I had been here, I would not have allowed it. But here you are. Be cheerful and enjoy your youth. Don't let me see another tear."

He left the room. Hortense stopped crying, but she was deeply, tragically wounded. She had been looking forward so to being comforted by her stepfather! She cried out to her mother against his cruelty. "I see that he is only irritated by my grief. I didn't ask to come here. I want to go away!"

Joséphine soothed her. "You don't understand the Emperor," she said. "He thinks that you have only added to your suffering by giving in to it. He told me earlier that he was going to speak to you severely, as the only way of curing you. Believe me, he *has* shared our grief. He has often spoken of it to me, and, if he seems harsh, it is only because he has your welfare in mind."

Nevertheless, for sometime Hortense felt uneasy in Napoleon's presence and could hardly find a word to say to him.

XVII

PERHAPS DIVORCE

SOME eight months earlier, on December 31, 1806, when Napoleon was on his way to Warsaw, he received word of a birth that had taken place recently in Paris. To quote the city register, a son, Léon, had been born to Eléonore Dénuelle de la Plaigne, spinster, and to an unknown father. Napoleon had reason to believe that he was the nameless parent. He had had sexual intercourse with many women, but this was the first time that a child had resulted.

Eléonore Dénuelle was a school friend of Caroline Murat, at Saint-Germain. Her parents, a rather raffish pair, married her to an officer, who proved to be a rascal and went to prison for forgery. Pending divorce, Eléonore was taken into Caroline's house as a lesser lady in waiting, a reader. It was there that she and Napoleon met. She made every effort to attract his attention and was quite willing, with Caroline's connivance, to visit the secret room in the Tuileries. Since she never left Caroline's house except to make these visits, and was carefully chaperoned to and from the palace, there was little doubt that Léon Dénuelle was the Emperor's son.

The next day, New Year's day of 1807, Napoleon made his entry into Warsaw. At a small town near the capital, his carriage stopped while the horses were changed. It was immediately engulfed by a shouting, gesticulating crowd, which rushed forward to greet the liberator of Poland, the man who had just defeated Prussia and who would soon defeat the Russians. General Duroc went into the posting house to pay for the horses, and came back shepherding two ladies through the crowd. One of them was very young, very blonde, fresh-faced, and dainty as a child. She knelt on the step of the carriage and, as though she were speaking to a god, hailed the deliverer of her country. Napoleon picked up a bunch of flowers that had been tossed into the carriage and handed it to the girl, saying that this was only a foretaste of his good will. He would look forward to thanks from "her beautiful lips," when they met again in Warsaw.

On arrival, Duroc was commissioned to make inquiries, and had some trouble in identifying the blonde-haired lady. Maria Walewska had not, like Eléonore Dénuelle and so many others, wanted to make a personal impression. She was a passionate patriot, and had come to the posting station only to adore her hero from a distance. By the time Duroc discovered who she was, all of high society in Warsaw knew that she had been favored. She had become a person of supreme importance, for great things were expected of this visit from Napoleon. Poland, which had been partitioned for the third time in 1795, might regain her lost provinces and become again a vital nation. All of Maria's friends, including her elderly husband, Count Walewski, united to push her into the Emperor's arms. It took a concerted effort to get her to the first ball at which Napoleon was present. A letter, signed by the foremost men of Poland, asking her to remember the Old Testament story of Esther and Ahasuerus, was necessary to persuade her to appear at a dinner party, where she sat across the table from Napoleon, with Duroc beside her, wooing her for his master in a well-rehearsed monologue.

Maria refused the flowers—not to mention the diamonds—that her admirer sent her. Napoleon wrote her love letters as passionate as any he had written to Joséphine: "I saw but you, I admired but

you, I desire but you." and later, "Oh, come, come! Your every
wish will be gratified. Your country will be dearer to me when you
take pity on my poor heart."

Even after she had yielded to him, their love-making was
strongly flavored with politics. Maria never failed to plead her
country's cause. As proof of his devotion, Napoleon condescended
to argue with her. He told her that he couldn't do everything she
asked. As a matter of fact, the best that he could do for Poland was
to give back the territory that had been taken by Prussia, and
create a Grand Duchy of Warsaw. If she was unsatisfied, he, too,
was wistful. He often accused her of being incapable of loving
anything but her fatherland.

When Napoleon moved his headquarters to Finkenstein, he took
his so-called "Polish wife" with him. And at Finkenstein, he
learned of the death of Napoléon Charles. He told Talleyrand that
he couldn't afford the luxury of mourning the dead, but he was
nevertheless deeply moved. He offered a prize for medical research
into the causes of croup, and mentioned the death of "that poor
child" in all of his personal letters. In the midst of mighty events—
his battles, his creation of kingdoms, his entente with Alexander—
the idea was developing in Napoleon's mind that, for reasons of
state and world strategy, he must divorce Joséphine. His candidate
for adoption was gone; the birth of Léon Dénuelle had proved that
he could produce a son. The affair with Maria Walewska, also—so
young, so idealistic, so selfless—helped to wean him away from
Joséphine.

But how could he force himself to discard his Empress? Joséphine was a habit. She had been the great love of Napoleon's
youth, and she had been his companion for more than ten years of
incredible success. Twice he had almost shaken her off, but she
had clung to him. She still could fascinate. When he returned to
France in the summer of 1807, the bond between Napoleon and
Joséphine was strengthened. For her children, he felt also a renewed sense of responsibility.

After his first cold douche of severity, Napoleon went out of his way to be kind to Hortense. He usually took an afternoon drive alone with Joséphine, but now he insisted that Hortense should go with them, and he talked of things that he thought would interest her, such as the school for the daughters of members of the Legion of Honor that he was about to found at Écouen. Madame Campan was to be its director, and Hortense its imperial patroness. Though he usually never spoke of politics to his womenfolk, Napoleon entertained Hortense and Joséphine with anecdotes of the meeting at Tilsit, of the Czar Alexander, whom he liked so much, of Queen Louise, who was beautiful, but "mincing" and "not the equal of my Joséphine."

One day after dinner, when Joséphine who had a headache had gone to her room, Napoleon told Hortense to get her hat and to put on a simple dress; he would take her to see the fair that was being held in the park of Saint-Cloud. They went on foot with only General Henri Bertrand, the aide-de-camp on duty for the day. Napoleon hated being hustled and cheered by a crowd, but he liked to mingle with it, if he was unrecognized. He often went to masked balls, and, in the early days of the Consulate, when he was less well known by sight, would play Harun al-Rashid with his secretary, Monsieur Bourrienne, on the boulevards of Paris. Today, with a young woman clinging to his arm, he passed unnoticed. He and Hortense visited some of the side shows, where the crowd was thick. They were so roughly jostled that they took refuge in a tent, where waxworks were on display. The meeting at Tilsit was shown, with Napoleon, the Czar Alexander, and all of the imperial family seated—improbably—around a large table. For good measure, the Sleeping Beauty slumbered in one corner of the council chamber. The showman pointed out the figures to Hortense, one by one, and said that the Queen of Holland was a particularly good likeness. Hortense admired her waxen self, but suggested that a string of pearls that had fallen over the doll's eyes should be put back in its place. This made Napoleon laugh at what he called a "personal vanity."

Hortense laughed, too, at the Emperor's growing anxiety to be gone. It was getting late, they hadn't paid for their side-show admission, and neither of them had any money. The aide-de-camp, who was the purse bearer, had been separated from them in the crowd. They had just decided, in whispers, that the only way of getting out of the tent was to tell the proprietor who they were, when General Bertrand appeared perspiring, very much worried at having lost them.

It was good for Hortense to laugh for an hour, for, in general, she found little reason to be light-hearted. Louis was again becoming difficult. He was unhappy at Saint-Cloud and insisted on their going to their house in Paris, where everything reminded Hortense of Napoléon Charles. Louis wanted Hortense to go back with him to Holland immediately, but she had discovered that she was pregnant, and seemed and looked so unwell—she had grown thin and had developed a cough—that Joséphine protested. It took the intervention of Napoleon to get Hortense a short reprieve. Even so, Louis, when he said good-bye to his wife, told her harshly that he expected to see her within two weeks.

Louis had had some unpleasant conversations with his brother about Dutch affairs. Napoleon wanted Holland to build up an army of forty thousand men and to maintain the Continental system of blockade against English goods, even when carried in neutral ships. Louis, who had closed his eyes to a good deal of smuggling, protested that his country was being ruined. There was much wrangling, nothing was settled; and Louis felt that he was being persecuted. Hortense had chosen a poor time to invoke the Emperor's authority for staying in France. Once more, her husband felt that she had betrayed him by going over to the enemy.

After Louis was gone, Hortense felt the same feeling of relief and the same prick of conscience as on earlier partings. Her pregnancy was proving difficult and she was told by her doctors that she must spend most of her time in bed or on her chaise longue, if she was to avoid a miscarriage. She rather welcomed her discomfort, since it gave her a valid reason for not doing as Louis wished. He acquiesced, but with poor grace, in her remaining where she was until after the birth. He saw no reason, however, why his son should not be sent to him in the early spring.

Hortense froze at the suggestion. Napoléon Louis was with her constantly, and had come almost to take the place of Napoléon Charles. No, no, she would not send him to Holland; Holland was the place where children died of the croup!

At her next private interview with the Emperor, Hortense brought the matter up.

Napoleon reflected for a moment. "A father is asking for his child," he said slowly, as though he were thinking out loud. "Your son isn't seven years old yet, and I have no legal right to keep him here. But he is the only boy in the family. If he goes back to Holland, he might die, as his brother died, and then all of France would want me to get a divorce. . . . Only a child of my own would solve the problem. If I have done nothing about a divorce so far, it is because of my affection for your mother. The nation as a whole would welcome such a move."

It was the first time that Napoleon had spoken to Hortense of divorce, but nothing that he had said was new to her. She had heard it all from others, from Joséphine's friends as well as from her foes. Hortense was startled by what came next.

"It was quite plain at the time of your son's death," Napoleon said, "that everyone thought he was mine. You know how absurd such a notion was, but it couldn't be helped; all of Europe thought that the child was my son."

He paused, as Hortense made a movement of surprise and revulsion. "The public didn't think the worse of you for that," he said. "Perhaps it was just as well that people thought as they did. I, too, felt that his death was a great misfortune."

Hortense remembered the remarks that both Napoleon and Bourrienne had made about the British scandal sheets. She remembered Napoleon's insistence that she should dance at La Malmaison, when she was carrying Napoléon Charles, and the foolish verses in the *Journal de Paris* on the subject. All the flattery and attention she had received since might have been due not merely to the fact that she was thought to be the mother of the successor to the throne; she had been thought to be the Emperor's mistress as well.

For a moment Hortense loathed her stepfather for having taken advantage, even momentarily, of a rumor that put her in such a poor light. It took time for her to conquer her repugnance and to realize that the most important feature of their conversation had been the mention of a separation from Joséphine. Was Napoleon preparing in this way for immediate action?

Hortense was even more disturbed, when she learned from her mother that Joseph Fouché, Napoleon's crafty Minister of Police, had advised her to write a letter to the Senate, saying that she would take the first step herself toward dissolving her marriage. Joséphine, following her policy of passive resistance, refused. Although Napoleon told Fouché sharply to mind his own business, Hortense continued to see signs of his struggle to come to a decision. How unlike the Emperor it was to temporize, to look at things as they might be, instead of as they were!

"It hurts me to see you like that," Napoleon said to Hortense, when he saw how misshapen she had become in the final months of her pregnancy, "but how I would love your mother if she were in the same condition!"

All during the winter, Hortense got information of the state of affairs in Holland from Adèle de Broc, who had left to join her husband soon after she and Hortense returned from the Pyrénées. Adèle no longer thought that Hortense's marriage could be patched up. Louis was once more embittered. He allowed prayers to be said in Dutch churches for the preservation of the Queen from the perils of childbirth, but made biting, sarcastic remarks about his wife to his courtiers.

In March, he sent one of his medical men to Paris to escort Napoléon Louis to Holland. At the same time, Hortense received a package from Adèle and found in it, hidden in a shoe, a letter saying that Louis had asked the doctor to discover if she were pregnant, or if she had already been delivered. Hortense found satisfaction in letting the doctor know that she was aware of the real reason for his visit, and in sending him back to Holland without her boy.

On April 20th, Caroline Murat gave an elaborate children's party at her home in the Elysée Palace. Hortense, though she was feeling poorly, went with Napoléon Louis. Part of the entertainment was a performance by tightrope dancers, who made their airy leaps and pirouettes directly above the heads of the children. This made Hortense very uneasy. The Archchancellor of the Empire, who followed all her movements closely, since he was supposed to be on hand for the birth of her child, came to her and asked permission to go home to bed. Hortense dismissed him, saying reassuringly that she was sure he would not be called upon that night, but the Archchancellor had hardly disappeared, when she began to feel the onset of labor. She hurried home, and at two o'clock in the morning of April 21, 1808, gave birth prematurely to a son, who was so small and feeble that he showed no signs of life until he had been sponged with wine and wrapped in cotton wool.

Hortense was disappointed by his sex. This time, she had hoped for a girl. She sent one of her equerries to Holland with the news and another to the Emperor, who, with Joséphine, was at Bayonne near the Spanish border. Napoleon was never sorry to hear that a baby Bonaparte had been born, particularly if the baby were a boy. All along the dividing line between France and Spain a cannonade announced the birth.

XVIII

ONE FRIEND, MANY ENEMIES

THE birthday of Hortense's child, April 21, 1808, was also the day when some Spanish visitors arrived at Bayonne. Napoleon had gone to the frontier to fish in muddied waters for yet another kingdom. Control of the Iberian Peninsula, with its long coastline, was essential to the maintenance of his Continental system of blockade. Hitherto, he had managed to make use of the dull-witted and feeble Spanish King, Charles IV, who was controlled by his termagant wife and by his chief adviser, Manuel de Godoy. Godoy managed to be at the same time the Queen's lover, the King's favorite, and Napoleon's tool. Because of the French alliance, Spain became involved in a war with Portugal, England's oldest ally on the Continent. As a result, all that remained of her sea power was swept away at Finisterre and Trafalgar.

This, as well as the cession to France of the Louisiana Territory in North America, which Napoleon promptly sold to the United States, was a body blow to Spanish pride. A party violently opposed to Godoy and all his works, took shape. It was headed by Ferdinand, the Prince of Asturias and heir to the throne, who was no more intelligent than his father and who also tried to curry favor with Napoleon. In the autumn of 1807, French troops were poured into Spain on their way to Portugal. In February and March, the four most important Spanish strongholds were occupied and a French army, under Joachim Murat, was advancing on Madrid. Rioting broke out, and the King, who was forced to abdicate in favor of his son, fled to Bayonne. Ferdinand was induced also to come there for a conference. He was confronted unexpectedly with his raging parents, slapped in the face by his father in Napoleon's presence, and forced to give back the crown. This was immediately laid at Napoleon's feet, in exchange for a pension and a safe conduct to Italy for the ex-King, his wife, and Godoy. Ferdinand was also pensioned and removed to a château in France, that belonged to Talleyrand. There he was to remain indefinitely as a "guest" of the Empire.

The throne being vacant, Napoleon offered it first to Joseph, who, well satisfied with his Neapolitan kingdom, refused. Louis was next on Napoleon's list. The Spanish climate, Napoleon wrote, might be better for a rheumatic man than the chilly fogs of Holland. But Louis also declined. He was not, he said, the governor of a province who could be shifted about at will. "The only promotion for a king should come from Heaven," Louis added, with a touch of mysticism that his brother did not appreciate. Napoleon, after considering other possibilities—Jérôme, even Lucien, who might thus be lured back into the fold—returned to Joseph. After what seemed inordinate delay, the elder brother yielded and started for Madrid. In the royal game of musical chairs a seat was now empty. Who would fill it? Who would become the ruler of Naples?

The choice fell upon Joachim Murat, ever anxious for something bigger and better than his Grand Duchies of Berg and Clèves. Napoleon valued his Gascon brother-in-law chiefly as a soldier; in making his new offer, he pointed out that if Murat were called away on military duty his wife would be quite capable of ruling during his absence. Caroline left in May for Bayonne, and returned to Paris in triumph—a queen.

She came to snap her royal fingers under the nose of Hortense. Hortense was unimpressed. She couldn't understand Caroline's

elation. Why should she want to exile herself? Hadn't she everything here to make her happy—husband, children, wealth?

Hortense was making a slow postpartum recovery. She had
caught a bad cold, by getting up too soon and going herself to hunt
for a wet nurse for her puny baby. In her weakened state she was
oppressed by the thought of Holland. Louis no longer seemed to
be anxious for her return and, though he had duly announced to
the nation the birth of a second royal prince, named somewhat confusingly Charles Louis Napoléon, he took no interest in this new
addition to his family. He was becoming more and more insistent
and short-tempered in his demands for his elder son. He wrote to
Napoléon Louis' governess, Madame de Boubers, and to Madame
Mère, asking her to come for a visit and to bring the child with
her. Hortense's only hope was again in the Emperor, but the reply
to the message she sent him by Caroline, was not encouraging.
Napoleon said that Hortense might wait a little longer, until she
had fully recovered her strength, but that in the end, she must come
to some sort of understanding with her husband.

This was only putting off a very evil day. Without Adèle, without
her mother, and without Eugène, Hortense was in need of someone to whom she could tell all of her miseries. The someone whom
she wanted most of all and whom she had hoped to see, appeared.
In midsummer, Charles de Flahaut was once again in Paris.

Charles and Hortense had not met for more than two years, and
in that time how much had happened! Charles had fought in the
Prussian campaign of 1806 and had gone into Poland with Murat
in pursuit of the Russian army. While Napoleon was wooing Maria
Walewska at Warsaw, Charles was having a flirtation with a
Countess Anna Potocka, in whose house Murat and his aides
were quartered. Murat, vain and crudely boastful, was not an easy
man to have as a superior. He wanted to put his staff into a uniform
that was of the same color and design as those worn by his servants.
This offended Charles's aristocratic sensibilities. He was not a
jockey; he was a cavalier. He asked for and obtained a transfer

to a regiment of mounted chasseurs, that survived the slaughter of Eylau and won great glory at Friedland. After its last, most deadly, yet most successful, charge Charles was one of fifteen who were still left in the saddle.

For this he received the ribbon of the Legion of Honor and hoped to win even greater favor from the Emperor, but Napoleon was prejudiced against him. He had heard of Charles's affair with Caroline and considered the young man "a libertine." Once, when Joséphine praised Charles to Napoleon, he said that he didn't see what she saw in De Flahaut. "Wit? No more than most. He sings well? That's a fine recommendation for a soldier, who is apt to be hoarse just on that account! Ah, he is a pretty boy—that is what you women like! I can't even give him credit on that score. He looks to me like a spider, with those long legs of his!"

After the campaign, Charles remained on garrison duty in Germany, cruelly bored and at times discouraged. He wrote to his mother asking for her help. Since letters sent by post were often opened by the police, Charles and Madame de Souza had worked out a code of communication. Charles wrote that it would be very useful if "my aunt" (Joséphine) could be encouraged by "my cousin" (Hortense) to take an interest in his career. The greatest care must be exercised, however, that "my uncle" (Napoleon) didn't know what was going on.

Charles urged his mother to speak of him often to "Sophie"— another alias for Hortense—and to give her some amber which he had picked up on his travels. He was distressed to hear of the death of Napoléon Charles—De Flahaut had been very fond of the little boy—and he managed, through his mother, to send Hortense a letter of sympathy.

Was it pity, was it ambition, was it loneliness that keyed up his courtship? "A thousand, thousand tender things to my dear cousin," he wrote in December of 1807. "Is her father going to take her to the country this winter, or will she be in Paris?" In other words, was Louis going to insist on Hortense's following him to Holland? Charles was beginning to feel possessively hostile toward the husband of his beloved. The news that Hortense was again pregnant caused him "more pain than I can express. But don't tell her that, for she is unhappy enough as it is. Give me news of her constantly. I am very uneasy about her; I don't know why, but I fear some great misfortune. All I want is for my cousin to be well. Nothing else counts, for you and she are the only ones I love."

In March, he repeated his vows of unique devotion and said how much he treasured the little keepsakes that Hortense had sent him from time to time: an aigrette, a seal, a chain and cross, some of her songs that had recently been published. When he was re-called to France, he gave Hortense all the credit for his rescue, though he was sent directly from Germany to Spain.

There, a letter from Hortense reached him that made him think that someone had been telling her tales of his amorous diversions in Poland. He was very much worried. "If she doesn't love me, there will be no more happiness for me," he wrote his mother. Only a short time later a great reward came to Charles, for which he was sure that Hortense was chiefly responsible, though actually his mother and possibly Talleyrand, whom Charles now knew to be his father, might have had something to do with it. In August, De Flahaut was appointed to the staff of Marshal Louis Berthier. Berthier's aides were cream of the crop; from them were selected officers who would serve directly under the Emperor.

Charles wrote to his mother that he "could not live without my aunt,"—Hortense had yet another pseudonym. "Have a little seal made for her, a leaf of aloe and the device around it, *Praemium aevi aurea dies* (A day of gold is the reward of a century). I am very proud to get this position and to owe it to the one to whom I owe so much."

Before taking up his new duties, Charles was given a furlough, and was in Paris on his way to a vacation in the Pyrénées. He and Hortense had a few happy hours together. Hortense insisted that their relations were still to be purely platonic. She gave Charles a lecture on the superiority of friendship over love, to which he listened with an ironic smile. Anyone could be in love, Hortense said; friendship was much more difficult. It required tolerance, a perfect understanding. However painful it would be for her to hear, Charles must never hesitate to tell her of his tender feeling for another woman.

When she said this, Hortense was not only thinking of Charles's Polish involvements, past and present; she was also thinking of Caroline. After Charles was gone, she went to see her sister-in-law and found her in the midst of preparations for moving to Naples. The Elysée Palace, which the Murats had inhabited lately, was being stripped of its magnificent furniture: the paintings, the Aubusson carpets, the crystal chandeliers that Caroline had collected. The baggage vans were being packed. At first, conversation was constantly interrupted by the hostess running away to give an order to her major-domo or to the porters. She was all smiles and vivacity, but when she at last settled herself down beside her visitor, her face took on a semitragic expression.

"Hortense," Caroline said, "you know how sad I am to leave France, in spite of my having a crown to assure the future of my children. What you don't know is the feeling that binds me to Monsieur de Flahaut. How often I have been afraid that he might be just a little bit in love with you! You are the only woman in the world whom I fear. At one time he seemed to be much taken with you, but then I saw how foolish that was. He's young, he's a flirt, but he could never really love anyone but me. He is so sad to see me go, however, that he might try to console himself with you. Promise me not to listen to him! . . . I don't like to think of his caring even a little for someone else."

Hortense could hardly breathe during this speech. "Why should you fear me?" she murmured. "No one is interested in me!"

"But you are the very one I am afraid of," Caroline exclaimed, with growing vehemence. "I don't know how you do it, but you have the secret of attracting people. There are many women more beautiful than you; I myself am very much prettier, but you must have something that I lack. I have often tried to force De Flahaut to say that he doesn't like you, but I have never been able to do it. . . . I saw him when he was here, you know. I was wearing a new bracelet, and that seemed to trouble him, for he can be very jealous, as well as very much in love. Your name flashed into my mind and I said that it was you who gave it to me. Promise not to tell him, if you should see him again!"

Hortense promised, and left the Elysée in great distress. All the soothing effect of De Flahaut's visit was gone. Her lecture on friendship seemed pedantic, when she found herself face to face with a rival. Charles was only deceiving her, when he said that he loved her and no one else.

De Flahaut was back again in Paris, briefly, before Caroline left for Naples, but Hortense did not see him. She had gone to stay at Saint-Cloud with her mother, who had recently returned from Bayonne. De Flahaut wrote Hortense from Spain that Caroline had told him of their conversation, adding that she was sure now Hortense could never love him. She was much too romantic!

It seemed as if Caroline were determined to scratch as often and as deeply as possible before her departure. At Hortense's house one day she saw a young man named Élie Decazes, who had come from Holland with a letter from Louis, appointing him as the Queen's secretary. Hortense had met Decazes at Cauterets the preceding summer, and felt a sympathy for him when she learned that he, too, had a sorrow; he had just lost his young wife.

"Did you know," Caroline said reflectively, "there is a rumor going around that you're very much interested in that young man? I had heard it so often I wasn't sure, but after seeing you together, I know there is nothing in it. He must be very stupid and presumptuous, for it was Fouché himself who told me that Decazes has been boasting of having been very kindly received here."

Hortense, hearing the name of Policeman Fouché, who had spies in every social strata and who had so many ways of influencing public opinion, was alarmed. She refused to accept Decazes as her secretary, though she saw him occasionally on business. Decazes remained for some time in Paris, however, as an agent of Louis.

The world seemed to be full of enemies, and the most bitter enemy of all was the man to whom Hortense was married. Throughout the summer, Louis wrote less and less often and with growing spite. In August, after Hortense had seen Charles de Flahaut, a letter came for Napoléon Louis, reproaching the child, who was not quite four years old, for having failed to wish his father a happy birthday, "It is *maman's* fault," Louis wrote. "She doesn't want Napoléon to love Papa, nor Papa to love Napoléon—this must never be!"

The accompanying letter to Hortense glowed with hatred. Louis said that only a miracle could reunite them. "It is a consolation to live far from you, to have nothing to discuss with you, nothing to do with you, nothing to expect from you. If I have anything to fear, at least it is not from you!"

After that, Louis wrote no more, and Hortense's letters to him, she learned from Adèle, were thrown on the floor and came back to her unopened. But still, everyone, everyone in Paris—even Eugène in far off Italy—wondered why the Queen of Holland lingered in France. Hortense wrote sadly to her brother of how difficult her position had become. "I think," she said, "that I was born to be a good woman, but the world will judge me otherwise."

The doctors hinted that Hortense might be consumptive. It was because her daughter looked so ill that Joséphine insisted that she should come to stay at Saint-Cloud; she herself, however, was in need of comfort. Ever since Fouché had spoken to her of divorce, Joséphine felt that her days as Empress were numbered. While they were at Bayonne, Napoleon was like a lover, but, once more in Paris, he was too immersed in affairs to pay her much attention. He was constantly at work, and was more than usually silent at mealtimes or during the drives that, come wind or rain, he took daily with his two female companions.

In September of 1808, Napoleon left for a meeting at Erfurt, with the German princes and the Czar Alexander. Joséphine was very much worried. Was he looking for a wife? The Czar had two unmarried sisters.

Napoleon, however, had other, more pressing problems on his mind than matrimony. He had overestimated the ease with which he could carry all before him in Spain. Elsewhere, he had brought the revolution as a welcome gift to the oppressed masses; in Spain, the gift had been rejected. Napoleon's open quarrel with the Pope —diplomatic relations had been broken off and French troops occupied Rome—was an affront to Spanish piety. When, in July, Joseph entered his new kingdom, expecting to be as cordially received as in southern Italy, he found a patriot army barring his way to Madrid. He was only able to enter his capital under French protection, and stayed just long enough to proclaim himself king before retiring to a safer position at Burgos. Joseph wrote to his brother, suggesting helpfully that he, Joseph, should abdicate and return to Naples.

At the same time a French force, which had been sent to Cádiz to take over what remained of the Spanish fleet, was totally defeated and surrendered to the enemy. In August an English army, headed by Sir Arthur Wellesley, the future Duke of Wellington, landed in Portugal, and the French were forced to retreat from the country.

These setbacks, the most serious that France had suffered in a generation, severely hampered Napoleon's conversations with the Czar at Erfurt. The contagion of national resurgence had blown with the wind from Iberia to Germany and Austria; there were leaders there who were quick to make use of it. Alexander was not so easily captivated as at Tilsit. He did not choose to preside over the partition of Prussia. Napoleon could only persuade him to be his ally in case Austria declared war on France. Both emperors addressed an appeal to King George III of England to make peace on a basis of the status quo, but both realized that this would have small effect.

Before the end of October, Napoleon was back in France and almost immediately left for Spain. He had sent some of his best troops and generals there—among them was Charles de Flahaut's General Berthier—but he saw that nothing would be accomplished unless he was on the spot.

"Are you never going to stop making war?" Joséphine inquired wistfully.

"Do you think I like it?" Napoleon asked. "Do you think I wouldn't prefer to stay here, where I can have a good bed to sleep in and a good dinner? . . . Nonsense! I know how to do other things than to make war, but I must yield to necessity and to my duty to France. I don't control events; I have to make the best of them."

It was the reply of a burdened man, a man who could still drive himself to vigorous action, but with greater conscious effort than of old.

XIX

THE DISINHERITED

THERE was little enthusiasm for the war in Spain, even on the part of fire-eaters and inveterate glory seekers. Talismans against death were much in fashion. Hortense's well-stocked cabinet of jewels contained a number of engraved semiprecious stones, that she gave to friends who were going to the front. It seemed as if everyone she knew was going, except those who, like Charles de Flahaut, were already there. Hortense's talismans were accepted with the greatest seriousness. Many of the school friends whose marriages she had arranged, came to ask her solemnly for good-luck stones to give to their husbands.

The Emperor's presence in Spain had its usual prodigious effect. After only a few weeks, Madrid fell to the French, Napoleon would have driven on to Lisbon, and was in pursuit of a British force that had pushed in from Portugal, when he heard of mobilization in Austria and what might be sedition in Paris. It was reported that frequent meetings were being held between two former enemies, Talleyrand and Joseph Fouché.

Napoleon had never entirely trusted these two supremely clever men, though he had made ample use of their talents. For him, they represented the two hostile elements that he had had to deal with in the past: Talleyrand the old nobility, Fouché the Jacobins. In January of 1809, Napoleon hurried back to Paris. He could find nothing amiss with the way that Fouché had behaved, and nothing worse on the part of Talleyrand than that he had been talking down the Spanish war among his royalist friends. Napoleon gave Talleyrand a ferocious tongue-lashing, interspersed with the French equivalent of four-letter words, and relieved him of his post as Grand Chamberlain.

Hortense first learned of this when she had a visit from Madame de Rémusat, one of Talleyrand's devoted friends, asking her to intercede with the Emperor. Talleyrand also called and, though he feigned indifference, showed that he would be glad of Hortense's help. She had no great affection for the ex-minister, but she knew that he had some undefined connection with Charles de Flahaut. Hortense went to the Tuileries that evening and said to Napoleon that she had just seen someone who was in disgrace, but who was still devoted to the Emperor. She declined to say who the someone was, but Napoleon guessed immediately.

"It's Talleyrand you are talking of," he said. "Talleyrand can chatter as much as he chooses!"

"But, sire," Hortense protested, "how can a man be accused of talking too much who never says more than two words at once? He must have been misrepresented to you."

"You don't understand the world, my girl," Napoleon replied. "I do."

Talleyrand, he added, might look down his nose and say little in Hortense's presence, but he made up for his silence in the salons of the faubourg Saint Germain. "I am not going to hurt him," Napoleon concluded. "I just want him to keep his fingers out of my affairs."

It was Napoleon's policy never to discard anyone completely, whom he thought might be useful in the future. It was this, perhaps, rather than Hortense's plea that led to a dubious reconciliation. Since it was also Napoleon's policy not to discuss world events with women, Hortense could only predict the future from trivialities.

There were games of whist played at the Tuileries after a concert or a play in the palace theater, and it was always an honor to be asked to play at the table of the Empress or of the Queen of Holland. Madame Talleyrand came to ask Hortense that her husband should be chosen. There was a similar request from the wife of the Austrian Ambassador, Madame von Metternich. Hortense noticed that the Emperor, who never played himself and who walked about among the tables, stopping now and then to chat, avoided her when Metternich was one of her partners. As relations between France and Austria deteriorated, the Ambassador and his wife were shunned by the rest of the court.

Then suddenly, in April, the Emperor vanished without warning. He had left at four o'clock in the morning for Strasbourg, taking Joséphine with him. A week later, Hortense followed with the children. Fighting had already begun. As she passed through Lunéville, Hortense heard of a victory; a second was announced to her by an imperial page, as she was driving into Strasbourg. Again, as at Mainz, Hortense distributed money to prisoners and to the blood-stained wagon loads of wounded that passed through the city.

Hortense's health—still uncertain—took a turn for the worse. She went with her children to Baden for a cure, and received a sharp reprimand from the Emperor for taking her boys beyond the frontiers of France. They were precious to the Empire. Napoléon Louis was not only Crown Prince of Holland; he had been given the Duchy of Berg after the Murats were exalted to the throne of Naples.

Driven from one watering place to another, Hortense made the long journey to Plombières, and soon was joined by Joséphine. There they heard of a battle won by Eugène at Raab, and of the still greater victory of the Grand Army at Wagram in July. An armistice was called. Again Napoleon was on his way to Vienna, to impose his terms of peace.

While he was watching a review of his troops at Schönbrunn, a young man who had been trying to come suspiciously close to him was arrested and found to have a long butcher's knife hidden under his coat. He was questioned by the Emperor. After learning that the prisoner's name was Staps, that he was a student at a German university and the son of a Protestant minister, Napoleon asked what Staps had meant to do with his knife.

"Kill you," was the brief reply.

"You are crazy, young man," Napoleon said. "Why should you want to kill me?"

"Because you have harmed my country."

"Have I done any harm to you personally?"

"To me, and to all Germans."

Napoleon tried to get Staps to say who was behind his attempt, and whether he belonged to one of the national secret societies that had mushroomed in Germany. Staps denied connections of any kind. Napoleon said again that he must be crazy, and called in Dr. Corvisart to examine the prisoner for any abnormal symptoms. Napoleon told Staps that he would grant him his life and would pardon him, if he would say that he was sorry for his intentions.

"I don't want a pardon," Staps replied. "I am only sorry that I was unsuccessful."

"The devil you are! Then crime means nothing to you?"

"It isn't a crime to kill you. It is a duty."

Napoleon asked who was the young woman whose miniature had been found in Staps's pocket.

"She is the girl I love."

"She will be sorry to hear of your adventure," Napoleon said.

"She will be sorry only to hear that I have failed. She hates you as much as I do."

Napoleon was more concerned by this attempted assassination than the circumstances seemed to warrant. In discussing it with his staff, he kept insisting that Staps must have been the agent of someone in power, of someone in Berlin. He found it hard to believe that an ordinary man would want to kill him for political reasons; he was the friend of the ordinary man. The only sign of emotion given by Staps during his imprisonment was a nervous shiver, when he learned that peace had been made with Napoleon. He died, crying, "Long live liberty! Long live Germany—and death to the tyrant!"

Knowing that he might be some time at Schönbrunn, Napoleon sent for Maria Walewska. She was kept in great seclusion and no one was supposed to know that she was there, but Joséphine was informed at once and learned with anguish that the "Polish wife" was pregnant. Again it had been proved that Napoleon could have a child.

Walewska and the Staps affair made dismal subjects of conversation at Plombières. The summer was rainy, and Joséphine stayed only a short time in the mountains. She went back disconsolately to La Malmaison, and was so low spirited that she begged Hortense first to send her the children and then to come herself. Hortense had been with her mother only a few days when they heard that the Emperor had arrived at Fontainebleau. Joséphine went to the hunting lodge palace with fear in her heart. She found that the communication between her suite of rooms and her husband's had been walled up. Did she remember the locked door in the house in the rue de la Victoire after Napoleon's return from Egypt? This time she knew that however abundantly she wept, however pitifully she begged, the barrier would not be broken down.

The court returned to Paris in November, and Hortense went to her own house in the rue Cerutti. One morning she received word that the Emperor wanted to speak to her. She hurried to the Tuileries, only to find that Napoleon was in conference with his cabinet. She went in search of her mother and found her in a state of collapse.

The evening before, the terrible words had been spoken. Joséphine had fainted, but not so deeply that when she was being carried to her room by the aide-de-camp, whom Napoleon summoned, she felt the man's sword hilt pressing into her side. "You are holding me too tightly," Joséphine said.

Hortense had thought so long of how she would meet this calamity that she was fully prepared. She told her mother calmly that when she, Joséphine, had left the palace, she could live in peace. "But what will become of you, my children?" Joséphine wailed.

"We will go with you. My brother will think as I do. For the first time in our lives, we will have a family life of our own, a private family life. We will be happy!"

Hortense spoke so resolutely and brought forward such definite plans for their future, that Joséphine was soothed and for the moment reassured.

That evening, as Hortense was having dinner, a page came again to tell her that the Emperor would like to see her. Still resolute, still determined to show no emotion, she returned to the palace. She met Napoleon just as he was coming out of his study. His face was pale and stern.

"You have seen your mother," he said brusquely, as though he were dictating a communiqué. "She has told you. My mind is made up and cannot be changed. Nothing will make me reverse my decision, no tears, no prayers."

He had expected, perhaps, that she would fall at his feet, that she would clasp his knees.

"You are the master here, sire," Hortense said coldly, "and can do what you want. No one will try to oppose you. . . . Don't think it strange, however, if my mother should shed a few tears; it would be strange if she didn't, after thirteen years of marriage. She will submit, I am sure of that, and when we have all left you, we will only take with us the remembrance of your kindness."

While she spoke, the Emperor's embattled look had vanished. His eyes had filled with tears. "What," he cried with a sob, "you are all going to leave me! You are going to abandon me? You are not going to love me any more? If it were my own personal happiness, I would sacrifice that, but this means the happiness of France! You should be sorry for me, for having to give up what I love best."

Hortense, who had intended to be so inflexible herself, wilted. "Be brave, sire," she said gently. "We will need courage to give up being your children, but we will be courageous—I swear it. We will only think, in leaving you, that we will no longer stand in the way of your plans."

"But you mustn't leave me!"

Napoleon combated the idea of a parting, with passion. He went over again the argument for the divorce: The pressure that had been brought on him, not by intriguing courtiers, but by responsible people who had the welfare of the country at heart. His work for France would endure only if he left someone in his own image to gather in the harvest of his labors.

"As for you," he said, "the interests of your own children, the greatest incentive any woman can have, should keep you here. Don't talk to me again of leaving!"

Hortense was nevertheless determined to go—and to go far. Later, when she spoke again to her mother, she was disappointed to find that Joséphine, who had been worked upon by Napoleon, no longer thought as she did.

Eugène was summoned from Italy by semaphore. Hortense traveled to meet him, their carriages crossing at Nemours. It was the first time in more than four years that Hortense had seen her beloved brother. Eugène's first words were, "Is the reason for our meeting good or bad?"

"Bad."

Has our mother the courage to go through with it?"

"Yes."

On their way back to Paris, Hortense told Eugène everything that had happened recently, and all of her own sad story; she had refrained from writing him a detailed account of her troubles. He told her that he had read much between the lines of her letters. She had changed so much in appearance, that when he first saw her, he hardly knew her. Eugène agreed with Hortense completely on their line of action.

"Yes, we will go finish our lives, that have begun so badly, somewhere else," he said. "But why did they marry me to a princess? My poor wife is the one to be pitied. She expects crowns for her children; that is the way she was brought up. She thought I was being called to Paris to be made the heir of France. But now she will show a brave spirit; she loves me, she is good, and she will see that if one only does the right thing one can never be too unhappy."

Eugène's marriage had been as fortunate as Hortense's had been disastrous. His Augusta, the Bavarian princess whom Napoleon had had to cajole into accepting what she called "her sad fate," had proved to be an ideal wife. It had not been easy to be the Italian satrap of the Emperor. Eugène had had to bear the brunt of Napoleon's conflict with the Pope, whose estates were now annexed to France, and who had been carried off a prisoner to Savona. Eugène had found much consolation for his difficult job in a happy home life and in his two little girls, one of whom had been named Eugénie Hortense.

The meeting with the Emperor and Joséphine was tearful. Eugène showed the greatest self-control of the four who were present. He spoke strongly for an immediate and complete separation. This would entail his leaving the Emperor's service.

Napoleon protested. "Haven't I been a father to you?" he cried. Napoleon could not promise Eugène the inheritance of Italy, but he was quite ready to create a kingdom for his stepson in Illyria or in the Tyrol.

"I don't want anything," Eugène said. He would refuse any honor that might be interpreted as the price paid for his mother's rejection.

At this time, a number of public events had been scheduled to celebrate the victory over Austria: a reception at the Hôtel de Ville and at the Tuileries, Te Deum at Notre Dame, a grand review of the army. Joséphine presided at all of these functions, wearing her crown. Napoleon intended that she should be spared all humiliation. She would retain her title of Empress; her style of living at the Elysée Palace and at La Malmaison was to be unchanged. Not only would she have a large allowance, but her debts would be paid in full.

The divorce itself was a minor matter. The civil courts could easily dispose of the ceremony that had taken place in 1796; the ecclesiastical courts could find that the marriage performed by Cardinal Fesch in 1804 was illegal, because Fesch was not a parish priest. The important step was the announcement of an accomplished fact to the nation and the world.

Napoleon had invited all the family to come to Paris for the signing of the deed of separation. This meant that Hortense would be brought face to face with Louis. He was the first of the absent ones to arrive, and, with a retinue of more than twenty people, went to stay with his mother, a disturbing experience for an elderly woman and a parsimonious housekeeper. Napoleon suggested tentatively that Louis might move into his own house in the rue Cerutti, but at Hortense's cry of horror the subject was dropped, though it was plain that the Emperor was hoping for a reconciliation. "Louis is a good man," he said, "though nobody seems able to live with him."

Hortense sent the children regularly, every other day, to see their father, and called on him herself once when he was ill. She and Louis were both present at various public functions, but avoided one another assiduously.

On December 15, 1809, at nine o'clock in the morning, all of the family gathered at the Tuileries, not only the Bonapartes themselves, their wives and husbands, but also representatives of the families into which they had married. Only Joseph and, of course, Lucien were absent. Each was seated according to his or her rank. Napoleon read the written articles of divorce. He spoke loud and clear until he came to the phrase, "She has adorned my life for thirteen years; the remembrance of those years will remain engraved upon my heart." His voice broke. Joséphine tried to read her statement, but was too overcome to pronounce more than a few words, and the reading was finished by the Grand Chamberlain.

After the documents had been signed by everyone, Napoleon kissed Joséphine's hand and led her from the room. A few minutes later he returned and asked Hortense to go to her mother. She found Josèphine prostrate, surrounded by her weeping maids and ladies in waiting.

The following afternoon mother and daughter drove in a royal coach, poetically named The Opal, through a driving rain to La Malmaison. They were silent during their drive. As she walked into her beautiful house, Joséphine looked about her and sighed.

"If he is only happy," she murmured, "I will have no regrets."

XX

THE AUSTRIAN BRIDE

THE day following the divorce, Napoleon came to visit Joséphine and, as in earlier days, walked alone with her for a long time on the terrace of La Malmaison. The visit was repeated. Joséphine and Hortense were invited to dine at the Trianon, where Napoleon was staying. Every day a page would arrive with an inquiry for Joséphine's health, or a letter telling her how much she was missed. Gradually, the visits were wider spaced, the letters less frequent, but Joséphine did not lack for company. Her salon was crowded all day long with visitors, high and low, from marshals and ministers of state to the tradespeople who had always found the Empress a dependable outlet for their goods. Since she was still a very rich woman, it was presumed that she would continue her purchases.

Joséphine began slowly to recover her equilibrium, perhaps even to enjoy a little her state of bereavement. She made it a household rule that no piece of furniture, no relic, however small, should be moved from the spot it had occupied when La Malmaison was the Emperor's home. Whenever there was to be an imperial hunt in the forest of Saint-Germain, Joséphine would watch at her window to see the Emperor's carriage pass in the distance, and she would wait for its return when the day's sport was over.

Joséphine was curious, of course, to know who would be her successor, and did not have to wait long to learn that a choice had been made. Madame von Metternich, the wife of the Austrian Ambassador, who was grateful to Hortense for having shown her friendship when she needed it so much, came to call early in January, and hinted that the handkerchief would be dropped at the feet of the Archduchess Marie Louise. Metternich himself was working for the match in Vienna. Talleyrand had been sent to negotiate its terms.

Napoleon's family, and in particular Madame Mère, had thought that a Bonaparte should marry only a Bonaparte. A tentative move had been made to induce the Emperor to take for wife Lucien's fifteen-year-old daughter, Charlotte, but this idea seemed impractical for other reasons than those of consanguinity and difference in age. Napoleon had also abandoned all thought of a Russian alliance, since the Czar no longer seemed anxious to have him for a brother-in-law. Only the bluest blood in Europe would satisfy him now. Marie Louise, of the ancient house of Hapsburg, was a great-niece, twice over, of Marie Antoinette. She was nineteen years old; she was healthy and came of a prolific race, her mother having borne thirteen children and her great-grandmother twenty-six. Everything that Napoleon heard of her was satisfactory.

Marie Louise had been very carefully brought up, watched over day and night by dragon governesses. Her education had consisted chiefly in learning many languages: French, German, English, Bohemian, Turkish, Spanish, Italian, and even a little Latin —for who knows in what country a female Hapsburg might find herself a queen! In religion, the Archduchess had been taught no dogma, so that if necessary, she could be easily switched from Catholic to Protestant. Her life at Schönbrunn, or at the various places to which she had been evacuated when Napoleon invaded her father's realm, was as secluded as that of a nun: no sociabilities, except an occasional visit to an elderly aunt or uncle, no luxuries. A great deal of ingenuity had been shown in concealing from a not too inquiring mind the duality of sex. Marie Louise's pets, furred and feathered, were all female; in the few books she was allowed to read, all dubious passages had been carefully excised with a sharp knife. The most important thing that this daughter of the Emperor Francis II had been taught was that her father should be obeyed in every particular.

The engagement ratified, Napoleon became very anxious to know whether his fiancée was plain or pretty. Talleyrand later told Hortense of a conversation that the Emperor had had with a young aide-de-camp, who had had the rare privilege of seeing the Archduchess at Vienna.

"Tell me frankly," Napoleon said. "What did you think of her?"

"Sire, she is very nice."

"Very nice doesn't tell me anything! How tall is she?"

"Sire"—a moment's hesitation—"she is about as tall as the Queen of Holland."

"Very good. What color is her hair?"

"Blonde. Very much the same color as the Queen of Holland's hair."

"Good. And what is her coloring?"

"Very pink and white, like the Queen of Holland."

"Then she looks like the Queen of Holland?"

"No, sire, not in the least, but I have tried to answer your questions absolutely truthfully."

Napoleon dismissed the aide-de-camp and shook his head. "I can't get a word out of them," he said. "I think my wife must be very ugly, for none of these young devils can be brought to say that she is pretty. Well, as long as she is good and makes me some fine, big boys, I will love her as if she were the most beautiful woman in the world."

The *corbeille* that was sent to Austria consisted of twelve dozen of every conceivable kind of undergarment, elaborately laced and embroidered, and costing almost 100,000 francs. Jewels and trinkets came to half a million more. This was certainly enough to dazzle an archduchess who had shared in the austerity of her nation's war years and had never had more for ornament than a string of seed pearls or a bracelet of braided hair.

The marriage was performed by proxy in Vienna, and in March the bride set out for France. Napoleon was as eager and as high-spirited as a boy. One evening, when Hortense was at the Tuileries, he said, "I have got to make myself more attractive. My serious, solemn ways won't do for a young wife. She ought to enjoy the pleasures of youth. Come, Hortense, you are our Terpsichore; teach me how to waltz."

Everyone burst out laughing, but Napoleon was in earnest. Hortense gave him a lesson then and there and another later, but he made a very poor showing and laughed at his own awkwardness.

"You can't teach an old dog new tricks," he said. "I am too old. Besides, I can see that I was never cut out to be a dancer."

Eugène had left for Italy, to bring his wife to the wedding. Hortense went to meet them at Fontainebleau, very anxious to make the acquaintance of her sister-in-law. Augusta was tall, slender, and very beautiful. Hortense was prepared to love anyone who made Eugène so happy, but she found Augusta attractive in her own right. If Hortense felt any jealousy of Eugène's good fortune, compared to her own, she dismissed it as an unworthy thought.

Joséphine had been given an estate, Navarre, in Normandy, and went there so as to be out of the way of the wedding festivities. Eugène and Hortense were in duty bound to be present, although they looked upon this as an ordeal. Hortense went with the Emperor, all of the imperial family, and a large company to Compiègne, to wait for Marie Louise. Caroline Murat had gone a short way into Austria to conduct her new sister-in-law to France. As Marie Louise approached, her progress announced by a series of couriers, who carried daily messages, flowers, and gifts of game from the groom, Hortense thought of the probable state of mind of this poor young girl—homesick, no doubt, frightened—on her way to marry the man who, a short time ago, had been represented to her as an ogre, the war scourge of her country. Though realizing that a princess had been trained from the cradle to look on marriage from a purely political point of view, Hortense could not help identifying the unknown Marie Louise with herself, who had expected so much and got so little from the marriage market.

The Emperor was to meet Marie Louise at Soissons on the 27th of March, 1810, and ride with her to Compiègne, but he couldn't wait to begin his love-making. He went to Soissons a day in advance, left in a downpour of rain, and was waiting under the shelter of a church porch at Courcelles-sur-Nied when the great traveling coach, drawn by six horses, rolled and splashed into the town. Dripping wet, Napoleon sprang in to embrace his bride. Marie Louise did not resemble Hortense, but she was far from ugly. Her eyes were bright blue, her complexion, though a little marred by smallpox, could pass muster as brilliant, and she had the rather prominent chin and pouted underlip of the Hapsburgs. The pace of the cortege was quickened; it rattled through Soissons and the other towns, where disappointed crowds had been waiting in the rain to receive it, and arrived late that evening at Compiègne.

The court was given only a glimpse of their Empress-to-be before she was hurried off to Napoleon's bedroom suite. The next day he said to one of his generals, "My friend, marry a German girl. They are the most charming of all women—sweet, gentle, fresh, and as innocent as roses."

He was ready to meet the criticism that he should not have slept with his bride before the French marriage ceremony, by saying that he was only following the example of one of his predecessors, the good King Henry of Navarre.

The wedding party left for Saint-Cloud, where the civil ceremony was performed on April 1st. The next day the procession entered Paris, a Paris that had been elaborately decorated. The half-finished Arc de Triomphe at the Étoile had been completed in wood, so that the coach could drive beneath it. There was little enthusiasm shown by the crowds that lined the streets. The Austrian marriage was unpopular, and the Paris public, which had seen so many parades, was always apt to be blasé; there were many older folk who could remember when Marie Antoinette came to France.

The big square salon in the Louvre had been transformed into a chapel for the Nuptial Mass. Hortense, Elisa, Pauline, and the wives of Joseph and Jérôme bore the Empress' train, while Caroline, Augusta, and Stéphanie of Baden went ahead carrying candles and insignia. The mantle that Marie Louise wore was the same that Joséphine had worn at her coronation. While the ceremony was in progress, Hortense felt that many hostile eyes were fixed upon her and on Eugène, to see how they were taking this event.

Hortense was determined to keep a stiff upper lip, but she was too absorbed in a sorrow of her own to take much heed of what was going on. The very worst had happened. She knew that as soon as the imperial wedding was over, she would have to return to Holland. Again she had become the victim of a political expedient.

One day before she went to Compiègne, Hortense was visited in Paris by one of Louis' Dutch ministers, who complained of the Emperor's severity in insisting that Holland should maintain the blockade of English goods. While disclaiming any influence that she could have, either with Napoleon or with her husband, Hortense pointed out that if Holland had an army strong enough to resist the Emperor, well and good. Since the Dutch army was so weak, Holland should go along with the Continental system in the hope of better days to come. Otherwise, the Master of Europe would lose patience and annex the kingdom outright to France.

This was the dilemma that had faced Louis when he came to Paris early in December. He had been so afraid of coercion, that he told those he left in charge of affairs at home that any decree he might send back from France signed "Louis" should be disregarded; only one signed with his Dutch name, "Lodewyck," would be genuine.

At their first interview, Napoleon said, "Holland is nothing but an English colony, more hostile to France than England herself. I intend to eat up Holland!"

If Louis would go along with this cannibal program he could return to live in France as a prince and constable of the Empire, or another throne could be found for him in Germany. If he showed fight, he would be overwhelmed and would receive no compensation. Louis asked for time to consider.

Negotiations followed. Offers were made, compromises were suggested, but Louis was always the loser. His discussions with his brother were further embittered by a demand that Louis made, early in the game, for a separation from Hortense.

On December 24th, a family council was called at the Trianon to consider the matter. Such meetings were now formal affairs, with representatives of the state and of the legal profession present. The decision reached was satisfactory to Napoleon: There was to be no open break. Napoleon did not want another domestic upheaval in the family so soon after his own divorce, and he did not want it to seem as if Joséphine's daughter was being repudiated. Hortense did not attend the meeting, but she was given to understand that she and her children could stay in France.

All during the preparations for the wedding, however, the battle for Holland continued. French troops were constantly moving into the country, and controlled not only the coast but the inland waterways. Dutch smugglers were arrested and taken to France. The towns of Bergen op Zoom and Breda were occupied, and when Louis ordered them to show a passive resistance, Napoleon was outraged.

At last, on March 16th, Louis, in desperation, signed a treaty that left him only the shadow of sovereignty over a small part of his kingdom beyond the Maas River. He had not got rid of Hortense, but he had at least obtained one thing that he wanted: his elder son. Louis was not interested in his other child. Since Charles Louis Napoléon, soon to reach his second birthday, had been born prematurely, Louis either believed, or pretended to believe, that the child was not his.

At Compiègne, Louis was scandalized when he found that the room assigned to him was close to that of Hortense, but Hortense did not guess what was intended until she lunched one day with Jérôme and his wife in their apartments. Hortense was chilled to find herself sitting down to table with Jérôme, Catherine, and Louis—no one else. After lunch, Jérôme and Catherine disappeared.

"Madame," Louis said, "I have been wanting to speak to you for some time. The Emperor will not consent to the separation that we both want. Consequently, you can't keep on living by yourself and apart from your husband."

"What possible good can you expect from our living together?" Hortense asked.

"I know that happiness is impossible," was the austere reply. "I don't ask for that. But you are the Queen of Holland, and it is there that you should be. I can't allow you to live anywhere else."

Hortense pleaded with Louis to let her make her home with Joséphine; she could understand why he would not want her to remain at court. "I can't make you happy," she said, "so let me live in peace. Don't think of me any more. Think of me as dead."

"That would be quite another matter," Louis said. From something that he added about the Emperor of Austria's marrying immediately after the death of Marie Louise's mother, Hortense gathered that Louis would not be sorry if he himself were a widower.

She would do all that she could to frustrate him. Life itself, she felt, was at stake. Since she had no chance of speaking privately to Napoleon, she wrote him a letter, to which there was no reply. She went with tears in her eyes to Eugène, but for once Eugène was against her. Though he was deeply sympathetic, he begged her to make one more trial and to show the world how brave she could be. If she failed, she would have won the right to live alone.

Hortense could not accept this as a challenge, but neither could she go against her brother's advice. Eugène offered to have an interview with Louis and to lay down certain conditions for Hortense's return. She was to live in the same palace as the King and the Crown Prince, and was to be allowed to go to a watering place if her health required. She was to take her own personal maids with her, since Louis would not permit her to have any French ladies in waiting. Little Charles Louis Napoléon was to remain, for the present at least, in Paris.

Hortense could not face saying good-bye to her mother, and wrote a letter to Navarre. Her parting with Adèle de Broc was heartbreaking. Adèle's husband, General de Broc, had, like all of Louis' French staff, been dismissed, so that his place could be taken by a Dutchman. De Broc took service with Eugène in Italy, and within the past two weeks had died of a fever at Milan. Adèle, so recently widowed, clung to Hortense and begged her to give up this suicidal idea of going to Holland. Yet another parting, the most difficult of all, was from Charles de Flahaut, who had never recovered from a wound he had suffered in the last campaign and was being nursed by his mother.

On April 6th, Louis left for Amsterdam, which was now the capital of Holland. He told Hortense that he trusted her to follow shortly with Napoléon Louis. The Emperor and Marie Louise were honeymooning at Compiègne. Hortense stopped there to say farewell. The palace was crowded; everyone was gay; there was dancing every evening. Hortense, who loved so to dance, stayed only overnight. This was no place for her; the gloating, crocodile sympathy shown for her by the Bonaparte sisters was more than she could bear.

"What, you are going so soon?" Napoleon said. He seemed truly sorry for her, but he was so absorbed by his bride that he had only a moment to give to her—a bitter moment for Hortense. He was no longer her protector, she felt; she was no longer his child. Cutting short their interview, she ran to the traveling carriage where Napoléon Louis and his governess, Madame de Boubers, were waiting for her.

XXI

SET FREE

THE journey to Holland was funereal. Hortense remembered how she had traveled this way four years earlier. She had been sad enough then, but then she had had Napoléon Charles with her; now she was afraid that Napoléon Louis would be taken from her also. She thought continually of death, and when, soon after they had crossed the border, they passed a coffin on its way to the cemetery, she wondered morbidly if this were not a sign.

They came to Utrecht. Louis had chosen this city for his capital, after he had come to the conclusion that the Hague was too dangerously close to the coast. It was soon abandoned, however, for Amsterdam. Nobody was expecting the travelers at Utrecht. There was only a single candle in the room into which Hortense was shown by the concierge; that soon had guttered out, and she was left in the dark until the carriage in which her servants were traveling caught up with her.

Louis appeared two days later. He greeted his son with great demonstrations of joy, but had hardly a word for Hortense. His palace at Amsterdam, to which they soon transferred, had formerly been the City Hall. It was a great, gloomy place, with echoing corridors. Hortense's salon had been the criminal court, and was decorated by a frieze of death's heads in black-and-white marble. The windows looked out on a churchyard and, when opened, admitted a clammy smell of sewer and stagnant canal.

In this unappetizing spot, Hortense passed her mornings alone, writing unhappy letters to Adèle and reading the Gothic romances of the English novelist, Ann Radcliffe; she couldn't seem to keep her mind on anything less macabre. She seldom saw Napoléon Louis. His father had taken complete possession of him. In the later afternoon, she was summoned to dine in silence with her husband. After dinner, Louis would play the piano and recite French poetry or hum a tune to his own accompaniment. He kissed and fondled his little boy and sometimes took him out on the balcony to be cheered by passers-by in the street. Later, candles would be brought; the household would be summoned; tables were set up for a dreary game of cards. At nine o'clock Hortense would retire, after having said a ceremonial good night to the King, who had pointedly refrained from speaking to her throughout the evening.

Hortense's Dutch ladies in waiting were pleasant enough, but they were all strangers and they seemed to be afraid of becoming too intimate with her. Others of the court avoided her. She had a comforting visit from Abbé Bertrand, her old teacher at Saint-Germain, whom she had brought to Holland four years earlier as her chaplain. He told her, who was always so eager for approbation, that people were sorry for her because she looked so ill. They had been led to suppose that she had stayed in France merely to amuse herself. Hortense didn't dare to keep the Abbé with her long or to see him again, since it was plain that anyone whom she favored might be suspect.

The only way out of Amsterdam was to be carried out on a sickbed. Hortense did not have to feign illness. Every day she felt that she was growing weaker. She at last plucked up her courage, complained to Louis of the charnel house smell in her apartments, and reminded him of the promise to Eugène that if she wished, she could go to a health resort. Very reluctantly, he gave her leave to go to another royal residence at Loo, to the northwest of Amsterdam. There was no hope of taking Napoléon Louis with her; Hortense had to trust that Madame de Boubers would take care of him. She spent only a week at Loo and then wrote Louis that her only chance for recovery was to get to the mountains where, three years earlier, she had regained her health.

As she set out again for Plombières on the 1st of June, she wondered if she would get there in time. She was not as ill as she imagined, but when the carriage stopped for a change of horses, people would look in through the window at the pale, emaciated young woman lying back upon her cushions and would say, "See how sick she is! She's dying!"

As she sped westward, Hortense had little pity for Louis, though in the turmoil of emotions he aroused in her, she felt an occasional faint twinge of compunction for having, perhaps, abandoned him in a moment of crisis. But how could she help him, she asked herself, when he would not even speak to her? He had broken his silence twice. Once, he asked her to write to the Emperor to beg him to stop sending troops into Holland. Hortense did so, but knew that it would be useless. In his latest communication—Hortense received it just before she left for Plombières—Louis told her how much was at stake for their children, in this quarrel with his brother; Hortense shared with him a responsibility in trying to save the Dutch throne for Napoléon Louis and his brother.

But these were only counsels of despair. In the six weeks that Hortense had been in Holland, Louis had almost reached the end of his resources for combat, such as they were.

When Louis returned to his kingdom in April of 1810, his one thought was how to avoid carrying out the terms of the treaty that he now wished he had never signed. He called a conference of Dutch statesmen, past and present, to ask their advice; he suggested abdication. The consensus of opinion was that he should remain as King. Things were bad enough as they were. Louis' subjects, republican at heart, knew that he was on their side, but were sceptical of what he could accomplish. The only hope that he could hold out to them was that, while he was in France, tentative moves had been made toward a peace with Great Britain. A good peace—and Holland's troubles might vanish overnight.

On May 5th, however, Louis went to Antwerp and had a brief interview with Napoleon, who was touring the northern provinces with Marie Louise. Louis was told that the peace negotiations had not survived even the preliminary stage, and that the terms of the treaty must be carried out to the letter. Napoleon accused Louis of stirring up anti-French feeling.

This, in part at least, was as unjust as most of Napoleon's accusations. The anti-French feeling existed already in every town, on every minor waterway where the Dutch came in contact with French customs officers, who confiscated their goods, made arrests, and gabbled at them in a language they could not understand. Louis, however, had countered with severities toward alien underlings whenever he dared. There were unfortunate incidents. One of the most petty, and the most disastrous, concerned the coachman of the French Ambassador, De La Rochefoucauld, a man whom Louis detested. The coachman, on his way to Sunday Mass in Amsterdam, resplendent in his uniform, was threatened and mauled by a gang of roughs and had to seek the protection of the police. Napoleon demanded that the guilty parties should be punished, but Louis replied that it was impossible to find them.

The result of this was a final exhortation from Napoleon for his brother to mend his ways; Napoleon said that Louis was "incorrigible." The word suggested the old, festering relationship, the punishments that the big brother had once meted out to a twelve-year-old, who both loved and feared his mentor.

Meanwhile, the military penetration of the country continued. Leiden, Utrecht, and the Hague were occupied. On June 28th, after the foolish affair of the Ambassador's coachman, Louis was told by a French commissioner that Amsterdam would be taken over on the 4th of July. Too late, much too late, Louis thought of appealing to the European powers, to Russia and Austria. Too late also, he consulted with his military men about defending the city. He was told that, if the decision had been made earlier, the country could have been flooded, but that now the French controlled the dikes.

In that case, Louis said, he would retire to Haarlem and would abdicate in favor of his son.

He had six days of grace. Louis made preparations for the entry of the troops into Amsterdam; they would not be welcomed, but there would be no hostilities. He sold, privately through a banker, some Dutch real estate he had bought. He sent a trusted man out of the country with his diamonds. On July 1st he went to Haarlem, and for two days was secluded in his study, writing with his rheumatic hand his abdication messages to the Council of State and to the nation. These would be his justification to the world and to the historians of the future.

Louis went on record as protesting the unlawful and violent acts of the Emperor, and what he now described as the forced signing of the treaty of March 16th. Hortense was mentioned, but only because, according to the constitution, she would be regent for the six-year-old King. In both of his messages Louis wrote that, "I abdicate in favor of my well-beloved son, Napoléon Louis, and in default of him of his brother, Charles Louis Napoléon." The "his brother" cast a subtle doubt, malicious in intent, on the paternity of the little boy who had been left behind in France. The abdication act, however, ended on a note of noble emotion that, at the moment, was sincere. "Whenever my life shall close," Louis wrote, "the name of Holland and my most ardent prayers for her happiness will be my last words and occupy my latest thought."

On the evening of July 3rd, Louis received his ministers and handed over to them his documents. The proclamation to the people was to be posted on the walls of Amsterdam, before the French troops came tramping in on the morrow.

That evening, dinner was served in royal state at the Haarlem pavilion and was followed by the usual social hour. There was music, card-playing, and conversation—languid, artificial conversation, since all unpleasant topics were taboo. At half-past ten the guests were dismissed, and the King retired to his apartments where he was joined by two of his aides-de-camp—one French, the other Dutch—whom he had let into the secret that he was going to leave the country at once, that very night.

With the help of his aides and his valet, Louis packed up his papers and a few belongings. At midnight he went into the room where Napoléon Louis was sound asleep and kissed the child gently, without waking him. A carriage was waiting in the lane that ran along the garden wall of the château. Louis emerged from the garden gate with his three companions and his dog, a mongrel water spaniel, a waif he had befriended and cherished. Louis, who could be so insensitive, at times, in dealing with human beings, was always kind to animals.

After the party had climbed into the carriage, Louis remembered a portfolio that had been left behind in his study. He went back himself to fetch it. As he was crossing a plank that was laid over the ditch, close to the garden wall, he slipped and fell into the muddy kennel. He was helped out—wet, besmeared. His aides wanted him to go back and change his clothing, but he said no. Too much time had been lost already. The carriage drove off along the bank of a canal that led toward Amsterdam, skirted the city, and turned inland. Before daylight, it was well on its way to the German border.

At one of the posthouse stops, the spaniel jumped out of the open window while the carriage was still in motion, fell under the wheels, and was crushed to death. To the poor, fugitive King, who felt that he was friendless and persecuted by all the world, the cruel death of his dog seemed the final, the gratuitous stroke of misfortune.

回

It was not until July 8, 1810, four days later, that Napoleon, who was at Rambouillet, heard that Louis had abdicated. He was neither surprised nor sorry. It had been his aim for months that his brother should step down from the throne, but for Louis to abscond, to vanish, no one knew whither—that was quite another matter! The clansman in Napoleon was outraged. He might bully and belabor Louis, but he did not expect him to desert the family standard, just because he had been abused. Napoleon was as shocked as when, six years earlier, Lucien roared his defiance and went to live in Italy.

Louis' disappearance coincided with a further defection of Lucien, who, in spite of Madame Merè's many efforts, had maintained his independence. Being rich, he had helped the Pope, who was in financial difficulties, by buying from the Holy See the principality of Canino. He had done much for his estates: established iron works, introduced the cultivation of cotton from Calabria, and carried on interesting archeological excavations. He was in high favor with Pius VII, who—an almost unheard of distinction—asked to stand godfather to one of Lucien's many children by the former Madame Jouberthou.

When French troops occupied Rome in 1808, when the papal states were united to France and the Pope was carried off a prisoner to Savona, Lucien became restive and talked of going to America. He asked for, and obtained, passports to cross the frontiers of the Empire. Napoleon did not think that Lucien would actually leave Italy, but now he wondered if Louis had joined his brother on a trip to the United States. He was soon to learn that Lucien and his family had indeed sailed, that their vessel was captured by the British, and that they were interned as prisoners of war in England. There, Lucien was made much of as "the good Bonaparte," the one who had had the pluck to stand up to his satanic brother.

Napoleon, when he wrote to Hortense at Plombières on July 8, 1810, realized how miserable she had been, and felt that he owed her a recompense for what he was taking away from her and from her children.

"You must have received a courier from Holland to tell you of the King's latest act of folly," he wrote. "My will is to unite Holland with France. I will send you a copy of the letter you should transmit to the Regency, if you have not already done so. . . . You are set free by this step that the King has taken. You can now live tranquilly in Paris. All I want to know is that you are completely well again and that you have nothing more to cause you the slightest unhappiness."

PART

IV

(July 10, 1810–August 28, 1814)

XXII

A DAY OF GOLD

ON THE same day that Hortense received the Emperor's letter, telling her that she was no longer a queen, she heard from Madame de Boubers that Louis had left Holland. Official notice of the abdication followed. Hortense obeyed without question Napoleon's instructions in regard to the regency. She heard from him several times during the next two weeks. He told her that he had sent for Napoléon Louis to be brought to Paris, and that he had no word of Louis' whereabouts. By July 20th, Napoleon had learned, to his great dissatisfaction, that his brother was in Austria at Töplitz, a Bohemian spa. The little King of Holland, whose reign had not even been proclaimed by the authorities, had arrived at Saint-Cloud, and he and his brother were given a wing of the palace, the Pavilion d'Italie, as their home for the present. There was no reason for Hortense to return immediately. Joséphine was at Aix-en-Savoie and wanted her daughter to join her there.

As Hortense approached the town of Aix, she saw two horsemen galloping toward her. One of the riders was her mother's equerry, who had been sent to meet her; the other was Charles de Flahaut. The meeting with Charles was not unexpected. He had stopped off at Plombières on his way to Aix to take a cure, for he was still feel-

203

ing the effects of the wound he had gotten in the Wagram campaign.

With De Flahaut riding beside her, Hortense made a triumphant entry into the town. She was greeted by Joséphine and her friends, as though she had just been released from prison. She was wrapped in a warm blanket of solicitude. Everyone worried about her health, everyone thought of little ways to give her pleasure—and Charles de Flahaut came to see her every day. Hortense was as shy with him as a young girl. She was embarrassed when he gave her all of his attention, but she suffered when she saw him talking gaily to another woman; there were all too many pretty women at Aix. Hortense was still so weak physically that tears were always close to the surface, but, for the most part, they were tears of happiness.

A month slipped by deliciously. Flahaut's leave was up and he had to go back to Paris. Joséphine went to a small house that she had bought, Prègny, on Lake Geneva. Hortense stayed on for some time at Aix, almost alone, for it was now September and the season at the watering place was over. A letter came from the Emperor, saying that it was time for his daughter to return to her children.

When she reached Fontainebleau, Hortense found that all the court, including her two little boys, were there. She had hardly arrived, when the Emperor and Marie Louise came to her room. Marie Louise was obviously pregnant. "See how large she is," Napoleon said proudly. "If it is a girl, she will make a nice little wife for your son Napoléon, for we couldn't let *her* marry outside the family or France."

Napoleon was anxious that Hortense and Marie Louise should be friends. "Come to see my wife in the mornings," he said. "You could sketch together, or make a little music. She would like it very much, but she is too shy to ask you."

Hortense passed over this invitation with a smile. Though she went regularly to evening receptions and Marie Louise seemed always glad to see her, she did not force herself upon the Empress.

It would have only increased the rage of the Bonapartes, who were held at arm's length and allowed no intimacy. It was hard enough for them to bear, that Hortense had turned up again in Paris and was favored by Napoleon. How often they had thought that she was gone for good! She seemed to be as indestructible and to have as many lives as a cat. Pauline was the only one of the sisters or brothers who was on the spot, but she spoke for all when she accused Hortense of having driven Louis into exile and having lost Holland as an inheritance for her children.

Against her will, Hortense was forced to think of Louis. Madame Mère wanted to send him the Monsieur Decazes who had been his agent in Paris and whom Hortense had refused to accept as her secretary. She was asked to write a letter, urging Louis to return, saying that the Emperor would provide for him and would give him the chance of future employment. Louis, however, was nursing his wrongs at Töplitz and had a new one: Napoleon had given Hortense the house in the rue Cerutti and the estate of Saint-Leu, with an ample income for her and for her sons. Louis forbade her to accept anything.

"Your husband is crazy," Napoleon said. "He deserves to have me do nothing for his children. It is lucky I am so soft-hearted—people always count on that. It's not the poor children's fault. They would be pitiful, if they only had their father to look out for them!"

Hortense saw that she was indeed free, that she no longer needed to obey Louis. She paid his debts, pensioned his servants, and financed the two trips that Decazes made to Austria for futile negotiations. From the second of these journeys, Decazes came back to announce that Louis, though he had been told to leave Austria by the authorities, had gone to Gratz, the capital of Styria, and bought himself a house.

Hortense had already settled down in Paris for the winter, and for the first time in her twenty-seven years was living exactly as she chose. She had her household—her chaplain, Abbé Bertrand, her chamberlains, her equerries, her ladies in waiting—but the only ones who were constantly with her were her two boys, her dear Adèle, now a widow, and Mademoiselle Louise Cochelet, a Saint-Germain girl, who for several years had been Hortense's reader. The greatest harmony existed in the rue Cerutti. It was only threatened by petty jealousies of the Queen's attendants, who competed for first place in her affections. If she complained mildly that her bed had been poorly made, the young woman who made it burst into tears and went about looking as if she had been beaten.

In the morning, no visitors were admitted. Hortense and Adèle devoted themselves to drawing and painting. They dined alone. In the evening, the doors of the house were thrown open to Hortense's friends. One could enjoy a little music, or one could play billiards—and one could always talk. At ten o'clock tea was served, and the conversation was often so enthralling that it was midnight or one in the morning before the party broke up.

Hortense had always disliked the stiff pattern of the old-regime salon, a circle of chairs around the fireplace, with seats for the ladies, while the gentlemen stood uncomfortably. There was a big round table in the middle of Hortense's room, at which everyone could sit down and on which books and fancy work could be spread out. The men did not need to wear tight-fitting uniforms; the women did not need to display a complete harness of jewels. The Bonapartes criticized the informality of Hortense's way of entertaining, and she was afraid that the Emperor, with his growing fondness for ceremony, might disapprove, but he only said, "I hear that at your house you have an open market for wit," and she knew he would not interfere.

Though she had a large reception every Monday and occasionally gave a ball, invitations to Hortense's small evening parties were much sought after. She had many visitors, and Charles de Flahaut, who was stationed now in Paris, was one of those who came most often. The evening glowed when he was there, though Hortense was still embarrassed in his presence. Small talk seemed to die upon her lips when he entered the room. She found it difficult to be natural with him, even to speak in a natural voice. It was easier to write him a love letter than to tell him that she loved him.

While Hortense was in Holland, Charles had had another encounter, this time in Paris, with his Polish flirt, the Countess Potocka. He told her, as he had once told Hortense, that he loved her, but that he was bound by gratitude and affection to another. Hortense, though unaware of this episode, was never sure that she could believe Charles's protestations. In a moment of doubt, she gave back to him the seal that he had had made for her, with its device of "A day of gold is the reward of a century." She had had another facet cut, with an anchor, the symbol of constancy, appearing through clouds, and the words, "*Soleil, je t'implore*" (Oh sun, I implore you).

Charles, Hortense felt, was too facile, too anxious to shine for all the world. When she complained to Adèle of the pain he caused her, Adèle said, "Look about you—whom do you see who is perfectly happy? . . . After long slavery you are free. You have your children, you're rich, and you can do a great deal of good. . . . Why should you complain?"

Adèle, who from the first had known of Hortense's feeling for Flahaut, was an ideal chaperone. If Charles and Hortense remained too long tête-à-tête by the fire, Adèle would come to say that there were other guests who needed a little of the hostess' attention. A look or a word from her friend was enough to warn Hortense that she was making her growing infatuation too public. Flahaut held no official position in her household, but all of the habitués of Hortense's salon could not help knowing that he was favored.

Hortense would have been glad to live privately, but, as a member of the Emperor's family in good standing, she had to make frequent appearances in public. The imperial school for girls at Écouen, of which Napoleon had spoken two years earlier, was a going concern; Hortense was its patroness. The school was intended to be an imitation of the school that Louis XIV had founded at Saint-Cyr, where Elisa Bonaparte had been a pupil before the Revolution. In all of his undertakings, Napoleon was determined to outshine his predecessors. Saint-Cyr had had an enrollment of two hundred and fifty; Écouen must care for twice that number. The main building, a remodeled château, was surrounded by five orphanages, for small children of heroes who had died in battle.

Madame Campan, in her sixties, but still indefatigable, was the headmistress. "If I were establishing a republic for women," Napoleon said, "I would choose Madame Campan for First Consul." It was a proud day for the former lady in waiting of Marie Antoinette, when the institution was formally opened—the Emperor present, the pupils in virginal white, Madame Campan with the Cross of the Legion of Honor shining on the bosom of her black dress, surrounded by queens, princesses, and duchesses whom she had taught at Saint-Germain.

Caroline, Queen of Naples, who thought nothing of making the long trip from southern Italy to Paris, was there, and said to her former teacher, "I think it is surprising that you are not more embarrassed in dealing with us. You talk as easily to us as if we were still in school."

Madame Campan was not to be cowed. "The best thing for you to do is to forget all about your titles when you are with me," she said. "I certainly am not going to be overawed by queens whom I once made stand in the corner!"

Écouen was near Saint-Leu and Hortense had a private road cut through her property, so that she could reach the school quickly and easily. She liked to think that in the prayers of the little girls of Écouen her name was mentioned with that of the Emperor.

Hortense also made frequent trips to La Malmaison, where Joséphine kept open house for her faithful friends, always glad to see her daughter and her grandchildren, to whom, at every visit, she gave extravagant presents. Joséphine was an indulgent grandparent, so much so that Napoléon Louis said to Hortense, "You spoil me when I am good, but grand'maman spoils me all the time."

For Joséphine, life had changed less than one might have imagined. She still had her visitors, her flowers, her lap logs, and her debts, which had again begun to accumulate, with less likelihood than formerly of Napoleon's shouting with rage when settling day came around.

Joséphine was always eager to hear talk of what was going on at the Tuileries or at Saint-Cloud. Hortense could keep her informed, for she was present on all state occasians, and also at the family dinners that took place every Sunday. Napoleon's court was very splendid, very decorous, and very dull. He was a great stickler for propriety; any young man rash enough to pay too obvious attention to a married lady was sent away to the army. Marie Louise, who might have enlivened the gorgeous scene, was a nonentity, a stiff little doll, with her china blue eyes, her wooden gestures, her mechanical courtesies.

Napoleon was far more considerate of his young wife, Hortense noticed, than he had been of Joséphine. If she kept him waiting, as often happened, he was patient, and when she appeared would say, "Ah, here you are! You have been making yourself still more beautiful!"

He made touching efforts to keep her amused. "If you like to dance, have the musicians in," he said. "Or go to see the carnival processions. Go visit workshops and public buildings."

"I don't want to, unless you will come with me," Marie Louise replied.

"But I haven't the time," Napoleon protested. "Go with Hortense. The people of Paris would be delighted to catch a glimpse of you."

The answer was always "No. I would rather stay where I am."

The only person, except Hortense, for whom the Empress showed any liking was her chief lady in waiting, the Duchesse de Montebello, who had been chosen for her post because she was of the loftiest, the most impeccable moral character. Napoleon found

her a bore, but put up with her for Marie Louise's sake. The
Duchess, Hortense thought, was not well fitted for her position and,
separated from a family of growing children, did not enjoy it. For
one thing, she failed to coach her mistress in the proper thing to
say to the people who were presented to her, something which
Joséphine had never needed. Marie Louise, for example, would
sometimes inquire for the health of the husband of a widow recently bereaved. Her flat voice, her German accent made everything she said seem ungracious.

◻

But though a social failure, Napoleon's wife was fulfilling her
biological function to the admiration of all. As the time for the
birth of the heir to the Empire approached, suspense developed,
deepened. At ten o'clock on the evening of March 19, 1811, a page
came to tell Hortense that the Empress had felt her first pains. Hortense hurried to the Tuileries. All of the palace was ablaze with
light. There were at least a dozen persons in the bedchamber, including Madame de Montebello, Madame Mère, the ladies who
had been selected to be governesses of the child who was about to
be born, and a corps of doctors and nurses. In the anteroom, two
young women from Écouen had been installed as messengers.

The protocol for this occasion had been carefully worked out.
Hortense's place was in the salon nearest to the anteroom, with
Pauline; Julie, Queen of Spain; and the Grand Duke of Würzburg, Marie Louise's uncle. The salons beyond were filled with
state officials and with courtiers, who were grouped about tables
at which wine and hot chocolate were served. The atmosphere was
that of a party, a party at which voices were kept at sotto-voce
level and no one dared to laugh.

Napoleon was back and forth between the bedroom and the first
salon, very pale, appalled by the crude realities of birth, which he
had never before witnessed. He seemed to have prepared himself
for a girl, though from certain questions that he asked, it was evident that he hoped against hope for a son.

The birth would be long, apparently. At four o'clock in the morning, it was announced that it would not take place for some time and all were urged to retire for what remained of the night. Hortense, who was exhausted, went to the room of one of the Écouen girls and threw herself down, fully dressed, upon the bed. At eight o'clock the owner of the room burst in upon her and, tears streaming from her eyes, said that the Empress was screaming horribly. The child was in an abnormal position and must be delivered by forceps. The Emperor had been asked what should be done and had said that the mother's life should be saved rather than the child's.

Hortense, with the feeling that she had wakened to nightmare, stumbled down the stairs and met Napoleon, who was just coming out of the bedroom. He was breathless, trembling from head to foot. "It is over," he said. "She is safe."

"Is it a boy?" Hortense hardly dared to ask the question.

"Yes."

Hortense would have kissed him, but he pushed her away. "Ah, I can't realize any happiness yet," he muttered. "The poor woman suffered so terribly!"

He went away to give the order for the salvo of a hundred guns that was to announce the birth of a son. Hortense went into the bedroom to see the child, and was glad to find that it was normal and unharmed by the instruments that had been used. There were so many about the bed of the Empress, that she could not get near enough to congratulate Marie Louise.

As the cannon roared, the empty outer rooms began to fill with the watchers who had been wakened from their short sleep. Napoleon remained grave in the midst of the rejoicing. Some thought him unfeeling, but not Hortense, who could appreciate the effort he made for self-control. She felt that people were looking at her as curiously as at the time of the imperial wedding, a year earlier. It seemed unlikely now that her sons would inherit the throne, but she had made up her mind to that long ago.

The son of an Emperor could be nothing less than a king, the

King of Rome. That evening, the child was anointed in the chapel of the Tuileries. His public baptism was to take place in Notre Dame on June 9th. The Emperor of Austria was to be godfather and would be represented by the Grand Duke of Würzburg. The godmothers were Madame Mère and Caroline, who, unavoidably detained in Naples, nominated Hortense to take her place.

When General Duroc came to announce this arrangement to Hortense, she declined. She thought that Caroline might have found someone else to represent her. She dreaded the thought of going to Notre Dame, which she had avoided since the death of Napoléon Charles; his small coffin was still lying in the cathedral, its final resting place—the restored Tomb of the Kings at Saint-Denis—being still unfinished.

Napoleon was annoyed by Hortense's refusal; he took it for granted that she thought it beneath her dignity to act as substitute. The matter was considered important enough to be discussed at a council meeting, and it was decided that there was no precedent for the stand Hortense had taken; she would have to serve. The evening before the ceremony, she went to the palace and, saying that she was ill, begged the Emperor to let her off.

"I didn't mean to humiliate you by asking you to hold my son at the font," he said coldly.

Hortense went home in great distress, having agreed to be at Notre Dame. She told Adèle that she was sure she would break down the following day. Perhaps, if they two went alone now to the cathedral she might be fortified. It was very late, almost midnight. Adèle tried to dissuade Hortense, but a hired carriage was summoned and the two women drove to Notre Dame.

The doors of the cathedral were locked. They had to go to the archepiscopal palace to find a doorkeeper who could let them in. The great building had been splendidly decorated. Late though it was, some workmen were putting the finishing touches to a remote corner; the only light was from their feeble lanterns; the only sound was the occasional echoing tap of a hammer.

All the sorrows of the past swept over Hortense. She fell on her knees before the altar and wept. Finally, Adèle coaxed her to her feet and led her away, assisted by the doorman, who was curious to know why this strange woman should be so overcome by grief the night before the King of Rome was to be baptized.

The following day, Hortense went through with her part in the ceremony without a tear. She bore up bravely through the even more tiring festivities that followed at the Hôtel de Ville and at Saint-Cloud. When all was over, the last rocket fired, the last drop of wine spurted from the public fountains, Hortense left with Adèle for Aix-en-Savoie. There was an urgent reason for her wanting to escape from Paris and from further public display; there was another cause for her emotional state of mind than remembrance of the past. Hortense was almost six months pregnant with De Flahaut's child.

XXIII

THE PRIME MINISTER

There would be no cannon fired to celebrate this birth. Every precaution had been taken to keep it secret. In this, Hortense had the devoted coöperation of Charles de Flahaut and his mother. Charles had got a three months sick leave from the army, which dated from the 28th of June, 1811. It was given out to his friends that he was going to take the waters at a spa in southwestern France.

During his absence that summer, Charles carried on yet another enigmatic correspondence with Madame de Souza. "I agree with you," he wrote on July 19th, "in all that you think concerning the Prime Minister. However difficult it may be, I would be very happy to have him in my own home." Somewhat later, he informed Adélaide that he was going to take a little trip in the latter part of August and that she could reach him through "my cousin. . . . My own health is good, and it is only fair that I should now take some care of hers."

On the 20th of August, De Flahaut was about to start on his trip, and let his mother know that he would be back in Paris in September. "After the 23rd, write me at my cousin's at Prègny. Unless something unusual comes up, don't make any arrangements for the chatelaine before my return."

The hidden meaning in all of this was that Charles was going to be with Hortense when her baby was born. He was going to meet her at Joséphine's house at Prègny on the Lake of Geneva. As soon as possible, the child would be brought back to live under Madame de Souza's care in Paris or its environs. If she did not hear from Charles, she was not to engage a nurse until the "Prime Minister" had arrived.

Meanwhile, Hortense was living with Adèle in a rented house outside the town of Aix. She gave a little party for a few friends on August 15th, the Emperor's birthday—a duty she could not shirk—but later she was invisible, and on August 31st she left for Prègny. From there, she wrote to Madame de Boubers, her children's governess, saying that she was going to visit her brother and his family on Lago Maggiore. Eugène was the only one, besides Adèle, in whom Hortense had confided; she could not trust entirely to her mother's discretion. Eugène, loyal brother that he was, came to see Hortense at Aix, and suggested the visit to Maggiore as a plausible announcement to be made to the world of the Queen of Holland's movements.

But it was not intended that the visit should actually take place, though a festival was arranged for her reception. On the day after writing to Madame de Boubers, Hortense and De Flahaut, whom she had found waiting for her at Prègny, left the villa on their supposed journey to Italy. At their first stop, on either the 15th or the 16th of September, Hortense gave birth to her fourth son. If there were any rejoicing it was muted by the hard realities of the situation. There was little time for Hortense to make the acquaintance of her child. Soon, father, mother, and infant had to go their separate ways.

On the 21st of September, Charles was back in Paris. Less than three weeks later, Hortense was again in the rue Cerutti; and on October 22nd, Dr. Claude Martin Gardien, a physician not listed in the medical almanac of 1811, registered the birth of a male child in the Third Arrondissement of Paris. The parents were August Jean Hyacinthe Demorny, an old soldier who was a pen-

sioner of Joséphine, and his wife, Émilie Coralie. The names given
to the baby were Charles Auguste, for the Comte de Flahaut who
had died so bravely during the Terror and whom Charles liked to
consider his father; to these were added Joseph, another of
Charles's names, and—rather oddly—Louis.

When, also in October, a baby appeared from time to time in
Madame de Souza's house in the rue Verte, she merely explained
its presence by saying that it was a protégé of her husband. She
was rather flattered, when some people wondered if she, who was
in her fifties, were not its mother. With tongue in cheek, Madame
de Souza wrote to one of her correspondents that Hortense had
had lumbago while she was away, which had made her scream with
pain. "But one doesn't die of lumbago. Now she is back again and
is well, although she has grown dreadfully thin. May God watch
over her, for she really is an angel!"

Hortense's son was in good hands; Madame de Souza, who had
such a tolerant attitude toward illegitimacy and whose own love
child had been the joy of her life, would give him every care, but
Hortense herself did not dare to visit him and could only hear of
him through his grandmother or through Charles.

Her other boys had been at Saint-Cloud while she was gone, and
their uncle had been very attentive to them. Every day they had had
lunch with the Emperor, a meal hastily eaten at a little round table
at which there was just room enough for the three of them to be
served. Napoléon Louis had recently passed his seventh birthday.
This meant that he should have a male tutor, Napoleon insisting
that a Prince of France should not be brought up by a noble of the
old regime, but by a gallant military man of the present era. Hortense put off a decision, since she could think of no one who met all
of her requirements. For the present, Abbé Bertrand, formerly
Hortense's teacher at Saint-Germain, served as tutor.

On her return to Paris, Hortense found that her old enemy,
Caroline, was in town. The reason for Caroline's visit was political. King Joachim Napoléon of Naples had, in the past two
years, set up a sumptuous court, and organized a large army and a

fleet, with which he made an unsuccessful attempt to conquer Sicily. He blamed the ill-will of his French subordinates for this defeat. Wishing to pose as an independent sovereign, he demanded the withdrawal of French troops from his kingdom, and that the Frenchmen who remained in his service should become naturalized Neapolitans. Napoleon's "No" to this proposal was emphatic; Murat was showing signs of following in Louis' footsteps. Caroline had come to mediate.

"I am really even more unfortunate than you are," Caroline said to Hortense. "Louis couldn't have been more jealous and more hateful in his way of doing things than Murat. It is only natural for me to want to know what is going on in my kingdom. Every once in a while my *valet de chambre* goes on a mysterious errand. Down at the harbor, he has a meeting with the Minister of Foreign Affairs or the Minister of Police. If there is any news, I get word of it at once, but the ministers are so afraid of the King that, when I see them, they are pale and shaking all over and can't wait to ask me if I have burned their letters. Tell me, do you think that is a nice way of treating people?"

Hortense failed to commiserate. Her sympathies were all with Murat. He was a braggart and, with his Gascon accent and his flamboyant costumes, rather ridiculous, but his intentions were good—and he was a brave soldier. Murat's military success and sudden rise had gone to his head. He could lead a cavalry charge, but he was never meant to be a king. It was plain to Hortense that Caroline wanted to get the royal power into her own hands, and that she would stop at nothing.

The Emperor had decreed that two large balls were to be given at the Tuileries that winter, one in full court dress, the other a masquerade. Caroline and Hortense should each arrange an elaborate quadrille.

Caroline took care that Hortense did not hear of this fiat until after she had sent out written invitations to all the prettiest women and the most attractive men to take part in her ballet. That evening, when General Duroc came to the rue Cerutti to announce the Emperor's pleasure, Hortense was surrounded by her friends, who urged her to take immediate action. Charles de Flahaut and several other young men left at once to recruit for Hortense in person, and, in consequence, many of Caroline's invitations were refused. Caroline could see that De Flahaut was no longer hers to command. During the weeks of rehearsal, an intense rivalry developed between the two dance groups.

The first ball, the ball in full dress, was given on February 6th in the palace theater, its boxes crowded with spectators. Caroline had dreamed up an elaborate allegory, representing the union of Italy with France. She herself was France, wearing a helmet and carrying a diamond-studded shield; Pauline was an even more beautiful and radiant Rome. The other female dancers were charmingly disguised as naiads of the Tiber and the Seine, rainbows, and hours; but the costumes of the men, who had to figure as stars, winds, and Apollos, were quite absurd. There were titters from the audience. Napoleon was displeased, and said later to Caroline, "Why did you have to mix up politics with dancing?" He turned to Hortense and asked her testily what sort of foolishness she was meditating for the next ball.

Hortense maintained a demure silence. Her ballet had no political significance; its plot was based on a story by Jean Marmontel, and she was sure that it would be all the more effective because its dancers would be masked.

On the evening of February 11th, Hortense, in a costume of glittering silver cloth, appeared as High Priestess of Peru. She led twenty-four Priestesses of the Sun and twenty-four assorted Peruvian lords and ladies through a set of elaborate figures, that had been coached by the ballet master from the Opera. The applause left no doubt of her success. As, still masked, she moved through the crowd, she heard compliments from all sides.

A short, thick-set domino came up to her and said, "Ah, you are so brilliant! I cannot look at you!"

"I would be quite a prize as I am now, covered with diamonds," Hortense said.

"You know very well," was the muffled reply, "that the best diamond of all, the diamond without price, is the one hidden by your costume."

Hortense had recognized Napoleon, who had an almost childlike faith that no one knew him in disguise. It was so unusual for him to pay compliments that she would treasure this one.

回

Hortense did not—and could not—know that this ball of February 11th, ushering in the carnival season of 1812, was to be the last great gaiety in the Tuileries for many a year.

Her oldest son appeared at one of the costume parties, dressed in the miniature, braided uniform of a Polish lancer that his grandmother Joséphine had given him for a New Year's present.

Napoleon had told Caroline so frankly that her ballet was inferior to Hortense's that he tried to even the balance between them by scolding Hortense in Caroline's presence.

"What is the matter with you?" he asked. "Where could you have got the idea of dressing your son as a Polish lancer? Do you know that I might have a war on my hands because of you? Already Kurakin"—Kurakin was the Russian Ambassador—"has complained to me. Already they are saying that I want to make your boy the King of Poland."

The reincarnated ghost of Poland, the Grand Duchy of Warsaw, had been enlarged and strengthened after the last war with Austria. Its very existence was an affront to its northern neighbor. Since that rapturous meeting at Tilsit in 1807, the Czar Alexander's love for Napoleon had dwindled steadily. The partition of the world into two equal spheres of influence and the march toward India had not materialized. Napoleon's Austrian marriage was another irritant. More than a counterirritant to Napoleon was the failure of the Czar to enforce the Continental system of blockade. Russia had no factories and had desperate need for English goods. Napoleon's grand strategy to weaken England, the strategy that had driven Louis from Holland and was the cause for the war that was devastating Spain, was the one in which he was the most determined to persist.

A subtle change had taken place in Napoleon's mentality, as well as in his physical make up. Even before his marriage, he had developed an unhealthy layer of fat; his will to power had hardened into a stubbornness that was often blind. Having played the autocrat so long and so successfully, he was less acute than formerly in judging the feasibility of his plans. It was more difficult now for him to accept advice. His two most able advisers, Talleyrand and Fouché, were in eclipse.

In June of the preceding year, when the French Ambassador to Russia, Armand de Caulaincourt, returned to Paris, Napoleon tried to get De Caulaincourt to admit that Alexander was a warmonger, an aggressor, and as "treacherous as a Greek." When De Caulaincourt refused to subscribe to any of these ideas, Napoleon laughed derisively and, giving the General's ear a painful tweak, told him that he had turned into a Russian. De Caulaincourt reassumed his duties as the Emperor's Master of Horse, but he was so obviously out of favor that neither Caroline nor Hortense thought of inviting him to dance in their quadrilles.

The first sign to Hortense that war was inevitable was Eugène's being summoned once again from Italy, on April 22nd. Eugène, in his talks with the Emperor, insisted that a Russian war would be very unpopular, not only in France, but in all the countries through which he had traveled recently. Napoleon would not listen to him. Eugène had been brought to Paris to be offered the regency of France during the Emperor's absence. Forseeing difficulties with the Bonapartes, Eugène said that he preferred to command a corps in the army. On May 2nd he left for Mainz, to take over his military duties.

A week later, Napoleon and Marie Louise went to Dresden to confer with the Emperor of Austria and the King of Prussia. The one was cajoled, the other threatened into safeguarding Napoleon's rear and contributing troops to the great army that was gathering in Central Europe. It was made up of 250,000 French veterans;

150,000 Germans; 80,000 Italians, 60,000 Poles; and detachments of Dutch, Swiss, Danes, and Serbo-Coats—more than half-a-million men in all. There was a babble of tongues about the bivouac fires. This was a very different Grand Army from the one with which Napoleon had manuevered in earlier campaigns. Those of his own family involved were Joachim Murat, Jérôme, and Eugène.

Even after he had started for Russia, Napoleon made abortive overtures for peace with the Czar; but on June 24th, the Neman, the same stream on which the raft had floated at Tilsit, was crossed. On its farther bank a minute catastrophe occurred. Napoleon was riding a horse named Friedland, one of the mounts that were specially bred and trained for him at the imperial stud farm. A rabbit popped up out of the grass beneath the horse's feet, the horse shied, and Napoleon, always a careless rider, was thrown. He was up in an instant and had remounted before anyone could come to his assistance, but the incident was buzzed about the camp and was taken as an evil omen.

Napoleon's plan was to move with his usual swiftness and to obliterate the enemy in a great battle, or else to spend the winter in Lithuania, inciting the population to revolt and moving on to Moscow in the spring. The Russian plan was to avoid a major engagement and to retreat, leading the invaders deep into the country, across barren steppes, where hunger and the heat of summer would be more deadly than bullets. An epidemic of colic broke out among the horses, due to their being fed on unripened grain, and a third of the cavalry was immobilized, helpless when attacked by raiding bands of Cossacks. There were many deaths from sunstroke, many desertions. The tactical advantage that Napoleon hoped to gain in his first advance was completely ruined by Jérôme's failure to obey orders. Nevertheless, the fortress of Smolensk was taken on August 17th.

At home, a restless gloom had settled over France. The young men of the country were all in Russia; to their anxious friends they seemed to have vanished into the underworld. Hortense had a troubled summer. She went to Aix with the children, and while they were there Napoléon Louis came close to dying of scarlet fever. In September Hortense was recalled to Saint-Leu, to be a companion to the lonely and apprehensive Marie Louise.

Hortense herself lived in daily fear of what she might hear from the front. In a letter that reached her through Madame de Souza, she read that not long after the crossing of the Neman a bullet grazed Charles de Flahaut's breast and, missing his heart, cut in two the shoulder knot of his uniform. A slight deviation of the projectile, and the father of Hortense's son, Charles Auguste Demorny, would have been dead and buried on the farther shore of the Russian river.

XXIV

THE YEAR OF DEATH

AFTER the taking of Smolensk, the decision was made to move on to Moscow. The bloody victory of Borodino was the first step in that direction. The capital of the Czars, almost empty of inhabitants and already in flames, was entered on September 14th. It was not abandoned until more than a month later, Napoleon hoping that Alexander would ask for a truce. He heard, instead, that two Russian armies were gathering in his rear at the Berezina River.

The great retreat began—one of the mountain peaks of history, viewed in terms of human suffering and in waste of human life. At fearful cost, the engineers working in icy water up to their armpits, the Berezina was bridged by pontoons on November 26th. The crossing took three days. Though the pontoons broke under the weight of the artillery and had to be repaired during the night, all were over by the evening of the 27th, except a single corps and a horde of stragglers who had refused to leave their campfires.

The following day, the Russians attacked on both sides of the river. There was a rush for the bridge, a panic scramble for foothold, comrade slashing at comrade to force a way. Charles de Flahaut distinguished himself by swimming his horse back and

223

forth across the river more than once, under fire, with dispatches, and taking part in the melee on either bank. When darkness fell, the fighting died down. De Flahaut discovered that one of his friends, Alfred de Noailles, also a bearer of dispatches, had disappeared. He went out to look for him and at last found his body, naked, so horribly mutilated that it could only be identified by a scar on the arm. A few days later Charles rescued his own servant, who was among the sick, carried him on his shoulders through the snow, and at last found a place for him on a sledge.

On December 4th, the young man's gallantry was rewarded by his being advanced to the rank of brigadier general and by being appointed chief aide-de-camp to General Berthier. Charles wrote to his mother that she would be glad to hear of his promotion, but that her son was in rags. His uniform was "one great hole." He begged her to send him a complete replacement, including breeches, an overcoat, and a pair of boots.

What was left of the Grand Army after the Berezina, perhaps fifty thousand men, was at Smorgonie, not far from the well-stocked town of Vilna. It was Napoleon's intention to take the town and spend the winter there with his forces. He put Murat in supreme command, and on December 5th left for France. He had been recalled by a seemingly farcical episode in Paris, that might have been the first act of an opéra bouffe. An ex-general of republican sympathies, General Claude de Malet, who had been arrested on suspicion of conspiracy in 1808 and confined, not in prison, but in an insane asylum, escaped on the night of October 22nd. He went to a barrack of the National Guard, announced the death of the Emperor, and presented a number of orders that he had forged and signed. For a few hours, the government of Paris was in his hands. The Prefect of Police, General Savary, Duc de Rovigo, and the minister whom Napoleon had left in charge, were arrested.

Hortense, when she heard of what was apparently a coup d'etat, jumped into her carriage and drove at top speed to Saint-Cloud, to see if the Empress and the King of Rome were safe. She had a plan ready to preserve them: She would take them and her own children to the nearest fortified town, buy up all the grain she could lay hands on, and stand siege until rescued.

As it turned out, this dramatic move was unnecessary, but when the news of the bubble conspiracy reached Russia, it was not enough for Napoleon to learn that De Malet was once more in prison and to send back word that he himself was in the best of health. The Emperor must return to show that he was alive and to take control of the complicated machine of empire that only he could operate.

"The French are like women," Napoleon said with a shrug to General de Caulaincourt, who was with him in the sledge that took them to Warsaw. "You cannot stay away from them too long."

With Napoleon's arrival on December 18th, the magnitude of the Russian disaster burst upon Paris. Hortense went at once to the Tuileries. She could see signs of physical exhaustion on Napoleon's face, but none of collapse in morale. How often had she heard him explode with irritation if a door were left open or if there were not enough candles in the room; but when the great moment came, he could meet it calmly.

She asked him if the catastrophe to the army was as great as had been reported in a bulletin printed in the *Moniteur*.

"I have told the whole truth," Napoleon said.

"But surely we are not the only ones who have suffered. The enemy must have had some losses."

"That may be true, but that is no consolation to me."

Hortense asked for news of Eugène. She was concerned to hear that her brother was now under the command of Murat, his mortal enemy, but this was only a temporary state of affairs. No sooner had Napoleon left Russia than Murat abandoned Vilna without a fight, abandoned also thousands of sick and wounded, who were massacred by the town's inhabitants. He rushed his exhausted troops for the Neman which was crossed without serious opposition. As soon as he was in east Prussia, Murat was off for Naples,

saying that he was ill with fever and jaundice. To Eugène was left
the heartbreaking task of putting together the splintered fragments of the mighty force that had crossed into Russia in June. He
was constantly harassed by Cossack raiders, who had penetrated
Prussia; he was so short of cavalry and staff that he had to lead
tours of reconnaissance in person.

The only consolation that Hortense could find was in the stories
of individual heroism she heard from survivors who came limping
home. One of the few who did not limp was Charles de Flahaut.
He had been given a place on the Emperor's staff, the position he
had coveted for thirteen years, from the time when he wrote, as
a boy, to the First Consul to tell him that he was big and strong
for his age. To be on the staff of General Bonaparte in those days
was a small affair compared to the honor that had come to Charles
now. He would have an income of twenty-four thousand francs a
year and would have a number of subordinates working under him.
His mother was overjoyed. When he made a surprise appearance
on February 10, 1813, he was in vigorous health and had even
grown fat; the uniform Adélaide had sent him was bulging at the
seams. Charles's father, Talleyrand, said, with raised eyebrow, that
the young man looked as if he had come from the land of Cockaigne
where pies grew on trees, instead of from hungry, frozen Russia.
All of the first floor of the house in the rue Verte was turned over
to General de Flahaut and his aides.

The new staff officer was constantly at the Tuileries, and that
spot seemed less sad to Hortense because she met Charles there so
often. She herself spent much of her time at the palace. Napoleon
wanted all to go on as usual. Caroline and Elisa were in Italy;
Pauline was in the south of France, entertaining two lovers at once;
and Hortense was the only one who could appear with Marie Louise
at state functions. She was so busy that her devoted friends, Adèle
de Broc and Louise Cochelet, were afraid that her health—she was
tortured by sinus headaches—might break under the strain.

Hortense's program for New Year's Day, which happened to be
a Friday and which ushered in the thirteenth year of the century,

was typical. At nine o'clock in the morning she, her children, and her household, all be-diamonded and in court dress, had to go to the Tuileries to wish the Emperor and the Empress a happy new year. Hortense remained there for the Mass, which was celebrated at noon. She then hurried home to receive well-wishers, changed her clothes, and drove out to La Malmaison to visit her mother. After her return, she had hardly time to dress again for the family dinner at the palace. The hairdresser, who took his art seriously, was in despair because the Queen would only give him a few minutes to comb out her long golden hair and arrange it elaborately. He was much impeded in his work by the two little princes, who kept running back and forth between him and their mother's chair. Hortense soon was running downstairs, trailed by her excited children, who bore her train, her evening bag, and gloves.

There had to be weekly balls and receptions in the rue Cerutti that winter, though all of Paris, it seemed, was wearing black. As carnival time drew near, Napoleon sent Duroc to tell Hortense that he wanted her to repeat the Peruvian ballet, which had been such a success a year earlier. Hortense was dismayed. Many of the young men who had danced in 1812 were dead; three or four of the living were minus a leg or an arm; of the female dancers two were widows and in mourning for their husbands.

"Your Majesty's ball will look like a hospital," Duroc said ruefully.

Nevertheless, the ball was given, with all invited who had taken part the first time, the legless, the armless watching from their chairs.

What would happen now? What would Napoleon do to strengthen his position? Hortense was surprised when these questions were put to her.

One evening, when she was alone with her ladies, Prince Karl von Schwarzenberg, the Austrian Ambassador, and Count Ferdinand von Bubna von Litie, an Austrian envoy, entered her salon. Napoleon frowned on ambassadors being received, except on state occasions, and Hortense wondered how the two Austrians had got past her doorman.

Schwarzenberg drew Hortense aside and said in a low voice, "Madame, you know the Emperor so well, do you think there is a chance for peace? We all want it. Europe is exhausted."

Hortense replied, somewhat ambiguously, that she was sure that victory was necessary to restore confidence and to make up for past disasters, but she was sure also that Napoleon wanted peace. He was a great administrator, as well as a great general. He would work for the well-being of his people, and in the end he would give his people what they wanted.

"Haven't you enough influence with him to convince him of this?" Von Schwarzenberg asked.

"Only public opinion can persuade him," Hortense said. "I have never dared to give him advice. I am too young. I am his daughter and have to obey him."

Schwarzenberg persisted. "Well then, there is Prince Eugène," he said. "He governs a great country; he knows the will of the people. Let him speak firmly to the Emperor and tell him the truth."

"My brother knows better than anyone else the need for a breathing spell," Hortense said, thinking of Eugène and his thankless labors in Germany. "I will write to him. I will tell him what you have said, but let me say again that the Emperor is too sure of his own judgment to listen to others. If he has only one more victory, he will devote himself to reforms that will bring prosperity to all the nations that he governs."

Hortense had made a guess at Napoleon's intentions; only he knew to the full his predicament. Whichever way he faced, an enemy lay in his rear. There was Spain—that "ulcer of a war" in Spain. Joseph, in trying to make headway against the insurgents and the British, had been much impeded by his own military incapacity, his pigheadedness, and the insubordination of the marshals whom Napoleon sent him, hard-bitten, quarrelsome veterans, who were loath to take orders from anyone except the Emperor himself. During the past year, all of the west, south, and center of

the country had been lost. Wellington and his British army entered
Madrid and held it for a fortnight, until a bumbling attempt to
take Burgos, as well, failed. Joseph, when he could once more
occupy his capital, clung to it, though Napoleon sent him repeated
orders to make a stronger stand at Valladolid and hang on, at all
cost, to the northern provinces.

There was even more serious trouble on the Rhine. An alliance
had been formed between the Czar and the King of Prussia. The
Russians crossed the Vistula on February 18th. Westphalia was
open to attack, but Jérôme, ever since he was relieved of his command in Russia, had devoted all his time and resources to giving
extravagant palace entertainments. When Napoleon told him
bleakly that he must build up and equip a new army, he was quite
willing to oblige, but where was the money coming from? His
treasury was empty; his credit for borrowing was exhausted.

Early in the new year, Jérôme sent his wife, Catherine, to France
against the Emperor's categorical command. The Westphalians,
Napoleon thought, would take this for a sign that their playboy
King was planning to abscond. The excuse given for Catherine's
visit was that she wished to be present at the coronation, which had
been tentatively planned, of Marie Louise and the King of Rome.

The coronation, however, was postponed indefinitely. Pope
Pius VII was once more in France, a prisoner at Fontainebleau, but
Napoleon was unsuccessful in getting him to sign a new concordat.
The only thing that could be done to emphasize the importance of
the Empress and her son to the nation was to confer the regency on
Marie Louise. On March 30, 1813, Hortense was told that she was
to appear at the Elysée Palace in court dress. She, Catherine, Ma-
dame Mère, and a few of the highest officials watched, as Marie
Louise knelt before her husband and, putting her clasped hands in
his, promised to be his true and loyal representative.

The ceremony was a signal for Napoleon's departure for Germany. Already Charles de Flahaut had been sent with instructions
for Eugène, who was to coöperate with the new army which had
been formed in France. The Emperor left Paris on April 15th. Two

weeks of suspense followed; then there was news of a victory at Lützen. A few weeks later, there was yet another victory at Bautzen.

In this battle, General Duroc was mortally wounded by a cannon shot that killed the officer with whom he was talking, at some distance from the firing line. He was carried to a farmhouse, where he survived in great pain for three days, constantly visited by Napoleon. After Duroc's death, Napoleon bought the farm and erected a monument to the friend, who, for years, had worked so quietly and efficiently under his direction. Hortense mourned the faithful servant of the master and the husband of one of her good friends at Saint-Germain—not the man she might once have married. Her intimacy with Duroc was a thing of the past. Since assuming the cloak, the plumed hat, and scarf of Palace Chamberlain, Duroc's sense of punctilio had never failed him.

This was a year of death, and death soon struck very close to Hortense's heart. The allies, twice defeated, consented to an armistice, and for those at home in France tension slackened.

At the end of May, Hortense went for one of her therapeutic holidays to Aix-en-Savoie, taking Adèle and Louise Cochelet with her. On June 10th, they went for a drive to visit a waterfall that Adèle wanted particularly to see. They left the carriage on the highway and walked to a mill at the foot of the falls. In order for them to get a nearer view, the miller came out and put down a plank over a deep cut in the rocks, through which the water was rushing at tremendous speed. Hortense, swift and sure-footed, crossed the plank in a single stride. She turned back just in time to see Adèle, who was following her closely, slip, the plank turn over, and both disappear into the cut.

Hortense ran back over the rocks, slippery with spray from the falls, snatched off her shawl, and threw one end of it into the water, calling to her friend, but there was no answer. Adèle had vanished.

Help was close at hand. Hortense's equerry, the miller, and his men came running, but it was twenty minutes before Adèle's body was dragged out of the whirlpool into which the millrace emptied. While the search continued, Louise Cochelet tried to persuade Hortense to go back to her carriage, but she had sunk down on the ground and covered her face with her hands. She would not leave until Adèle had been found.

Attempts were made on the spot to revive the dead woman, and were continued after she had been taken back in the carriage to the town. Hortense knew from the start that there was little hope. Adèle was gone, and she wondered how she could learn to live without her. They had spent the greater part of their lives together; for the past three years they had been almost inseparable. There was added to Hortense's sense of bereavement, of having lost a part of herself, regrets for her own shortcomings in this long friendship. Adèle had given of herself so generously. Hortense had accepted all as if it were her due.

In an agony of self-abasement, she said to Louise Cochelet, "I must be very wicked. I am sure that Adèle never knew how much I loved her; it is always so hard for me to say what I feel. And I was forever complaining of my own troubles and forgetting hers."

She remembered, perhaps, the dismal letters she had written during her last stay in Holland, when Adèle had recently been widowed and should not have been burdened with another's woe. Hortense didn't like to think of how often she had spoken to her friend of remarrying and having a life of her own, though these suggestions had been well meant. Perhaps Adèle had thought that Hortense was anxious for a parting. On the very day of the accident, they had been talking of a little country house that Adèle thought of buying and of Hortense's offer to contribute to its purchase. Had Adèle gone to her death with a misunderstanding of the motives behind the offer?

Hortense had expected to stay only a short time at Aix, but she couldn't bear to leave a place where her friend still seemed so near. She made arrangements for Adèle's body to be taken to Saint-Leu, where a chapel would be built and a monument raised, such as Napoleon had erected for Duroc. Since Adèle had been living in the rue Cerutti, most of her small income had been given to charity. As a memorial, Hortense added ten endowed beds to a hospital run by the Sisters of Mercy at Aix, and had a footbridge built over the treacherous millstream, with the inscription: "Take care, you who pass the abyss. Remember those you love."

In the last week of August, Hortense went back to Saint-Leu, where Joséphine and her children were waiting to console her. She had a sorrowful meeting in Paris with Adèle's two sisters, Antoinette and Eglé, with Adèle's elderly father, and with Adèle's aunt, Madame Campan.

One day in September, Hortense went to Joseph's country estate at Mortefontaine. There she was brought face to face with what she had almost forgotten during her weeks of mourning: the crumbling of empire, the peace of Europe, which still, to an incalculable degree, depended on the will of a single man.

XXV

MALBROUK S'EN VA-T-EN GUERRE

WHILE Hortense had been absent from Paris, the Emperor was for the most part at Dresden, taking advantage of the armistice to collect reinforcements from France and Italy, whither he had sent Eugène. His two victories over the allies, except for having given those at home a false illusion of security, had been barren. After Bautzen, the battle in which Duroc was killed, Napoleon should have pursued the demoralized Russian and Prussian armies and annihilated them, but he was so short of cavalry that this was impossible.

Reinforcement was his major need. Before the campaign began, Napoleon tried without success to lure his father-in-law, Francis II of Austria, into providing him with 100,000 men, the bait being the Prussian province of Silesia. A sizeable Austrian army was building up in Bohemia under Prince von Schwarzenberg, Hortense's one-time visitor in the rue Cerutti. Count von Metternich, another acquaintance of Hortense and now the Austrian Minister of Foreign Affairs, offered armed intervention to stop the war in May, if France would dissolve the Grand Duchy of Warsaw and withdraw from northwestern Germany and the coast of Illyria.

Napoleon haughtily rejected these terms. "You say you cannot act with me," he said. "It seems that you can only be strong against me."

On the 21st of June, Jérôme came to Dresden. The brothers had not met since Jérôme's lamentable performance in the Russian campaign, but Napoleon let bygones be bygones. He was cool, however, to Jérôme's request for an important military command and for French troops to be sent to Westphalia. He was exasperated when Jérôme revealed the reason why he had hurried Catherine off to France earlier in the year. Jérôme wanted to divorce his present wife so that he could marry his latest mistress, the Princess von Löwenstein. Jérôme had no criticism to make of Catherine except that she had not yet given him a child. This defect could be remedied by the Princess, who was already pregnant by her lover. Napoleon gave his opinion, in no uncertain terms, of the folly of Jérôme's marital plans and of his frivolity in suggesting them at such a moment. Jérôme was sent back to his capital at Kassel in short order, and was told to stand fast.

This was what Napoleon had told Joseph to do in Spain, but on the very day that Jérôme arrived at Dresden, Joseph was being disastrously defeated at Vitoria by Wellington. He came within a few feet of capture by the British. Joseph had to make a rain-soaked, rugged journey through the mountains to reach the French frontier. When Napoleon heard from him on July 1st, he was at Saint-Jean-de-Luz and asking for help.

Help, what help was possible? Napoleon now knew that Austria would be against him when hostilities were resumed. He had had a last interview with Metternich on June 26th—Metternich, whom he had come to loathe as a double-dealing diplomatist and as a representative of the old kingly order in Europe. Metternich again proposed peace on the terms earlier laid down.

Napoleon cut him short. "What do you want of me?" he asked. "Dishonor? Never—I know how to die, but I will never yield an inch of my territory! Your sort of sovereign, born to the throne, may be beaten twenty times and return to his palace. I cannot. I am a child of fortune, and my reign will be over when I have ceased to be strong."

The conversation lasted for hours, ranged far and wide, and touched more than once on Napoleon's marriage. "Does the Emperor intend to dethrone his daughter," he asked. "When I married an archduchess I tried to weld the new with the old, the conceptions of my own century with Gothic notions. I deceived myself; now I see how great a mistake I made. It may cost me my throne, but I will bury the world beneath its ruins!"

Of the two contestants, Metternich had the advantage of the cooler head, the scalpel tongue. The question of morale in Napoleon's army was brought up. Metternich said that he had seen the French troops. They were boys. He asked Napoleon what he would do when his present collection of raw recruits had melted away like the Grand Army of Russia.

The old wound, never completely healed, had been slit open. Napoleon turned tallow white with rage. He hurled the hat he was holding into a corner of the room. "You are not a soldier," he shouted. "You don't know what goes on in the soul of a soldier. I have grown up on the battlefield. A man such as I am cares little for the lives of a million men!"

He seemed sorry later to have spoken so wildly, and regained his self-control, but Metternich had the final word. It had grown dark in the room. Neither man could see the face of the other distinctly. Napoleon went to the door when the Austrian was taking his leave, and laid his hand lightly on Metternich's shoulder. "We will meet again? . . . You will not make war on me?" he questioned, as though he more than half-believed that the answer would be what he wanted.

Metternich refused to be spellbound by the great magician. He drew back. "You are lost, sire," he said harshly. "I thought so when I came here; now that I am going, I am certain of it."

On August 14, 1813, the day before Napoleon's forty-fourth birthday, the armistice came to an end. From every side, Napo-

leon's enemies began slowly to converge upon him, but still in
France the talk was all of peace. At least, they were talking peace
at Mortefontaine, when Hortense visted it late in September. She
found not only Joseph, but Catherine there. Joseph had been
ordered by the Emperor to stay close to his own home and to
remain incognito. He still considered himself, however, the King
of Spain. He was only waiting for a general settlement in Europe,
to return—with his brother's help—to Madrid. Catherine, who
knew about the Princess von Löwenstein, but not about the divorce
scheme, was still very much in love with Jérôme, and was expecting either to go back to Westphalia or else to lead a princely life
with her husband in France.

Hortense, badly informed though she was, felt less sympathy
for Joseph or Catherine than for Joseph's plain, self-effacing little
wife, Julie, who had never set foot in her kingdom beyond the
Pyrénées and whom Joseph often humiliated by his affairs with
other women. Hortense thought that she herself was luckier than
either of these Bonaparte wives, bound to men who showed so
little consideration for them. She at least was free and had her
children. She remembered how Adèle had once told her that she
should count her blessings.

Hortense went back to the rue Cerutti. She was pleased to see
how prettily her bedroom had been done over during her absence,
and said lightly to Louise Cochelet that she hoped the Cossacks
wouldn't come to turn her out of it. She began immediately to
see through the press a beautifully bound collection of her songs
and ballads, for which she had drawn illustrations, and which she
would give to her friends at New Year's. She began also to receive visitors again in the evening, though the atmosphere of her
salon was not what it had once been. There was no Adèle; Louise
Cochelet, an adoring handmaiden, bubbling over with good intentions, tried to take Adèle's place, but that was impossible. And
there was no Charles de Flahaut; Charles was with the Emperor
in Germany, where the game of attrition was being played to its
bitter end.

The allies, cautious in spite of their superiority in numbers, weakened their adversary by a series of blows, that were successful when struck at the Emperor's marshals, but not when he himself was their target. Napoleon triumphed for the last time over Schwarzenberg near Dresden, but for some reason—was it lack of physical energy in himself, of verve—he failed to follow it up. For a month he marched and countermarched his troops, using Dresden as a pivot, searching for an opportunity for a breakthrough and one of his lightning-bolt attacks. On October 16th, his forces were concentrated around Leipzig. The battle thundered fiercely all that day, through the surrounding villages. A rainy Sunday followed; there was a lull. To the dismay of his subordinates, inertia seemed again to have fallen on the Emperor. He sent a letter to Austrian headquarters, proposing an armistice, hinting at concessions, but there was no reply.

On the 18th, fighting began again and the French were pushed back steadily toward the city. The drums were beaten for retreat at four o'clock in the afternoon. All during the night, troops were pouring through the town toward their one avenue of escape, the river. The next morning, Napoleon was standing by the single bridge that spanned the Weisse Elster, watching his broken army, a confused flood of humanity, streaming above the dark, reflecting water. A stranger, who had never seen the famous Emperor before, wondered who the stubby little man was, in his plain gray overcoat like that of any ordinary civilian. Napoleon seemed to be thinking deeply of something—was it of the Berezina, was it of other rivers he had crossed? Meanwhile, he softly whistled to himself the tune to which so many Frenchmen had marched to their death, *Malbrouk s'en va-t-en guerre.*

"The Grand Empire no longer exists; it is France that we must now defend."

On November 14th, Napoleon thus announced to the French Senate that—for the moment, at least—he had accepted the inevitable. Swiftly, almost simultaneously, the structures on which the Emperor's power had rested outside of France collapsed. For friendship, he could only count on the Grand Duchy of Warsaw, Saxony, and the Kingdom of Italy. Eugène's father-in-law, the Elector of Bavaria, whom Napoleon had made a king, was one of the first to join the allies, and sent word to Milan that Eugène could be sure of having the throne of Italy if he would go over to the anti-Bonaparte camp. Hortense was proud, when she heard of her brother's refusal; his wife, Augusta, had loyally upheld him.

Another united couple were Caroline and Joachim Murat, but they were united in treachery to Napoleon. Murat had fought at Leipzig, but he secretly made a separate peace with the allies that would save him his crown. Throughout the campaign, both he and Caroline had been corresponding with the enemy.

Other members of the Clan were hurrying home to France. Jérôme, who had made a precipitate exit from Kassel as soon as he heard of Leipzig, joined Catherine at Compiègne early in November. Before the crash, he had privately sold to speculators some of the crown lands of Westphalia, and with the proceeds intended to buy himself a fine estate at Stains, near Saint-Denis.

Hortense was disturbed to learn that Louis was on his way to France. Louis had been living for the past three years at Gratz, nursing his health and devoting himself to literature. He had rewritten and brought out a new edition of his novel, first composed in 1800, *Marie, or the Pains of Love*. It was now titled *Marie, or the Dutch Women*, a confusingly romantic tale, full of adventures —duels, battles, rescues of captive maidens, complicated love affairs—and abounding in characters, some of whom could be identified as being drawn from life. Jules, the persistently heroic hero, was obviously Louis himself; Marie, the heroine from whom Jules was cruelly separated, was Émilie de Beauharnais, Hortense's cousin, for whom Louis had felt a tenderness when she was a schoolgirl at Saint-Germain. An unflattering picture of Hortense was given in Amelie, the girl Jules was tricked into marrying. Amelie was very worldly, very popular in society, and only laughed when Jules tried to reprove her. Louis had also written much poetry and an essay on versification, in which he advocated the revolutionary technique of unrhymed verse.

But, like Joseph at Mortefontaine, like Jérôme at Compiègne, Louis still thought of himself as a king. He had kept in touch with a few friends in Holland, and on very slight encouragement had developed the delusion that his return there was eagerly awaited. He wrote a curious letter to Napoleon after Spain had been lost and Austria had joined the Coalition, offering his services, and suggesting that he should go back to Holland as soon as his brother had made peace with England. Napoleon paid no attention to the proposition.

After Leipzig, Louis became more insistent in his demands for restoration to royalty. Napoleon was so afraid of what his brother might do in France, that he sent home instructions that Louis was to be arrested, if he were foolish enough to claim the title of king.

Though Hortense tried to give her husband credit for rallying, in his own peculiar fashion, to the Emperor, she could not help being apprehensive at the thought of his being so near to her and to her children. All her world was tottering; she had a single joy: Charles de Flahaut had been in the thick of the fight at Leipzig and had come through without a scratch. He had had another promotion to General of Division. The Emperor took Charles into his confidence; he asked him to persuade Talleyrand again to take over the Foreign Office. Charles's father, however, was not to be wooed. Like Murat and Caroline, he had unrevealed plans of his own.

As an inducement, perhaps, to Talleyrand, Napoleon considered appointing Charles to the position left vacant by Duroc's death, that of Palace Chamberlain. It was ironic that the two who had done the most to help Charles on his way, his mother and Hortense, should be stumbling blocks. Napoleon disliked Madame de Souza; she was a female scribbler and an intellectual. He now learned from his Minister of Police what he had known only vaguely before: that there was a very special bond between Charles and Hortense. Napoleon wanted, from his right-hand men, the sort of unique, unfettered devotion that he had had from Duroc; the appointment of Chamberlain went to another of his aides, General Henri Bertrand. Armand de Caulaincourt, Napoleon's former envoy to Russia, reluctantly accepted the post of Minister of Foreign Affairs.

It was a hazardous, but not at first a hopeless position. There was a universal, passionate desire for peace. After Leipzig, Metternich proposed that France should retain her natural boundaries of the Rhine, the Alps, and the Pyrénées. On December 2nd, De Caulaincourt was told to negotiate on these terms, though Napoleon was not sure that they represented the will of all the allies. What he had once told Metternich, he felt was true: He could only hope to reign as long as he was strong, and, personally, he longed to take revenge on Austria for having betrayed him. The negotiations hung fire. In the Senate, there was such a loud demand for constitutional reforms that Napoleon adjourned the chamber's sessions sine die on December 31st.

On New Year's Day, 1814, the enemy entered France. Hortense heard of it first when she went to Mass at the Tuileries. The Duchesse de Montebello, the Empress' chief lady in waiting, told her in a frightened undertone that the allies had crossed the Rhine. Marie Louise, ordinarily so phlegmatic, seemed much troubled. "I take bad luck with me wherever I go," she said sadly. "Everyone who comes near me has to suffer for it. Since childhood, I have spent most of my life in flight."

She was thinking, no doubt, of the number of times she had had to make a hurried departure from Schönbrunn; then the ogre in pursuit was her present husband, now it was her awe-inspiring father.

In the evening, Hortense went back to the palace for dinner. She found the Emperor and Empress alone. Marie Louise was in Napoleon's arms and was weeping.

"Well, Hortense," Napoleon said, with a smile, "they are frightened to death in Paris, are they? They are seeing Cossacks everywhere. Ah, but they are not here yet, and we haven't forgotten how to handle them!"

"Don't be afraid," he said, turning back to Marie Louise. "We will go to Vienna yet to beat Papa Francis."

He said the same thing later to the little King of Rome, who came in at dinnertime when the dessert was being served, and the child took up the phrase. He marched about shouting, "Go beat Papa Francis." Napoleon roared with delight.

After dinner, he sent for General Berthier. "Come, Berthier," he said, motioning the General to sit down at a table," we will have to begin the campaign of Italy all over again."

While Hortense and Marie Louise listened, Napoleon dictated, without notes, the organization of the army that would gather in the flat country around Châlons. The four generals of the imperial guard were summoned. Napoleon questioned them for some time, as to the number of sick that they had, the number of men who were available, and went into the most minute detail of their commands. After the officers had been dismissed, Napoleon turned to his audience.

"Well, ladies, are you satisfied? Do you think now that we will be caught napping?"

The allies were in no hurry to overrun France. They were like mountain hunters, advancing cautiously into a bear den. Napoleon had time—but all too short a time—to make his preparations. His treasury was empty, but enough gold, saved from his privy purse, was stored in the vaults under the Tuileries to finance the government for the present. Marie Louise, as regent, should have a chief executive, one of the family—who but Joseph? Louis had arrived from Switzerland on the same day that France was invaded, but Louis could not be counted on. Jérôme was in disgrace. Napoleon was so scandalized by his brother's purchase of an estate, when all of France was girding for defense, that he refused to see him.

Before Joseph could be appointed lieutenant general, however, he must relinquish his claim to the Spanish throne. Napoleon had taken the easiest way to rid himself of the Spanish incubus, by recognizing Prince Ferdinand, who for the past five years had been detained in France. Joseph would have none of this arrangement and stubbornly refused to give up his title. It was not until France was deeply penetrated, that he could be persuaded to abdicate and accept his new responsibilities.

On January 24th, Napoleon was ready to go to his army at Châlons, a pitifully small army to pit against the invaders. He wished to make a solemn ceremony of his leave-taking and to present the King of Rome to the nation as his successor. Napoleon carried the child, in his arms, into the great Hall of the Marshals in the palace, where all of the family and representatives of the government and of the National Guard of Paris were assembled. To them, Napoleon entrusted the safekeeping of the city and of his heir.

That evening, Hortense was again alone with Napoleon and Marie Louise in the Emperor's study, where he was going over his file of private papers. Many were to be burned. Each time that he approached the fireplace to toss in a handful, Napoleon stopped to kiss and caress his wife, to tell her not to cry. He would beat Papa Francis yet. He would soon be back.

The following day he was gone.

Napoleon's first engagement with the allies was a defeat. De Caulaincourt was sent to Châtillon to talk peace with Metternich. The demands of the Coalition were stiffer now. France must return to the boundaries she had had before the Revolution, and she would have no part in any congress called to resettle Europe. Napoleon was informed of the terms and was urged by his staff to accept them. He seemed on the point of yielding, but that same night he heard that the Austrian army under Schwarzenberg and the Prussian army under Blücher were drawing apart. Napoleon was discovered by one of his generals bending over a map, which he had dotted with pins.

"I am going to beat Blücher tomorrow," he announced. "I will beat him the day after tomorrow also. Then we will see what is what!"

The next two weeks were miraculous. The campaign swung into vigorous action. There were four victories in quick succession, now against Blücher, now against Schwarzenberg. Napoleon seemed to be everywhere at once. Large numbers of prisoners were taken, and were sent to be paraded on the streets of Paris in the pale sunshine of February.

Schwarzenberg asked for an armistice. Charles de Flahaut, in spite of his youth, was sent to parley at Lusigny. He was told to stand solidly upon a demand for the natural boundaries of France—short of that, no armistice. While Charles was arguing with the foreign generals, fighting continued. There were more victories, but there were also reverses, and it was plain to Napoleon's assailants that his potential for attack was dwindling. The allies captured a courier from Paris, with dispatches from Joseph to Napoleon begging for peace at any price. Charles came home to French headquarters with nothing signed.

On the day after he left Lusigny, a message from Charles's father, Talleyrand, reached the Czar Alexander, telling him to come with his army to Paris, for "friends" would be waiting there to collaborate with him. The Czar hesitated. The way to Paris was open, but Napoleon had moved eastward in a daring maneuver to cut in behind the allies and sever their communications with the Rhine. After estimating the risks involved—he was short of ammunition—and spending an hour on his knees asking for divine guidance, Alexander gave orders for his army to advance.

XXVI

CATASTROPHE

BY THE third week of March, only a feeble beginning had been made to safeguard Paris. Shallow entrenchments were being dug around the outer walls. Some of the elegant strollers in the Bois de Boulogne were afraid that the Bois would be completely ruined. Though many of the well-to-do had begun to leave the city, there was no universal panic. Theaters were well patronized; there was much joking about where to hide one's valuables from the Cossacks. Hortense's salon had become a workroom, where old linen was being scraped into lint for dressings, and she had set the schoolgirls at Écouen to scraping also.

On the 28th of March, Hortense's maid came early to her bedroom and, all atremble, told her that the enemy was not far off. French casualties were being brought into the city. Hortense could hardly believe that this was so. The evening before she had spent at the Tuileries, and had heard nothing there to disturb her. Hortense had played a game of whist with Talleyrand, who was a member of the Regency Council. In his nonchalant way, he made fun of all this talk of the allies coming to Paris.

Hortense decided to see for herself. She rode on horseback to the outer boulevards and saw wagonloads of wounded soldiers, who were being taken to a hospital at Versailles. She came home feeling that the moment for testing her own courage was coming soon.

That evening, Hortense went early to visit the Empress. Marie Louise was just going in to a meeting of the Regency Council, at which, she told Hortense, the question was to be decided whether or not she was to leave the capital. But the Empress Regent must not turn tail and run, Hortense protested. If she stayed, her presence would give the entire city—the entire nation—a feeling of security.

Hortense was talking eagerly in this vein, when Joseph entered the room. She repeated all her arguments to him, but he, though he listened, said nothing in reply.

Hortense stayed on alone in the salon, after Joseph and Marie Louise had gone, and presently was joined by the Duchesse de Montebello. Knowing how great an influence the First Lady in Waiting had, Hortense tried to win her over to her side. A short time later, Marie Louise returned. She laughed nervously, as she said to Hortense, "I am going to leave, and I advise you to do the same, for the Minister of War assures us that it will be impossible to defend Paris."

"At least, sister, you must realize that this will mean losing your crown," Hortense exclaimed. "I am glad to see that you can give it up so gaily!"

The room was filling with those who had been present at the council meeting. Marie Louise stepped closer to Hortense and said in a low voice, "I think perhaps you are right, but that is the way it has been decided. If the Emperor is angry, he will not be angry with me."

Apparently this descendant of the warrior-empress, Maria Theresa, had inherited none of her ancestor's fortitude.

A dispute had begun as to when the imperial party should go. Some said immediately. Others protested that there would be no time to pack the Empress' trunks, or the gold that still remained in the palace vault. To save a double escort, gold and Empress must leave at the same time.

The departure was put off until the morrow. Hortense asked Joseph if anything had been said at the meeting about herself and her children. He replied vaguely, and as though the subject did not interest him, that at a moment such as this each must decide for himself. No one, it seemed, had given a thought to Joséphine, who was at La Malmaison. Before leaving the Tuileries, Hortense sent off a messenger, telling her mother that Paris was in danger and that she should go at once to her estate in Normandy.

Very tired, very impatient with the spinelessness of all concerned, Hortense went back to the rue Cerutti at one o'clock in the morning. She found Louise Cochelet waiting up for her, and also Madame Ney, Adèle's sister, and the Comte de Lavalette, Émilie's husband, who was now the head of the French postal service. She told them the discouraging news, and they agreed with her that it was a double folly for the Empress to leave in broad daylight, when all the city could see.

Hortense had gone to bed and had just fallen asleep when she was roused to receive a letter from Louis, whom she had not seen since he had been in Paris and who was staying with his mother. The letter told her what had happened at the palace. She sent back word that she herself had been at the Tuileries and fell asleep, only to be roused a second time. Louis informed her that he had been delegated to accompany the Empress to Rambouillet, thence to Blois, and invited Hortense to join the train. Hortense replied that she would consider that proposition in the morning. She was just dropping off again, when a third letter arrived. This time it was a sharply worded command for her to leave Paris with her children.

The day that followed a night of broken rest was exhausting. Hortense was up early and did not have a moment to herself. Various people came to offer her their help, one being Charles de Flahaut's cousin, Charles de la Bédoyère, whom Hortense had met at Aix and who—this seemed a very long while ago—had once told her that he was in love with her. She heard that Marie Louise had left at eleven o'clock, and that the King of Rome had had a tantrum and was carried to the carriage, screaming that he didn't want to go away. Madame Mère had driven out of the city and was hooted by a crowd. Worst of all, Louis had not gone with the Empress. He was waiting in Paris to see if Hortense would obey him.

She was very loath to put herself again in Louis' power, very anxious to show that at least one member of the imperial family was stout-hearted. A report reached her that the Emperor would soon be in Paris, but it was growing late. Louis had delivered his ultimatum: If Hortense didn't leave before morning, he would come and take the children away from her by force. He had posted a servant at her door to keep watch upon her movements.

At eight o'clock in the evening, Hortense ordered the carriages to be brought around. She got into the first one with her children; she would trust no one else to guard them. Some of the servants and Louise Cochelet, who carried a bag in which she had packed all of Hortense's jewelry, followed.

A friend had offered a night's lodging near Versailles. Hortense had hardly arrived, had hardly put the children to bed, and was trying to sleep herself when she heard the sound of cannon. This was not a ceremonial cannonade, she said to herself; these shots were meant to kill. She lay awake, tossing about, wondering what was happening in Paris, her beloved Paris; all its inhabitants now seemed to be her dearest friends.

Hortense didn't think it wise to stay long in a private house, and the following morning went to the Trianon. She sent word to the general of a cavalry regiment at Versailles that she was there. As she and Louise were walking about the palace garden, they heard again the sound of distant explosions. Suddenly all was quiet. Hortense saw a soldier coming toward her on foot. He seemed so calm, so leisurely, that she couldn't believe at first what he had to say: Paris had surrendered; Joseph, Jérôme, and the high officials of the government had swept through Versailles that morning; the Versailles regiment was to be withdrawn; Hortense herself must leave at once.

The horses were put to in a hurry. Some of the servants had gone off to the town, in spite of Hortense's orders to the contrary; they would have to be left behind to shift for themselves. The children were delighted to hear that they were going somewhere else; they liked this wandering life. As the carriages rattled down the long avenue leading from the royal palace, Versailles stood empty. There was not a human being, soldier or civilian, to be seen in its streets. The inhabitants were waiting for the enemy behind closed doors and shuttered windows.

It was late in the afternoon when Hortense and her party reached Rambouillet. Marie Louise was no longer there. She had gone on to Chartres on her way to Blois. Joseph, Jérôme, and their companions were just finishing dinner. They were much surprised to see Hortense. When she asked if it were true that Paris had fallen, Joseph would not answer yes nor no, but Jérôme gave all the details and produced a proclamation that, he said, had been drawn up by Prince Schwarzenberg, urging the people of Paris to imitate the inhabitants of Bordeaux, where a representative of the Bourbons had already been received.

No one offered Hortense anything to eat. Louise Cochelet, who was plump and had a hearty appetite, managed to get a loaf of bread, which she took to her room. Soon the Bonaparte brothers were off for Chartres, and told Hortense to follow them. She turned up her nose at their advice; she was too disgusted with their cowardice to believe that danger was imminent; also, her horses would have to be rested before they could make another long journey.

She was about to go to bed, when an officer burst in upon her with a letter from Louis. Louis had gone straight through to Chartres and was furious to find that she was not already there. His letter, telling her to come at once, was so violent that Hortense rebelled. She sent the man back with letters both to Louis and Marie Louise, saying that she had intended joining the Empress, but now she was going to her mother at Navarre. While she was writing, she was interrupted by yet another officer, a colonel, who said that he and his regiment had been ordered to follow the princes from Paris to guard their retreat, and now he didn't know what to do or where to find them. He cursed the War Minister for having left no orders. Hortense said that she would give him his orders herself. He and his regiment could stay to guard her during the night.

After she had blown out her candle, Hortense was wakened by someone pounding at her door and shouting, "Quick, quick, let's be off," but it was only a false alarm. The château of Rambouillet had become an inn. Refugees from Paris were arriving at all hours.

As soon as it was light, Hortense was ready to take the road. She studied the map she had brought with her from Paris. The most direct route to Navarre was through the forest of Rambouillet. She sent a rider ahead of her as scout. Just as the carriages were about to enter the wood, another man rode up to say that a band of Cossacks had been seen moving in this direction.

Hortense ordered her driver to turn around and to take the open highway. They had not gone very far, when they saw a lone Cossack ride out of the forest. The little boys were excited; they had heard so much of the wild horsemen of the steppes that they wanted to see one. This specimen was not as terrifying as the grownups had feared. One of Hortense's mounted servants bravely charged him at a gallop, and the Russian disappeared among the trees.

The travelers pushed on as fast as they could, though the highway was crowded with westward moving traffic. In one of the towns, through which they passed, they met an imperial courier, who told Hortense that he had only recently left Napoleon and that the Emperor was on his way to the capital. Hortense was so overwrought that she burst into tears. It was just as she had expected. If only the city could have held out for a day or two! What would happen now? Would there be a fight outside the walls? Would the Emperor be killed, and Paris, like Moscow, go up in flames?

Soon all signs of war were left behind. The travelers passed through valleys that were so peaceful, so beautiful, with the first touch of early spring, that it was hard to believe that there was a foreign enemy in all of France.

That night, however—it was the 30th of March—a carriage and a small troupe of mounted men dashed up to the inn and posting station at the Cour de France, ten miles south of Paris, not far from Fontainebleau. Napoleon sprang out of the carriage. He had heard of the Russian advance and had been on the road for forty-eight hours. He had brought with him five of his generals, among them Armand de Caulaincourt and Charles de Flahaut.

It was ten o'clock, very dark, very quiet around the little inn. While the tired horses were being unhitched and others brought out to replace them, Napoleon paced back and forth in the roadway. He heard—the others heard also—the multiple beat of horses' hooves in the distance. Cossacks? Napoleon sent an aide to investigate, and in a few minutes the man returned with the word that this was a detachment of French cavalry, coming from Paris. The cavalry commander, General Belliard, soon rode into the circle of light from the lanterns.

Napoleon poured out his questions. "What are you doing here? Where is the enemy? Who is holding Paris? What has become of my wife and son? Where are Prince Joseph and General Clarke [the Minister of War]?"

Belliard at last was allowed to speak, to say that although there had been fighting on Montmartre that morning, and Generals Marmont and Maret had given a good account of themselves, Paris had fallen. All for whom the Emperor had asked were either at Blois, or on the road to Blois.

"Has everyone lost his head here?" Napoleon shouted. "This is what comes of counting on people who have neither energy nor common sense! That pig of a Joseph, who thinks he can command an army as well as I do! And that cursed old fool of a Clarke, who is utterly incapable once he is taken out of his office routine!"

Napoleon turned to De Caulaincourt. "You heard what Belliard says. We must get on to Paris." He had started impulsively to walk in the direction of the city.

De Caulaincourt and the others hurried after him, protesting how futile, how dangerous it would be to go to Paris now. It was too late for that. But it was not too late, Napoleon insisted, to send word to General Marmont that he must break off negotiations with the enemy. Charles de Flahaut was given a fresh horse, and set off at top speed to Marmont's camp at Essonnes, some five miles distant.

Charles had a wild ride through the night; a candlelit conference with Marmont, and was back again at the Cour de France at four o'clock in the morning. Napoleon had fallen asleep over the maps he had been studying, in planning his defense of Paris. All that De Flahaut could tell him was that the capitulation of the city had been signed. He brought a letter to the Emperor from Marmont and, from his conversation with the General, knew what it contained. Marmont thought that resistance would be useless. He had only held his own against the first wave of invasion; the sea was yet to come.

Napoleon and his party turned their horses' heads toward Fontainebleau. Dawn was breaking as De Flahaut went to his room in the empty palace. Exhausted though he was, he could not sleep. He must let his mother know, the first thing in the morning, that he was still alive.

"Good God," he wrote, "how I dread what is coming now! I can't really believe that the enemy will enter Paris. What will they do there? What are we going to do? We have beaten them once, but that was only a part of their army. At least, we have shown them that there are some good Frenchmen left, for I know that our soldiers put up a brave defense."

Charles remembered that this was the 31st of March. "How long this month is!" he lamented. The month had begun with desperate hope and desperate triumph; it was ending in despair.

The following day, the allies marched into Paris. A provisional government was set up under the presidency of Talleyrand. The reconvened Senate voted for the deposition of the Emperor, and De Caulaincourt, whom Napoleon had sent to talk with the Czar, returned to Fontainebleau to say that Alexander demanded Napoleon's abdication. The question of the accession of the King of Rome would have to be discussed later.

Napoleon balked at these terms. His army had begun to catch up with him. He held a review of the Guard in the courtyard of the palace, and told his men that Paris would "become the tomb" of those who had been rash enough to enter it. In the military action that he planned, he was counting heavily on Marmont and his division at Essonnes.

But Marmont had already been approached by siren Talleyrand. Napoleon could understand the defection of one who, he had once said in anger, "would sell his own mother," but the news of Marmont's surrender was hard to grasp. Marmont had been with Bonaparte in Italy and Egypt.

"He was brought up in my camp," Napolen said. "He forgets under what flag he won his promotions."

On April 6th, a treaty was drawn up and was sent to the allies for signature. Napoleon renounced the throne for himself and for his son. In return, he demanded that he should be given sovereignty over the island of Elba and that a specified income should be paid to him and to each of his family.

Charles de Flahaut wrote to his mother that he was ashamed now to say he was a Frenchman. He no longer wanted to serve under a banner that was "shrouded with crêpe." Charles had never blindly adored the Emperor, but he had been trained to identify all patriotism, all honor, with loyalty to a single man. His anguish was increased, when he considered that it was his father who was the arch betrayer, and that, unless he himself went to Elba with Napoleon, he would have to turn to Talleyrand for help.

Adélaide de Souza, in every letter that she sent to Fontainebleau, urged her son to return to Paris and to sign an act of submission to the temporary government. Charles would not leave until Napoleon had left. "All the abuse that is heaped upon him in the press only attaches me to him more firmly," he wrote. "Never have I seen such courage."

But the days lengthened. To Charles, they seemed a lingering illness that could end only in death. He told his mother that he didn't know if Monsieur Bégo—this was a pseudonym for Talleyrand, taken from a character in one of Madame de Souza's novels —was still interested in doing something for him, but he had written Talleyrand a letter. He longed for peace and retirement and for something more—a home of his own, fireside love. When he had fulfilled his duty here, he would return to "enjoy a great happiness," if Henriette (Hortense) "should decide to make me happy." Hortense was the mother of his child; now that the world was upside down, she might also be his wife.

"Write to her," he begged his mother. "Tell her as best you can that she should arrange this matter with her family, that she should no longer consider her husband. . . . A little place in the country with her and with you, dear mother—that is all I need to be perfectly content."

XXVII

A KINDLY CONQUEROR

WHEN Hortense arrived at her mother's house at Navarre on April 1, 1814, she found the little château crowded with refugee women and children, some of them of the royalist stripe, who openly and tactlessly rejoiced that a Bourbon king was soon to be reseated on the throne of France. This in itself seemed no great calamity to either Hortense or Joséphine; only the Emperor's fate was tragic. When Joséphine heard that Napoleon was going to Elba, she threw her arms about Hortense's neck and vowed that, if it were not for Marie Louise, she would go to Elba herself.

But Joséphine could stay in France, if she so wished. She was no longer a Bonaparte; anyone who bore that name would be a pariah.

"I have just had an idea," Hortense said to Louise Cochelet, "of what I am going to do. My only fortune now is in my diamonds. I will sell them and go to live in Martinique, on a plantation that my mother owns. I was there as a child and have happy memories of the place. It would be a great sacrifice to leave my mother and all my friends, but at least I could live an untroubled life. . . . I could give my children a wholesome education."

254

Louise Cochelet seized Hortense's hand and, kissing it, vowed that there was one friend who would not be left behind. She, Louise, would be glad to share in the Martinique adventure.

Though the inspiration was so sudden, Hortense was very much in earnest; so also was Louise. The following day, Mademoiselle Cochelet left for Paris, to break the news to her mother and her two brothers that she was going on a great journey. Hortense undertook to prepare her children for a new outlook on life.

"You are no longer royalty, no longer dukes and princes," she said. "Perhaps you will amount to more in the end, but it will mean being very good and working very hard."

To put things on a level they could understand, she told them that, from now on, they couldn't expect to have dessert with their dinner.

The boys reacted heroically to this privation. Napoléon Louis, who was going on ten, said he would like to be a soldier. Someday he would be a colonel.

"But, my poor child," Hortense exclaimed bitterly, "perhaps they won't let you be a soldier in France."

Louis, aged six, asked if he could keep his hobbyhorse. Hortense warned him that he might have to give that up also.

Soon Hortense began to hear from Louise Cochelet in Paris. Louise had found the house in the rue Cerutti occupied by Swedish soldiers, but in good condition. No one was making use of Hortense's beautifully decorated bedroom, and in her library, where she had left her papers lying about in cardboard cartons, nothing had been touched.

Louise got her mother's blessing on the Martinique scheme, but that was mentioned only in passing in the almost daily bulletins sent to Navarre. Something very much better was in prospect. Armand de Caulaincourt, who was at this time in Paris, negotiating the Emperor's treaty of abdication, came to see Louise. She was also visited by Count Karl Nesselrode, the Foreign Minister of Czar Alexander, and by Prince Leopold of Saxe-Coburg, likewise a member of the Czar's official family. All these men spoke with respect of both Hortense and Joséphine. In planning for the future, they said, the ex-Empress and her daughter would be considered on a different footing from that of the Bonapartes. Talleyrand had expressed approval also. At one of the allied meetings, he said how much he admired Queen Hortense. Both ladies must return at once to La Malmaison, where the Czar, who was anxious to make their acquaintance, would come to see them.

Joséphine was eager to get back to her house and its treasures, which, she had been told, were quite unharmed, but Hortense did not like the idea of fraternizing with the enemy or accepting their patronage. The attitude of some of her mother's house guests had deepened her sense of solidarity with the Emperor. Like Charles de Flahaut, she was revolted by the abuse with which Napoleon was spattered in the daily press and wanted to make a gesture of sympathy. She wrote a letter to Napoleon, which De Caulaincourt would take to Fontainebleau; she announced that she would also go to see Marie Louise, who was again at Rambouillet, and for whom no provision had as yet been made.

Joséphine tried to dissuade her daughter. Louise Cochelet was in despair when she heard of Hortense's plan. But when Joséphine left Navarre for La Malmaison on April 14th, Hortense took the road she had traveled two weeks earlier in coming from Rambouillet. On her way, she met some dispirited French cavalry going to a garrison in Normandy; they were some of General Marmont's men. She felt a pang, when she saw the Russian uniform of the guards at the door of the château. To her great relief, she learned that all of the Bonaparte family were in Switzerland, except Pauline, who was in the south of France. Marie Louise and her child were alone, though two other visitors had arrived that same day, messengers from the Emperor, who had come to get some of the gold that had been taken from the Tuileries when Paris was abandoned. Napoleon needed money to take with him to Elba.

Hortense asked to be announced to the Empress, and, to her great surprise, was told that Marie Louise was ill and could not see her. She went to the nursery, where the King of Rome was playing by himself, quite contented, quite unconscious of how pathetic he seemed to his visitor, who pressed him to her bosom and tearfully kissed him. When Hortense had gone to her own room, a servant came to say that the Empress would see her.

She found Marie Louise propped up in her bed, a disconsolate figure—far from joyful at sight of Hortense. Marie Louise asked anxiously how long her sister-in-law intended to stay at Rambouillet. "I am expecting to see my father tomorrow," she said, "and I would like to see him alone. He has never met you. I think he would be vexed if he found that you were here."

Offended by the suggestion that she would be so officious as to intrude between father and daughter, Hortense assured Marie Louise that she had only come to be helpful. If there was nothing she could do, she would go back next morning to her mother.

This seemed to take a load off Marie Louise's mind, for thereafter she talked more freely. She could tell little of Napoleon that Hortense did not already know, but she complained piteously of the way she had been treated by Joseph and Jérôme Bonaparte. They had wanted her to go away with them from Blois to Bourges —perhaps farther still. When she refused, Joseph became so angry that she was frightened. At one point she thought that Jérôme was going to strike her, and called out to the guard that she was being kidnaped.

"You are luckier than I am," she sighed. "You haven't been abandoned, and I—why I haven't even my own guard of honor left!"

The thing that seemed to be weighing most heavily upon Marie Louise was the coming interview with her father. Hortense tried to be reassuring.

"But, sister,"—there was real alarm in Marie Louise's voice —"*do* you think that my father will tell me that I have got to go to the island of Elba?"

Hortense said nothing. Her lips had parted, but no words came. She had thought that, strange as it seemed, Marie Louise was really in love with Napoleon. She remembered how, only a few months ago, the Emperor had comforted his weeping wife by saying that he would soon be back. It was not her husband that this little waxwork of a woman had been afraid of losing, it was her crown!

In the morning, the good-byes on either hand were cool. Hortense found that she had not left the château a moment too soon. She had driven only a short way when she passed a small open *calèche*, in which were riding Count Metternich and a man who must be Marie Louise's father, the Emperor of Austria.

As she looked back upon it, the trip to Rambouillet seemed to Hortense a waste of time and sympathy, but she had just had an experience that ought to have made her a little less harsh in her judgment on Napoleon's wife. The problems faced by all those connected with the fallen titan were complex. Hortense had seen not only Marie Louise, but the two messengers who had come from Fontainebleau to get the money that Napoleon needed. They were Armand de Caulaincourt and Charles de Flahaut.

Charles had asked Hortense to marry him. She had told him how impossible that was. If she could get a divorce from Louis, she would have to forego the promise of a settlement that Napoleon had extracted from the allies. Worse—much worse—she would have to lose her two sons; the court would surely hand them over to their father. Even if Charles's dream of a house in the country were realized, Hortense could not acknowledge as her own the little "prime minister," Charles Auguste Demorny. And Charles himself, could she be sure that he would make her happy?

As Hortense drove into the courtyard of La Malmaison, she saw that it was full of soldiers—Russian soldiers. Hortense could now recognize the bright blue, baggy trousers and the belted tunic of the Cossack uniform. She was told that her mother was walking in the garden with Czar Alexander.

Trailed by her children, who had rushed out to meet her, Hortense went to look for Joséphine and her guest. She caught sight of them standing near one of the greenhouses. Joséphine was no longer slim, but at a distance one could still mistake her for a young woman; the Emperor was impressively tall. On closer view, one saw that he was blond, that his face had a deceptively naïve expression, and that his pale, myopic eyes were blue.

Joséphine hurried forward to embrace Hortense. "Here is my daughter," she said to Alexander, "and these are my grandsons. I will hand them over to you."

The Emperor offered Hortense his arm, and they walked slowly back toward the house. She found it difficult to make conversation. She had heard a great deal of Alexander, not only from Napoleon, but from many others, Duroc among them, who had seen him at Tilsit. Duroc had once prophesied that if the Czar and Hortense ever met, she would be swept off her feet; but Duroc, dead now a year, had never foreseen a meeting such as this! Hortense still felt that Alexander was the enemy of her country; even if he were a generous enemy, she must not grovel in the dust before him.

When they reached the house, Hortense was more at her ease. Joséphine was pleasantly talkative, and Alexander paid great attention to the children.

"What would you like me to do for them?" he asked. "You must let me be their chargé d'affaires."

Hortense thanked him, but said that she wanted nothing for her sons.

Shortly after, the visitor took his leave, and Joséphine scolded Hortense for having been so haughty. She was afraid that her daughter might have given offense to someone who could do so much for her and for her brother.

The Czar having called, there was a freshet of visitors to Joséphine's house. The King of Prussia came, and all the German princelings who were in Paris; only the Austrians stayed away. The children were rather confused by so many new royal acquaintances. They wanted to know which of them they should call uncle. "Aren't kings always uncles?" Louis asked.

The governess, Madame de Boubers, said that, unfortunately, these royal persons were not relatives. They were conquerors.

"But if they are enemies of Uncle Emperor, why do they kiss us?"

Madame de Boubers explained that it was all because the Czar of Russia was a very kindly conqueror. He wanted to help them and to help their mother.

"Then I suppose he is the one we ought to love," Napoléon Louis said.

Soon after April 20th, the day when Napoleon left for the south of France and the ship that would take him to Elba, Charles de Flahaut came to La Malmaison. He brought a letter for Hortense from Napoleon, in which he thanked her for her visit to Marie Louise. It was signed, "your affectionate brother," not "your affectionate father." Napoleon apparently had abdicated his paternity and the protection it implied, along with his crown.

Charles told Hortense of the final hours at Fontainebleau, though he had not been present at the most dramatic moment. On the night of April 11th, after the treaty with the allied signatures had been delivered, De Caulaincourt was called to the Emperor's room. He found Napoleon writhing in his bed. He had just swallowed the contents of a little bag of poison, that he had worn about his neck since the Russian campaign and that he had intended to use if there was danger of his being captured. It was better to die, he panted, than to sign the treaty, an ignoble treaty, since it was only concerned with his own interests and not with those of the nation.

De Caulaincourt tried to leave the room and call for help, but Napoleon held him fast. The mixture he had taken, which consisted largely of opium, induced vomiting. Napoleon survived, and found a reason for survival, that he expressed in the farewell to his guard in the courtyard of the palace. Charles de Flahaut was there. He was one of the few who stayed until the end.

"Soldiers of my Guard," Napoleon said. "I have come to say good-bye. During twenty years, I have always found you on the path of honor and glory. . . . With men like you, our cause was

not lost. . . . You, my friends, must continue to serve France. . . .
Do not pity me. If I have consented to live, it is to increase your
fame. I will write of the great things that we have done together.
Good-bye, my children. I wish I could embrace each one of you.
Instead, let me kiss your standard. May that kiss sound on for-
ever in your hearts."

After Napoleon had gone, the flag that he had kissed was
burned. The ashes were swept together and were divided among
the weeping guardsmen, each of whom swallowed a morsel.

De Flahaut was still living in the shadow of that strange scene
in the courtyard and the words that had been spoken there. He
could not quite forgive his mother for having persuaded him to
sign the oath of submission. He could forgive Hortense for not
wanting to marry him; he told her that he would come to see her
often, but—this implied rebuke—he would never come if there
were any risk of his meeting Czar Alexander.

For Alexander was laying siege to La Malmaison. He had noticed Hortense's coldness at their first meeting, but had taken no
offense. He came a second time and, when Hortense went to Paris
for a few days, dropped in at the rue Cerutti. He also called on
Louise Cochelet, who had a little parlor of her own in the house,
where she could receive her friends. Louise was giddy with excitement. Never before had an emperor sat upon her sofa! She served
tea to the Czar and, when he admired her china, begged him to accept her set of tea plates as a gift.

Alexander told Louise that he counted on her to persuade Hortense to accept his services. He would offer her asylum in Russia,
but he was afraid that the climate was too rigorous for a lady
whose health was so delicate. By the terms of the treaty between
Napoleon and the allies, Hortense and her children would receive
an income of 400,000 francs. Alexander and his minister, Nesselrode, wanted the French King to create a Duchy of Saint-Leu for
Hortense, that would yield this revenue and which her sons could
inherit after her death.

Alexander seemed, to Hortense, to have an almost feminine desire to make himself liked for his own sake, and a feminine fondness for exchanging confidences. He told her of the disappointment he felt on meeting the Bourbon royal family: the Comte d'Artois, his son, the Duc de Berry, and Louis XVIII, who, when he arrived at Compiègne, declared this to be the nineteenth year of his reign. The Bourbons seemed determined to ignore all that had happened in France during their long exile. Even the King's niece, the Duchesse d'Angoulême, the daughter of Louis XVI and Marie Antoinette, for whose past sufferings one felt great sympathy, was repellent. She was an angular woman, with a harsh, masculine voice and none of the charm of her martyred mother.

Though Alexander had no love for the Bourbons, he always spoke with respect of Napoleon. It warmed Hortense's heart also to hear him express admiration for Eugène as "the Prince of Chevaliers"; Eugène, who had remained faithful to the Emperor and who had had to stand fast in Italy against Murat's Neapolitan army, as well as the Austrians.

On May 9th, Eugène arrived at La Malmaison. After his surrender, he had taken Augusta and their children, including a month-old baby daughter, who was born in Mantua while the city was under siege, to Augusta's father in Bavaria. A clause of Napoleon's treaty specified that Eugène was to be given a principality outside of France, but this claim would have to be validated at the congress, which would meet in the autumn at Vienna. Alexander could make no promises, but he and Eugène were soon the best of friends.

The Czar told Hortense that he had heard so much of her beautiful estate at Saint-Leu that he wanted to see it. A day was settled upon, May 14th, for a small "family party" there, consisting of Joséphine, Eugène, Hortense, Madame Ney, Alexander, and one of his military staff, General Tchernycheff.

While they were having lunch, Alexander told Hortense that there was going to be a religious service that day in honor of King

Louis XVI and Marie Antoinette. All the foreign sovereigns should attend, but here was the Emperor of Russia enjoying himself at Saint-Leu. "I was saying to Tchernycheff, as we were driving out here, what a strange situation this is. I came to Paris full of hatred for your family, and it is only with you that I feel at ease."

The afternoon was spent in a long drive through the forest, part of which was no longer Hortense's property, the half of the estate which had belonged to the Duc d'Orléans having been returned to its original owner. In the evening, after the others had gone in, Hortense and Alexander walked for a long time back and forth under the great trees that surrounded the château. Alexander said that he admired Hortense's serenity, in face of recent reverses. She replied that she was not really serene, that she always feared the worst. What had happened to her during the last few weeks had not affected her deeply; the real sorrows of her life had made her apprehensive. She told him of her calamitous marriage and of the deaths of Napoléon Charles and Adèle.

Alexander listened attentively. Several times he interrupted her to say, "You do not trust, as you should, in the goodness of God."

He, in turn, told her of his own tribulations and of the consolation and guidance he had always found in prayer. He gave as example the time he spent on his knees before the attack on Paris, and how he had risen to his feet certain of success.

When Hortense said that she could think of God only as a God of Vengeance and that there was little chance for happiness in this world, Alexander cried out again at her lack of faith. There was strength in a clean conscience; his was clean except for a single weakness that he hoped God would forgive him. For years, his marriage with the Czarina, a Princess of Baden, had been a mere formality. He had had a long standing liaison with Princess Narychkine. He loved his mistress and the children she had borne him passionately.

To Hortense's objection that he ought to have legal heirs, the

Czar said that he had three brothers to succeed him. His wife had no better friend than he, but reunion with her was impossible.

Darkness had fallen while Hortense and Alexander were talking. They went back into the house, Hortense feeling that she had found a true friend. Hadn't they just revealed their inmost secrets to one another?

ഇരുരുരുരുരുരുരുരുരുരു

XXVIII

THE DUCHESS OF SAINT-LEU

It was soon known that Hortense had entertained the Czar at
Saint-Leu on May 14th. One of her friends, who belonged to the
court circle, came to ask her why she had chosen that of all days
for a fête.

It was not a fête, Hortense protested, it was a small gathering
of six persons, and the date had been set before she knew of the
Requiem Mass for the dead King and Queen in Notre Dame.

Her friend warned her that the partiality shown by Alexander
for the Beauharnais family was causing jealousy. It was said that
La Malmaison was a gathering place for discontent, and that spiteful things were said there of the royal family. It was rumored also
that Joséphine was distributing money to the working people in
the suburbs of Paris, where Napoleon had always been so popular.

Hortense laughed at the absurdity of this canard. At the moment, both she and Joséphine had little money to distribute. Their
allowances from the Emperor's privy purse were in long arrears.
At Blois, 600,000 francs, a portion of the gold which was taken
from the Tuileries when the government fled, was deposited for
Joséphine and Hortense with the city treasurer. A few days later,
however, the Duc d'Angoulême passed through the town and confiscated the money to pay his troops.

Hortense was not sure that her story was believed. She noticed that her mother's royalist friends, for whom Joséphine had done so much, neglected her. The determination of the Bourbons to blot out the past was plain when, toward the end of the month, the patent for the Duchy of Saint-Leu was delivered to Hortense. In it, she was named as Mademoiselle Hortense Eugénie de Beauharnais. She felt that she couldn't accept the grant under a name that took no account of the fact that she was married and had been a princess of France and a queen. Louise Cochelet was deputed to take up the matter in Paris with Alexander's minister, Count Nesselrode, and a new patent was issued to "Madame Hortense Eugénie, as described in the treaty of April 11th." Thus the hateful name of Bonaparte did not appear, but the recipient's former status was recognized.

Before the matter was settled, Hortense had almost forgotten it; she had other concerns. Joséphine had worn a light, gauzy dress to the party at Saint-Leu and caught a cold that she seemed unable to shake off. She was much depressed. Whenever the name Napoleon was mentioned, her eyes would fill with tears. She was glad that Hortense and her children were provided for, but she was worried about Eugène, and about the readjustments she would have to make in her own way of living. Though her income still was large, it had been reduced by two-thirds. Joséphine couldn't bear to dismiss any of her servants or cut down on the pensions she paid to various people, amounting to 300,000 francs a year. She admitted to Hortense that she had a few debts. If she sold her diamonds, perhaps they could be settled.

Joséphine, whose health had always been so good, had never been one to coddle a cold. Her active social life continued. There was a dinner party every day at La Malmaison. Now it was for German royalty, now it was for the younger brothers of the Czar, well-behaved young men who admired Joséphine's treasures, particularly a snow scene in her picture gallery that they said reminded them of home.

It is only a cold, Hortense said to herself. She went to Paris for a few days to attend to business, and for another meeting with Alexander. Eugène recalled her to La Malmaison. Their mother was worse, he said, and she was very much distressed by an article that she had seen in a newspaper, saying that the body of Napoléon Charles was to be removed from Notre Dame and buried in a public cemetery.

Hortense had not seen the article. She hurried back to La Malmaison to tell her mother that she would see that her son's coffin was taken to Saint-Leu. She found that Joséphine was so hoarse that she could hardly speak.

The patient was coaxed to bed, and a blister, the panacea of the day for all infections, was applied to the neck. Alexander sent his personal physician, who advised further blistering, blistering en masse. Hortense's worries were increased, when Eugène also came down with a fever and had to take to his bed.

It was the 28th of May. The Czar, who was leaving for England shortly, was expected for dinner. Hortense had just sent off a message, asking him to put off his visit, when he arrived earlier than expected. Hortense led him to Eugène's room. She wanted to hide his presence in the house from her mother, for fear that Joséphine would insist on getting up to receive him.

When she said that the Czar had sent his excuses, Joséphine murmured sadly, "I am sure that is because he is embarrassed at not having anything new to tell us about your brother's future."

The doctors—Hortense had asked for a consultation—assured her that this would be a long illness. A schedule was drawn up for those who would take turns at spending the night in Joséphine's room. Her doctor and one of the maids would watch the first night. but Hortense found that she could not sleep. She got up twice to go to her mother. Joséphine seemed to be sleeping, but her dreams were troubled. "Bonaparte," she muttered, "the Island of Elba— the King of Rome."

Early the next morning, Hortense and Eugène, who was still feverish, entered the sickroom. Joséphine held out her arms to them and said something, a mere babble that they could not understand. For the first time, Hortense realized that this was not going to be a long illness. It was Sunday, the Feast of Pentecost. Hortense and Eugène went to Mass. When they returned, Hortense prepared herself to speak calmly, so as not to alarm her mother, of the last sacrament, but she found that it had already been administered on the advice of the doctor.

Joséphine had gone beyond the point where death is feared. She was comatose. Her features seemed to have shrunken. Hortense could not bear to see her so changed; she felt faint and left the room. A few minutes later, Eugène came running to tell her that it was all over. There was a rushing sound in the corridor, as all of the household burst in upon her with their grief.

Joséphine had died at high noon. Two hours later, Hortense and Eugène left for Saint-Leu. They wished to avoid the period of public mourning. For three days, Joséphine's embalmed body lay in state in a candlelit chamber, which was hung with black, without imperial insignia. The road from Paris was choked with traffic. Twenty thousand people passed through the room.

On June 2nd, the coffin was carried between a line of Russian soldiers and National Guardsmen, that stretched all the way from the château to the village church of Rueil-Malmaison. It was followed by royal princes, generals, officials of all sorts, except those of the Bourbon court, and a vast crowd of ordinary people for whom Joséphine was the good Empress, the generous chatelaine. If she had her faults, they did not know them. They had only seen her virtues: her facile kindliness, her desire to please, "that indescribable something," as Napoleon had once written to Hortense, that set her apart from all the world.

"The death of Madame de Beauharnais," so read the bulletin that the police sent daily to Louis XVIII, "has caused general regret. This lady was endowed from birth with gentleness, and elegant and amiable manners. . . . Desperately unhappy during the reign of her husband, she sought refuge from his brutalities and neglect in the study of botany. . . . The public was aware of the battles she fought to snatch the victims of Bonaparte from his grasp. It is grateful to her for having fallen at his feet in an attempt to save the life of the Duc d'Enghien."

The King, whom Eugène had informed of the death, sent a letter of condolence, one among thousands. Neither Eugène nor Hortense attended the funeral; the conventions of the day allowed for the absence of the chief mourners. They were represented by Hortense's two sons, and the Czar of Russia by one of his staff. Alexander had made himself one of the family. He spent June 2nd at Saint-Leu, and stayed there until the evening of the following day, when he left for England. He walked with Eugène, dined alone, with brother and sister, in Hortense's boudoir; and his sympathy could not have been more delicate, more unobtrusive.

While he was staying in Hortense's house, the Czar worked at his own affairs, and received several couriers from Paris. One of them brought him the revised patent for the Duchy of Saint-Leu, which he tactfully handed over to Louise Cochelet, telling her to give it to Hortense when the proper moment came. She did not need to thank the King, he said. He, Alexander, had had to exert pressure to get this new document drawn up. In the evening, when the Czar left, he said to Hortense that he hoped to hear from her constantly, and to Eugène that he would meet him in the autumn at Vienna.

Eugène was anxious to return to his family in Munich, and felt that the sooner he left France the better. But there was Joséphine's estate to be settled, a vastly complicated affair. Joséphine owned La Malmaison, Navarre, the house at Prègny in Switzerland, and the plantation in Martinique; she had a small number of government securities, and a very valuable collection of pictures, objets d'art, and jewelry. When the drawers of the desks at La Malmaison were emptied and their contents sifted, it was discovered that her debts amounted to three million francs. It was hard to know where to find the cash to meet these obligations. The business agents, who had been put in charge of the estate, suggested that a sale of the Empress' effects would be very profitable, since the public would be willing to pay high prices for souvenirs.

Hortense and Eugène, however, could not bear to see their mother's things put up for auction. They divided her personal belongings among her maids and ladies in waiting, giving the securities as dowry to those who were not married. Joséphine's collection of shawls was scattered far and wide; her horses and carriages went to her equerry and her maids of honor. Then there was the difficult business of pensions for the servants, and providing for those whom Joséphine had subsidized for years. It was inevitable that some were dissatisfied.

The inheritance that finally came to Hortense was half of her mother's pictures and half of her mother's diamonds. It was a sizeable legacy, worth perhaps two million francs, but far short of the fantastic figures in the press, that liked to contrast the luxury of Napoleon's court with the penury of the royal family during their exile. The Duchesse d'Angoulême ostentatiously appeared in public without jewels and wearing a dowdy hat that she had bought in England.

Eugène took his leave on the 24th of June, and suggested that Hortense should meet him and his family at Aix-en-Savoie, in July. Hortense heard from the Russian Ambassador in Paris, Pozzo di Borgo, a Corsican and a long-time enemy of Napoleon, that the French government would look askance on her going to Aix, because the Empress Marie Louise would be there. Hortense decided to go to Plombières instead. She no longer had ladies in waiting and equerries to fill a caravan of carriages; she took only Louise Cochelet with her. Every day she hoped that she would see Eugène and Augusta arrive at the spa, but after two weeks a letter came, urging her to come to Baden, where she would find many friends, as well as her cousin Stéphanie, whom Napoleon, when the Federation of the Rhine was forming, had married to the reigning grand duke.

Stéphanie's mother-in-law, the Dowager Margravine, had married her daughters well. They surrounded their mother that summer: the Czarina of Russia, the Queen of Bavaria, the former Queen of Sweden, and the Grand Duchess of Hesse-Darmstadt. The one who interested Hortense the most was the Russian Empress whom the Czar so pointedly neglected. Hortense, when she felt herself on sufficiently intimate terms with the Czar, had tried a second time to discuss his marital problems with him, but he asked her never to mention them again. The Czarina was tall, dignified, and, as befitted a rejected wife, melancholy. One could see that she had once been beautiful, but her complexion, it was said, had been ruined by the cold Russian climate.

All these royal ladies were rather stiff in their manners, and their conversation tended to be stuffy. They made much, however, of Hortense. They had heard that she was talented. They wanted to see her sketches, her book of songs, and, if she had not been in mourning for her mother, they would have asked her to dance. Their attitude toward her was very different from their attitude toward Stéphanie. Stéphanie, the gay little flirt, whom Napoleon's politics had raised so high, was an intruder in their midst. They would like to see her repudiated by her husband.

The Princesses at Baden were all devout. The national movement in Germany had had its religious aspects, and some rather queer personalities had come to the fore. One day, Louise Cochelet was alone in the salon of the little house that Hortense shared with her brother and sister-in-law, when a small, shabbily dressed Russian lady entered the room. She was skeleton thin, and her eyes, under a thick mop of untidy ash-blonde hair that fell across her forehead, had a fanatic gleam.

Louise, recognizing an old acquaintance, sprang up to embrace the Baroness von Krüdener, but the visitor gestured to her to keep her distance.

"I have come to see your Queen," she said solemnly. "I must save her from a danger that menaces her. I wanted to come as soon as I heard that she was here, but God would not let me. Those who are even more unfortunate than she required my services."

Behind Barbara Juliane von Krüdener lay fifty years of high-colored eccentricity. She had had her flaming youth when she was lavishly extravagant, flaunted a lover in the face of her elderly husband, and wrote, like so many ladies of exhibitionist tendency, a semi-autobiographical novel. In 1804, she experienced a conversion at the hands of her shoemaker, a member of the Moravian Brethren. She lived among the poor in various religious communities in Switzerland, in the Vosges mountains, and in Germany. When Louise visited Baden with Hortense in 1809 and first met Madame von Krüdener, the Russian lady was devoting herself unobtrusively to charitable work. Her Pietist associates looked to the millennium and the second coming of Christ. The Antichrist, the beast of the Apocalypse, had been identified as Napoleon, then at the summit of his power. Now that Napoleon had fallen, several inches had been added to Juliane's diminutive stature, in the opinion of the public and of herself.

"What do you want to say to her?" Louise asked. By "her" she meant Hortense.

"I have come to reveal to her what God wants her to know. . . . I have not seen her since 1809, but I have often prayed for her. . . . Since I last saw her, she has lost her crown, a brilliant position, a dear friend, and a tender mother. . . . God loves her, but he wishes to put her to the test. . . . She is not yet at the end of her misfortunes."

Hortense would be happy because her soul was pure, Madame von Krüdener continued. "But she must not look to man; God will be her only protector. Above all, she must not return to France. She must go to Russia. Czar Alexander will give refuge to the unfortunate."

"You frighten me out of my wits," Louise quavered. "What worse things can happen than have happened already?"

"The year 1815 will be a fearful year," the prophetess announced. "You think that the congress at Vienna will accomplish its purpose. Don't deceive yourself! The Emperor Napoleon will come from his island. He will be even more powerful than before, but those who take his part will be hunted, persecuted, punished! They will not know where to lay their heads."

All this time the little Russian lady had remained standing, though Louise was continually motioning her to a seat. If she would only sit down, Louise thought, she wouldn't talk so strangely.

"The Queen is out," Louise said. "Come back tomorrow. I know how pleased she will be to see you, but, I warn you, if you speak of her mother, you will make her cry."

"What do tears matter?" Madame von Krüdener asked of the universe. "God loves those who weep; they are his chosen. But if the Queen wants to see me, she must be at home tomorrow, for I can't come often. I no longer have a will of my own. I belong to those to whom God sends me as comforter. But remember what I say, she must not go back to France!"

When Hortense came in with Eugène, Louise gave them a vivid account of what they had missed. The following day, Hortense received the Baroness and was moved to tears by a mention not only of Joséphine's death, but the deaths also of Adèle and Napoléon Charles. She dried her eyes, however, when Madame von Krüdener said mysteriously, "If you wish, you may know where those you have loved and lost are now."

Hortense failed to ask the question that was expected of her. She told Louise later that she thought their friend was a little mad, though not because she advised against a return to France. That might be sound advice for the Duchesse de Saint-Leu.

At the end of August, Hortense and her companion left for France. Eugène rode a short way beside them. When he said goodbye, he told Hortense that as soon as he had a home of his own she must come to share it.

The travelers were going straight through to Paris without stopping for the night. At six o'clock in the evening they had passed the frontier and halted for a change of horses at Saverne. A carriage, in which were four French officers, was waiting in the stableyard. Hortense heard someone say, "That's Queen Hortense. There's never a French officer who wouldn't recognize her!"

Hortense didn't want to be drawn into conversation and told the driver to hurry on. They came to a point where the road—it was one of the many fine highways that Napoleon had built in France—climbed over a high ridge. Louise suggested that she and Hortense should get out and walk. They hadn't gone far when the carriage, seen at the posting station, came up behind them. The four officers got out and offered to escort Hortense to the top of the mountain. She was their queen, and they wanted no other.

"I will accept your escort as a woman," Hortense said, "but I don't want to claim a title that no longer belongs to me."

"What do you mean, doesn't belong to you?" one of the young men cried. "Do you think that we recognize the abdication of the Emperor?"

Hortense reminded him that he had another sovereign now and had taken another oath of loyalty.

"Loyalty to people who were brought back by the Cossacks!" was the reply.

The man said that he had been one of the guard of honor when Napoléon Louis was christened by the Pope at Saint-Cloud. Another, the oldest of the group, said that he had been a prisoner for six years in England, had worn chains and done forced labor, but he would rather go back to slavery than to see his country as it was now.

"The Emperor will return, and he will find us ready for him. He can't leave us in the lurch."

But they were talking of civil war, Hortense protested. There was nothing worse than that.

It would not be civil war, because in the army there was unity, she was told. All of the officers had drunk the Emperor's health on his birthday. Their soldiers had drunk it also. They would shout, "Long live the King," when they were ordered to do so, and then would add, sotto voce, "the King of Rome and his little father!"

There was a village at the top of the hill, and a triumphal arch, decorated with flowers, had been put up for an expected visit from the Duc de Berry. "You will be the first to consecrate it," Hortense's military friends cried. They seized her by the arms and dragged her under the arch, shouting, "Long live Queen Hortense!"

Hortense was frightened for them. There were guards standing by the arch. She begged the officers not to be so rash, and to leave her. When they heard she was going to travel all night, they wanted to follow her, but she wouldn't hear of that. Before parting, they wrote down their names and addresses and told her that if she ever wanted them, she need only say the word.

Hortense was relieved when she saw the last of her bodyguard and had no intention of communicating with them, but one day she would remember that they, as well as the seeress, Madame von Krüdener, had prophesied that Napoleon would return to France.

PART

V

(August 28, 1814–June 1, 1821)

꿴꿴꿴꿴꿴꿴꿴꿴꿴꿴

XXIX

THE LAWSUIT

EVEN before the Emperor had left for Elba, the members of the
Bonaparte Clan went their separate ways. Quarrelsome though
they were, they kept in close touch with one another, and their
misfortunes gave them an even greater sense of cohesion. Louis
spent the summer of 1814 in various health resorts in Switzerland,
though his brother Lucien, who had returned to Italy from
England where he had been held as a prisoner of war, offered
him a Roman refuge. Louis wanted to stay close enough to France
to wage war on Hortense. Again she had openly defied him, and
she could no longer hide behind the colossal figure of the Emperor.

In April, 1814, Louis wrote to Hortense, suggesting a legal
separation. He had had no reply, when he heard in June of the
donation of the Duchy of Saint-Leu. This was piling grievance
upon grievance. Hortense had not only disposed of her children's
future without consulting him, she had robbed him of his name;
since his abdication, Louis had used the title of Comte de Saint-
Leu. He published, in a Lausanne newspaper, a formal rejection
of any arrangements made under Napoleon's treaty with the
allies for himself or his family, the treaty having stipulated that

Hortense should have an income independent of her husband. While soaking in the medicinal waters of a Swiss Baden, Louis meditated further aggression.

As a result, Hortense, before she left for Plombières and Baden, had a call from Monsieur Decazes, Louis' former secretary and business agent, who sounded her out on the subject of divorce. She told him that she would make no move herself in that direction, but would consent, if she could keep her children and their inheritance of Saint-Leu. Decazes was so pleasant spoken and seemed personally so sympathetic to her ideas, that Hortense went away for her holiday with the not very substantial hope that all would be well.

After her return, she decided to spend the winter in the country and to keep out of the gossip-laden atmosphere of Paris. For a few weeks, life was pleasantly humdrum. Then, in the latter part of September, a Monsieur Briatte, a lawyer, very stiff and pompous, dressed in professional black, appeared before Hortense. Louis had dimissed Decazes as negotiator, because he thought that Decazes would be too easy going. Briatte handed Hortense a letter, in which his client demanded that his eldest son should be handed over to him immediately. Louis pointed out that it was within his rights to demand both of his children, but that he would allow Hortense to keep the younger of the two boys. He wanted no scandal, he said, but he was determined to have his way. If he didn't receive a prompt and satisfactory answer, he would have recourse to the law.

Hortense replied at once, and as temperately as she could. She would not speak of her own feelings, she wrote, but she listed the advantages that Napoléon Louis would enjoy by remaining in France. Louis, an exile and an invalid, who had managed to do without his children for some time now, had little to offer in comparison. Hortense said that she didn't mean to separate him from his sons forever; as soon as he had a settled home and it was feasible for the children to leave the country, she would send them to visit him from time to time.

Hortense knew, however, that nothing she said would deter Louis. She was fighting a delaying action, but fight she would! She wrote to both Alexander and Eugène to tell them of this development. She decided also to see what help she might find nearer home. Though Eugène had been to court while he was in France, Hortense, following the Czar's advice, had avoided the Tuileries. Now she asked for an audience with the King on October 1st, and was told to present herself the following day.

It was a strange experience to find herself again in the palace where she had once lived. Nothing in its décor had been changed as yet. The eagles, the golden bees, and the letters N that were sprinkled over the walls, woven into carpets and upholstery, had not been deleted. The changes were all in the human beings, who moved in ceremonial fashion against the palatial background; the courtiers of the day seemed elderly and decrepit, as compared with the vigorous young people who surrounded the Emperor.

Hortense was received by the King in his study—Napoleon's study. Louis XVIII was sixty-nine. He had found compensation for the frustrations of his life in hearty eating and drinking, and had grown enormously fat during his exile. There were brains inside his pear-shaped head; he was said to be both learned and subtle, and Hortense discerned a flicker of malice in some of his remarks. He asked her to sit near him and said how sorry he was never to have met her mother. Hortense replied that Joséphine had done a great deal of good in France, and some of the good had been for supporters of the King.

"Yes, I know," Louis said. "At Martinique, she was a good royalist."

Thus praise was discounted for Joséphine, the wife of the Emperor and the wife of the First Consul. When Hortense said how much she appreciated the favors that had been granted her, the King asked her if it were true that she had once said to Napoleon, when he was clad in his regalia for some state occasion, that the sword and mantle of a Constable of France would be more becoming.

"I have been said to say a great many things that I did not say," Hortense replied. "What is true of me today is that I only want to live quietly and to educate my children."

She added that she considered herself now an old woman and preferred to be an onlooker. The King laughed at the notion of anyone who was thirty-one claiming old age. During the rest of their conversation, he was much more genial. When he rose to dismiss Hortense, he kissed her hand and asked if he could kiss her on the cheek.

Later, Hortense heard that she had made a very good impression. The King spoke so admiringly of the Duchesse de Saint-Leu that one of his courtiers had to remind him that she and her friends were troublemakers. Later still, the secret police, a branch of Napoleon's administration that the Bourbons had retained in full activity, was requested to write a bulletin of Hortense's daily habits and of the people who came to her house in the rue Cerutti.

Hortense had abandoned Saint-Leu, when she was officially notified that the suit for the surrender of her son had been registered. It was necessary, she found, to be in Paris to consult her lawyers. She knew nothing of legal procedure. It was painful to have to hand over all of Louis' letters to strangers, and to go over the depressing details of his abdication, his quarrels with his brother and with herself. She had little encouragement from Alexander or Eugène, both of whom urged her to offer no defense. When Hortense petitioned the King to intervene, his prime minister replied that it was not the policy of His Majesty to interfere in legal matters. If her son left France, however, he would automatically lose his inheritance.

The police reported that Hortense received a few friends, very informally, on two days of the week. To be in Paris and not to have a salon was unthinkable! There was a wide variety in the folk who came to sit around the big table in Hortense's drawing room. To the private eye of the government, "the house of Madame la Duchesse" seemed to be run on very simple lines, "without magnificence. There is no disorderly conduct there. Madame la Duchesse is much beloved by those who surround her."

Paris, as in the early days of the Consulate, was full of foreigners. Many of the newcomers to the rue Cerutti were English. One was the Duke of Wellington, now the English Ambassador to France. There were Russians, of course, and a scattering of other nationalities. But those on whom the police intended to keep an eye were French officers. The government was disturbed by signs of disaffection in the army, where promotions were being given to returned émigrés, who had never seen a battlefield. The King's nephew, the Duc de Berry, occupied himself with military affairs, tried to imitate Napoleon's manner by being brusque and dictatorial, and only succeeded in making himself unpopular.

When Charles de Flahaut went to court, the Duke asked him in what campaigns he had served.

"All of them, *Monseigneur*."

"What was your rank?"

"Aide-de-camp to the Emperor Napoleon."

The Duke turned on his heel. He considered service under Napoleon to have been "fifteen years of brigandage."

Charles was often indiscreet. At social gatherings he sang duets, but he also sang the *Marseillaise* and the *Ça Ira*. One day, he said in the hearing of his father, Talleyrand, that Napoleon had expected Paris to be true to him; he had not counted on treachery.

Even more rash was Charles's cousin, Charles de la Bédoyère. He came, as he had often told Hortense, of a royalist family. Recently, he had married a young lady, Georgine de Chastellux, of an even more rigidly traditional background. De la Bédoyère shocked his in-laws by his anti-Bourbon talk; they considered him a Jacobin. He came to Hortense's house nearly every evening to let off steam. She reproached him for leaving his young wife alone night after night, but he said that if he stayed at home, Georgine would only be upset by family wrangling. She was pregnant, and he would introduce her to Hortense after her child was born.

One evening, a group of hotheads, among them De Flahaut and his cousin, appeared without their crosses of the Legion of Honor, all of which had been earned for gallantry in action. They said that now that the cross was being given indiscriminately to highwaymen, their decorations no longer had any significance. One of the young men had fastened his to the tail of his horse. Hortense tried to persuade them not to be so petulant and foolhardy. All she was able to get out of them was a statement that they would wear their crosses in her house, but nowhere else.

In other salons, royalist salons, Hortense was represented as a siren to sedition and as a dangerous subversive. Petty jealousies played their part. An elderly lady, the Duchesse de Mouchy, who lived opposite and was at home on the same evening as Hortense, was miffed when she saw how many more carriages were lined up across the way than stood before her own door. Her daughter, Madame Alfred de Noailles, though she had been a schoolgirl at Saint-Germain, was dagger-tongued. Her sayings were reported to Hortense by Charles de Flahaut, who was very attentive to Madame de Noailles. She was the widow of his friend who was killed in Russia at the crossing of the Berezina and whose body he retrieved. There was personal rivalry here, as well as a difference in political outlook.

On Christmas Eve of 1814, Hortense and her friends were making a little music in her salon, when they were interrupted by a call from a clerk in the office of the mayor of the Arrondissement. Hortense had done him a personal favor of some sort, and he had come to warn her, that the government was about to confiscate all the property that the Bonaparte family owned in France. The next day, officials would come to put their seals on everything in the house. If Hortense wanted to save any of her personal belongings, she must get rid of them at once.

Louise Cochelet again packed up Hortense's diamonds in two stout boxes. One of them was given to the secretary of the Russian Ambassador, the other to a friend who had no Bonapartist connections. Hortense registered a declaration in the mayor's office that everything in the house, except some papers of her husband, belonged to her, and the seals were not applied; but she thought that if Napoleon's treaty with the allies was going to be broken in one respect, it would be broken in all. She knew that Napoleon had taken little money with him to Elba. If his promised income of two million francs were unpaid, he might have to dismiss some of his guard and might no longer be safe. She invited the English Ambassador to dinner, and, when she told him her fears, was glad to hear Wellington say that England would consider itself dishonored, if the obligations of the allies were not faithfully discharged.

The police took cognizance of the Duke's visit. "It was remarked"—so ran the bulletin—"that he [the Duke] stayed in her [Hortense's] study for more than an hour, and during the entire evening showed the Duchesse the greatest deference, and to her other guests the greatest affability. This is unlike his usual manner, which in general is very haughty and very solemn."

With the people of Paris, Hortense was more popular than ever before. When carnival time came around, she was visited by a band of mummers who never called on any but royalty. Louise Cochelet, who had a better opportunity than her friend of hearing what was being said, noticed that Hortense was always spoken of as Queen, never as Duchess. Napoleon was "the little corporal" or "the little shaveling," (le petit tondu). He was also called Père Violette, because he would come back in the spring, when the violets were in bloom. Violets happened to be Hortense's favorite flower. A box of them was sent to her regularly from the greenhouse at Saint-Leu. She wore them constantly and gave them to her friends—a trifling circumstance, but trifles were now significant.

Though in many ways Hortense's life was satisfactory, though she carried on a fascinating correspondence with Alexander, in which he confided to her the details of a new love affair at Vienna, she could not forget her lawsuit. The case was opened on January 7, 1815, and continued for two months and a day. Hortense attended none of its sessions, but sent Charles de la Bédoyère, Charles de Flahaut, and others combined to cover all the hearings.

One had to be at the courtroom early to get a seat, for the public flocked to the trial, as if to a matinée. Louis' lawyer, Monsieur Tripier, had made his reputation in civil cases, and had never shown any political bias; Hortense's lawyer, Monsieur Bonnier, a royalist, was a star of the criminal court. Both played up the emotional features of the case. How, Monsieur Tripier asked, could the Duchess, who had been united to her husband in prosperity, be so cruel as not to console him in the hour of his adversity? When Monsieur Bonnier had his innings, he tore mother love to tatters, and wanted to know how anyone could consider snatching an innocent child from the arms of his maternal parent, his fatherland, and his king.

The papers were full of the case. The *Journal de Paris* published a long article, titled "The History of a Great Trial between a King and a Queen for a Little Duke." There was so much abuse of Louis in the article, that Hortense got one of her friends to write a letter to the *Journal* saying how unfair the attacks were. Later notices were unfriendly to both parties, and turned the whole affair into a farce. Hortense was continually at loggerheads with her lawyers, because they paid no attention to her requests to speak respectfully of Louis and always to give Napoleon his title of Emperor. They seemed to her to be interested only in increasing their fame as orators.

Hortense could not be sure whether her position, as wife of a Bonaparte, would work for or against her. According to the law of the land, a father had full control of his children, but Louis was, from a political point of view, an outlaw. On the other hand, it might seem a good thing for a male Bonaparte, even if he were only ten years old, to be removed from France. During the summation of the case, when the courtroom was so packed that those in the rear could not hear what was being said in the front of the room, Hortense was hopeful. Her lawyers had the final say, and she thought that they did well.

The decision was to be given on the last day of February. Hortense was told that it would be deferred for a week, and she waited in great suspense. Perhaps the government was bringing pressure on the judges, for or against. On March 8th, Hortense learned that she had lost her case. She was ordered by the court to hand over her elder son to Louis, within three months.

She barely noticed her defeat. Two days earlier, on Monday, March 6, 1815, Hortense was returning from a drive, and as she crossed the Pont Royale, a horseman drew abreast of her carriage window. She recognized one of her English acquaintances, Lord Kinnaird.

"Have you heard the great news, Madame?" he cried. "The Emperor Napoleon has landed at Cannes."

☙☙☙☙☙☙☙☙☙☙☙☙☙

XXX

FROM STEEPLE TO STEEPLE

NAPOLEON was again in France! For a moment Hortense thought that her informant, Lord Kinnaird, was playing a practical joke, or had been hoaxed himself. The Englishman, however, had just come from the house of the Duc d'Orléans, and so what he said must be true. The Palais Royale was buzzing with alarm. The Duke and his cousin, the Comte d'Artois, had left for Lyon, to prepare for defense.

"Do you think that there is any danger to my children?" Hortense asked.

"Not unless they should be held as hostages," Kinnaird replied.

Hortense could hardly wait to get home to put her children out of reach. She was having a reception that evening and had engaged two singers from the opera. She considered calling off her concert, but, on second thought, decided that it would be better to behave as if she had heard nothing. She told Louise Cochelet to take the children to the house of a friend, as soon as it was dark. Unless one of the boys were ill, she did not want to hear anything from them.

Louise, the children, and Louis' nurse, carrying a small bag,

288

slipped out through the garden gate into the street that ran along the rear of the house. Napoléon Louis, who remembered their flight from Paris a year ago, wanted to know if there were any danger.

"Only to you," Louise said cheerfully. "Your mother will be safe at home."

That seemed to satisfy the boys. They asked no more questions, and enjoyed the excitement of being out at night and riding in an ordinary cab.

By the time Louise returned, the guests had begun to arrive. Louise let Hortense know by a nod of the head that the children were safe. The evening passed without incident. Though some of those present must have known what had happened, no one mentioned the news of the day. Later, Hortense learned that it was being said all over Paris that there had been a great celebration at her house, that toasts had been drunk and Bonapartist songs sung.

The following day there were many visitors. De Flahaut, Lavalette, and De Caulaincourt came—three perplexed and worried men. They were so used to seeing all that the Emperor touched turn to gold, that they couldn't believe Napoleon was insane, as some said, or that he would be tracked down like a wild beast. They wondered what their friend, de la Bédoyère, who was with his regiment at Grenoble, would do. Hortense advised them not to come to see her again, and to stay quietly at home.

A visitor, whom Hortense had not expected to see, was the Duc d'Otrante, otherwise Joseph Fouché. Napoleon's former Chief of Police lived next door to Hortense; his garden adjoined hers. They rarely met, however, for Hortense had never forgiven Fouché the part he played in her mother's divorce. Now, it seemed, they were allies. Fouché told Hortense that he was sure the Bourbon cause was lost, but for the moment, they were both in danger. Hortense was supposed to have been in direct communication with the island of Elba.

Fouché wanted two things. One was the key to Hortense's garden gate; he might have to make a quick escape if officers came to arrest him. He also wanted Hortense to communicate with the Russian chargé d'affaires and, through him, to send word to Alexander in Vienna, suggesting that it would be wise for Eugène to be sent to France to negotiate.

Hortense complied with both requests. News came from the south that Napoleon had reached Grenoble. Whenever, on his way from Cannes, he met a regiment, he would get out of his carriage and advance alone on foot. When he was within speaking distance of the first soldier, he would call out, "Don't you recognize me? Are you going to fire on your general?" He would be answered by shouts of *"Vive l'empereur!"* Charles de la Bédoyère had led his regiment into the Bonaparte camp, as had also Marshal Ney, who was sent to bring "the monster" back to Paris in a cage. As Napoleon had prophesied, in his first speech after landing, his eagle was flying "from steeple to steeple to the towers of Notre Dame."

Hortense was told by her royalist friends that her arrest was certain. On the 10th of March, she went to the house of a couple whose marriage she had arranged and who owed her much, but finding that they were afraid to harbor her, stayed but a single night. She was at home early the following morning. What should she do now? Hortense thought of a Negro maid, Mimi, who had come with Joséphine from Martinique and who had been Eugène's nurse. Mimi was pensioned by Joséphine and married to a Monsieur Lefebvre, a former usher at the Tuileries. She lived in the rue Duphot, at the corner of the boulevard.

It wouldn't be safe to wait until nightfall to go to Mimi's apartment, for the police might arrive at any moment. Adrien Cochelet, one of Louise's brothers, had come to see her. He offered, rather reluctantly, to be Hortense's escort. The spies, who were watching the house, had surely seen him enter and were probably familiar with the street clothes of Louise, who was constantly going out or coming in.

A few minutes later, Hortense, wrapped in an overcoat that

was much too big for her, since it had been tailored to fit the
buxom Louise, her golden hair hidden by Louise's hat, walked
out of the front door of the mansion, leaning on the arm of Adrien
Cochelet. Luckily it was raining, and a big umbrella gave protection as the pair scuttled past the watchers in the street. Hortense had not taken time to change her dress, and Adrien was
even more nervous than she, when he looked down and saw that
the lace of Hortense's morning gown was showing under the
hem of her coat.

They reached the rue Duphot safely and climbed to the fourth
story apartment of Monsieur and Madame Lefebvre. It consisted
of a parlor, a dining room, a bedroom and a large storage closet.
Mimi greeted Hortense with cries of joy and kisses. There was
no doubt of where her loyalty lay! The little apartment was decorated with mementos of the Beauharnais family. There was a
cabinet of china, in which Hortense recognized a coffee cup that
had belonged to her father and another that she herself had given
to Mimi when she was eight years old. Hortense could share the
bedroom with her old friend, while Monsieur Lefebvre would sleep
in the closet. There was an attic room on the floor above, where
Hortense could hide when the Lefebvres had company.

During the next nine days, Hortense spent a great deal of her
time in the attic, for the Lefebvres were sociable. From her
window, Hortense could look down on the boulevard. She could
see a recruiting station where volunteers, mostly very young or
very old, were signing up for a royalist army corps. The oldsters
looked as if they could hardly shoulder their equipment; the
youngsters strutted in their new uniforms and shouted, *"Vive
le roi!"* Very different was the look of a regular cavalry regiment
that passed by; its members failed to join in the shouts and stared
sternly and contemptuously ahead of them. They were probably
wondering if there were going to be a fight and if, in the end,
they might not be pitted against these noisy amateurs.

Mimi warned Hortense to keep very still, for the neighboring
apartment was occupied by royalists. She mustn't show herself at

the window, because across the way was the studio of a royalist painter.

Hortense was visited constantly by Louise, who, among other things, brought her a number of anonymous letters that had been delivered in the rue Cerutti, warning of plots to assassinate Napoleon. All of Hortense's friends were in hiding. De Caulaincourt had taken shelter with his cook; Lavalette had chosen Hortense's house as the place where nobody would think of looking for him. He had borrowed a wig and the butler's uniform.

Hortense also learned that the police had visited the house of the Duc d'Otrante. Fouché excused himself for a moment, ran out into the garden, climbed over the wall into Hortense's premises, and then discovered he had forgotten the key that Hortense had given him. He smashed the lock of the garden gate with a stone to let himself out into the street.

What was going on at the Tuileries was reported to Hortense by her *valet de chambre*, Vincent Rousseau, the son of her old nurse. Vincent's father-in-law was a royal mail carrier. He had witnessed the arrival of Napoleon at Lyon, and after his return to Paris was summoned to the palace to tell the King that he had seen Bonaparte greeted with wild enthusiasm. "My faith, sire," the mail carrier said disgustedly, "your nobility are very cowardly! I saw your brother [the Comte d'Artois] on his way home with only two gendarmes; all the rest had deserted him." At this, Louis XVIII groaned and covered his face with his hands, and Vincent's father-in-law was hustled out of the room by the courtiers.

The time in the attic began to seem long; Hortense's legs ached for exercise. In spite of Mimi's warnings, she found it hard to keep away from the window. On the morning of March 20th, she saw the royalist recruits about to march away and saying good-bye to their families. They were far less cocky than they had been at first. The royalist painter, opposite, appeared on his balcony. He no longer wore in his buttonhole a white rosette, the insignia of the Bourbons. He and his skinny wife, who seemed to be

giving him a vehement lecture, were dusting off a portrait of one
of Napoleon's ministers.

Something must have happened overnight. Hortense fretted
with impatience, until her man of affairs, Monsieur Devaux, came
to tell her that the King had fled. He advised Hortense to stay
where she was, for the present. There was no government; there
was no one to keep order in Paris today. Hortense, as she waited
for release, couldn't help feeling sorry for the King—old, fat,
and infirm, once more a wanderer. She wrote a letter to Louis,
thanking him for his kindness and telling him she had had no part
in Napoleon's return. She gave the letter to Louise Cochelet to
give to an officer in the King's bodyguard, who had not yet left
the city.

In the afternoon, Devaux came to conduct Hortense to the rue
Cerutti. They met no bands of bloodstained demonstrators. The
population of Paris was going quietly about its business, and the
only sign that there had been a change of dynasty was that shopkeepers on the boulevard were painting out the fleur-de-lis above
their doors and substituting eagles or golden bees.

It was said that the Emperor would enter the city before the
day was over. At seven o'clock Hortense went to the Tuileries.
The great garden of the palace was filled by a crowd that was
orderly, but ready for excitement. A cheer went up, as Hortense's
carriage appeared. The guard presented arms. Hortense realized
that the belief that she was responsible for Napoleon's return was
not restricted to the Bourbon court; it was universal.

The crush was as great within the palace as without. There
was hardly room to stand, in the state apartments. The ministers
were there, the military, many women. Julie Bonaparte, Joseph's
wife, who had not gone with him to Switzerland, arrived soon after
Hortense. As it grew dark, some of the sightseers in the garden
began to drift away. They remembered, perhaps, Napoleon's
habit of entering or leaving Paris in the small hours of the morning. Others, who knew that this was the fourth birthday of the

King of Rome and therefore a golden day in Napoleon's calendar, were sure that he would arrive before midnight.

At nine o'clock his carriage, with only three people in it, Napoleon and two of his aides, drew up before the entrance to his private apartments. There was a great push forward. For a moment, it seemed as if Napoleon might be crushed to death. He didn't walk up the staircase; he was carried up, shoulder high, by the close-packed crowd. Lavalette, a burly man, was walking backward before him and repeating, as if in a trance, "It's you, it's you, it's you."

After the first hubbub of excitement had died down, a way was cleared for Hortense and Julie to enter the room in which Napoleon was standing. He greeted them very coldly and said to Julie, "And how do *you* happen to be here?"

To Hortense he said, "Where are your children?"

"Sire, I have had to send them away from home. I ask your permission to bring them to you tomorrow."

"I see by the papers," Napoleon said, "that you lost your lawsuit. I could have told you that. In such cases, paternal authority counts for everything."

Without saying another word to either of his sisters-in-law, Napoleon went into his study, whither his ministers were summoned, one after the other, to speak to him. It was growing late, and Hortense, perturbed by the chilly reception she had received, wondered if she should go home without saying good-bye. De Caulaincourt, who was one of those priviledged to speak alone with the Emperor, came out of the study and told Hortense that Napoleon was very angry with her for having accepted the Duchy of Saint-Leu. While he was in Elba, Pauline and Madame Mère, who had come to share his exile, had done all they could to turn him against Hortense. De Caulaincourt had spoken a good word for her. He advised her to go home and to come back next morning with her children.

Early the next morning, Hortense sent for her two boys. They

had been enjoying a two weeks' holiday from lessons with Abbé
Bertrand, and were pleased when told that they were going to
see Uncle Emperor. Hortense's heart was beating painfully. All
the old fear that she had felt of her stepfather, when she was a
young girl and expected to be scolded by him, revived.

She found Napoleon alone. He was standing by an open window
and was gesturing a reply to the shouts of a crowd in the garden.
He gave Hortense one of his piercing looks of displeasure, but
he embraced the children as affectionately as of old. While the
boys remained at the window, looking out into the garden, Hortense and Napoleon walked up and down the room for some time,
without exchanging a word. At last Napoleon broke the silence.

"I would never have believed," he said, "that you would have
deserted my cause."

"Deserted your cause, sire," Hortense cried. "Why would I
want to do that, and how could I?"

"You had no right to fix the fate of my nephews without my
permission. Your husband has good reason to be angry with you."

"Sire, you don't know all the circumstances that made me stay
in France. My mother wanted me to stay. I was all that she had.
My husband, as you know, was no help to me. I could have no
confidence in his opinion. Where could I go?"

"With your brother."

But Hortense protested that she would not have been allowed
to go to Vienna with Eugène. The Czar of Russia was generous
and wanted to insure the future of her children. "How could I
refuse? Did anyone refuse the Duchy of Parma for your son?"

Napoleon winced. That was different, he said. Parma was an
independent principality. "You should not have stayed in France.
A piece of black bread by the roadside would have been better
than that. Don't think that your children would have benefitted.
They would have been gotten rid of somehow. You have behaved
like a child. When one has shared in the rise of a family, one
should share in its downfall."

Hortense began to cry, and acknowledged that she had made a great mistake. She thought that she was doing the right thing, in seeing that her children could stay in their native land.

"There, there, you see how it is! You haven't a single good excuse," Napoleon said more gently. "But you know that I have always been a good father to you. I want to forgive you. We will say no more about it."

Then he spoke of her mother and of wanting Joséphine's body to be buried in Saint-Denis, "but not now. Later, and without any fuss." He spoke of wanting Eugène to come from Vienna.

Other visitors were announced, came, and went. One of them was the Comte de Molé, to whom, Napoleon said, he had offered the foreign office, but who refused it. Hortense exclaimed that she had supposed, of course, he would appoint De Caulaincourt foreign minister. De Caulincourt had always stood strongly for peace; his nomination would prove to the world that the intentions of France were peaceful.

"Ah, so you talk politics nowadays!" Napoleon pinched Hortense's ear, a certain sign that she was back in favor. He dismissed her, saying that she could come to see him any evening she chose after dinner. He was about to review a parade of the troops in the Place du Corrousel.

Hortense, exhausted by her talk with Napoleon, would have been glad to go home, but her boys begged to stay for the parade. There had never been anything like it seen before, not even in the greatest days of the Empire. The streets leading to the square, the windows and roofs of the houses, every foothold, every toehold, was occupied. The spectators joined in the roars of "Long live the Emperor," as the soldiers took off their shakos and twirled them on the points of their bayonets. Conspicuous heroes were the little band that had come with Napoleon from Elba, deeply tanned by the southern sun, their clothes still white with dust gathered on their long march from the south.

When Hortense reached the rue Cerutti and was sitting down to dinner, she was joined by Charles de la Bédoyère. He told her of his motives in joining the Emperor. "If France can be independent," Charles said, "if the Emperor grants a liberal constitution, and if freedom is assured to all by law, then I will feel glad to have contributed something to the salvation of my country."

XXXI

A CENTURY OF DAYS

IN THE TEN MONTHS he spent at Elba, Napoleon put his little kingdom in order and made ready to receive his wife and child. With them, he might perhaps be reconciled to a life of quiet, of narrow horizons.

But Marie Louise did not come. If the wife of Napoleon could be said to have a will of her own, it was all against a reunion with her husband. Her promised Duchy of Parma had not yet been handed over to her. She had spent the summer visiting Aix and traveling in Switzerland. To guard against a sudden change of heart, that might lead her to Elba, her father and Metternich provided her with a male escort, a *chevalier d'honneur*, General Adam von Neipperg. Neipperg was almost forty, had lost his right eye in battle, and had a wife and five children, but the part of his face that was not concealed by a black silk patch was handsome; he had charming manners; he could play the piano. Before they returned to Vienna in September, Neipperg had become Marie Louise's lover.

Of this, Napoleon as yet knew nothing. He only knew that his "good Louise" had failed to respond to any of his urgent letters, not even when he sent one of his guards secretly to Aix to bring her back to him. He still had faith in her constancy. An important part of his plan in returning to France was based on Marie Louise's joining him, and bringing with her the King of Rome. Papa Francis might be lured again into an alliance with the country in which his daughter was Empress, to which his grandson was heir. If the worse came to the worst, Napoleon I could abdicate in favor of Napoleon II.

The day after the Emperor's arrival in Paris, De Caulaincourt came to Hortense and asked her to write an enticing letter to Marie Louise. She did so, and by the same courier sent a note she had written the night before to Eugène, telling him of Napoleon's reception at the Tuileries, and hoping that he was about to leave for France with the Empress. Later, Hortense learned from Napoleon that her courier was arrested at Stuttgart, that the letters were opened and read before the congress, which had already declared Napoleon an outlaw. The results were serious for Eugène. There was talk of his being sent to a prison in Hungary or Transylvania, and only the intervention of Alexander saved him.

To Alexander, Hortense wrote after she had had a call from Boutiakim, the Russian chargé d'affaires. He, and all the other representatives of foreign powers, had been stranded in Paris by the sudden exodus of the Bourbons. Boutiakim was afraid of being interned, until Napoleon gave him his passport. He was also given a document found among the papers of Louis XVIII, a secret treaty between England, France, and Austria against Russia and Prussia. It was hoped that it might cause greater dissension than already existed at Vienna.

Hortense's letter to Alexander showed that she had learned to talk the language of diplomacy. It was a plea to the Czar to be the friend of France. "The nation as a whole is for the Emperor," she wrote, "but it wants peace. He will be wise enough to bow to public opinion, for he has had proof—the Bourbons are a good example—that one cannot remain in power by running counter to the sentiment of the nation. That is my own political outlook, but it is one I am sure he will follow. . . . He promises a liberal constitution, the liberty of the press; he wants to satisfy all parties, and if he does not do so he cannot continue to rule."

While she waited for an answer that she hoped would be favorable, Hortense was kept busy by petitions, addressed to her by her royalist acquaintances, for favors from the Emperor. She went daily to the Tuileries. Napoleon, who had need of friends of every sort, was lenient and open-handed. He was ready to welcome those whom he had exiled, among them Madame de Staël and her sometime lover, Benjamin Constant. Constant, a liberal, who once had dubbed Napoleon a second Attila or Genghis Khan, was appointed a member of the committee to draw up the new constitution, modeled on the British system, with a Chamber of Peers and a Chamber of Deputies. These bodies had been in the one case appointed, in the other elected, and were in session before the writing of the constitution was finished.

As Hortense had feared, members of the Bonaparte Clan began to drift back to Paris, though some of them, notably Elisa, Pauline, and Jérôme's wife, Catherine, had not been nimble enough to elude the long and restraining arm of the allies. Joseph was the first to arrive, having escaped arrest in Switzerland by twenty-four hours. The next to appear was Lucien. He and Napoleon had met only once since that night in 1804, when Lucien hurled his watch on the floor and stamped upon it, prophesying that Napoleon and his empire would be smashed to pieces. With Lucien, many more republicans would rally to the new constitution. He was given a fraternal welcome, the title of Prince of France, and the Grand Cordon of the Legion of Honor.

Yet to come were Jérôme, Madame Mère, and Cardinal Fesch. Only Louis was absent, though Napoleon had put his name down for the Chamber of Peers and had written to him at Rome. Louis had set a price on his return: permission to divorce Hortense and thus to get full control of his children. Hortense was relieved to find that the Emperor was against divorce, but she shivered when he spoke of a reconciliation. Louis was older, he said, and would be more reasonable. When she told him that there was an insurmountable barrier between her and her husband, he told her not to be so childish.

Though she was thus left uncertain on what, to her, was the most important question, Hortense's relations with the Emperor were on their old, affectionate footing of father and child. He liked to chat with her about the past. He asked her why he was called Père Violette, and laughed when she told him about the language of flowers that had developed under the Bourbons. He told her in confidence that all of the army, up to the rank of captain, was for him; the rest might fear him, but he could not count upon them. Hortense asked him why, since he was trying to reconcile everyone, he didn't make a greater effort with women, who had a far greater influence on public opinion than he realized.

"I don't know what has got into the women," Napoleon said. "They talk of nothing but politics. In my time"—he spoke as if this were very long ago—"they were only interested in their clothes. Do you know that you are quite a personage nowadays? They talk about you in Paris with awe. They even say that you are the leader of a party, a conspirator."

Hortense lightly brushed aside the compliment. She was unable to admit, even to herself, that she had any interest in politics. Finding Napoleon in such a mellow mood, however, she ventured to speak about the Czar Alexander, of his kindness to her and Joséphine, of his desire for peace, of his repugnance to putting the Bourbons back upon the throne.

This put an end to their conversation. Napoleon gave Hortense a long, steady look. "The Emperor of Russia talked to you like that, did he?" he said. "If he did, he is a very deceitful man!"

〔▣〕

Spring had come to Paris with a rush. Napoleon moved to the Elysée Palace, where he could walk in the garden during the short respites he allowed himself from work. One day in April, he let Hortense know that he would like to visit La Malmaison, and told her whom to invite to meet him there. Hortense had not seen her mother's house since the death of Joséphine. She went out the night before to accustom herself to a place that seemed so empty now, so silent. The Emperor arrived at nine o'clock in the morning. With Hortense, he walked about the garden, which had never been more beautiful.

"How every spot recalls her to me!" he said. "I cannot believe that she isn't here."

Before he left, Napoleon wanted to see Joséphine's room. "You stay here," he said to Hortense. "It might be too painful for you."

When he returned, there were tears in his eyes. To Hortense, it seemed ironic that when they reached the Tuileries that evening, they found there Charles de Flahaut, who had been sent with a last vain appeal to Marie Louise and to her father. Like the courier whom Hortense had sent earlier to Eugène, De Flahaut got no farther than Stuttgart. Marie Louise had promised the congress that she would read no more of her husband's letters. The reply to Hortense's letter to Alexander came not to herself, but to Louise Cochelet, via Boutiakim. Three copies of the Czar's reply on the subject of Napoleon were enclosed. One was for Hortense, one for De Caulaincourt, and one for Louise:

"No peace, no truce, no reconciliation with that man. All of Europe shares this feeling. Without that man, what seems best for all, with no preferences shown. Once he is out of the way, there will be no war!"

And so, after all, there was to be a war, what all of France, all of Europe, feared the most. Napoleon had been preparing for it, as best he could. De Flahaut had been given an important job of reorganization at the War Department. There was fighting already in Italy, where Joachim Murat had attempted rashly, and against the advice of Caroline, to bring all of the peninsula under his control. He did great harm to Napoleon's attempt to placate Austria, by saying that Napoleon had egged him on. On May 2nd, he was beaten at Tolentino and fled to the south of France, while Caroline and her children, falling into the hands of General Neipperg, Marie Louise's cavalier, were carried off to Trieste as prisoners of Austria.

In France itself, there was a royalist revolt in La Vendée, near revolt in Brittany and in certain sections of the south. To dramatize a national unity that was far from firm, a great ceremony was arranged to celebrate the inauguration of the new regime. Delegates from the electoral districts of the provinces came to Paris for a week of festivities. At a reception, given by the Minister of the Interior, the chorus of the Paris Conservatory sang one of Hortense's ballads, that had a patriotic refrain. On June 2nd, thousands of spectators gathered in the Champ de Mars, where an altar had been set up. Mass was celebrated, and Napoleon, wearing his imperial robes and crown, swore to preserve the constitution. He was flanked by his brothers—Joseph, Lucien and Jérôme. In the tribune, directly behind his throne, were Hortense and her sons.

All of this pageantry was reminiscent of the ceremony that had taken place in this same spot more than twenty years earlier, when Louis XVI swore to obey the first constitution ever written for France. How much bloodshed and sorrow had followed that attempt to create a more reasonable and tranquil world! Hortense was heavy hearted. Joseph Fouché approached and asked her why she was so sad.

"After all this—war," she said.

"The Emperor has missed a great opportunity," Fouché replied. "I advised him to abdicate today. If he had done so, his son would reign and there would be no war."

Fouché, though he was back in office again as Minister of Police, was secretly corresponding with Metternich in Vienna, and his words echoed the ultimatum that Alexander had sent to Hortense.

The vanguard of the allied army, under Wellington and Blücher, had already arrived in Belgium. It was better to go to meet them there, before the Austrian and Russian contingents were ready to take the field. Even so, Napoleon's forces would be outnumbered two to one.

The day of departure was June 12th. The 11th was a Sunday, and the traditional family dinner party was held at the Elysée. All except Jérôme, who had already left for the army, were there. Napoleon was high spirited. Next Sunday, he said, he would be in Brussels. He was much more talkative than usual; he joked with Hortense's boys and with the two daughters of Joseph, Zenaïde and Charlotte, who were also present. Hortense felt, however, that his gaiety was forced. In the evening, the ministers came to say good-bye, and it was late when the informal reception broke up.

At four o'clock the next morning, Napoleon left for Waterloo. In the hurry of his final preparations, he had not forgotten Hortense. His parting gift to her was a letter, written two days earlier, giving her permission to live apart from her husband.

卍

During the following week, Hortense knew the fortunes of war only by what she read in the newspapers. Joseph, who was President of the Council of Ministers, and Lucien ignored her completely. On the 18th, the cannon of the Invalides thundered for a victory over Blücher at Ligny. On the 20th, Hortense had made an appointment with Benjamin Constant. He was to come to her house, and read to her and a few friends a little manuscript he had written some years earlier and expected soon to publish. It was a short novel, *Adolphe*, based on Constant's long and tumultuous love affair with Madame de Staël. Hortense was given a preview of what was to become a landmark in the history of psychological fiction.

As the tale drew to its conclusion, it became so pathetic that both the author and his audience were misty-eyed. The reading was interrupted when Hortense was called out of the room to speak to a gentleman who wanted urgently to see her. The gentleman was General Savary. Like the messenger, who in classic tragedy reports doom off stage, he told Hortense of the defeats at Quatre Bras and Mont-Saint-Jean. With a heroism that was worthy of a daughter of Joséphine, Hortense returned to the salon and, without telling anyone why she had left the room, listened to the concluding pages of *Adolphe*.

The following morning, she was at the Elysée. Napoleon had arrived at eight o'clock, haggard, weary from the physical punishment of the past three days. He had been suffering from an inflammation of the bladder, that made the long hours spent in the saddle torture. Since he was closeted with Joseph and Lucien and was about to go to a meeting of the Council of Ministers, Hortense could not see him. She spoke with General Bertrand and his wife, both of whom had been with Napoleon at Elba. The General thought there was some hope yet; the Emperor had sent his aides to rally the retreating army. The two women were sure that this was the end.

"Why did we ever leave Elba?" Madame Bertrand moaned. "What will become of the Emperor now?"

Hortense was so restless that she felt she must do something, even if it were only to send her carriage to wait for her at the Place de la Concorde and to walk down the Champs Elysées with Louise Cochelet. As they passed the walled garden of the palace, they saw a woman, very gaily and elaborately dressed, speaking to the sentinel, a *cocotte* trying to lure the guard off duty. Hortense heard the woman say, "They are deceiving you. He is lost forever. He has abandoned his army." The soldier's reply was, "Go away! I will never desert him!"

At six o'clock, Hortense returned to the palace. Napoleon was alone in the garden. She hurried toward him, with arms outspread. He recoiled from her pity. "What on earth have they been telling you?" he asked.

"Only that you have been very unfortunate, sire."

For a few minutes he said nothing, and then beckoned Hortense to come back with him into his study. He dropped down in his chair by the desk, as though utterly exhausted. He picked up a packet of letters, slit them open, but did not have the energy or curiosity to read them. A servant came to tell him that dinner was ready. Napoleon asked Hortense to keep him company. There was comfort in her presence, apparently, though during the meal he spoke hardly a word, and immediately after was called into conference with Lucien and Joseph.

From others, Hortense learned of the burden that the day's events had laid upon Napoleon. He had come home to ask for dictatorial powers from the chambers created by the constitution. An opposition party had developed in the Chamber of Deputies. It was led by an old warrior for democracy, the one time Marquis de Lafayette. On his motion, the Chamber declared itself in permanent session and asked for protection by the National Guard.

While Hortense was with Napoleon, Lucien and the Minister of War visited the Chamber of Deputies and tried to convince them that defense was possible. A motion calling for abdication was made by a Deputy who was a stooge for Joseph Fouché. The allies, he said, would make peace with France, but never with Napoleon.

Lucien rose to protest. He was once more the spell-binder, the orator who, fifteen years earlier, had sparked the coup d'état of Brumaire. His passionate plea for the nation not to desert its great leader was having its effect. However, he made the mistake of saying that if France failed Napoleon now, it could be accused of faint heart and fickleness.

Lafayette was quick to retort. "That's a calumny!" he cried. "No one can charge the French with fickleness toward Napoleon. They have followed him through the sands of Egypt and the deserts of Russia. Because they have followed him, they have had to mourn the death of three million Frenchmen!"

There was long applause. When Lucien came back to the Elysée to report his lack of success and to urge a coup d'état with bayonet and beat of drum, Napoleon was too weary to make up his mind. It was not until the following day and after another meeting of the Council that he asked Lucien to sit down at his desk and write a message to the chambers at his dictation. When Lucien realized that the message was an abdication, he threw down his pen. There was silence in the room. Shouts of *"Vive l'empereur!"* could be heard from the street. Lucien would only continue writing when Napoleon added a clause declaring that he was yielding the throne to his son, Napoleon II.

On this subject, there was more furious debate in both chambers. In the Peers, De la Bédoyère, De Flahaut, and others spoke with fervor for a regency, but without effect. The matter was left undecided; a temporary government commission was chosen; Joseph Fouché was elected as its president.

From the street, cries of *"vive l'empereur"* still continued to sound. People climbed over the low wall of the Elysée garden when Napoleon was walking there and, with tears in their eyes, begged him not to abandon them. It would have taken only a word to have set a mob marching on the chambers, as in the bloodiest years of the Revolution.

Hortense, who spent all her days now at the Elysée, was worried by the Emperor's torpor. He seemed, once his decision had been made, to be indifferent to his own fate. Hortense took her courage in her hands, for she had never ventured to advise him before, and told him that he must make up his mind to something. If he wanted to go to America—an idea that she herself favored— he should go at once to a port, before all ports were closed to him. If he were going to surrender to one of the allies individually, he should make his choice, before they took concerted action. She would like to see him write to the man who had once been his friend, the Czar of Russia.

Napoleon listened without comment to what she had to say, and asked her what she expected to do.

"Oh, don't think about me, sire," Hortense cried, vexed by his indifference. "Think about yourself. The very worst suggestion I have made is better than doing nothing!"

The following day, the 24th of June, Napoleon said that he would like to go with Hortense to La Malmaison.

◫◫◫◫◫◫◫◫◫◫◫◫

XXXII

IN JOSÉPHINE'S HOUSE

THERE was outcry from Hortense's household, when she told them that she was going to La Malmaison with the Emperor. This would confirm all rumors; this would bring reprisals if, as seemed likely now, the Bourbons should return. But Hortense knew that she was compromised already, and nothing could keep her from comforting Napoleon as long as he had need of her. She felt that she had taken her mother's place, and was touched that he wished to find refuge in Joséphine's house.

Again she must hide her children. The same lady who had sheltered them in March offered to take them again, but Hortense didn't want to impose on her friend's generosity a second time. The children would be safer in an obscure hideout. She sent them to a woman from whom she bought her stockings and who owned a house on the boulevard Montmartre.

Hortense set off at once for La Malmaison. Napoleon had said that he didn't want to occupy Joséphine's room. For his use, Hortense made ready the farther wing of the château. She told him that there he could be alone as much as he wished, but she would be ready at any moment to come at his call.

Napoleon arrived on the morning of June 25th, and later Joseph, Lucien, and Jérôme, who, for once, had fought with real and surprising valor at Quatre Bras, came to see him. A number of young officers had followed the Emperor. They took counsel in Hortense's salon as to how they should protect the house from a royalist attack. A round-the-clock guard was set. None of Hortense's male guests went to bed that night.

In the morning, Napoleon sent for Hortense to come to him in the garden. This was the place in which the ghost of Joséphine walked.

"Poor Joséphine, how strange it seems," Napoleon said, "to be living here without her! I think every moment that I am going to see her appear on one of the garden paths, picking the flowers that she loved so much."

He saw how sad an impression his words had made on Hortense. "But," he added, "she would be unhappy now. . . . There was only one thing about which we ever really quarreled, and that was her debts. How I used to scold her! She had more allure than anyone else I have ever known. She was a woman to her fingertips—all that that implies—so quick, so gay, and so kind-hearted. You must have another picture of her painted for me. I would like it to be a medallion."

That afternoon the brothers and Madame Mère, who seemed much afflicted, came to stay. More of the military arrived, among them Lavalette, De Flahaut, and De Bédoyère. News came also of a plot to assassinate the Emperor. It was said that five hundred royalists would march on La Malmaison, and the night watch was doubled. Hortense wondered how she would behave, if blood should flow in her mother's house. She had lived on the fringe of combat all her life, but had never actually seen it.

The young men who surrounded the Emperor wanted—and more than half-expected—that he would put himself in command of the French army that was returning from Belgium. The wiser heads knew that it was much too late for that. Hortense spoke repeatedly to Joseph about Napoleon's leaving while there was yet time. She suggested that he should slip away in disguise, with a forged passport, to Le Havre, while she continued to hold the fort at La Malmaison, as if he were still there.

But Napoleon's lethargy—so strange, so out of character—continued. The temporary government, that was as anxious as Hortense to see him go, sent word that two frigates were waiting for him at La Rochelle. Charles de Flahaut went to Paris to get the details from the Minister of War, General Davout, who had been one of Napoleon's marshals. There were high words between the two men, when the Minister threatened to arrest Napoleon if he didn't leave.

"I am not surprised to hear that kind of talk from someone whom I have often seen licking the dust before the Emperor's feet!" Charles said with scorn. He was ready to give Davout his resignation from the army on the spot.

Napoleon, when he heard of the interview, merely shrugged his shoulders and said that if Davout wanted to arrest him, he should come to do it in person.

On the second day of his stay Napoleon sent for Hortense at noon. Again he was in the garden, and with him was a man, a stranger, and a beautiful boy, who was nine or ten years old. Napoleon drew Hortense aside.

"Hortense, look at that boy. Whom does he resemble?"

"He is your son, sire. He's the very image of the King of Rome."

"You think so? Then it must be so. I didn't realize that I was so sentimental, but at sight of him I felt a great emotion. You seem to know all about his origins. Who told you?"

Hortense had heard—was it perhaps from Caroline—of the child that Napoleon had had by Eléonore Dénuelle, Caroline's protégée and her friend at Madame Campan's school. "Sire, it was much talked of," she said discreetly. "His likeness proves that the talk was true."

"I was not quite sure that he was my child," Napoleon continued, "but I sent him to a boarding school in Paris. The man who has charge of him wrote me to ask what my intentions were. I wanted to see the boy and, like you, I was struck with his looking so much like the King of Rome."

"What are you going to do with him?" Hortense asked. "I would be glad to take charge of him myself, but that might lead to more hateful gossip."

"Yes, you are quite right," Napoleon said. "I would like to think that he was with you, but everyone would say that he was your child as well as mine. When I have established myself in America, I will send for him."

Napoleon went to speak with the boy's tutor and Hortense to talk with Léon Dénuelle. She asked him if he liked his boarding school and what sort of games he played. The boy said that for some time now he and his friends had been playing war. There were two sides, one called the Bonapartists and the other the Bourbonists.

Hortense asked which side Léon was on. "The King's side," he said.

"And why is that?"

"Because I like the King, and I don't like the Emperor."

Hortense pressed him for a reason for not liking the Emperor.

"There isn't any reason," Léon said. "It's just because I am on the other side." He apparently had no idea of the identity of the short, stout man, whom he had just met in the garden.

All during the lunch that Hortense ate with Napoleon, he spoke of how much he had been moved by seeing his bastard son. Behind his words Hortense sensed his resentment, directed, not at Marie Louise, but at the Austrian government, for having withheld his child. Although Napoleon had mentioned Napoleon II in his abdication message, he could not believe that France would consent to be governed by a four-year-old boy, who was prisoner of a foreign power.

There was to be yet another reminder of the absent King of Rome. As soon as she awoke on the morning of June 28th, Hortense was told that Madame Walewska, Napoleon's "Polish wife," who had also visited him at Elba, had arrived at an early hour. Hortense asked the little Countess, still pretty, still fresh and virginal, to come to her room. Maria and her son had already seen Napoleon. Her eyes were so red with weeping that Hortense kept the young woman with her until she was ready to face the world again.

Hortense herself, on coming downstairs, learned that all was set for departure the following day. The frigates were ready at La Rochelle. Napoleon was in the stableyard, inspecting the traveling carriage that the government had sent for his use. He found it so dilapidated that he decided to travel in a small *calèche.* Hortense spoke to him of money. He had little with him, and she insisted that he should take a string of her diamonds. She would sew them into a belt that he could wear about his waist. The diamonds were his, she said, since he had given them to her, but he, in his turn, insisted that she should take a note for 200,000 francs.

He told her definitely that he was going to the United States. In time she must come there also. "It will be the only thing for your children," he said. "If the Bourbons come back to the throne, they will stay on it for a much longer time than you think."

While they were talking, they heard a great shouting on the highway. They walked in that direction; all who were on watch in the château came running. Some hundred soldiers were marching by on their way to Saint-Germain. As they passed the gate of La Malmaison they shouted, *"vive l'empereur,"* and threw their caps in the air.

"It's not cheers I need; it's deeds," Napoleon said. He went back quickly to the house before he was recognized.

There were many farewells throughout the day. Hortense sent for her boys to be brought from the boulevard Montmartre, to say good-bye to Uncle Emperor. In the late afternoon, she and General Bertrand's wife, who was planning again to follow her husband and Napoleon, walked for a long while in the garden. It was very still; the air was so perfumed, the play of light and shadow so enchanting, that it was hard to believe there could be any trouble in such a place. Hortense and her companion sat down on a bench to rest. Presently they saw the Emperor coming toward them. As though he, too, were weary, he dropped down beside them.

"How beautiful La Malmaison is," he murmured. "How happy we would be, Hortense, if we could stay here forever!"

Hortense did not trust herself to speak. Never before had she heard Napoleon express attachment to any particular place. The world was his home. His restless spirit did not feel the pull of earth. If he felt it now, it was only because La Malmaison represented the past toward which he yearned. Here, his flight to glory had begun; here, he had been strong, and youth and strength had both seemed limitless.

His mood could change, however, without warning. Early the next day Hortense received a letter from Louise Cochelet, that was brought to her by Vincent Rousseau. Louise was panic-stricken. The Prussian army was so close to Paris she was afraid that it might have reached La Malmaison, or that it lay between the château and the city. The bridge over the Seine, that Hortense would have to cross on her return, was already barricaded.

Hortense hurried to Napoleon's study, where he was talking to Joseph. The Emperor took her news very calmly. Things were not as serious as she supposed, he said, but it might be a good idea for her to go back to Paris now, and to take all the women with her. Hortense had no intention of leaving before he did, but she begged him to go at once. He had everything to fear from the Prussians.

"Why, what could they do to me?" he asked.

He shrugged his shoulders, when she said that they might kill him, but he sent one of his aides to reconnoiter in the neighborhood. The man returned to report that the Prussians were in a village nearby, and had set a bridge on fire. From the windows of La Malmaison one could see the smoke.

The light of battle kindled in Napoleon's eyes. He turned to De Flahaut and Lavalette. "Go to the provisional government,"

he said. "Tell them that I can still unite the army, halt the enemy
advance, and give time for the government to bargain for the
rights and liberties that they are certain to lose. I promise, on my
honor as a general, a citizen, and a soldier, that I will leave on the
very day that I have saved the capital."

The two messengers hurried off. Hortense had no sooner seen
them gallop away, than she began to count the minutes until their
return. Every moment of delay was a moment lost. She was
alarmed by the talk of the young men who were going to travel
with the Emperor. They were prepared to resist any attack, any
insult, from the Prussians. One of them, Colonel Gourgaud, said
that, if necessary, he would kill Napoleon himself rather than let
him fall into the hands of his enemies.

The post horses, that had been engaged for the journey, arrived, but still there was no word from Paris. In the early afternoon De Flahaut returned. He had had no success at the war office.

"Why not?" Napoleon asked. "Are they still afraid of me?"
He rose to his feet. "Since they have refused, let us go. . . . I
wanted to make a last effort to save France, but they have thrown
it away."

He went into his room with Joseph, and when he returned
they saw that he had taken off his uniform and had put on a plain
gray overcoat. He kissed Hortense's tear-wet cheeks. He said a
Spartan good-bye to his mother, his brothers, to all who would be
left behind. They were gathered at the door, to see him go down
the steps. Before he plunged into the dark hole of his carriage,
Napoleon turned to take a last look at La Malmaison, its ivory-
tinted walls mellowed by the gentle light of afternoon.

Now, at last, he would be safe. Hortense was almost light-
hearted. Her own problems had been neglected for the past four
days. Before leaving the château, she walked through its picture
gallery and remembered that these paintings were an important
part of the inheritance of herself and of her children. She should
have given orders for them to be packed up and sent to some
safe place; now it was too late.

Hortense, Madame Bertrand, and two other ladies, who had made themselves useful during the Emperor's stay, drove back to Paris by a roundabout route, that led through Saint-Cloud. The bridge over the Seine at Neuilly had been closed to traffic and was guarded by Prussian soldiers.

XXXIII

THE HUNTED

IN THE rue Cerutti they had almost given Hortense up for lost. They thought that she had been captured by the enemy. After her return on June 29th, Hortense stayed close within her own four walls, but had little time for her personal concerns. In this hour of defeat, she, rather than Napoleon's flesh and blood, had become the rallying point of the Bonaparte cause.

Hortense had hardly had a good night's sleep when, on June 30th, she was visited by an old-guard republican, a man she had never seen before. He said that he represented a group of colonels of the French army, that was encamped just outside of Paris. There was a movement afoot to capture the provisional government and recall the Emperor. Was it really true that Napoleon had left La Malmaison?

Hortense assured the man that by now the Emperor was far away. She combated the idea of an army coup d'état. There were good men in the government, she said; De Caulaincourt was one. She believed that even Fouché, whom her visitor said should be hung as a traitor, would never surrender France to the enemy. There had been talk of offering the throne to the Duc d'Orléans, who was more popular than his cousins of the elder branch of

the Bourbons, or else to some foreign prince: a brother of the
Czar, the Prince of Orange, or the King of Saxony. Hortense
was told that Eugène's name had been mentioned in the Chamber
of Deputies, but she said she was sure that her brother would not
accept for himself; he would uphold the claims of the King of
Rome.

On July 2nd, there was fighting near Versailles between the
French and Prussians, in which the Prussians were defeated;
to Hortense it seemed a tragic, senseless bloodletting. The following day, the French army marched in orderly fashion through
Paris, headed for the valley of the Loire. That evening, Hortense's
house was full of officers who urged her to go with them; they
would protect her from every danger. Hortense declined this
madcap offer, with thanks. Sooner or later, she said, she would
have to leave France. She would go to Joséphine's house at Prègny
on the Lake of Geneva, and to do so, she would have to get a
passport from the allies.

One curious suggestion made her seemed to imply that she
was practically in command of the French army. A certain Baron
Hyde de Neuville, who had been accused of complicity in the
gunpowder plot to assassinate Napolen in 1800, sent her a list
of French generals, all of them her friends. If she would undertake to get them all to sign a pledge of allegiance to the Bourbons,
De Neuville said, no harm would come to her.

Hortense had not considered the possibility of bodily harm,
until, on July 6th, Louis XVIII arrived at Saint-Denis. In the
afternoon Hortense was in her garden, when a procession of cabs
passed by in the street, filled with rowdy royalists going out to
greet the King. They recognized Hortense, brandished fists, and
shouted curses. It seemed as if they were going to leap out of
their carriages and swarm over the wall on which she was leaning.

Hortense retired quickly to the house. Her neighbor, Fouché,
sent word that it was unsafe for her stay where she was. In the
name of a Russian acquaintance, Hortense rented the ground
floor of a house in the rue Taibout, just behind her own. There,

she and the children spent several days in complete seclusion, visited only by Louise Cochelet, who reported that stories were current of Queen Hortense having been seen in the poorer sections of the city, where she was inciting the workers to revolt.

It was not until the allied armies entered the city on July 10th and Prince Schwarzenberg selected Hortense's house as his head-quarters, that she felt it prudent to return. She expected no callers and was startled when De la Bédoyère, wearing civilian clothes and dark glasses, walked into her room. She thought that he had either joined the army on the Loire or had left the country. He told her that he had been in Paris with his wife and child. Prussian soldiers were quartered in his house, and there was so much shouting and thumping overhead that he went upstairs to complain of the noise.

"Do you want to be arrested?" Hortense cried.

She begged him not to be so rash and to get out of Paris immediately. When she first met him, he told her that he wanted to live dangerously, but that was nine years ago and he was hardly more than a boy. Now he was a man, a married man with a family to consider.

"Your're right," De la Bédoyère said. "I mustn't let myself be be taken. I would be condemned to death, and then they would pardon me because of my wife's family. I don't want that kind of pardon! They [the Bourbons] are going to do a lot of harm in France, but her defenders are not all dead, and I will be among those who will deliver her."

This sort of exalted talk filled Hortense with fears for her friend. She had noted the effect that the fall of the Emperor had had upon his devotees. They had all become a little fey; they had lost touch with reality.

She herself was making preparations for departure, dismissing all but a few of her servants, selling her horses and also some of her paintings, for she was in need of ready money. From Fouché, she got passports for Switzerland. He told her that Louis XVIII had spoken kindly of her and said that he didn't believe all those stories about the Duchesse de Saint-Leu; if she went away for a short time she would be able to return. Hortense felt that she could not count on the old man's indulgence. Louis was too deeply in debt to the allies to be a free agent.

The most powerful man in Europe now was the Czar Alexander. From her scout, Louise Cochelet, Hortense learned of his arrival in Paris, his figure in the military procession eclipsing all others. Should she, the partisan of a lost cause, receive him if he came to call? There was no need to debate this delicate point. The Czar came to see Prince Schwarzenberg and, though he must have known that the mistress of the house was there, he did not ask for her. His attitude was revealed to Hortense by Maria Walewska, who had gone to see Alexander to interest him in the fate of Madame Mère. Alexander said impatiently, "How can you expect me to show consideration for any of that family? Look at Queen Hortense! I protected her in 1814, and yet she has been the cause of all the misfortunes that have befallen her country."

In an article that appeared in the *Moniteur*, Hortense's name was listed among the enemies of France, but she was much more deeply wounded by Alexander's accusation. Alexander was her friend. She had established relations with him on the plane that she valued above all others. Those delightful conversations she had had with him, walking under the great trees of Saint-Leu or in the gardens of La Malmaison, his delicate sympathy at the time of her mother's death, the confidences given and received— did none of this mean anything to the Emperor of Russia?

Hortense made a bundle of the letters Alexander had written her during the past year, and sent them to him, saying that she no longer wished to keep them, since she no longer believed in the expressions of friendship they contained. There was no written reply, only a call from Boutiakim, Alexander's man, who told her how angry the Czar was with her for having assayed a political role. There was no reply at all to a long letter that Hortense wrote, defending her actions in detail. When a newspaper paragraph announced that the Czar had visited the Duchesse de Saint-Leu,

there was a curt, printed denial that there had been any communication between them.

On July 17th, Hortense was notified that she must leave the
city within two hours. The order came from the new Prefect of
Police, who, oddly enough, happened to be Monsieur Décazes,
Louis' former agent, with whom Hortense had had so many con-
ferences. She was told that she would be guarded to the gates of
Paris, and Schwarzenberg deputed a handsome young Austrian,
Count Woyna, to go with her to her destination.

Just as Hortense was getting into her carriage, she received a
confidential warning that she must take no valuables with her,
for she might be robbed during her journey. She left all of her
jewelry with Louise Cochelet, who was staying behind for a
few days and would join her at Geneva. While driving out of the
city, Hortense noticed that mounted soldiers were stationed at
intervals along the boulevards. This was the guard of which
she had been told, but there was no sign of hostility.

On the third day, the train of carriages entered Dijon, where
some Austrian troops were quartered. Hortense was going upstairs in the inn, when a woman's head popped out of a door;
Hortense heard her say to someone in the room behind her,
"Here she comes!" Count Woyna went out to see the sights of
the town; Hortense was talking with an Austrian captain to whom
Woyna had introduced her, when three French officers, wearing
the uniform of the King's bodyguard, clumped into the room.

"Madame," one of them said, "we have orders not to let you
leave this town."

"Very well then, gentlemen, I'll stay." Hortense was cool; not
so the Austrian captain.

"Who do you think is in command here?" he bawled. "*I* am!
And Madame can leave whenever she chooses!"

The Frenchmen retired, but soon a crowd, made up mostly of
old men, children and a few well-dressed women of Dijon's demi-
monde, gathered about the inn to shout, "*Vive le roi!*" When
Woyna returned, the crowd was dispersed; only the guardsmen

remained. Throughout the evening, they took turns in picketing Hortense's carriage and in drinking noisily in the tavern. Their commander, who was little more than a boy, marched up and down before the inn, letting his saber rattle against the paving stones.

Hortense guessed that these were the robbers against whom she had been warned in Paris. In the morning, Woyna went to see a French general, who had just arrived to take over the command of Dijon. The new commandant had received no instructions to arrest the Duchesse de Saint-Leu, but not wanting to run into trouble with the Paris high command, called a review of the troops, in which all of the military, including the guardsmen, would have to take part. When Hortense walked to her carriage through a line of Prussian soldiers, only the youthful commander was left, almost in tears to see that his victim was escaping him.

"I'll send a courier to Paris," he shouted after Woyna. "You will have to answer for my orders not being carried out. A woman who has done us so much harm—to let her go free, it's a crime!"

Hortense noticed that the townsfolk were unimpressed by his antics; they looked at her with silent sympathy. At the next stop, there were active signs of partisanship. Red carnations were thrown into the carriage. Tears stood in the eyes of a woman who shouted out in her rough, peasant voice, "Can you believe it! It's enough to make you puke the way the good ones go and the bad ones stay!"

A man, wearing a blouse, standing at the gate of his farmyard, took up the theme. "Yes, we have to give in now," he said, "but our day will come, the day when the lion will awake."

For the first time in all of her journeys, Hortense was relieved when she crossed the frontiers of France.

◫

Meanwhile, in Paris, Louise Cochelet was doing what she could to help her friend and patron.

When the Czar entered Paris, he brought in his train the

Baroness von Krüdener, the religious enthusiast with whom Hortense and Louise had associated at Baden in the summer of 1814. There was a pronounced strain of guilt and melancholy in Alexander's psyche. The curse of the Romanovs was upon him, for he had ascended the throne over the body of his murdered father. He might be, as Napoleon had said, "a very deceitful man," but the most sincere words he had ever spoken to Hortense were those concerning his religious strivings.

Alexander was going through a period of deep depression when, on his way to France with his army, he was visited by the prophetess at Heilbronn. For three hours, Juliane von Krüdener preached her doctrine of salvation, while Alexander sat sobbing, with his face hidden in his hands. At the end, he told his visitor that he had "found peace." He accepted the Krüdener dictum that God had sent her to him.

In Paris, the Baroness was installed in a house behind the Elysée Palace, which Alexander had taken over. Every evening he would cross the intervening gardens, with only a single Cossack following at his heels, and would spend several hours with his spiritual adviser. Alexander wished to keep these tête-a-têtes secret, but it was soon noticed that he, who had been so worldly at the time of his earlier visit, was never seen at social gatherings. When the reason was known, all of intellectual and high society in Paris wanted to meet Madame von Krüdener and to be present at her religious gatherings.

Louise Cochelet, rather than Hortense, had been the lady's friend at Baden, and had kept in touch with her. On the very day after Hortense left Paris, Louise went to call on the Czar's adviser and was affectionately received. When Louise spoke of Hortense, the Baroness said that she knew there had been a misunderstanding between the Queen and Alexander, but that she was sure it was only a passing shadow. Alexander was so good, so noble, a soul "worthy of heaven." Louise must come to see him at the time of one of his nocturnal visits.

Louise jumped at the chance. In advance she was nervous,

thinking that only a year ago the Czar had sat upon her sofa, drunk her tea, and chatted with her as cozily as though he were a neighbor who had just dropped in. How would she find him now?

She found him very cold and stiff, every inch the monarch. Both he and Louise remained standing throughout the interview. Alexander only relaxed a trifle when, in pleading Hortense's cause, Louise said that Hortense had acted as a woman and not as a politician when she consoled Napoleon at La Malmaison. Alexander offered to send Hortense's diamonds safely to her in Switzerland, but this was not the sort of service—a trifle for a man in his position—for which Louise was angling. She thanked the Czar, but said that the diamonds were to be left with the Queen's lawyer in Paris, where they could be sold as necessity arose.

Though so little had been accomplished, Louise thought it just as well to keep the Russian line of communication open. She went to kiss Madame von Krüdener good-bye, just before leaving Paris in company with Abbé Bertrand and her brother Carli, who, having been an army paymaster, was out of work. Louise found that Hortense had run into fresh trouble at Geneva. The authorities would give her only a short-term visa; she could not live at Prègny. She had seen briefly Cardinal Fesch and Madame Mère, who, passing through to Italy, were not allowed to stop over even for a few hours' rest.

Hortense had decided to go to Aix-en-Savoie, where she had spent so much time in the past, where Adèle de Broc had met her death by drowning. While Hortense waited there, her Austrian guardian, Count Woyna, who was now her champion and thought she was being unjustly persecuted, would go back to Paris for fresh instructions.

At Aix, Hortense rented the only house that was available at the height of the season. It was ugly and badly situated, but it had a large courtyard, where the Bonaparte boys and some friends they made in the neighborhood could play soldiers. Hortense's friends of better days, when the Queen of Holland was the most sought-after member of the resort colony, avoided her.

There was one friend who had not forgotten her. As in the past, Charles de Flahaut appeared suddenly and without warning. Again, he offered to devote his life to Hortense in any way that she wished, as husband or as lover. Both realized, however, that this was not the moment to join forces. They were being closely watched and must not remain together long. After only a day in Aix, Charles moved across the border into Switzerland, where he could communicate easily with Hortense. His visit to her was noted by the police and was mentioned in a French newspaper article, saying that the Duchesse de Saint-Leu was surrounded by a group of army officers, with whom she was plotting mischief. It was also reported that she was drilling soldiers in her court-yard, the sound of the boys' toy drum having been heard beyond its walls.

By this time the fate of Napoleon was known: his surrender to the British, his transportation to Saint Helena. In France, his followers were being hunted down. On July 24th, an ordinance was passed that would put under police surveillance all who had had government employ during the Hundred Days. A long list of military men was summoned to appear before a court martial. De Flahaut's name was omitted, out of deference to Talleyrand, but not the name of his cousin, Charles de la Bédoyère.

On one of his stolen trips to Paris, De la Bédoyère again courted danger by riding in a public conveyance. He was recognized and denounced to the police by a man who had been his valet. As foretold to Hortense De la Bédoyère was condemned to death. No pardon was forthcoming, but, with the connivance of Talleyrand, the prisoner was given a chance to escape, which he refused to take. On August 19th, he fell before a firing squad.

With less sense of personal loss, but still with horror, Hortense heard of the death of Joachim Murat. He had tried to imitate Napoleon, by landing with a few companions on the shores of Calabria, but he met with no popular support in what had once been his kingdom. Captured on the seashore, as he was trying to launch a boat for escape, he was sentenced to death as a disturber of the peace, under a law that he had himself promulgated. At the last, Murat showed the courage that was his when charging the enemy on the battlefield. He wrote a brave letter of farewell to Caroline and, facing his executioners with eyes uncovered, gave the order to fire himself.

Charles de Flahaut, who had brought some of this ill news to Aix, was not allowed to stay in Switzerland very long. He went back to France, to Lyon. Some letters addressed to him came to Hortense. She didn't want to risk sending them on to him unless they were important, and opened one. It was a letter from an actress, Mademoiselle Mars, a passionate love letter.

Hortense was thrown into a nervous fever. She had almost persuaded herself that she and Charles might someday be happy, if they could find a spot to lay their heads, but here she was faced again by the problem of the Other Woman. There had always been another woman: Charles's Polish countesses, Caroline, Madame Alfred de Noailles, now Mademoiselle Mars. Hortense realized that she, perhaps, expected too much of masculine devotion—but why had Charles again deceived her? If he had told her of this entanglement, she felt that she could have forgiven him.

She wrote a letter of reproach, while she was still too angry to choose her words. Charles's reply was desperate. He said that he wished a bullet had found him at Waterloo. He swore again that she was the real love of his life, and that his liaison with Mademoiselle Mars had been prolonged only because the actress threatened to tell Hortense if he should leave her. Charles wanted to come to Aix, in spite of the danger to them both, but this Hortense would not allow.

Indecision had always been a torture to her. The distance that lay between them, the time that it took for letters to travel back and forth added to her miseries. Hortense wanted Charles's affection too much not to have moments of weakness. She was suffering from nervous indigestion and occasional cataleptic seizures, such as those that followed the death of Napoléon Charles, when she had yet another shock. In the last week of September, the chamberlain of Louis' household in Rome and Monsieur Briatte, Louis' lawyer in Paris, converged on Aix. They had come for Napoléon Louis; the chamberlain to take him to Italy, the lawyer to see that the deed was done.

There was nothing to do but yield. Hortense was saved from complete collapse by having to nurse and comfort her remaining child. Seven-year-old Louis, who had thrived on the excitement and uncertainties of the past twelve months and more, was so upset by the parting with his brother that he fell sick and developed a case of jaundice. Before he was completely well, Hortense was told that she would have to leave Savoy. She heard from Charles de Flahaut that, though he was going to escape from the poisoned atmosphere of France to England, he would come to her as soon as she had found a resting place. But where, she wondered, would that be? She felt as if every door in Europe were closed against her.

XXXIV

A RESTING PLACE

THE town of Constance, standing on the left bank of the Rhine, just as it issues from the Lake of Constance, was, in 1815, in a state of picturesque dilapidation. It had its memories of famous events: of Friederich Barbarossa, of the Great Council of all of Christendom, and of John Huss, burned at the stake; but now its medieval splendors and cruelties were only legendary. Its streets were almost empty of traffic; when Hortense first saw them, on a December afternoon, they were covered with snow. Hortense had suffered cruelly from the cold on her way from Aix.

To reach Constance, she had had to pass through Switzerland. To save expense, she spent a night at Prègny, and was awakened at cockcrow by a call from the police, who searched the house from top to bottom, hunting for French generals. One of Hortense's maids unfortunately had a very masculine appearance, and Louise Cochelet had great difficulty persuading the gendarmes that this was not Joseph Bonaparte in disguise—Joseph, who at the moment was in America. There were other gendarme incidents along the route; Hortense was held prisoner for two days in a dirty unheated inn just outside of Berne. That she was able to accomplish her journey at all was due to Louise's having courted Madame Krüdener in Paris. The Russian Ambassador at Berne was a son of the prophetess, and saw that Hortense was allowed to continue on her way. She carried with her a passport, signed by Alexander and by others of the Allied Council, giving her permission to reside at Constance.

The paper was put to immediate use. Constance was just within the borders of the Grand Duchy of Baden. Hortense wrote to the Duke, the husband of her cousin Stéphanie de Beauharnais, to tell him of her arrival. A court chamberlain came from the capital at Karlsruhe to say politely that Hortense must move on. He brought a sad little note from Stéphanie, expressing her sorrow that politics should be allowed to interfere with kinship. Her husband, as Hortense knew well, was under great pressure from his family to put Stéphanie aside. Not wishing to do so, he had to make at least a formal gesture of banishing Stéphanie's undesirable relatives. Luckily, the passport issued by the Czar impressed the local authorities. Hortense was told that she could remain for the present, but not indefinitely.

She and Louise set out to find a house to rent at once, for every stove in the inn smoked, and the food was almost inedible. The best that could be found was a ramshackle wooden structure, all its rooms opening on an uncovered veranda. It was set high, with a fine view of the lake, but blown upon by all the winds of winter. Hortense sent for some furniture from Prègny, that, being of fine workmanship, looked odd against the bare, whitewashed walls.

At first, nearly everything that made for comfort was lacking, including books. Abbé Bertrand found, in a second-hand bookshop, a worm eaten copy of *Anecdotes of the Court of Philip Augustus*, that he read aloud to the ladies. They were able, eventually, to get some French newspapers, none of recent date. In one of them, they read of the arrival, in October, of Napoleon at Saint Helena. They read also of the trial for treason and execution of Marshal Ney; Ney, whom Napoleon had called "the bravest of the brave," the husband of Adèle de Broc's sister, Eglé.

Another of Hortense's intimate circle, her good friend La-valette, was also condemned to death, but was saved from the guillotine by the heroism of his wife. Hortense's cousin, Émilie de Beauharnais, had learned to love her husband, after she recovered from her schoolgirl passion for Louis Bonaparte; no one suspected, however, that she, who was so gentle and subject to long attacks of lethargy and melancholy, could act with daring. Émilie came to see her husband two days before the date of execution and, while she remained in the cell, Lavalette, wrapped in her cloak and scarf, made his escape from the prison in a sedan chair.

But the White Terror in France was not merely something of which one read with dismay in the newspaper; its results could be seen here by the wintry Lake of Constance. Hortense soon discovered that there were other refugees besides herself in the town, members of the Revolutionary Convention that more than twenty years earlier had voted for the death of Louis XVI. They were elderly men now; many were destitute. Hortense helped them to the extent of her resources, which at present were limited. Already she had had many petitions and had given generously. In answer to one appeal, that came to her by letter, she sent a valuable diamond, only to learn later that she had been hoaxed.

In April, Hortense was overjoyed by a visit from Eugène. He, of all Napoleon's relatives, had been the most fortunate. At the congress of Vienna, he was not given a principality, as stipulated in Napoleon's first abdication treaty, but, due to his friendship with the Czar, he was allowed to claim all his estates and personal property in both Italy and France. He was living now with his father-in-law, the King of Bavaria, unmolested by spies or police. He was soon to receive the title of Duke of Leuchtenberg.

Hortense thought no title was too grand, no reward too munificent for Eugène; he was her ideal of the good man—as opposed to the great—without personal ambition, ever generous, ever loyal. With his practical good sense, Eugène was able to help Hortense in her business affairs, contributing substantially to her relief projects himself, and arranging a credit account for her with the House of Rothschild in Frankfort, her jewels to be the collateral on which she could borrow.

When Eugène went back to Bavaria, he worked upon the sympathies of his father-in-law, King Maximilian. In June, Hortense was allowed a traveling permit to visit her brother, not at Munich —that would cause too much flutter in foreign embassies—but at a country house on Lake Stahrenberg. There, for the first time, Hortense met Eugène's children, a boy and four charming little girls.

Though the visit to Bavaria was brief and unobstrusive, it again focused attention on Hortense and her household. Louise Cochelet learned that some letters she had left with a friend in Paris, among them letters from the Czar, had been confiscated by the police. At this time, an attempt was made to lure Hortense into Austria, where she could be more closely watched. She received a polite invitation from Metternich to settle near a beautiful lake in the Tyrol. This was too obvious a case of the spider asking the fly to walk into its parlor. Hortense replied that she still hoped she would be allowed to live in Switzerland.

And she still hoped that somehow, somewhere, she and Charles de Flahaut would be able to join forces. She heard from him regularly from England. In her daily walks, Hortense found herself moving instinctively in the direction from which his carriage would come. She watched for it, as she had once watched for his gray saddle horse in the Bois de Boulogne.

She could not think of his coming, however, without many misgivings. Would Charles be happy here? He was made to shine in society, and here there was none. Perhaps his love for her had burned itself out and he had made his offer of self-sacrifice only from a sense of duty. After all that had passed between them, Hortense wondered whether she herself would be able to play her part and hold her jealousy in check.

In September, Hortense received a letter that brought her long-

standing love affair to a crisis. It came not from England, but from
Rome.

In Rome, Louis Bonaparte had had the satisfaction of having
his son under his control for many months, and of trying to
eradicate the faults that he thought due to the boy's upbringing.
In Hortense's house and subject to Abbé Bertrand's easy-going
tutelage, Napoléon Louis and his brother had been allowed great
freedom of expression. Louis, senior, was shocked to find that a
boy of eleven could talk so much and could give an opinion on so
many subjects, including matters of religion. Since his misfortunes, Louis had become very devout. He insisted that Napoléon Louis should be exact in all religious observances and that
he should learn to serve as acolyte at Mass.

Every hour of the young scholar's day was scheduled for some
activity. He was cut off entirely from companions of his own age.
Rules of health and hygiene were laid down, such as the wearing
of shoes that were large enough to fit either foot, and suspenders
long enough to insure good posture. The use of eau de Cologne
was forbidden, and even of soap; hands should be washed with
bran, nails cleaned with lemon juice, and the head with a dry
sponge. Bordeaux wine could be consumed in moderation, but
no coffee, no liqueurs, and not more than a quarter of a square
of chocolate per day. Napoléon Louis must wash his feet at least
once a week. Tucked in among these precepts, some sound, some
a product of Louis' hypochondria, was the cardinal injunction:
Every rule must be obeyed, even when it seemed unjust.

Hortense had sent a tutor with her son to Rome, but he was
dismissed a few weeks after his arrival. To carry out Louis' educational ideas, a series of pedagogues came and went between
Italy and France. None of them gave satisfaction for very long.
The French embassy in Rome, that kept a close watch on everything that went on, not only in Louis' household, but in those of
Lucien, Madame Mère, and Cardinal Fesch, thought that these

young men might be political agents, and for a time duly reported their names to Paris. Since there were so many of them and all seemed to be so dissatisfied with the way their employer had treated them, this precaution was relaxed.

The French Foreign Office was informed, however, that "Monsieur Louis"—Louis' various titles were now taboo—wanted to divorce his wife, so that he could marry again. He had selected, for a second experiment in matrimony, a girl of sixteen, his junior by more than twenty years, a daughter of the distinguished Roman family of Odelscalchi. Louis' acquaintance with her was slight, but he tried to improve it by writing her letters of courtly sentiment. The young lady giggled when she read them, and her relatives soon put a stop to the correspondence.

The grounds upon which Louis was going to petition the Pope to annul his marriage were that it had been forced. He wrote to all those with whom he had associated at the time of his marriage, asking them to come to Rome and testify that he, Louis, had been threatened with banishment by his brother unless he married the daughter of Joséphine.

He got some very unsatisfactory answers, for he had quarreled with most of his old friends, just as he had quarreled more recently with his son's teachers. One of his correspondents said with brutal frankness that the failure of his marriage was due to his "insane jealousy." No comfort was forthcoming from Louis' family, to whom he also wrote. His sisters—Caroline, Pauline, and Elisa—rejected the idea of a divorce. It was essential, they said, that the family should remain united and give no cause for scandal by disinterring the past.

At last, on September 16, 1816, Louis wrote to Hortense. "All of France," he declared, "knows that our marriage was contracted against our wishes and for political reasons. . . . I remember how, during the nuptial benediction, I gave—and you received—the ring with trembling. . . . The irresistible will of my brother put me in the painful situation of obeying, or going into exile. . . .

Since then, fourteen years have gone by and never for a moment
have we been of like mind."

This was indeed true, but Hortense, out of loyalty to her
mother, had never admitted to anyone that she had been over-
persuaded by Joséphine. If pressure had been brought to bear
upon Louis by Napoleon, Hortense was unaware of it. On the
contrary, in the early years of their marital disunion, Louis'
complaint had always been that he loved his wife and that she
failed to love him in return.

To be free of Louis, to be able to marry Charles de Flahaut—
the temptation to coöperate in the divorce proceedings was allur-
ing. It would entail only a slight tampering with the truth, but it
would mean an end to Hortense's hold, however feeble, upon her
children. Louis would see to that. He would never allow his sons
to be brought up by his wife's second husband or by her lover.
When the Chapter of the Cathedral of Constance came to question
Hortense and asked her to put her hand upon the Scriptures and
speak true, she said that Louis' allegations were false. She declared herself the defendant in his suit before the papal court.

Life with Charles, on any terms, now seemed impossible. At
best, it had been only a dream. Charles had promised Hortense,
after their last quarrel over Mademoiselle Mars, that he would be
perfectly frank, and wrote her fully of his experiences in England.
There, he had picked up connections made by his mother when
he and she were refugees to London in 1793. Charles wrote Hortense of meeting a young woman who seemed to be very much
pleased with him, Miss Margaret Elphinstone, the daughter of
Lord Keith, who was commander of the Channel fleet at the time
of Napoleon's surrender to the British. Miss Elphinstone was
handsome, was rich, was an intimate friend of Princess Charlotte,
the heir to the throne, and was a peeress in her own right. Charles
said he would still like to come to Constance, but Hortense could
see that he was weakening; he would be glad to have her give
him his dismissal.

She could not bring herself to write the letter. She must have support and encouragement, a badge of virtue, such as had been represented in her school days by Madame Campan's rose. Though Hortense had made her first communion under Madame Campan's care, she was not a practicing Catholic. She had lived in a world of free thinkers and anti-clericals. Some of the remarks made by Napoléon Louis, that so shocked his father in Rome, had no doubt been overheard in Hortense's salon. Once, when Abbé Bertrand, that mild ecclesiastic, asked her why she didn't go to confession, she said flippantly, "What should I say in the confessional? Bad things about other people, good about myself?"

But within the past year, Hortense had felt a drawing toward the Church. While she was in Aix, she frequently visited the hospital that she had endowed as a memorial to Adèle de Broc. She was impressed by the self-abnegation of the Sisters of Mercy, who cared for the sick. One day, when she was there, a case of gangrene was brought in. Hortense was almost overpowered by the smell of decaying flesh, that filled the room. She thought she was going to faint, and marveled how the Sisters went on about their work, untroubled. Hortense had always prided herself on being charitable, but her charity, she reflected, had consisted only in giving money here and there, money that she did not need. She had been generous to those who came to ask for help, but she had never gone in search of misfortune.

In her walks along the main highway that led to Constance, Hortense often saw bands of pilgrims on their way to the Benedictine abbey of Einsiedeln, in the Swiss canton just across the border. Hortense did not believe that prayer was any more efficacious in any particular spot, but perhaps she might find something she craved at Einsiedeln. In late October, she and Louise Cochelet made a pilgrimage to the abbey.

They drove through beautiful country along the shore of Lake Zurich. Toward evening, they began to go up into the mountains. The cliffs seemed to close in above them and Hortense's mood, which had been one of gentle melancholy, changed to fear. She felt as though she were going to say good-bye to all the joys of life. It was quite dark when she arrived at the abbey, where word had been sent in advance of her visit. A French monk met her at the door, carrying a lantern. Before taking her to her room, he wanted to show her the church, where a wonder-working black Madonna was enshrined. Over the portal was inscribed, "Here all sins are forgiven."

The next morning, Hortense made a confession of her entire life to a kindly and gentle-spoken priest. She found it easy to say that she forgave all those who had done her wrong, but when the priest told her her love for Flahaut had alienated her from the love of God, that she must renounce it completely, she began to weep. The priest left her for a time, saying she must make this sacrifice herself, without his help.

When, at last, she was given absolution and was about to take her leave, her confessor said, with some embarrassment, that news of the world penetrated even to this secluded spot. He had sometimes read in English newspapers things about Queen Hortense, which he was now sure must be calumnies. In future, he would be glad to set the record straight and speak the truth of her.

"Father," Hortense said, "you can say what you like, but you will not be believed. In the passionate times in which we live, truth counts for very little."

Once more in Constance, Hortense wrote her letter of farewell to Flahaut, urging him to be happy and to marry his English noblewoman. Even as she wrote, however, she hoped that he would not follow her advice, that he would return.

XXXV

HOUSES OF EXILE

AGAIN the winds blew cold off the lake and drove the snow around Hortense's ill-built house. The winter of 1816 was, for her, a sickly season. She suffered from sinus headaches and wore a black velvet mask to protect her cheeks and forehead, whenever she went out. While she was spending so much time housed, if not actually in bed, to keep warm, she heard from Paris that she was supposed to be hidden somewhere in the French capital, going about diguised as a man, busy with her plots to overthrow the Bourbons.

These stories boomeranged to the embarrassment of Monsieur Decazes, now the chief minister of Louis XVIII; being so high in royal favor, he had developed some enemies of his own. It was remembered that Decazes had once been Louis' secretary; it was said that it was he who was hiding Hortense.

Hortense herself paid less attention than formerly to these damaging fables. Her pilgrimage to Einsiedeln had given her a more serene outlook. She felt she had done the right thing, both in regard to her children and in regard to Charles de Flahaut. This was his opinion also. He continued to write to her affectionately and gratefully. In the spring, she learned that he was to be married in June to Margaret Elphinstone.

With the return of warmer weather, Hortense came out of hibernation. She often walked to a point of land where she could imagine herself building a house and planting a flower garden. She would again grow roses and violets, though not on the lavish scale of Saint-Leu. When she made overtures to buy the land, she was told she could not own property in Baden. This led to expeditions farther up the lake into Swiss territory. There was a a house that seemed to Hortense to have an ideal location, set up high on a promontory jutting out into the water. It was called the Castle of Arenenberg, Arenenberg being a corruption of Narrenberg, Fool's Hill. The title of castle was extravagant. The house, a two-story square pavilion, with a pillared portico, was small, and had been built in the seventeenth century. Being in poor repair, the price was modest. Hortense bought Arenenberg and, although she was told she could not live there, she was at least allowed to keep it, hoping that in future the ban might be relaxed.

During the past year, Hortense had heard frequently from her cousin Stéphanie. Stéphanie and her husband, the Grand Duke, told her that they were coming to Constance to see her. Unfortunately, the French Minister at Baden got wind of the visit. The so-called Holy Alliance of the great powers of Europe—of which Madame von Krüdener, incidentally, considered herself the architect—so dominated the lesser states, that nothing could be done without its sanction. Instead of being visited by Stéphanie and her husband, Hortense had an interview with one of the Grand Duke's courtiers, who told her, with many apologies, that she must leave Baden altogether.

There was again the problem of where to go. Eugène again had recourse to his father-in-law, King Maximilian, who apparently could refuse him nothing. Hortense was told that she could live in Bavaria and that the King would vouch for her good behavior. There were the usual protests from France, but they were quashed by the all-powerful Czar. Alexander, it seemed, had decided that Hortense had been sufficiently punished. He was about to do her and Eugène another good turn, by buying, at a generous figure, most of the art collection of La Malmaison, half of which Hortense had inherited from her mother. This would ease her financial situation considerably, though she thought it expedient to sell all of her silver- and gold-plated ware to pay for the house Eugène bought for her at Augsburg.

At Augsburg—a pleasant, provincial city—Hortense would be out of the official glare and glitter of Munich, but she would be near enough to Eugène for him to visit her frequently. Her new home was on a comfortably large scale. With some feeling of permanence, Hortense gathered together her scattered possessions: her books, her grand piano, the portraits of her family, including those of Napoleon, and the big round table, about which her friends used to gather in the rue Cerutti. Hortense could begin to build up a salon. The society of Augsburg was limited, but the town was the seat of a university; it had its artists and writers, its occasional visiting celebrity. Since Hortense had no official position, she could be democratic in her choice of friends.

As soon as she was well installed, in the early summer of 1817, Hortense began negotiations for a visit from Napoléon Louis. It was almost two years now since she had seen him. She had heard from him every week, one of Louis' rules for his son being that the boy should write a correct and legible letter to his mother every Thursday; he was not allowed to leave his room in the morning until this had been accomplished. These weekly compositions told Hortense only a tithe of what she wanted to know. It took a great deal of correspondence and the intervention of Eugène, who sent his cousin, Colonel Tascher de la Pagerie, to Italy, to bring Napoléon Louis to Augsburg in October, for a two-month stay.

Louis wrote to Hortense that he hoped she would recognize that their son was now "more reasonable, more thoughtful, and more religious. If I have not been able to correct all his bad habits, it is not because they have developed since he has been with me."

Hortense saw only a distressing change for the worse. What had Louis done to their child? He looked frail; his health had not benefited by the ban on chocolate, soap, tight shoes, and tight braces. From a lively boy, who had been perhaps a little too self-assertive, Napoléon Louis had become subdued and noncommittal. When answering a question, he glanced aside. Hortense suspected that he had been either snubbed or coerced into being a hypocrite. She sent quickly to Paris for a tutor who would provide an antidote to Louis' educational poison, a Monsieur Vieillard, a veteran of the Grand Army; in religion, an agnostic, in politics, a republican.

Two months was too short a time, however, to undo the work of two years. Hortense was put on the defensive when Louis wrote that he would now like to see the younger of the two boys. His attitude toward Louis, Junior, had always been ambiguous. Hortense was not sure how much of it was genuine, how much intended to wound her own sensibilities. She would not allow her nine-year-old to go to Italy with anyone but herself. Another winter had come and gone, wires had been pulled, and large amounts of official ink and paper had been consumed before Hortense got Italian passports for herself, her son, Abbé Bertrand, and a secretary. The excuse given for the journey was that Hortense wished to visit the baths of Livorno.

Like all travelers from the north, Hortense was entranced by her first sight of Italy. How bright the skies, how gay the Italians seemed after the sober Germans and Swiss! Hortense marveled at the relics of Roman civilization, and felt that she herself had lived in times as great and constructive as those of antiquity. Whenever she asked when some old monument had been restored, some new road built, she was told that it had been done "when the French were here." She was proud to think that Eugène had been the ruler of this section of Napoleon's empire.

When Hortense arrived at Livorno, Louis was taking the waters near by at Montecatini. Hortense hoped that she would not have to see him, and sent Louis, Junior, to visit him; while, in exchange, she had Napoléon Louis with her. An unfortunate accident brought the father of the family to Livorno in a hurry. Napoléon Louis was playing with a gun, set fire to some powder, and burned his hand severely. This accident, of course, was all Hortense's fault! She had to put up with Louis' reproaches and his presence in her close vicinity, until the wound was healed.

Hortense, with the new outlook on life she had gained at Einsiedeln, had come to look on her husband's failings with greater detachment. Without benefit of depth psychology, she traced the defects in Louis' character to his close association as a child with Napoleon. Louis, like everyone else in the world, wanted to be loved, but at the first sign of deviation from the ideal he had formed, he came to think that the beloved was his enemy. As Napoleon had once said, "Louis creates a world of his own."

In Constance or in Augsburg, Hortense could be philosophic; exposed to Louis' faultfinding and gloom, she was in a constant state of irritation. Louis' suit for divorce, though soon to be abandoned, was still dragging on in the Curia; he nevertheless wanted Hortense to stay, not with, but near, him in Italy. A refusal was all the more difficult because the boys were, for once, on their father's side. It would do them no good, Hortense thought, to witness their parents' bickerings. In October she went back to Bavaria, with the understanding that, if she could afford it, she would come again the following summer; failing which, Napoléon Louis would be sent to her.

The trip to Italy had one important effect. Louis had become sufficiently interested in his second son to criticize him severely. "I was not at all satisfied at Livorno," he wrote Hortense, "with the way Abbé Bertrand handles Louis. I was distressed, and if I didn't make an issue of it, it was because . . . any correction I might have made would be only temporary and therefore useless. His [Louis'] willfulness, his extreme talkativeness, his puns and bad jokes—in this respect he is much worse than Napoleon— pained me. As for his educational progress, the letters he writes me now are worse written than a year ago."

Hortense could not think that Louis, Junior, who as a small child had always been the quiet but observant one, was too much of a chatterbox, but she began to see that he had outgrown Abbé Bertrand as a teacher. The Abbé was no longer young. He liked to sleep late in the mornings and lessons were held whenever he got up or whenever he could capture his pupil, who was given to wandering far afield. The child was not always bent on mischief; once he came home on a very cold day without his coat, shoes, and stockings; he had given them to a beggar boy. He was pert to his teacher sometimes, but never malicious. When the Abbé was explaining to him in the schoolroom, the meaning of the word metamorphosis, Louis said, "I would like to be metamorphosed into a bird right now, so that I could fly out of the window."

Seeing that the Abbé looked hurt, he added, "Not to get away from you, just to get away from lessons."

This child, who was to be Hortense's own creation and no other's, must be taught some sort of intellectual discipline. Fortunately, the Abbé agreed with Hortense. He would go back to France and end his days living near his old friend, Madame Campan, in whose school he had taught. He would come often for visits to Augsburg or Arenenberg, when Hortense was allowed to use it for a summer residence.

Hortense took some time in choosing the Abbé's successor. She finally engaged a Monsieur Philippe Le Bas, a young college professor, who combined a number of disparate qualities. His father had been a member of the Convention and a friend of Robespierre; he was a Free Mason and would have nothing to do with young Louis' religious instruction. On the other hand, he was a royalist in good standing, who had held a small government post after the restoration. His chief drawback was that he was married and would have to bring his wife with him into exile.

Monsieur Le Bas buckled with vigor to the task of making over Hortense's son. His first judgment was that the boy knew absolutely nothing, and that the only faculty he had developed was the faculty for avoiding work. The tutor mapped out a program that began at six o'clock in the morning and ended with bed at nine o'clock. Grammar, Latin, arithmetic, German, Greek, history, geography, and elocution were seasoned with brisk walks in the open air and lessons in swimming, horsemanship, and fencing. Le Bas was with his pupil constantly, and only allowed him an hour and a half each day in his mother's salon. Monthly oral examinations were held in her presence and in the presence of any of her friends, whom she might wish to invite.

This was a sudden and violent change from the Abbé's somnolent ways, but young Louis did not resent it, as had his brother in Rome. He learned to apply himself and became much attached to Le Bas. Hortense was proud of his progress. So was Abbé Bertrand, who was kept up-to-date on all that went on at Augsburg. Was it just an old man's partiality that led him to predict great things for his pupil?

"You may be very much surprised," the Abbé wrote to Le Bas, "if someday history should connect your name with his, as once the name of Socrates was connected with that of Alcibiades. Who knows?"

With her boy so busy, Hortense had more time for her life-long occupation of being what Madame Campan had once called "an accomplished woman." She did some serious reading and re-reading of the classics. She took up again her sketching and her painting in water color. She composed a whole new series of songs, which was published as *A Collection of Romances Set to Music and Dedicated to the Prince Eugène by His Sister.*

There was yet another activity that filled the morning hours of Hortense and her secretary. In the past, Hortense's friends had sometimes suggested she should write her memoirs. To all urgings, she replied that she didn't have the patience or the literary skill. She found it easy to write the music for her songs, for instance, but she always had to borrow the words. Once, when she was at Aix in 1812, she told a woman, who fancied herself as a writer, something about her childhood, her voyage to Martinique when she was hardly more than a baby, her parents' imprisonment during the Terror. The next day the author brought her a neat little narrative, a few pages in length. Hortense saw it was well and cleverly written, but it wasn't true. She could not recognize herself in the childish, aureoled heroine. If her own story was ever to be written, she would have to write it herself.

A beginning was made in the first winter that Hortense spent at Constance. She started what in time came to be her autobiography with the recent past, wanting to refute the unjust accusations made against her. Later, she filled in the earlier sections, writing and re-writing, adding an incident here, a reflection there. If she was not alway accurate as to chronology, events were put more or less in their proper sequence.

There was much that Hortense left unsaid: no reference to her mother's pecadillos, no reference, of course, to the existence of Charles Auguste Demorny; but on the whole Hortense was frank. She did not aim at publication. Her friends were the audience that she had in mind. "I will tell them all the details of my life, saying, 'Here I am. Judge me, pity me, for this is my true self. Love me and value me; that is the dearest wish of my heart; it will be the joy of what remains to me of life.' "

Though she was only thirty-three when she began her memoirs, Hortense's tone was valedictory. Youth was over. The world in which she had flourished was gone. The kind of happiness she had once imagined was impossible. "Let me live a little in the remembrance of my compatriots, in the hearts of my friends. Let me die in the arms of my children—that is my last wish."

The date that Hortense put at the end of her memoirs was Augsburg, 1820, the year that young Louis was beginning to respond to the vigorous ministrations of Philippe Le Bas. Her greatest satisfaction, she said, was watching over the development of her son; her greatest sorrow was the "dreadful fate of the benefactor of my family."

Hortense was well aware that, if she would be remembered at all, it was as the daughter of Napoleon. His masterful presence dominated her narrative from its earliest pages. Of her own father, whom she had known so little, Hortense made a one-dimensional character, paper thin, with about as much reference to reality as one of the heroes of her romances set to music. Eugène, whom she loved so much, she praised, but did not describe in any great detail. Even Louis and Charles de Flahaut, the one the evil genius of her life, the other the lover who had failed to meet all of her requirements, were seen in but a single attitude. Only Napoleon was appreciated in the round, in his many moods, his weakness as well as his strength.

Hortense showed a far deeper understanding of Napoleon's character than of her own. Her estimate of him as a world figure was unusual because of the time at which it was made, while he was still alive and before the flood tide of literary praise and vilification had begun. Hortense saw Napoleon as the Messiah of the Masses.

"With his strength, his will, and the prestige of his glory, he called all people to share in the vanities of this world. He gave them their due in human happiness. As Christ rescued them from moral slavery, so he freed them from the hindrances which prevented all but a privileged few from enjoying the highest honors. Before he became Emperor, the French Revolution, it is true, had destroyed much, but the excess energy needed for destruction had led to weariness . . . and to a return to the same unhappy situation that had led earlier to revolt. It was only the establishment of the Empire that confirmed the supremacy of merit over hereditary rank. Only the Emperor, who dictated laws to all of Europe, could bring about such a social change."

This was the theme that was being developed by Napoleon himself at Saint Helena, in the conversations that his homesick companions jotted down, in the moments when his old energy flared up and he shouted at someone to write at his dictation, write until the cramped fingers that held the pen grew spastic with fatigue. A messiah stands in need of martyrdom. Napoleon often said that he should have died at Waterloo, or even on the day he entered burning Moscow; but his final years, spent in a shabby, rat-infested farmhouse on an island two thousand miles from any port, assured him a more durable apotheosis.

Communication by letter was so difficult that Napoleon, who realized how carefully everything he wrote was scrutinized, gave it up altogether. His family only heard from him through those who returned from the rock in the South Atlantic. The first to reach Europe was Giovanni Santini, a rough-and-ready Corsican, who had vowed vendetta on Sir Hudson Lowe, Napoleon's jailer —Lowe who, Napoleon said, had "the eye of a hyena, caught in a trap." Santini had memorized a lengthy protest of the conditions of Napoleon's detention. He visited various liberals in England, went to see Eugène in Munich, and was on his way to Italy, when he was arrested and taken to Austria.

Later arrivals were the Comte Emmanuel de Las Cases, who had gone to Saint Helena with the express purpose of being the Emperor's historian, and the fanatically devoted Gourgaud, the young man who had so alarmed Hortense at La Malmaison by saying he would kill Napoleon with his own hands rather than allow him to be captured by the Prussians.

All of these, as well as other less well-qualified observers, were to have their say in print. The messages they brought had a single aim: to ease the prisoner's situation. When the last of them, Gourgaud, left the island, the cancer of the stomach that was to kill Napoleon had only just begun to declare itself, but was reported as a liver complaint, fairly common at Saint Helena and always fatal. It would be inhumane not to remove the sick man to a more healthy climate.

In 1818, just before she went to Italy, Hortense had a visit from Catherine, Jérôme's wife, and with her concocted a scheme for presenting a petition for leniency to a Council of the Powers to be held at Aix-la-Chapelle. Hortense took a rough draft of the petition with her to Italy, and sent it to Madame Mère at Rome to be signed by all the family. At the same time, Marie Louise, now Duchess of Parma, was approached by Las Cases to lend her voice;

but she, who had already borne a child to her lover, Baron Neipperg, and was under his control, would take no action.

Nobody wished to linger at Saint Helena; those who stayed made a sacrifice of their lives. General de Montholon, Napoleon's secretary, asked for replacements in 1818; and Madame Mère and Cardinal Fesch dispatched a cook, a Corsican doctor and two priests. They made an odd selection. The doctor, Francesco Antommarchi, was so inept that Napoleon called him an assassin and refused his services; one of the priests had suffered a stroke and was half-paralyzed, the other, who was to take the place of Montholon, was almost illiterate.

A strange delusion had taken possession of Letizia Bonaparte. She, who was so parsimonious, would give her all to rescue her son, and had offered herself to go to the island, but she had come to believe that this was unnecessary. Napoleon would be sent elsewhere by the British, perhaps to Malta. He might have already left, before the new recruits arrived. The old lady and her brother, the Cardinal, were being victimized by a seeress, who convinced them that their wish-fulfillment was fact. During the last two years of Napoleon's agony, they thought all letters they received, relative to his imprisonment, were forgeries of the British; that actually the invalid had been transported by the angels to a healthy, but earthly, paradise. His whole life had been a miracle, so why not this?

In vain, Louis and Pauline tried to convince their mother and uncle of the insanity of their ideas. The only results were painful, quarrelsome scenes.

On June 1, 1821, Hortense was writing a letter to be sent by another envoy to Saint Helena, asking Napoleon whether he had ever received a crystal box she had sent him, with a medallion picture of Joséphine upon its cover, the picture he had asked her to have painted during the final days at La Malmaison. If Joséphine were still alive Hortense wrote, "her great regret would be that she had only shared your days of good fortune."

The letter was never read by Napoleon. Already his body was

buried in the Valley of the Geraniums, a spot on the hated island, that he liked to visit to escape the summer heat. The news of his death rolled slowly, but thunderously, about the world. It reached Hortense at a health resort in Switzerland, where she had gone with Madame Campan and Abbé Bertrand. She wrote to Philippe Le Bas, in Augsburg with his pupil, to break the news to Louis, who was now thirteen. It was a great shock to the boy; he wept abundant, adolescent tears.

"What I am most sorry for," he wrote to his mother, "is that I never saw him again. At Paris I was so young, that I can hardly remember him. Whenever I do something poorly, I think of that great man, and I seem to hear his spirit tell me that I should make myself worthy of the name of Napoleon."

PART

VI

(June 1, 1821–October 5, 1837)

꙰꙰꙰꙰꙰꙰꙰꙰꙰꙰꙰

XXXVI

THE CONSPIRATORS

AFTER the death of the Emperor, Hortense felt that she must not lose touch with the Bonapartes. During the next few years, her life developed a new pattern. Her summers were spent at Arenenberg, her winters in Rome. She was there in the winter of 1823–1824, when she heard of the sudden death of Eugène. Though only in his early forties, Eugène had suffered a slight stroke the preceding summer. Hortense would never have put the Alps between herself and her adored, her "perfect" brother, if she had not thought him completely recovered. With Eugène gone, Bavaria had no further attraction for Hortense. She sold her house at Augsburg and concentrated all her relics of the past in her queer little castle above the Lake of Constance.

In Rome, the focal point of the Bonaparte family was the Palazzo Rinuccini, where Madame Mère lived in great seclusion, seldom going out, her dim-lit salon the gathering place of her children and grandchildren, who came to pay her their respects and to hear the latest news.

In Rome, Hortense could be fairly certain of not meeting her husband, for Louis had moved to Florence in 1820. In the same

351

year he published his *Historical Documents and Reflexions on the Government of Holland*; a French and an English edition being brought out simultaneously in London. This was Louis' Apologia pro Vita Sua, a paranoid cry of pain. It represented his life as having been a prolonged martyrdom to his unscrupulous brother. None of the family, least of all Hortense, could approve of it, and it seemed a bitter circumstance that the book came out in time for a copy to be read by the dying Napoleon at Saint Helena. Though Louis was on bad terms with most of his relatives, for this and other reasons, his motive in moving to Florence was to protect his son, Napoléon Louis, from becoming involved in one of the movements for social and political reform that had been driven underground in the Papal States and elsewhere. Tuscany was better governed and there was less political activity there than anywhere else in Italy.

The name of Bonaparte, however, had become associated with that of revolution, and the younger members of the family, who were now growing into man- and womanhood under the anxious eyes of their elders, all had leanings toward revolt. Unknown to his father, Napoléon Louis, while still in his teens, became a Carbonaro, a member of the secret society, dating, some said, from the Middle Ages, when Guelph battled Ghibelline, secret meetings of the oppressed minority being held in charcoal burners' huts in the forest. Though the movement was now led by veterans of the Napoleonic wars, its vocabulary remained rustic. A lodge was a *vendita* (a sale), members greeted one another as "good cousins," while the rallying cry was to "deliver the lamb from the wolf."

Napoléon Louis was inducted into the Carbonari, no doubt, by his latest tutor, a Colonel Armandi, who taught him military science and was with him for three years, a longer period than any of his predecessors. The boy had survived submission to his father's discipline surprisingly well. The fears Hortense had felt, of his being permanently warped, were unrealized. Having out-

grown his teenage furtiveness, Napoléon Louis became a charming, a very handsome young man.

When he reached the age of twenty-one, the question of a wife
was brought upon the family carpet. Napoleon, in his will, had
declared his wish that the family should inbreed. In 1822, a match
was arranged between Lucien's son Charles and Zenaïde, a daughter of Joseph. Two years later, Joseph, now living near Borden-
town, New Jersey, sent his other daughter, Charlotte, to her
mother in Florence, to be married to Napoléon Louis.

Hortense was at first disappointed by this match. Charlotte
was two years older than her intended fiancé. She was tiny and, like
her mother Julie, slightly deformed, one shoulder being a little
higher than the other. The dowry, however, would be ample, for
Joseph was rich. And Charlotte was a very intelligent girl. Napoléon Louis seemed to be genuinely in love with her. After his
marriage, which took place in 1826, he continued to live under
his father's roof, but was completely independent. He and Charlotte had many tastes in common. She was a good artist and
illustrated books that her husband wrote, one being a translation
of Tacitus' *Life of Agricola*, another a translation of a Latin poem,
The Sack of Rome, written in 1527 by a Jacopo Buonaparte, a
remote ancestor.

Napoléon Louis had also developed an interest, well outside
the family range, in science and technology. He worked out a
theory for a dirigible balloon—unguided balloon ascents having
been a daredevil sport for more than fifty years. He made ex-
periments in the manufacture of paper, in a small factory he
established near Florence. Soap-making was another subject for
research. Was this because, as a growing boy, the technician had
been forced by his father to wash his hands with bran?

Several of Hortense's Roman winters were spent in a beautiful
villa that was now the property of her son, a legacy from his
aunt, Pauline Borghese. Pauline had always had a great fondness
for handsome young men, and in the final months of her life—
she died in 1825, like Napoleon, of cancer—Napoléon Louis was

a comfort to her. The villa made a delicious setting for the kind of social life that was meat and drink to Hortense. Artists, writers, and most of Rome's foreign visitors, except those who hovered about the French Embassy, came to her salon. Napoléon Louis was often with her. Happy though he was with Charlotte, he had never ceased to envy his brother the privilege of living the year round with their mother.

Young Louis, on the other hand, went for frequent visits to his father in Florence. This was a great trial to his tutor, Monsieur Le Bas. The intensive study program was disrupted. Le Bas, like everyone else, found Louis, Senior, difficult, to say the least, and he was afraid that the visits might be prolonged indefinitely.

No one could say now that Le Bas' pupil was not well educated. In the final winters he spent in Augsburg, young Louis took courses at the Augsburg Gymnasium. He spoke German so perfectly that a slightly Teutonic accent overlaid his mother tongue. Louis had inherited Hortense's golden hair and her blue eyes. Though not as tall as his brother—his legs, a Bonaparte trait, were short in comparison to his head and torso—he was a good athlete, a strong swimmer, a spectacular horseman. Near his left eye was a scar, the result of a fencing accident.

Just as the Abbé Bertrand had once been superseded, so the time came when Le Bas must go the way of all tutors. Hortense gave as excuse for the parting that she had to economize, which was all too true, but actually, young Louis, now in his twentieth year, felt he had learned all that he could from the Professor. His head had been stuffed with Greek and Latin, nothing else. "Now," the young man said, "I will educate myself." For a year, Le Bas' place was taken by the Colonel Armandi, who had had such a pronounced effect on Napoléon Louis, teaching him not only tactics, but the language, the passwords, and the ritual of the Charcoal Burners.

Here was knowledge not to be shared with Father or even with Mother. Hortense had the confidence of her sons—she was not intolerant of youth, as was her husband—but she, like Louis, was afraid her boys might be exploited or led into some dangerous escapade. Both of them, for example, wanted to take part in the Greek war for independence, that began in 1821 and in which one of their cousins, Paul, the son of Lucien, was killed.

Hortense feared particularly for her younger child. He was dreamy; she could never be sure of what he was dreaming. Though affectionate and ready to yield on minor points, he could be extremely persistent. "Gentle, but obstinate," she said of him; this was a judgment that Eugène had often passed upon herself.

Even at Arenenberg, where Hortense and young Louis spent their quiet summers, there were influences at work upon a youthful, crescent imagination. The very pictures in Hortense's house mirrored the glories of the Empire. There was, in the neighborhood, a typical, a living relic of the Grand Army, one of Napoleon's "old grumblers"—and not so old at that. He was the husband of Louise Cochelet. Though Hortense had made many attempts to arrange a good match for her protégée, in the end Louise succeeded in making one for herself. She met, in a diligence in Switzerland, Captain Denis Charles Parquin, who had had to leave France suddenly as the result of an army mutiny in 1820. He was "traveling the world," as he put it, and was not intimidated by the fact that Mademoiselle Cochelet, though still flirtatious, was fat and forty. He remembered having seen her many years earlier at a military review, when he was a mounted escort to the Queen of Holland's carriage. The married pair set up housekeeping, not far from Arenenberg, in another castle, Wolfsberg, which they turned into a pension. Many of their paying guests were friends of Hortense, and their comings and goings were noted by the police.

To see Louise's husband, with his battle-scarred face and bayonet mustache, to hear him roar out as he introduced himself, "Captain Charles Parquin, Soldier of the Emperor!" was to find oneself back in the land of heroes. Hortense did not mind her son listening to Parquin's tales of the campaigns he had fought, from Russia to Fontainebleau; but she was sometimes uneasy when

she saw them going off alone for long strolls, giving their cigars
as excuse for their private talks, since smoke might be offensive
in the drawing room.

An idle life was perhaps even more demoralizing. In 1829,
young Louis was accepted as a student at the Swiss Artillery
School on the Lake of Thun. This would lead to a commission in
the Swiss Army. During the summer of 1830, he was on maneuvers and was writing his mother of long marches made on foot
in the mountains, when news arrived, both at Thun and Arenenberg, of fighting on the streets of Paris. The white flag of the
Bourbons had gone down; the tricolor had again been raised.
What did this mean for Louis and his brother, for Hortense, for
all of the Bonapartes?

For the first time since 1815, legitimacy, the darling doctrine
of the Congress of Vienna, had been challenged in one of the
major powers.

In 1824, the obese and crafty Louis XVIII died. He was succeeded by his brother, the Comte d'Artois, who took the title of
Charles X. Talleyrand must have been thinking of the new king,
when he said that the Bourbons came back to France having
"learned nothing and forgotten nothing." Fresh restrictions were
clamped upon the press; old privileges were restored to the
clergy. Worst of all, an indemnity, amounting to a billion francs,
was promised to the emigrant nobles who had lost their lands
during the Revolution. The indemnity was to be paid by a re-
duction of interest on government bonds. Businessmen and the
middle-class holders of the bonds became revolutionaries over
night. Charles appointed, as minister, the reactionary Prince de
Polignac and dissolved the Chambers when they refused to ratify
the appointment; the National Workshops were closed, throwing
thousands out of work, and barricades rose in the narrow streets
of Paris.

There was not much bloodshed during the July Revolution, as

it came to be called. The aged Lafayette appeared again upon the scene, reassumed his command of the National Guard, and persuaded the Republicans to join forces with the liberal Monarchists in accepting as King, Louis Philippe, the Duc d'Orléans.

Louis Philippe, to be sure, was a Bourbon, but with a difference. His father, the Red Duke, had sat in the Convention and voted for the death of his cousin, Louis XVI. Louis Philippe himself had held military office in the earliest days of the Republic. During his subsequent exile, he supported himself for a time by teaching school in Switzerland. Of late, he had made himself popular with the middle class by his anticlericalism and by sending his sons to middle-class academies. He charmed his supporters when, after becoming "King of the French," he was seen walking unattended on the boulevard, carrying a green umbrella.

It seemed possible that an umbrella-carrying king and his liberal backers might allow the Bonaparte family to return to France. Hortense remembered that she had been very helpful to Louise Philippe's mother and aunt in 1815. The Duchesse had broken her leg and was caught in Paris by Napoleon's return. Hortense petitioned the Emperor to allow the two elderly ladies to remain where they were and to grant them a pension. She was now deluged with letters from friends in France, who took it for granted that she would soon be back in Paris. Their congratulations were premature, for in September, the decree of banishment against the Bonapartes on pain of death, first issued in 1816, was renewed.

Hortense was very anxious, nevertheless, to get to Italy and to talk with her elder son. Louis, Junior, would go with her and a new secretary, whom she had just engaged, a young woman of thirty, Mademoiselle Valerie Masuyer, one of Joséphine's innumerable godchildren. The departure from Arenenberg on October 16th seemed routine. Those who were to be left behind crowded about the carriage to say good-bye. Vincent Rousseau, Hortense's foster brother, now the steward of Arenenberg, told the man on the box and everyone else to take great care of the

Queen. Madame Bure, Louis' nurse, kissed him a dozen times and wept. Louis himself seemed to have nothing more serious on his mind than saying farewell to his dog, Fido.

Hortense had decided to avoid Milan, where there might be repercussions of the July Revolution, and chose a roundabout route, through the Tyrol, Venice, and Bologna, to Florence. She would have a two-week visit there with Napoléon Louis and Charlotte, during the absence of Louis, Senior, who had gone to Rome to see his mother.

At the last posting station outside of the town, Napoléon Louis appeared on horseback. Hortense was to remember later how gallant and healthy he looked. He had much to tell her. His father-in-law, Joseph Bonaparte, had written from America to the French Chambers, protesting that in the choosing of a king, the claims of the Duke of Reichstadt, as Napoleon's son was now called, had been overlooked. Napoléon Louis himself had had calls from France and from Corsica, to head up a movement to restore his cousin. At first he was tempted, he said, but after thinking the matter over, his reply was that the French people had made their choice; even if he could do so, he did not want to start a civil war.

This was a realistic answer. Hortense was much relieved. It was a great satisfaction to her to see how well rooted Napoléon Louis was in domesticity. He was at work on a history of Florence, in which Charlotte took an interest. In his study was a large Etruscan sarcophagus, but there was also a little cabinet in which were displayed a few trumpery relics of Napoleon: an autographed letter, a silver eagle, a reading lamp, and some chipped chinaware that had been used at Saint Helena.

When her two weeks of grace were up, Hortense left for Rome. Halfway there, she met her husband traveling in the opposite direction. Their carriages stood wheel to wheel in the posting station, and they exchanged a few words, without either getting out. Mademoiselle Masuyer, the secretary, who had never seen Hortense's husband, thought that Louis had a handsome head, but his body, crippled by arthritis, was gross and unwieldy. She was prepared to dislike him, since she had come to love Hortense in the short time she had been with her.

In Rome, Hortense went to an apartment that she rented in the Palazzo Ruspoli. It was more central and less expensive to maintain than Napoléon Louis' villa. Before her trunks were unpacked, Hortense was off to call on Madame Merè, who earlier in the year had fallen and broken her hip. Though she had survived an accident that was usually fatal to a woman of eighty and her sight was dimmed by cataracts, she was still a vital, an awe-inspiring figure, her face as pale and as perfectly chiseled as the marble busts of her famous son, with which she was surrounded.

Hortense went regularly to read aloud to the old lady, who wanted to hear everything that was written about Napoleon. Most of it was sorry stuff, from a Bonapartist point of view. The latest book was a life by Sir Walter Scott, to which Louis had written a reply. This, to a certain extent, made amends for Louis' earlier work, his *Historical Documents and Reflexions*. He maintained that Napoleon was the greatest man who had ever lived, viewed as general, as conqueror, or as king. Louis had even transferred to his brother's case some of his own sense of all-pervasive treachery. Napoleon, he said, had been tricked by his enemies into undertaking the Russian campaign, into the war with Spain, and —this was certainly a change in point of view—into taking over Holland.

Though young Louis went to call on his grandmother the day of arrival, he was not often in attendance at family reunions thereafter. He gave, as excuse, a bad cold he had developed, though this did not seem to keep him at home to any great extent.

On November 30th, all the bells in Rome were tolling for the death of Pope Pius VIII, who had reigned for only a little more than a year. What a misfortune, everybody said! The cost of another election so soon after the last would be a burden, and there was a general feeling of uneasiness, a feeling that something untoward might happen before a successor was chosen. On the

10th of December, the cardinals went into conclave. Cardinal Fesch was ill and unable to join them. He was visited one day in his sickroom by Monseigneur Capelletti, the Governor of Rome, who requested his fellow churchman to see that the younger son of the Duchesse de Saint-Leu should leave the city immediately.

Uncle Fesch bristled. He did not have any personal affection for his great-nephew, Louis Bonaparte, but he was always quick to take offense at any slight given to the family. What had the young man done, he asked?

He had been seen constantly riding about Rome on a horse that had a tricolor saddlecloth.

Was that all?

The Governor shrugged. An interregnum was always a dangerous time, he said; one must take every precaution.

The Cardinal flew into a rage. He had never heard of anything so ridiculous, he sputtered. He would certainly take no action in the matter. He did, however, tell his nephew Jérôme, who told Hortense.

She came to the Cardinal's house in great alarm. She would be glad to have Louis leave Rome and to go his father in Florence, she said. Fesch told her not to give in so easily. She should ignore this spiteful incident.

As soon as Hortense reached home, she sent for her son, but before she could question him, a colonel of the papal army was ushered in. He had an order for the deportation of Charles Louis Napoléon Bonaparte. A post chaise and a guard were waiting in the street to take the culprit to Florence.

The sight of the papal uniform caused commotion in Hortense's household. A bag was hastily packed. Louis was hugged and kissed by the elderly servants, as though he were a small boy who was being unjustly punished. Just as he was saying good-bye to his mother, he drew her aside and whispered in her ear that there was a man hidden in his room who was wanted by the police. She must look out for him.

Hortense had no opportunity to ask the man's name, or to

investigate, for Louis had hardly left when Jérôme arrived, very indignant because his son, Jérôme, Junior, who was only sixteen, had been arrested also and had only been saved from deportation by an appeal to the Russian Ambassador. When at last Hortense was able to go to Louis' room, she found there an Italian officer named Pieoni. He told her that he had been in prison once and had suffered so horribly that he was determined to blow his brains out rather than be arrested a second time. When he learned that the gendarmes were on his trail, he came at once to Louis for protection. Four hundred others, less lucky than Pieoni, had been rounded up. The government announced that a plot for an armed rabble to take over the city had been squelched, just in time.

Hortense did not doubt that Louis was implicated, and was glad he had escaped so easily. She wrote her sons a letter, in which she analyzed the political situation. However great one's sympathies might be, she said, this was not the moment for a revolution to be successful. It was France that had liberated Italy from Austria in 1796; there was little hope of help from France at present. It must be remembered also that, though the elite might start a revolution, it was the people as a whole who must maintain it, and who would suffer if it failed. Hortense's mind was eased when she got a reply from Louis and his brother, saying that they both agreed with her entirely.

A period of calm succeeded the excitement of the first few days of the conclave. The problem of keeping a fugitive hidden in her house would have been difficult for Hortense, if she had not had the cheerful coöperation of her servants. They supplied Pieoni's wants unobtrusively and, since they did not know his name, nicknamed him Fido, after Prince Louis' dog, whom he had had to leave behind at Arenenberg.

On February 2, 1831, a new Pope, Gregory XVI, was chosen. At the same time, a chain reaction of revolution was set off in the Romagna—Bologna first, then Modena, Forli, Ravenna, and Ancona. The Grand Duchess Marie Louise of Parma had to fly to the nearest town in which there was an Austrian garrison.

The people of Rome, however, seemed to be interested only in the papal coronation and in the carnival that followed. Hortense always enjoyed this popular festival—the feeling that all men were brothers, the costumes, the confetti, the drives on the Corso in decorated carriages.

One evening she was having dinner with some French friends, when the group about the table was startled by a pistol shot, followed by the rattle of musketry. A small band of revolutionists had tried to disarm a regiment in the Piazza Colonna. There had been casualties. Hortense had a call from a Corsican named Pasqualini, who told her that his son had been one of the victims. He had been carried home, but the father was sure the police would come for the boy. The man fell on his knees before Hortense and cried, "Save my son!"

That night, Hortense sent her carriage for the wounded man and smuggled him into her apartment. A surgeon, who could be trusted, was sent for to dress young Pasqualini's wounds, two of which were serious. Pieoni was delegated to nurse him and was glad to do what he could for a comrade, but for several days, Hortense tried to keep from thinking what would be the result if her latest guest should die.

She felt that the press was making too much of the disorders at Rome, when she received a letter from her sons, saying they were worried for her safety. They begged her to come to Florence. She was very loath to go, but felt she could not refuse.

On February 19th, Hortense, Valerie Masuyer, and a French officer, who had offered to guard them on their way to Florence, drove out of Rome with Pieoni, disguised as a servant, seated on the box. His patient, Pasqualini, had begun to mend, but was in no condition to travel; Pasqualini had been left to the care of the servants. Hortense spent one night on the road. On the evening of the second day, as she approached the city, she began to look for two horsemen coming out to meet her. There was no sign of either of her sons.

At the posting station, Hortense found Charlotte waiting for her. Charlotte said her husband and brother-in-law had left earlier in the day, but she was afraid they had mistaken their mother's route and thought that she was coming via Perugia.

Hortense had no faith in this theory. She had another of her own. She could not share her fears with Charlotte, but when she got out of her carriage in Florence, she was trembling so that she could hardly walk into the inn.

XXXVII

ONE LOST, ONE SAVED

ON THE day of Hortense's arrival, February 20, 1831, the two young Bonapartes rode off to join the revolutionists. One of the leaders of the movement, Ciro Menotti, a rich industrialist of Modena, had come to Florence to persuade them that their name would be of help to the cause. In a letter from young Louis, delivered to Hortense at the inn, he said they had undertaken commitments which they must carry through. He asked her to let Charlotte believe that it was he who had led his brother on, for Napoléon Louis' conscience hurt him for having kept his plans secret from his wife. Hortense knew, however, that the political sentiments of her sons were identical. She understood now why they had wanted her to come to Florence; in Rome she might have been held as hostage for their good behavior.

But what could she say to them that, without hurting their pride and sense of honor, would make them turn back? Hortense sat up the better part of the night, writing letters and then tearing them up. When finally composed, her appeal was given to Pieoni, who would deliver it in person.

In the morning, Louis, Senior, arrived at the inn, in a pitiful state of agitation. His sons had always seemed so docile; he

364

couldn't understand why they had done this dreadful thing without asking his permission. To attack the Pope—Louis' piety was outraged! To put themselves in danger—Louis' chief parental sin was overprotectiveness. As usual, he blamed Hortense for everything. He wanted her to go at once to bring the rebels home.

"I can't," Hortense said. "If they come back, it will have to be of their own free will."

She added that if she went into the revolutionists' territory, everyone would say that she had done so to bring them the money they needed so desperately; she was still supposed to have millions at her command. Her presence might even be taken as an excuse for Austrian intervention.

Louis would give her no rest. It was like the old days, when he had tried to force her to say that she loved him better than anyone else in the world. Letters and messages flew back and forth between Louis and Hortense. At last, to pacify him, Hortense said that she would go as far as the borders of Tuscany. When, however, she found that Louis wanted her to lure the runaways across the frontier, by saying she was ill, she refused to be a decoy to their arrest on Tuscan soil.

Meanwhile, the young Bonapartes' action had been publicized. Cardinal Fesch and Jérôme had an audience with the Pope. Jérôme sent his secretary to his nephews, telling them to desist, and saying that the Vatican did not even know the demands of the insurgents. Napoléon Louis, in consulting with the rebel chiefs, drew up a list of grievances and the constitutional reforms needed to redress them. A copy was sent, not only to Rome, but to Louis, Senior, who, after reading it, called for the doctor to apply leeches to his forehead; he was fearful of a stroke. Across the top of the document that was handed on to Hortense, Louis wrote, "This is the work of an adventurer!"

The brief hope that the revolution might succeed was beginning to fade. On March 3, 1831, Gregory XVI signed a treaty of alliance with Austria. Austrian troops retook Parma and Modena. Colonel Armandi, the boys' former tutor, who was now Minister of

War of the revolutionary government, wrote to Hortense that her sons had been asked to resign their commissions. Their name, it was now felt, would only be a hindrance in getting the support of France. They had offered to enlist in the ranks, but that also was denied them. They were now at Bologna.

Hortense took heart. Though their cause would collapse, her sons would survive; but where could she take them to safety? They would have to leave Italy, of course. She feared that if they went to Switzerland, the Austrian government would force their extradition. She hunted the map of the Mediterranean world over for a refuge, and decided that one might be found in Turkey or in British-controlled Corfu. She consulted Louis and got his consent, though he would not hear of Corfu's being reached via Corsica, where there were so many friends of the Bonaparte family. Hortense would have to sail from the east coast, from Ancona, which was still in rebel hands.

While she was making her preparations for yet another exile, Hortense heard of an Austrian fleet in the Adriatic. Again she lay awake at night to worry. The worst thing that could happen would be for her sons to be taken by the Austrians. A bold idea came to her: She would go with them to France, in spite of the decree of outlawry, and would throw herself on the mercy of Louis Philippe.

It would never do to confide this inspiration to Louis, or to Charlotte, who had to stay in Florence because her mother was seriously ill. Hortense asked the English Ambassador, whom she had known in Rome, for a passport for an English lady and her two sons to travel through France to England. He was startled by her request, but said he would do as she asked, even if it cost him his place. Hortense was soon in possession of two passports, one for Italy in her own name, and one for England made out to Mrs. Hamilton, the mother of two sons, Charles and William.

On March 12th, Hortense and Valerie Masuyer set out for Ancona. As soon as they had crossed the border, the revolution that, viewed from a distance, seemed to be moribund, came to life again. Everyone was wearing the tricolor, everyone seemed to be smiling confidently. In the towns, Hortense was cheered and heard herself called "the mother of Napoleon," a title she had thought reserved for Madame Mère. In Perugia and Foligno, she met revolutionary officers, who told her how well her sons had done in their brief taste of soldiering. They had fought like veterans, in hand-to-hand skirmishes with the papal troops.

Hortense stayed for several days at Foligno and, hoping her boys would join her, sent a courier to them at Bologna. The man came back to say that he had found them at Forlì, well to the south of Bologna, which had been abandoned to the Austrians. The provisional government was retiring to Ancona. Young Louis sent word that his brother was in bed with a bad cold.

For a few days there was no further news. Hortense became very uneasy. She remembered that March had always been a fateful month for the Bonapartes, the month when Paris fell to the allies, the month when the Emperor returned from Elba. Twenty years ago in March, the birth of the King of Rome was being fêted in Paris, and the splendors of the Empire seemed eternal. Hortense could never have guessed then that someday she would be alone in a poor little inn in Italy, with the Austrians advancing and her children in peril of their lives.

She left Foligno for the coast on March 19th. At the first posting station, a carriage drew up beside hers and a messenger from Forlì sprang out to give her a note, not from one of her sons, but from a comrade, who wrote that Napoléon Louis was very ill and was asking for her. He had developed measles; a dangerous variety of the childish disease was epidemic. The man drew Valerie Masuyer behind the carriage, where Hortense could neither see nor hear him, and with tears in his eyes told the secretary that when he left Forlì, Prince Napoléon was thought to be dying. Hortense must be prepared to hear the worst.

It seemed as if the news had traveled faster by word of mouth than by messenger. As the carriage shifted its direction and took the shortest route toward Forlì, it passed through towns where people were saying that Napoléon, their young Napoléon, was dead. Hortense refused to believe what she heard until, after a twenty-four hour journey over the Apennines, she reached Pesaro on the coast. There, young Louis was waiting for her and threw himself into her arms, weeping hysterically and saying he had just lost the best friend he could ever hope for in this world.

Napoléon Louis had died on March 17th, after a five-day illness. Louis nursed him as best he could, but the only real comfort and distraction he could give the invalid was reading him the newspaper accounts of the progress of the revolution; he chose only those that were encouraging. When it was discovered that Napoléon Louis had the measles, as well as pneumonia, he didn't want his brother to come near him. The friend who wrote the letter, asking Hortense to come to Forlì, foresaw the end and sent Louis out on an errand so that he would be spared seeing his brother fight for the last breath from his clogged and failing lungs. In his final moments, Napoléon Louis asked for his mother repeatedly and paid a tribute to his brother.

"He is a deep thinker," he whispered, "more intelligent than I. He will be a great statesman."

The funeral was held in the cathedral at Forlì, with all of the town that could find standing room present. Immediately after, the tricolor ribbons and rosettes, that were as much in evidence as mourning black, disappeared. Many prepared to hide themselves, or to leave the town before the Austrians arrived.

Valerie Masuyer—in devotion to Hortense, she had become a second Adèle de Broc or Louise Cochelet—wondered how Hortense, exhausted as she was, could stand the stream of visitors, who came to offer her their sympathy. At night, she sat up in her bed to write an obituary of her son. She would leave it to no other hand than her own. There was no time to rest, no time to come to terms with grief. The only thing to be done was to move on at once to Ancona.

At Ancona, as at Pesaro, the finest residence in the town had belonged to Eugène de Beauharnais, when he was viceroy of Italy. It was now owned by his son, the young Duke of Leuchtenberg. Hortense could go there and thus avoid staying at an inn.

From her windows, she had a complete view of the harbor, for the palazzo was directly above the sea. A storm was blowing up, and the spray from the waves dashed against the windowpanes. There were only a few small ships tossing about at anchor. Hortense was glad that she had another avenue of escape. Since her English passport was made out for herself and two sons, she could take someone with her to France. She selected a young Italian, the Marquis Zappi, who would be sure to suffer if captured by the Austrians. He had dispatches from the revolutionary chiefs, asking for French assistance. Hortense told him that she would get him to France, if he wouldn't ask her how the feat was to be accomplished.

She intended to set out immediately, but Louis seemed feverish, went to bed early, and awoke the following morning with a face blotched red—another case of the measles! Hortense, cruelly frightened, had to reshape her plans. She gave out that it was she who was ill. She sent a servant down to engage a passage for her son on a ship bound for Corfu, and told him to talk of his errand to everyone he met on the way. When the ship set sail that evening everyone in the town thought that Louis was aboard.

A heartbroken letter arrived from Louis, Senior. He had heard of the death at Forlì, and begged Hortense to save the only child who was left to them. She could not tell him the truth, for her reply might be intercepted. She wrote reassuringly that all was well, and that Louis was on his way. She would join him at Corfu, as soon as she had recovered from a slight illness.

Though Hortense declined, on score of health, to see anyone, she did allow herself a call from Colonel Armandi. He had just made a difficult decision. He knew that further fighting would be useless, and wanted to save as many of the revolutionists as possible. There was a cardinal in Ancona to whom Armandi offered to surrender the town, in return for passports for all who wanted to go to France or the Ionian islands. Remnants of the revolutionary forces were pouring into the town, young men, still eager for battle. They shouted treason, when they heard of the bargain Armandi had made. Few of them could pay for a passage on the only two ships in the harbor. Hortense was able to come to the rescue. Some years earlier, she had bought a small farm in the marches of Ancona, as an investment. She had intended adding a little to her property and had sent a considerable sum to her nephew's palace. She now reserved only enough to pay her own journey, and gave the rest to be distributed to the refugees. Some would go by sea, others would go back on foot to their homes through the mountains and would need only a pittance.

Two days later, the Austrian troops marched into the town, though the Cardinal had sent them word of its surrender to the Pope. The palazzo was selected as headquarters for the general. He happened to be the same officer who had protected Hortense at Dijon, when she was fleeing France in 1815. When he heard that she was there and was ill, he sent a polite message, saying he did not want to inconvenience her; he hoped to see her when she was well. The house, however, was filled to the last inch with soldiers, and only two rooms were left for Hortense's use. The room in which Louis was bedded was separated from the next by a pair of folding doors. For fear that his voice might be heard, Hortense forbade him to speak; when he coughed, she would put her hand over his mouth.

By the end of the week, the measles had run their course without complication, and Hortense was ready to undertake the difficult masquerade of her departure. She had an interview with the Austrian general and told him she was on her way to sail from Livorno, to join her son at Malta. She would leave on April 3rd, Easter Sunday, very early in the morning, so that she could hear Mass at Loreto.

At four o'clock on Easter morning, Hortense and Valerie Masuyer groped their way through the dark anteroom of their chamber, in which soldiers were sleeping. They were followed by Louis and his comrade, Zappi, disguised as servants—an uncouth pair—Louis' head had been shaved during his illness; Zappi's livery was much too big for him.

The party reached Loreto for the earliest Mass, but only visited the church for a few moments. This was the start of a swift and nerve-wracking journey. To reach France, it was necessary to double back and pass through territory where Louis was well known. He was recognized several times, but only by those who wished him well. The most anxious moments were in the vicinity of Florence. At Pisa, Hortense thought it safe to use her English passport for the first time, and Louis and Zappi could change their disguise to that of two young English gentlemen, Charles and William Hamilton. At Lucca, there was a new complication; now it was Zappi's turn to develop a fever and spots. The best that could be done for him was to wrap him in blankets, make him a bed in the carriage, and trust that his measles would be no more serious than Louis'.

No halt was made until Pietrasanta was reached. There, Hortense and her son stayed over for a day to make an excursion to the little town where Napoléon Louis had established his paper factory and built a small house, designed by Charlotte, where he and his wife could spend their summers. As they skirted the Gulf of Spezia, Louis told Hortense that his brother had planned to build a naval base there, after they had liberated Italy. On such high hopes had youth been fed!

At last, only a week after leaving Ancona, the travelers passed through Nice and crossed, by a long wooden bridge, over the Var River into France. There, they felt that they were treading on holy ground. It seemed a miracle to hear French spoken everywhere. Young Louis' spirits, till now depressed, began to revive. Whenever they stopped for the night, he would go off for a stroll through the town, to chat with its inhabitants, to come back to tell his mother of the conversations he had had. Though he was supposed to be English, he was questioned more than once about the uprising in Italy and his brother's death. He and Zappi played schoolboy tricks on one another. They teased Mademoiselle Masuyer, by saying that all the French girls were ugly. They took a dislike to a hat she wore, and when it blew off her head into a canal, instead of fishing it out, they pelted it with stones until it sank.

Hortense, meanwhile, was reliving the past. It was at Cannes that Napoleon had landed from Elba. It was at Nemours that she had met Eugène, when he was summoned from Italy for her mother's divorce. At Fontainebleau the party visited the palace as tourists. Their guide was a servant who had been there during the Empire. Hortense let down her veil, though she did not think that there was much danger of her being recognized. She had just passed her forty-eighth birthday; she was an elderly woman, and the length of time she had been away was measured by the growth of shrubbery in the gardens planted by Napoleon.

The rooms that had been hers were pointed out to Hortense. She herself showed her son the chapel where he was baptized by Cardinal Fesch on November 4, 1810. He seemed to be most moved, however, by the great courtyard where the Emperor said good-bye to his troops, and the little round table at which the abdication was signed.

The following day, April 23rd, Louis was leaning out of the window of the carriage and gazing greedily as they drove into Paris, skirting the Jardin des Plantes and crossing the river by the bridge that had been named Austerlitz after Napoleon's greatest victory.

XXXVIII

A LONG WAY HOME

HORTENSE and her son had arrived in Paris at a fortunate moment. Louis Philippe, the King of the Green Umbrella, sat uneasily on his throne. He was unpopular with Legitimists, who sighed after the exiled Charles X and his heir, the Comte de Chambord. The republicans were disgusted that the Revolution had been allowed to die in Italy without the King of the French so much as raising a finger. On the other hand, Bonapartism had become a cult and a legend, seeded at Saint Helena, kept alive wherever old soldiers met, in the songs of the people's poet, Béranger, in peasant houses where the chief and only ornament was apt to be a picture of the Little Corporal.

At least four Bonaparte plays were running simultaneously in Paris, the most ambitious being *Napoleon Bonaparte, or Thirty Years of French History* by a rising young playwright, Alexandre Dumas. It covered the entire life of the hero, from Corsica to Saint Helena, and the actor who played the part of Sir Hudson Lowe, Napoleon's jailer, played it so well that he had to have police protection on his way home from the theater.

The travelers went to a hotel, the Hôtel d'Hollande in the rue de la Paix. From a balcony that ran along their suite of rooms,

373

one had a good view of the Place Vendôme, where a new statue of Napoleon was about to be raised to the top of the famous column, the old one having been pulled down and melted by the Bourbons.

Hortense had selected Colonel d'Houdetot, an aide-de-camp of the King, whom she had met in Switzerland, as her best prospect for getting an interview with Louis Philippe. Valerie Masuyer wrote the Colonel that she was in Paris with an English family, and asked him to come to the hotel on some business concerning Queen Hortense. D'Houdetot came and gave a bleat of surprise and alarm, when confronted by the Queen herself. He promised, however, to present her request to the King, who took such a serious view of the matter that he sent his Prime Minister, Casimir Périer, a hard-headed, unsentimental banker, to see Hortense, before venturing to see her himself.

All of this was done so rapidly that on the evening of April 26th, only three days after reaching Paris, Hortense was conducted by Périer to the Palais Royale, the home of the Orléans family, which Louis Philippe had not yet quitted for the Tuileries. She was taken in, by a side entrance, to a small room, occupied by Colonel d'Houdetot, in which there were only two chairs, a table, and a bed. Hortense sat on the bed and the King in one of the armchairs, while D'Houdetot stood with his back against the door throughout the visit, to guard against surprise.

Though the setting was informal, Louis Philippe was very polite. His manner was an unpretentious as his appearance, and he reminded Hortense a little of the good King of Bavaria, who had been so kind to her and Eugène. He spoke with sympathy of her exile—he had known exile himself—and said that the renewal of the ban on the Bonapartes was none of his doing. He must feel his way cautiously; his position was still uncertain.

Hortense assured the King of not wanting to add to his burdens. She intended to remain in Paris for only a short time, before going on to England. When she came back, she would like to pass through France on her way to Switzerland, and asked the

King to protect her in that country from any hostile moves made by Austria.

Hortense also told Louis Philippe that her son was with her. During their journey from the south, young Louis had written a letter to the King, asking that he might be allowed to enlist in the French army. "Send the letter to me," Louis Philippe said.

Unasked, he brought up a matter that Hortense had already mentioned to Casimir Périer. For years, she had vainly petitioned the French government for payment of the money, deposited for her and for her mother Joséphine at Blois in 1814 and confiscated by the Duc d'Angoulême. With interest running for seventeen years, her claim amounted to a million francs.

"Write me an account of what you think is due, and send it to me personally," the King said. "I understand money matters and will be your man of business."

He then asked if Hortense would like to meet his wife, Queen Amelie, and his sister, Madame Adélaïde. The ladies were sent for, and the Queen, seating herself on the bed beside Hortense, was very cordial, though when she heard that Hortense had been in Paris for three days she exclaimed, "Three days, as long as that!"

In spite of the lack of enthusiasm shown for her being in Paris at all, Hortense went back to the hotel feeling that she had accomplished something. She found Louis in bed with a fever. It seemed as if the measles had come back to plague him. His throat was red and swollen. During the next few days, Hortense stayed at home to nurse him and had several visits from Casimir Périer, who lived in the neighborhood and said that he only wanted to be useful to her. He spoke of the Law of Banishment being repealed at the next sitting of the Chamber. He suggested that the Duchy of Saint-Leu might be reconstituted, and that Louis, if he took the name of Saint-Leu, might be permitted to enter the army.

Hortense knew what her son's reaction to this would be. When she told Louis of it, he said simply, "I would rather lie down with my brother in his grave!"

Casimir Périer's visits ceased. Hortense wondered if this were due to an unfortunate slip of her tongue. At their last meeting, the banker offered to lend her some money for her journey. She declined, saying that she and her son had simple tastes and did not care about traveling in style. She added with a smile, "You see, we are very plebian royalty"—at least, that was what she meant to say, but after Périer had left, she realized she had said, "You see, we are very popular royalty." The 5th of May, the anniversary of Napoleon's death, was approaching, and the government didn't want any "popular royalty" to be living so near to the Place Vendôme, where a demonstration might be made.

Colonel d'Houdetot took over the task of keeping an eye on the Bonapartes. He came daily to the hotel, and showed a growing dismay because the visitors had not yet left for England. He always inquired for Louis' health and went into the bedroom to see if the young man was there, and if he was as ill as Hortense said he was.

Hortense herself was anxious to be gone. There were innumerable people whom she would like to see—Charles de Flahaut, for one, was in Paris, and was again a general in the French army—but she had promised Louis Philippe to remain incognito. She was afraid of going out except after nightfall, and was always heavily veiled.

Hortense's one daylight excursion came close to disaster. Louis Daguerre, the painter and physicist, who would soon present to the world the first photographic plate, had opened to the public his Diorama, a series of panoramic views, with elaborate lighting effects, of famous places. One of the subjects shown was Napoleon's grave at Saint Helena. Hortense and Valerie Masuyer visited the show on an afternoon when they thought there would not be many people there. Hortense was gazing mournfully at the desolate spot where Napoleon was buried, when she became aware that someone was gazing at her, a man who used to come to her house in Paris and whom she had seen more recently in Rome. Seizing Valerie by the wrist, Hortense fled into the open air and leaped into a cab. Before she could drive away, her friend of former days was at the door and put his finger to his lip, as if to say he would keep her secret. Nevertheless, he sent a boy to follow the cab on foot, and it was only after playing hide-and-seek in the shopping district of Paris that Hortense was able to escape.

Later, she regretted that she had yielded to instinct and run away; it would have been better to have spoken to her discoverer and asked his coöperation.

On May 5th, while Louis was still in bed and was being bled by leeches that the doctor had applied to his throat, Hortense watched from her balcony people coming to lay flowers at the base of the Vendôme column. They seemed to be sorrowful rather than belligerent and were on good terms with the soldiers on guard within the enclosure. It was not until late in the day that an argument arose between two spectators. Before more serious trouble could develop, fire hoses were brought into play to disperse the crowd. With somewhat the same intent, Colonel d'Houdetot came to call upon Hortense. She must go at once, he said, even if Louis had not yet recovered. This was a royal command, backed up by the ministry, all of whom were sure that Louis was in touch with disturbers of the peace.

The following day, Hortense set off for Calais, traveling by easy stages so as not to tire her invalid.

A seasick crossing of the Channel, a night at Canterbury, London; Hortense's first impression of England was that it was very much like her kingdom of Holland; it was neat, its roads well kept, its countryside was green. The first unusual sight the travelers saw was the campaign headquarters of a political candidate, for a general election was in progress. England had a new sovereign, William IV. The Tories were out, and the Whigs were in. A bill was in the making to reform Parliament by doing away with what Valerie Masuyer described in her diary as "*les bourgs pourries,*"—rotten boroughs.

Hortense had soon met Lord Grey, the courageous champion of

the Reform Bill. She had entrée to all the great Whig houses, for at Rome she had made the acquaintance of Charles Richard Fox, a son of Lord Holland; Holland, who was now a cabinet minister and who, while out of office, had protested in vain the rigors of Napoleon's imprisonment. Lady Holland had gone to great trouble to send books and comforts to Saint Helena.

There were Bonaparte plays running in London, as well as in Paris, and there were other representatives of the Bonaparte family in town, beside Louis and Hortense. One of Lucien's many children, Christine Egypta, was married to Lord Dudley Stuart; Achille Murat, Caroline's oldest son, had just arrived from America, where he had studied law, bought a plantation in Mississippi, and married an American wife.

The two natural sons of the Emperor were also in London: Léon Dénuelle, the little boy whom Hortense saw at La Malmaison in 1815, and Maria Walewska's son, Count Walewski. "How much you look like your father," Lady Holland said to the latter, somewhat to the young man's embarrassment. When Walewski came to call on Hortense, Louis was scornful of him.

"What is that pretty boy doing here," he asked, "while men are fighting and dying in Poland?"

This criticism was unjust, for Walewski had been in Warsaw, had taken part in the uprising against Russia that followed the French revolution of July; he was now in England, trying to get intervention or a loan for the insurgents.

Louis was not yet his usual, even-tempered self. It took some time for him to recuperate from his infected throat. When he was well enough to go about, he did not follow his mother's footsteps to Mayfair or to the palatial country houses to which she was invited. He had an orbit of his own. Hortense and Valerie Masuyer were worried about Louis' social activities and contacts. Where was he spending his evenings? Who were the ladies who wrote him so many notes, and who seemed to take such an interest in his affairs?

"Louis is not so seductive that all the women in the world

should be running after him," Hortense said, with a realism that was rare where her child was concerned.

Valerie was the pursebearer, and Louis came to her often for money. "Come now, own up," she said to him. "You are conspiring again. This money you want isn't for you; it's for some political factotum."

"Perhaps," Louis said, with a smile.

"You're ruining yourself," Valerie grumbled. "These people are deceiving you. They only want to empty your pockets."

She had in mind an Italian, Mirandoli, who often came to the little house in George Street, that Hortense had rented. Valerie was sure the man was an adventurer. Louis also seemed to be falling in love with a Madame Lenox, whom he had met through his cousin, Achille Murat, and who had nothing to recommend her except that her husband was in a French prison. Her dear Prince, Valerie thought—for Louis had become dear to her and she felt she should save him from himself—was a far more complicated person than he seemed. His gentleness concealed a passionate nature, his silences a restless mind. Valerie refused to give him the twenty-five louis he had asked for, saying that it was needed for a new carriage. The one that had brought them all the way from Florence to London was a wreck and must be replaced.

Valerie had taken over all of Hortense's business correspondence, and knew how closely finances must be reckoned. In the past three months, Hortense had spent almost 60,000 francs. She had made inroads into her capital at Ancona, and while she was in Paris, the banking firm with which she dealt failed. Hortense had brought with her to London a diamond necklace that had a sentimental as well as a cash value. Joséphine had worn it at her coronation, Hortense had given it to Napoleon in 1815, and it was returned to her after his death. Hortense tried to sell the necklace, but without success, to the Duchess of St. Albans, who was fantastically rich and a collector of jewels.

The payment of the claim that Hortense had lodged with the French government was now of great importance. As the weeks went by and no word came from France, it seemed less and less likely that anything would be realized. There was no word, either, of Louis' being allowed to enlist in the artillery regiment at Strasbourg, on which he had set his heart. He wrote a letter of sympathy to Madame Lenox' imprisoned husband, which fell into the hands of the French police.

In June, there was a series of riots in France. Again it was being said that Hortense was hiding somewhere in her native land. The English newspapers reported that she was scheming to get the Belgian crown for her son, Belgium having recently seceded from Holland. Once more the figure of Napoleon's stepdaughter, the mother of a male Bonaparte, was being inflated to menacing proportions.

It was time, Hortense thought, to go home to Switzerland, but it seemed as if even passports to travel through France might be denied. Talleyrand was French Ambassador in London. He made no effort to see Hortense and, though he answered politely a letter that she wrote him, he did not seem to have been notified of her conversations with the King and Casimir Périer. Hortense wrote to Colonel d'Houdetot; while she was waiting for a reply she went to Tunbridge Wells to take the waters and to remove Louis from the intriguing atmosphere of London. The passports were issued in late July, made out to Madame d'Arenenberg and son; they were not delivered until after Bastille Day.

Hortense thought it would be wise to by-pass Paris, but there were still remembered spots she wanted to show to Louis. They crossed the Channel in a steamboat. From Calais they went to Boulogne. Hortense had never forgotten that golden week in 1805, when she and Napoléon Charles visited the Grand Army, poised for its abortive invasion of England. The great camps of wooden barracks had disappeared, without a trace. The only proof that they had ever existed was an observation tower. Hortense and Louis climbed to its top, and while she was pointing out landmarks, they were joined by other sightseers, who looked at her curiously and marveled that she knew so much of what had happened here so long ago.

It would have taken too wide a detour to visit Saint-Leu, now in other hands, for Louis, Senior, had sold it many years earlier, without sharing the profits with his wife. La Malmaison was on the travelers' way. Its present owner was a banker, who had kept only the house and a small part of the gardens created by Joséphine; the rest had vanished as completely as the Boulogne camp. Hortense asked at the door if she would be allowed to visit the château, but was turned away because she had no ticket of admission from the proprietor. She and Louis went next to the church nearby at Rueil. Hortense saw for the first time the monument that she and Eugène had erected to their mother. It had been decorated with flowers—still fresh. Some old pensioner, some neighbor of the good Empress had remembered Joséphine.

Hortense and Louis went on their way slowly, lingeringly, with the feeling that at each stage of their journey a door was closing behind them. The immediate future called for a winter spent soberly and economically at Arenenberg. Hortense wondered how Louis would stand the long months of isolation and what outlet he would find for his energies. Had she done well or ill to summon up the past?

XXXIX

THE HEIR APPARENT

On July 22, 1832, Napoleon's son, the Duke of Reichstadt, died at Schönbrunn, and his corpse, clad in the white uniform of an Austrian officer, was buried in the tomb of the Hapsburgs. Hortense's son Louis, wrote to his old friend and teacher, Abbé Bertrand, that his cousin had left him "the sword of the Emperor. It is a precious gift, of which I hope I will be worthy."

Louis did not need to tell the Abbé that the legacy was purely figurative. He had become heir apparent to a phantom throne. Because he was young and vigorous, he had taken precedence over those who had rights of seniority: his uncle, Joseph, and his father, Louis.

Hortense tacitly recognized the new status of her child. Visitors to Arenenberg that summer noticed that the Prince was expected to lead the way into the dining room. There were many visitors to make up for the lonely winter months, when Hortense and Louis, each with a literary project in mind, were busy at their desks. During August, Alexander Dumas, the beautiful Madame Récamier, and Chateaubriand, the grand old man of French romanticism, were at Wolfsberg, the pension presided over by Louise Cochelet and her husband, Captain Parquin.

With the first frost of autumn, visitors vanished. In November, Louis went to London to see his uncle, Joseph Bonaparte. Joseph, as soon as he heard that the Duke of Reichstadt was dying, left America for Europe, to view at close range the Bonaparte position. Apparently Louis made a good impression on his uncle, for Joseph wrote Hortense that he found her son "gentle, tractable, and studious, a man of honor and delicate perceptions." Hortense hoped that Louis, with Joseph to guide him, would avoid the company of adventurers, male and female.

While Louis was in London, he had an interview with General Lafayette, one of the last survivors of the group that tried—and failed—to establish a constitutional monarchy in 1789. Lafayette felt that he had made a mistake in helping to put Louis Philippe on the throne of France. He also repented the stand he took in 1815, when he led the demand in the Chamber of Deputies for Napoleon's abdication.

"Only your name," Lafayette told Louis, "has any popular significance."

In June, the young man was back in Arenenberg. He had been working on a book in London, and the one he had written the winter before had just been published, with the modest title of *Political Reveries*. It was a brief work, hardly more than a pamphlet, and was intended to appeal to all who were dissatisfied with the repressive, middle-class government of Louis Philippe. It strongly echoed the opinions of Napoleon, as reported at Saint Helena. Louis paid homage to the philosophers who begot the French Revolution and declared himself a democrat in theory, but for all practical purposes, in a world unsafe for democracy, an imperialist.

Louis had taken to heart what Hortense had once written him, that "every form of government is good, sufficient, and legitimate, if it is orderly and effective." The empire that Hortense's son had in mind would respect national aspirations in all countries and would be safeguarded internally by a constitution. If the son or

other heirs of the emperor were unfit to rule, the succession would
be settled by a plebiscite.

Louis sent a copy of his *Reveries* to Chateaubriand, who, though
a royalist and loyal to the Bourbons, said that he would vote for
Prince Louis if an election for sovereign were ever held in France.
Very different was the reception given to Louis' work by his father. Louis, Senior's, feelings were hurt by a passing reference to
the affairs of Holland. It would have been better, the author of
the pamphlet said, if Napoleon had appointed a general to gov-
ern that exposed outpost of empire. "It seems that I count for very
little in your estimation," the aggrieved parent wrote. "You have
a frenzied desire for fame. Let me tell you that, without realizing
it, you are working against your own interests. The only real glory
lies in doing one's duty."

It was the duty of a junior Bonaparte to marry and to marry
well. This was a matter in which Father, Mother, Uncles, Aunts,
and Grandmother all agreed. In the spring of 1833, young Louis
was twenty-five, an overripe age in a family geared to early mat-
ings. While he was still in England, Hortense wrote her son that
she wished nothing better for him than a "good little wife," who
had been well brought up and was young enough to adapt herself
to his ways. She herself would like to have some grandchildren to
cherish. "Those who think I am ambitious don't know how little
I regret power, too dearly bought. All I ask for is you—and a
little sunshine!"

Father Louis expressed himself in somewhat the same vein, but
without endearments. He would be satisfied with any daughter-
in-law, he said, who was well born, of irreproachable morals, and
wealthy, for Louis must realize how small was his portion.

Louis himself was not eager for matrimony, though he was very
susceptible to women and spent far too much money, his mother
feared, on ladies whom she never met and whose names she did
not know. Louis told Abbé Bertrand that he did not want to marry
as long as he was an exile. He was indifferent, when various plans
made for him by his elders came to nothing, the most splendid

failure being a match with Maria Braganza, the youthful Queen of Portugal.

Louis went on his dogged way of acquainting the world with his opinions. His second book, *A Consideration of Swiss Politics and Military Affairs*, gave a good deal of information about its declared subject, but its real interest lay in its asides on French history. In 1834, Louis, who for two years had been a citizen of Switzerland, received his commission as captain of artillery. This entailed only part-time, seasonal employment. He started work at once on a *Manual of Artillery*, that would give him professional standing; getting himself out of a warm bed at five o'clock of a winter morning to write by candlelight.

"What a generous nature he has!" Hortense wrote to one of Louis' friends. "I am proud to be his mother. . . . He was born for great things and is worthy of them."

Hortense, convinced of her son's destiny, was touched by his uncomplaining acceptance of the fact that they were too poor now to leave Arenenberg except for an occasional short stay at Geneva, or some nearby resort. Her motive in editing her mother's letters and appearing in print in 1834 with an account of her recent travels, *Queen Hortense in Italy, in France and in England in 1831*, was in part at least financial. Hortense knew that Louis should marry money, but she hoped, as she had hoped in all of the many marriages she had made for others, that love would be included in the bargain. She might even settle for love alone.

In November of 1835, Jérôme's wife, Catherine, died. She had been heroic in her devotion to a husband who was consistently unfaithful to her. She left three children: Jérôme, aged twenty, Mathilde, aged sixteen, and Napoléon, aged thirteen. It was the youngest who would feel his mother's death most keenly, Hortense thought. She invited "Plon-Plon," as he was nicknamed, to live at Arenenberg. Cousin Louis tutored the boy in history and mathematics and took him skating on Lake Constance. Hortense shared in their fun, to the extent of being pushed in a sled over the ice by Louis.

Only Louis, Senior, who kept a dour eye on everything at Arenenberg, disapproved of Hortense's kindness to the family of Jérôme. He was very much afraid that his son would be inveigled into marriage with Mathilde. Jérôme now lived in Florence, but the two brothers never met. Louis was shocked by the reports of the lavishness of Jérôme's establishment, of the balls and dinners for thirty or forty guests that he gave. As long as Catherine was alive, she received a pension from her brother, the King of Würtemberg, and from her cousin, the Czar of Russia. These sources of income died with her. Jérôme, chronically in debt, had borrowed to the hilt on what he expected to inherit from his mother, who died in February of 1836.

When Louis, Senior, learned that Jérôme and Mathilde were going to Arenenberg in April, he guessed the reason for their visit. He gave his son a bleak outline of his expectations. Though he would be his father's heir, Louis could only count on an annual allowance of 6,000 francs during his father's lifetime; this was little enough, even for a bachelor. Louis was warned against becoming involved with a father-in-law who would squander a royal income —and several royal incomes, if he had them.

For once, the older head was the wiser, but on the very evening of her arrival at Arenenberg, Mathilde Bonaparte had an overpowering effect upon her cousin. Louis had not seen Mathilde for two years. When they last met, she was a child whom he could entertain by making faces under cover of his prayer book during Mass; she was now a beautiful young woman. Her evening gown was cut so low and showed so much of her white breasts and shoulders that her father, with the prudishness of the confirmed rake, scolded her for being so indecent. Louis, hot-eyed, devoured her nakedness.

Valerie Masuyer could see that he was ensnared. Hortense's companion and secretary loved Louis with the wistful protective love of a woman for a man who is not for her and who is ten years younger than she. Valerie disapproved of the Jérôme family, root and branch. The children were brats; the parent was shifty. Jérôme spoke of buying an estate in the neighborhood and visited all the fine houses that were vacant, though everyone knew how he hated the country and how little taste he had for the romantic scenery of Switzerland. He was only trying to impress Hortense with his solvency. She was ready to hand over all she had to her son; she had told Valerie to write to Paris, telling her agent there to sell the last important piece of jewelry, a turquoise diadem.

The visit lasted much too long for all but the budding lovers, whom "Plon-Plon" spied upon, as they were kissing in the garden. When Louis had to be away from home, Mathilde sulked and was rude to Valerie and others of the household. Her seventeenth birthday fell on May 27th, 1836. Louis arranged the entire celebration: a boat trip on the lake, a troupe of folk singers and musicians engaged to come from Constance, a ball in the evening, at which Mathilde wore her daring evening gown.

A few days later, she and her father left. Mathilde wept; Louis was glum. He tossed a bouquet into the carriage as it moved off, and galloped after it on his handsome mare.

Hortense had not shared in the jealous faultfinding of Mademoiselle Masuyer. She was blinded, Valerie thought, by the vision of love in springtime. She was planning how Arenenberg could be arranged as a two-family house, which rooms she would assign to her daughter-in-law and the grandchildren. Immediately after Jérôme's return to Florence, however, there was a meeting, the first in several years, of the two Bonaparte brothers. Jérôme revealed that Mathilde would have no dowry. Louis, though not forbidding the banns, reiterated that he could do no more for his son than he was doing at present. There the matter rested.

Hortense was chiefly sorry for the depression that the report of this interview caused in her Captain of Artillery. At the moment, he had no military duties to distract him. She could not begrudge him a little holiday at Baden, the Swiss Baden, though she was alarmed by the amount of money he managed to spend there in two months: six thousand francs, all of the yearly allowance given him by his father.

Hortense, that summer of 1836, was taking an interest in another love affair and in the future of yet another young man.

The memory of her child by Charles de Flahaut had run—a dark thread—through her years of exile. In spite of money difficulties, she had provided more than 40,000 francs for young Demorny's support and education. Once, she sent for him to come to her in Switzerland, but her messenger, Vincent Rousseau, found that the boy's grandmother was unwilling to give him up.

Charles Auguste Demorny was only four, when his mother left Paris in 1815. He was not quite six, when his father was married to Margaret Elphinstone in England. As a result of this, little Auguste, till then boarded out in the country, came to live permanently with Madame de Souza. He suffered none of the misfortunes that illegitimacy is supposed to entail. His *bonne maman*, as he called her, adored him. He was the pet of *papa*, her Portuguese husband. Whenever Charles de Flahaut—*Monsieur le comte* to Auguste—came to Paris, he was very attentive. Auguste, while still small enough to be led by the hand, was taken to call on a distinguished old gentleman at the Foreign Office, who looked, somebody said, very much like a dead lion. Talleyrand admired his grandson and predicted that someday he would be a statesman. When he was eighteen, in the summer of 1829, Auguste went to Aix with his father at the same time that a very gracious lady, Queen Hortense, was visiting the resort.

The relationship of these various persons to himself must already have been surmised by a bright boy, who was a pupil at one of the best schools in Paris. On a trip to Scotland, Auguste made the acquaintance of his father's wife and her five little girls, his half-sisters. After the July revolution of 1830, the De Flahauts came back to Paris, and Auguste lived with them in their magnificent house in the rue d'Angoulême. Margaret de Flahaut, in spite of her puritan background, was neither straight-laced nor jealous of her husband's past. The fact that she was a zealot of the Napoleonic cult may have accounted, in part, for her tolerance. A gift portrait of the former Queen of Holland hung in her bedroom. She herself may have suggested that her second child, and De Flahaut's favorite daughter, should be named Clementine Hortense.

It was a great advantage to young Demorny to be a protégé, if not the acknowledged son, of the Comte de Flahaut, who was high in favor with Louis Philippe. After graduating from a military training school, Auguste received a commission in an aristocratic regiment, the First Lancers. He saw service in Africa, where a long, debilitating war with Algiers had begun in 1831. Auguste was wounded in the leg, received the Cross of the Legion of Honor for bravery, and, after two attacks of dysentery, was sent home and given an honorable discharge.

He had earned the right to a little frivolity. A very elegant young man, with much of his father's charm and a wit that was all his own, he was invited everywhere. He soon had won the heart of one of the most attractive women in Paris, Madame Le Hon, the wife of the Belgian Ambassador. In July of 1836, Madame Le Hon paid a visit to Arenenberg.

She and Hortense had already carried on a correspondence that was almost as mysterious as that of De Flahaut and his mother during the Napoleonic wars. A third party, reading the letters, would never guess that Madame Le Hon's "grandfather" was Louis Philippe, that her "sister Augustine" was actually her lover, and that the Monsieur Dunant, so often mentioned, was Charles de Flahaut. Hortense was delighted with Fanny Le Hon when they met. She was beautiful, a dazzling blonde. Being three years older than Auguste, her feeling for him was slightly maternal. She was anxious to do all she could to further his career. Hortense saw an analogy between this youthful pair and herself and the De Flahaut of other days.

One of the subjects discussed during Fanny's visit was Auguste's desire to be legally adopted by his father. There was no son of Margaret Elphinstone for him to displace. It seemed a perfectly reasonable suggestion to Hortense. She promised to write to Monsieur Dunant and take the matter up with him in person, for she was expecting a long-promised visit from him and his wife later in the summer.

But the visit was again deferred, and Madame Le Hon came back to Arenenberg in October. Neither the adoption scheme nor Louis' marriage with Mathilde had been settled. Louis, home from Baden, seemed subdued and thoughtful, so much so that Valerie Masuyer, an interested spectator of all the drama of the household, thought he might be ill. He announced that he was going hunting on the estate of Prince Hohenzollern-Hechingen, the husband of one of his Murat cousins.

Louis and Madame Le Hon left Arenenberg on the same day, but were to travel in opposite directions. On her way home, Fanny stopped at an inn at Besançon. She heard the voice of a man, passing by in the corridor, that sounded very much like that of Prince Louis; but thought she must be mistaken.

Her ears had not deceived her. Louis was not at Hechingen; he was at Besançon on his way to Strasbourg, the most important military post on the eastern boundary of France. Just before leaving home, he went to Wolfsberg to call on Captain Parquin, who was now a widower; Louise Cochelet having been dead for more than a year. Wolfsberg had just been sold to an Englishman; its ex-proprietor was again at loose ends.

"Parquin," Louis said tersely, "I am going to bring the eagle back to our banners or die in the attempt. Are you with me?"

With equal brevity, the soldier of the Emperor replied, "My prince, you can count upon me."

XL

GENTLE, BUT OBSTINATE

THE return from Elba took place in 1815; to reproduce it in 1836 did not seem impossible to an adventurous mind, given the fact that, after twenty years, the French army was still strongly Bonapartist. Louis had been preparing for his coup for many months. His chief confidant and conspirator was a young man named Fialin de Persigny, who had come to Arenenberg with a letter of introduction from Joseph Bonaparte. De Persigny was a fanatic for the cause; he had been both soldier and journalist. Throughout the summer of 1836, he visited various garrison towns, testing the degree of disaffection to the government to be found in each. Louis, for his part, was associating expensively with officers on holiday at Baden and found one on whom he could work, Colonel Vaudrey, the commander of an artillery regiment at Strasbourg. Before he went home to Arenenberg, Louis paid a visit to the town and had a secret meeting with a score of officers, all of whom gave him encouragement.

On the evening of October 28th, Louis was again in Strasbourg with De Persigny and Parquin. The following day was spent in furtive visits to key personalities, and the night in writing proclamations. At six o'clock on the morning of October 30th, Colonel

Vaudrey's regiment was drawn up in the courtyard of its barracks. A light snow was falling. The Colonel drew his sword and shouted, "Soldiers of the Fourth Regiment of Artillery, a great revolution is about to take place. You see before you"—he pointed to Louis, who was there with his companions—"the nephew of the Emperor. He has come to reconquer the rights of the people. All who love glory and freedom should rally around him. The people and the army can trust him. . . . Soldiers, can the nephew of the Emperor put his trust in you?"

There were shouts of *"Vive l'Empereur"*; there were shouts of *"Vive Napoleon"* after Louis had spoken. He recalled that it was in this regiment his uncle had served as captain. It had opened the gates of Grenoble to the Emperor on his return from exile. Louis came to them with the testament of Napoleon in one hand and the sword of Austerlitz in the other. "Let us march together against the traitors and oppressors of our country. Long live liberty!"

The regiment, with its band playing, Louis, Vaudrey, and the others at its head, marched through the streets of Strasbourg. Early though it was, there were many onlookers to cheer, many to rush forward to kiss the banner that one of Louis' henchmen was carrying. There were cheers also from the gendarmerie, when the prefect of police was arrested by De Persigny. There were even cheers from the servants of the Commandant, when the procession halted at his house. The Commandant, General Voirol, was not yet up and, when interviewed, refused to recognize "the revolution." Parquin was left to deal with the General; when he tried to make an arrest, he found that his intended prisoner had escaped through a rear door.

There had been treachery somewhere along the line, as well as bungling. Voirol had not been taken by surprise. Forewarned, he had alerted the officers at the infantry barrack, toward which the parading regiment was heading. When it reached the spot, it was greeted by cries of *"Vive le roi!"* When Louis was introduced as nephew of the Emperor, someone shouted, "Imposter! He's the nephew of Colonel Vaudrey!" Or it might have been "the bastard of Colonel Vaudrey."

A scuffle took place, but only a scuffle; Louis had stipulated that no weapons should be used. He and his supporters were outnumbered, for only a few of the invaders had been able to squeeze into the courtyard. Louis' coat was torn in the melee, and he and Vaudrey were taken prisoner.

The drama had failed. It was not without its elements of farce, but to its author it was a veritable tragedy. De Persigny had escaped, but Parquin was brought in, a prisoner. He had fought back and his hands were bleeding.

"You are wounded," Louis exclaimed. "You have shed your blood for me!"

"I wish there was not a drop of it left in my veins," Parquin said. "I wish you were safe at home with the Queen at Arenenberg."

"We will be shot," he prophesied, "but we will die a good death."

Louis had been so convinced that the outcome would be either victory or death, that the night before he had written two letters to his mother: one announcing his having taken command of the garrison at Strasbourg, the other a last farewell. The victory letter was sent by mistake.

Hortense took the good news calmly. When Louis left Arenenberg, she knew nothing of his plans, but she guessed that the hunting expedition was a pretext; she gave her son Joséphine's wedding ring as a talisman. When word came of Louis' arrest, Hortense remembered the fate of Marshal Ney, of Charles de la Bédoyère, of so many others. She pictured Louis facing a firing squad, and receiving the traditional six bullets in the heart and one in the head.

Within the hour, Valerie Masuyer was on her way to Strasbourg. The father of Hortense's companion, a doctor, had taught in the Strasbourg School of Medicine, and Valerie had a married sister living in the town. As soon as she arrived, Valerie went to see General Voirol, and learned that Louis was being held in the citadel. Though she was not allowed to see him, she heard that he was making many friends by his quiet, pleasant manner and the serenity with which he accepted his predicament. There would be no chance for escape, but Valerie was told that Louis' life was not in danger. Her sister, married to an officer who had flirted with the plot and who was afraid of being found out, railed at the Prince and the foolish, dangerous thing he had done.

While Valerie was in Strasbourg, Hortense was on her way to Paris with Madame Salvage, a friend of Madame Récamier, who, during the past few years, had become a member of the Arenenberg household. They traveled night and day to Viry, just outside the capital. Because she had no passport, Hortense could not enter the city; she had to trust her companion to act as intermediary. Madame Salvage had an interview with the Comte de Molé, President of the Council of Ministers. He told her that there was no chance of Hortense being allowed to see him or the King. Louis, however, was to be treated with leniency, and was to be deported to America on a government cruiser. On November 9th, he was removed from Strasbourg; his carriage must have passed close to Viry on its way to the coast.

Hortense received a letter from Louis, written just before he sailed on November 14th. He told her that he had protested strongly his being separated from his friends, who were to be tried by court martial. He had no regrets for what he had done. She must not pity him, nor must she try to follow him. Life in America would be hard for her, and at home, she could help his comrades or their families.

Hortense went back to Arenenberg. In the press, Louis was ridiculed. His uncles, Joseph and Jérôme, had disowned him. His father had stopped his allowance and retained the proceeds from the sale of some property that belonged to his son. There was no chance now of a marriage with Mathilde Bonaparte. Jérôme had told his daughter—decidedly an afterthought—that Louis was a bastard.

"The human race is false and wicked," Hortense wrote to Fanny Le Hon, whom she had seen at Viry. "I would like to run away from it for good and all. Think of me sometimes, my dear child. Speak of me once in a while. Be happy. I will be thinking of you. At the moment I am so heartsick that I can only embrace you tenderly."

It was a great worry to Hortense when she heard that the police were to question Auguste Demorny, to make sure he had had no part in the Strasbourg affair; she was relieved when she learned he had been exonerated.

Not all of the human race was false and wicked. A young Italian friend of Louis', Count Arese, who had visited so often at Arenenberg that he seemed part of the family, offered to join the outcast in America. He left, laden with letters and personal belongings that Louis might need, the least practical, perhaps, being a sketch of Mathilde that Hortense had made during the springtime visit. All of the inhabitants of the castle rejoiced, when news came in January that Colonel Vaudrey and Captain Parquin had been acquitted. Even the members of a French court martial had such a strong Bonaparte bias that they were blind to mutiny.

Hortense told Fanny Le Hon that she was almost happy. She only needed to hear of her son's having landed safely in America; then she would relax and would pay attention to her health. She had not been well lately, though she was sure that there was nothing seriously wrong. Her symptoms were due, she thought, to an accident she had suffered on her way to France.

But her symptoms of vaginal hemorrhage and physical weakness could not wait. The ship that had taken Louis across the Atlantic was in no great hurry to reach the United States. It went first to Rio, where it spent a month, the prisoner not being allowed to go ashore. It was not until late in March that Hortense heard from Louis in New York. By then, her doctor, Dr. Conneau, who had followed her from Rome to Switzerland, took a serious view of her case. He had diagnosed a cancer of the uterus.

He called for a consultation of four doctors, one of them a famous surgeon, to meet him at Arenenberg.

April 3, 1837

My dear Son:

I may have to undergo an operation. If it is not successful, this letter brings you my benediction. We will meet, perhaps, in a better world where you will join me, I hope, after as long a life as possible. In leaving this world, you are my only regret; only your love for me has given life its charm. It should be a consolation to you, my dear, to know that your devotion has made your mother as happy as she could possibly be. Try to believe that all-seeing and loving eyes look down on those who are left below! This is a belief so necessary to our peace of mind that it must be true.

I give my blessing to your friend Arese. I feel as if he also were my son. I press you to my heart, my darling. I am very calm, very resigned, and I still hope that we may see one another again, but the will of God be done!

Your loving mother

Hortense had written before the medical consultation took place on April 7th. The surgeon found that the malignancy was too far advanced and that it would be impossible to operate. Hortense was so glad to escape the knife that she wrote more hopefully to Louis and told him not to be disturbed. She gave the letter to Valerie Masuyer to address. Underneath the flap to which the seal was affixed, Valerie wrote, "Come—come quickly!"

All about her knew, Hortense herself knew, that she was going to die, but not today, nor yet tomorrow. Undated death still lacked reality. As she grew weaker, Hortense spent more and more of her time in bed, but she thought how lovely it would be to have another winter in Italy and, quite as if she were able to make the journey, wrote to her cousin, Stéphanie of Baden, to ask if she could get her a passport.

Hortense had often been afraid of loneliness—it was one of her basic fears; she was far from lonely now. Letters inquiring for her health came from all parts of Europe. The house, as always, was full of visitors. Some stayed only an hour or a day, and went away in tears, shocked to see how changed, how emaciated the invalid had become. Others lingered. Among them was Monsieur Vieillard, who had been Napoléon Louis' tutor; a Lieutenant de Querelles, who had carried the banner at Strasbourg; and a young painter, named Cottrau, who, on Hortense's invitation, had come to sketch in the region.

The rudiments of a salon were still at hand. When she could no longer walk up and down stairs, Vincent Rousseau built a chair with carrying poles for Hortense, so that she could be brought down to the parlor or the terrace. She was visited there one day by an old friend, an archeologist and writer, who had brought his little boy with him. Hortense set the child to hunting four-leaf clovers for her. She had been hunting them all her life, she said, and they still might bring her luck.

Arese wrote Valerie that Louis had left New York on June 8th. Fast sailing vessels now went back and forth across the Atlantic, and Hortense heard in July that Louis was in London. He had tried to see his Uncle Joseph, but was rebuffed. Though he was traveling on an American passport, the French government knew of his whereabouts. Hortense wrote him she was sure he would be safe in his home canton of Switzerland—and she was feeling much, much better!

She had become so fragile, however, that her attendants were afraid the shock of Louis' arrival might be too much for her. Late in the night of August 5th, Valerie Masuyer, who was keeping nervous watch at the window, heard the sound of wheels on the drive and saw the light of the carriage lantern, as Louis drove up to the door of the castle. His coming was kept a secret until the morning. He had grown thin, Valerie noticed. He looked very pale as he entered the sickroom, but his coming had only a revivifying effect upon the invalid. Hortense said, as if she believed it, that she had turned the corner toward recovery. She actually got up, walked downstairs and made a tour of the garden, leaning on Louis' arm.

In the weeks that followed, there were some good days, but there were many bad. Hortense, when her son was absent, wept and said how cruel it was to leave him so alone in the world, so insecure, so rejected by his family. She was only fifty-four, and it seemed as if she might have been given a few more years to watch over her child. At the last, there was much pain. Hortense, whatever she might say or think, was too deeply rooted in life to die easily, and those who watched and suffered with her marveled at her stubborn resistance.

She seemed so near the end of her strength, on the night of October 4th, that all the household was awake and hovered about the sickroom. A priest had come to give Hortense the last sacrament. She seemed troubled, and anxiously asked her friends to pray for her. She was afraid of what might lie beyond the grave.

"I have done right whenever I could," Hortense said, "and I hope that God will be good to me. They say He is good, and yet"— here was a problem and its attendant doubt she had never been able to resolve—"He lets us suffer so."

As she drifted into semi-consciousness, Hortense murmured the names of her mother, of the Emperor, and of her sister-in-law, Augusta—though it might have been her son Auguste. She had not, however, slipped back into the safe and happy past. She still was living in the present and the future. Her fading mind was harassed by the dangers surrounding Louis.

"The French have treated us very badly," she whispered. "They have such little minds. They would make everything little—and yet they dare speak ill of the Emperor! . . . If you made a move on Paris, you would be lost. Be very careful. Think of your personal safety. They are very much afraid of us; they would hurt you if they could."

Again she spoke of her mother and the Emperor. Louis, who was kneeling by the bed, had told Valerie, at the time of his brother's death, that he did not believe in a future life. He would have foresworn anything, even, perhaps, his faith in the destiny of which Hortense was so sure and so apprehensive, if it could bring a moment's comfort to the dying.

"I will follow you to the better world to which you are going," he said. "You will find your mother there, and the Emperor, and my brothers. It is I who will be left alone. Give me your blessing, Mother."

There was no answer.

"I am here, Mother," Louis cried. "Can you hear me?"

Only the faintest whisper came back: "I hear you." A few minutes later, the doctor held a mirror to Hortense's lips to make sure she was no longer breathing. It was half-past five on the morning of October 5, 1837. The hour was noted so that it could be inscribed on the stone above Hortense's grave.

XLI

TO REMEMBER

HORTENSE had specified in her will that her body should be embalmed and buried beside her mother's, in the church at Rueil. A funeral service was held a few days after her death, at the cathedral at Ermatingen. People came from miles around, from Constance and from down the Rhine at Schaffhausen. Peasants came in their carts or on foot from distant mountain villages. Mass was celebrated by a mitred bishop. A discourse, praising the dead Queen's virtues and written by Monsieur Vieillard, was read in a German translation. Mozart's last *Requiem* was sung.

All during Hortense's illness, hidden tensions had existed in the group that surrounded her. They now came to the surface. Valerie Masuyer and all the women of the household detested Madame Salvage, who was dictatorial and tactless. They were sorry to find that she had been named executrix of the will and guardian of Hortense's unpublished memoirs.

The will itself was a lengthy document. It began with a preamble, in which Hortense spoke of Louis' mission in life. "I have no political advice to give to my son. I know that he realizes his position and the duties imposed by his name." Louis was to be sole legatee, but his inheritance would be small; the estate was burdened with pensions to all of the household and to many who had served Hortense in the past. Keepsakes were left to all of her friends. It was as though it were New Year's Day and Hortense were thinking of an appropriate gift for everyone she knew. Schoolmates were remembered, whom Hortense had not seen for many years. No one was overlooked, not even the British consul in Florence, who gave Hortense an English passport when she needed it so desperately in 1831. She willed that a cameo, surrounded by pearls, should be sent to him, "to remind him of my gratitude."

Valerie Masuyer, in addition to her pension, was given a ring, bracelets Hortense had worn, and a cashmere shawl. The faithful secretary was exhausted by her long vigil, and was very unhappy because Louis had been noticeably cool to her ever since his return from America. After the funeral they had a painful conversation, in which the reason was revealed. Louis thought that Valerie's sister and brother-in-law in Strasbourg were responsible for his failure last autumn. Madame Salvage had persuaded him that Valerie was involved.

The victim of this slander was too hurt to defend herself. Valerie ran away to hide her tears. When Louis came to her later and, holding out his hand, said, "Let's make it up," she flung her arms about his neck and kissed him. He wanted to give her Hortense's large collection of music. He opened up boxes, in which laces and furs were packed, and told her to take what she wanted. She refused. These things were valuable, she said; when he married, he would want to give them to his bride. How generous, he was, Valerie thought, how like his mother and grandmother before him.

Hortense had left no keepsake to her husband, but he was mentioned in the prologue to her will. It was one of the great sorrows of her life, she wrote, that she had been unable to make the man to whom she was married happy, and she hoped he would remember her with indulgence. Louis had been told that his father threw his letters in the fire unread; but he wrote to him from America, from London, and again on the day of Hortense's death. The strange man, who had shown himself at times so bitter and so vindictive to wife and child, wrote a reply that could not have been more tender.

My dear child:

I was not surprised, but I was saddened to hear of your poor mother's death. I can imagine the deep grief you must feel and share it as a Christian should, asking God to give her soul eternal rest. . . . I shall pray for her, as I would have liked to have her pray for me. I was touched by the few words concerning me, included in her will. With all my heart I will do as she asks. I do not want to keep alive any feeling that is contrary to the law of God.

You have lost her tender affection, but there is still mine, which will never fail you. . . . You must keep me informed of the ceremonies that will follow your mother's death. I wish to bear half of the expense of her monument and want it to be the work of our friend, the sculptor Bartolini. For my part, I have had a Mass celebrated for the repose of her soul in the Church of the Holy Spirit, where your poor brother is buried. I attended the service, as did also all of our family who are in Florence, and a large congregation.

In closing, let me give you again, dear child, my blessing and assure you of my love. I affectionately embrace you.

Louis gave Valerie the letter to read, because in it, she was mentioned by name and thanked for all she had done. Valerie asked permission to copy the letter. In doing so, she omitted several lengthy paragraphs of practical advice, the sum of which was that Louis should come to live in Florence with his father, should marry as his father wished, and give up all past ambitions. Valerie overlooked the high price to be paid for parental affection, and did not realize how typical it was of the writer. Forever after, she thought kindly of Hortense's husband. Whatever his faults, she felt that he had retained a feeling of respect for his wife.

Valerie was lenient in her judgment of the husband; she was

severe in her judgment of the lover. Soon after entering Hortense's service in 1830, the secretary learned from one of her predecessors of the existence of Charles de Flahaut and Auguste Demorny. She saw them both at the ceremonies that took place in the church at Rueil on January 8, 1838, a bitterly cold day. The church was filled with all who were left in France of the great folk of the Empire, elderly generals, festooned with decorations, faded beauties of the Imperial court. Louis was represented by his cousin, Tascher de la Pagerie. A son of Lucien and Caroline Murat—there was irony in this—represented the Bonaparte family. Caroline had grown enormously fat and was soon to die of the same disease as her rival, Hortense.

A few days later, Valerie, who was staying with Hortense's cousin, Émilie de Lavalette, had a call from the Comte de Flahaut and his son. Very politely, but with icy self-control, Charles questioned Valerie about Hortense's last days. It was an emotional moment for the devoted companion. Valerie's eyes filled with tears, when she saw how much young Demorny resembled his mother. He seemed to be more moved than Charles, though he said nothing to show that this was other than a formal visit of condolence.

Valerie voiced her disapproval later to Émilie's daughter, Joséphine de Forget. Monsieur de Flahaut, Valerie said, was a typical diplomat: cold of heart and cool of head. "And that is the man to whom the Queen gave herself, the wonderful woman that she was! Why on earth did he bother to come to see my modest self?"

"Oh, it was just a conventional gesture," Joséphine said. "Monsieur de Flahaut is well aware that people know about him and the Queen. He likes to hear them say, 'There goes the man who was Queen Hortense's lover.' He cares a great deal for his self-esteem."

"What vanity of vanities!" Valerie sniffed.

"Yes," Joséphine replied, "he may have some good qualities,

but I know all that my aunt [she meant Hortense] had to suffer on his account."

As the Laughing Cavalier, Charles had fascinated many women, but the devotees of Hortense were immune to his charm. They would never realize how unjust they were, or how much real sorrow was concealed by his diplomatic sang-froid. Within the past year, De Flahaut had lost the three beings who had meant the most to him in life: his mother, his daughter, Clementine Hortense, and the woman for whom the girl had been named.

When Valerie Masuyer left Arenenberg, Louis asked her what her plans were for the future. She replied simply, "To remember." She settled down to live in a convent, the Abbaye-aux-Bois, near the tomb of her dead mistress. Over the years, she saw the crypt beautified with stained-glass windows, in which glowed the arms of Holland; the flower that had become identified with Hortense, the hortensia; and various heraldic mottoes, among them being the one that Hortense preferred to all the rest: "Better known, better loved."

It was not until 1845, that Bartolini's statue of a veiled, kneeling figure was installed in the chapel. Eleven years later, this was replaced by a much more elaborate monument, representing Hortense, still veiled, but wearing a crown and being welcomed into Heaven by an angel. The inscription read: "To Queen Hortense, from her son Napoleon III."

For Louis had become Emperor of the French and, in doing so, had shown due regard for the traditions of the Corsican clan, of which he was an offshoot. On the night before his coup d'état, in 1851, one of the few who were informed of his plans was his half-brother, Charles Auguste Demorny, later the Duc de Morny and the Emperor's close associate. As Louis rode his horse through the streets of Paris the following day—December 2nd, the anniversary of Austerlitz—he was flanked on one side by the Comte de Flahaut, on the other by his Uncle Jérôme, the last survivor of the children of Letizia Bonaparte.

As for Valerie Masuyer, she, too, had received a well-earned reward. Her later years were spent in a luxurious apartment in the Tuileries, the palace where Hortense had lived as a young girl, dreaming of marrying for love, never seeing far enough into the future to realize that one day she would be the link between two empires, between two Napoleons.

BIBLIOGRAPHY

BIOGRAPHIES AND HISTORICAL WORKS

d'Arjuzon, Caroline. *Hortense de Beauharnais.* Paris: 1897.

Bordeaux, Henry. *Le coeur de la reine Hortense.* Paris: 1933.

Lacretelle, Pierre de. *Secrets et malheurs de la reine Hortense.* Paris: 1936.

Nabonne, Bernard. *La Reine Hortense.* Paris: 1951.

Taylor, Ida Ashforth. *Queen Hortense and Her Friends.* London: 1905.

Turquan, Joseph. *La Reine Hortense.* Paris: 1896.

Wraxhall, Lascelles, and Wehran, Robert. *Memoirs of Queen Hortense: Mother of Napoleon III.* London: 1862.

Atteridge, A. Hilliard. *Napoleon's Brothers.* New York: 1909.

Bac, Ferdinand. *Napoléon III, inconnu.* Paris: 1932.

Bernardy, Françoise de. *Charles de Flahaut.* Paris: 1954.

Bertaut, Jules. *Marie Louise, femme de Napoléon Ier.* Paris: 1952.

Boulenger, Marcel. *Le Duc de Morny.* Paris: 1925.

Bronne, Carlo. *La Comtesse Le Hon.* Bruxelles: 1952.

Cabanès, Docteur. *Légendes et curiositiés de l'histoire,* 2nd série. Paris: 1914.

Castelot, André. *King of Rome.* New York: 1960.

Charles-Roux, F. *Rome, asile des Bonapartes.* Paris: 1952

Du Casse, le Baron. *Les Rois frères de Napoléon Ier.* Paris: 1883.

Gallix et Guy. *Histoire complète et authentique de Louis Napoléon Bonaparte.* Paris: 1853.

Guérard, Albert. *Napoleon I. (Great Lives in Brief)* New York: 1956.

———. *Napoleon III. (Great Lives in Brief)* New York: 1955.

———. *Reflections on the Napoleonic Legend.* New York: 1924.

Hanoteau, Jean. *Joséphine avant Napoléon.* Paris: 1935.

Hastier, Louis. *Le grand amour de Joséphine.* Paris: 1955.

Jerrold, Blanchard. *The Life of Napoleon III.* London: 1874.

de Keratry, Comte Emile. *Le dernier des Napoléon.* Paris: 1874.

La Fuye, Maurice de. *Louis Napoléon Bonaparte avant l'empire.* Paris: 1951.

Leflaive, Anne. *Sous le signe des abeilles.* Paris: 1929.

Loredan, Jean. *Madame de Lavalette.* Paris. 1929.

Lucas-Dubreton, Jean. *L'évasion de Lavalette.* Paris: 1926.

Maricourt, Baron de. *Madame de Souza et sa famille.* Paris: 1907.

Masson, Frédéric. *Joséphine de Beauharnais.* Paris: 1899.

———. *Madame Bonaparte.* Paris: 1898.

———. *Joséphine, impératrice et reine.* Paris: 1899.

———. *Napoléon et sa famille.* (13 vols.) Paris: 1907.

———. *Napoléon et les femmes.* Paris: 1921.

———. *Petites histoires.* (1st série) Paris: 1910. (2nd série) Paris: 1912.

———. *Les Quadrilles à la cour de Napoléon Ier.* Paris: 1904.

Mitchell, S. *A Family Lawsuit.* New York: 1958.

Montagu, Violette. *The Celebrated Madame Campan.* London: 1914.

Réval, Gabrielle. *Madame Campan.* Paris: 1931.

Rheinhardt, E. A. *Josephine.* New York: 1934.

Roseberry, Lord. *Napoleon: The Last Phase.* New York: 1900.

Saunders, Edith. *Napoleon and Mademoiselle George.* New York: 1959.

Taine. H. *Les Origines de la France contemporaine, régime moderne.* (Tome I) Paris: 1891.

Turquan, Joseph. *Les soeurs de Napoléon.* Paris: 1925.

Zweig, Stephan. *Joseph Fouché: The Portrait of a Politician.* New York: 1930.

CONTEMPORARY MEMOIRS, LETTERS, AND OTHER WRITINGS

Hortense, la reine. *Mémoires de la reine Hortense.* (3 vols.) Paris: 1927.

———. *La reine Hortense en Italie, en France et en Angleterre pendant l'année 1831.* Paris: 1834.

———. "Lettres à Alexandre Ier," *Revue de Paris,* Septembre–Octobre, 1907.

———. "Lettres de la reine Hortense et de son fils, le Prince Louis-Napoléon, à l'abbé Bertrand," *Revue d'Histoire diplomatique*, Tome 37, 1923.

———. "Lettres de la reine Hortense à Eugène," *Revue des Deux Mondes*, Juillet–Août, 1933.

d' Abrantès, La Duchesse. *Mémoires*. (18 vols.) Paris: 1831.

Bausset, L.F.J. de. *Mémoires anecdotiques*. (4 vols.) Paris: 1827.

Bertrand, le général. *Cahiers de Sainte Hélène*. Paris: 1949.

Boigne, Countess of. *Memoirs*. (3 vols.) New York: 1908.

Bonaparte, Louis. *Mémoire sur la versification et essais divers*. Paris: 1831.

———. *Poésies*. Paris: 1819.

———. *Reponse à Sir Walter Scott*. Paris: 1829.

———. "Correspondance du roi Louis et de Louis Napoléon, interceptée par la police de Metternich (1833–1840)" *La Revue des Études Napoléoniennes*, Janvier–Juin, 1926.

———. *Historical Documents and Reflections on the Government of Holland*. (3 vols.) London: 1820.

Bonaparte, Mathilde. "Souvenirs d'Exil," *Revue des Deux Mondes*, Décembre, 1927–Janvier, 1928.

Bourrienne, L.A.F. *Mémoires*, Paris. 1830, 10 vols.

Campan, Madame. *Journal anecdotique*. Paris: 1824.

Castellane, Boniface de. *Journal du maréchal de Castellane*. (Tome I) Paris: 1896.

Caulaincourt, Armand de. *With Napoleon in Russia*. New York: 1935.

———. *No Peace with Napoleon*. New York: 1936.

Chastenay, Madame de. *Mémoires*. (2 vols.) Paris: 1896.

Chateaubriand, F.R. de. "Quatre lettres inédites de Chateaubriand," *Revue des Deux Mondes*, 15 Juin, 1926.

Cochelet, Louise. *Mémoires sur la reine Hortense et la famille impériale*. (3 vols.) Paris: 1836.

Constant, Louis. *Memoirs*. (4 vols.) New York: 1895.

Derosne, Charles Bernard. *Mémoires sur la reine Hortense, mère de Napoléon III*. Paris: 1863.

Duboscq, André. *Louis Bonaparte en Hollande d'après ses lettres*. Paris: 1911.

Dumas, Alexandre. *Impressions de voyage*. (Tome III) Paris: 1854.

Eugène, Prince. *Mémoires et correspondence politique et militaires*. (Tome I) Paris: 1858–1860.

Fleury de Chaboulon. *Mémoires*. (2 vols.) Paris: 1901.

Garnier, Athanase. *Mémoires sur la cour de Louis Napoléon et sur la Hollande*. Paris: 1828.

Hamelin, Madame. "Douze ans de ma vie," *Revue de Paris*, Novembre, 1926.

Hobhouse, John Cam. *Recollections of a Long Life*. London: 1910.

Jung, T. *Lucien Bonaparte et ses Mémoires*. (3 vols.) Paris: 1882.

Lacroix, Madame. "Mémoires de Madame Lacroix," *Revue de Paris*, 1 Avril, 1839.

Lansdowne, Lord. *The First Napoleon, Some Unpublished Documents from the Bowood Papers*. London: 1925.

Las Cases, Comte de. *Le Mémorial de Sainte Hélène*. (2 vols.) Paris: 1926.

Lavalette, Comte de. *Mémoires et souvenirs*. (2 vols.) Paris: 1831.

Lenormant, Madame Charles. *Souvenirs et correspondance tirés des papiers de Madame Récamier*. (2 vols.) Paris: 1859.

Le Pelissier, J.G. *La portefeuille de la comtesse d'Albany*. Paris: 1902.

Masuyer, Valerie. *Mémoires et papiers*. (2 vols.) Paris: 1937.

Metternich, Prince. *Memoirs*. (2 vols.) New York: 1880.

Napoleon I. *Lettres de Napoléon à Joséphine et lettres de Joséphine à Napoléon et a sa fille*. (2 vols.) Paris: 1833.

Napoleon III. *Oeuvres*. (Tome I) Paris: 1848.

Nesselrode, Comte de. *Lettres et papiers du chancelier comte de Nesselrode*. (Tome V) Paris: 1908–1912.

Parquin, Charles. *Souvenirs et campagnes d'un vieux soldat de l'empire* Paris: 1892.

———. *De la paix de Vienne à Fontainebleau*. Paris: 1911.

Potocka, Countess. *Memoirs of the Countess Potocka*. New York: 1897.

Rapp, General. *Mémoires*. Paris: 1823.

Rémusat, Madame de. *Mémoires*. (3 vols.) Paris: 1881.

———. *Lettres*. (2 vols.) Paris: 1881.

Roederer, Pierre Louis. *Bonaparte me disait*. Paris: 1942.

Sainte-Aulaire, Comte de. "Souvenirs sur Napoléon Ier," *Revue de Paris*, 1 Juin, 1925.

Ségur, Philippe de. *Un aide-de-camp de Napoléon*. (Tome III) Paris: 1894.

Thibaudeau, A.C. *Mémoires*. Paris: 1913.

MATERIAL IN PERIODICALS

Billiard, Max. "La maladie et la mort de la reine Hortense," *Intermediaire des chercheurs et des curieux*, Mai, 1913.

Bordeaux, Henry. "La reine Hortense au château d'Arenenberg," *Revue de Paris*, Mars–Avril, 1931.

———. "La reine Hortense, peinte par elle même," *Revue hebdomadaire,* Année 11, 1932.

Duboscq, André. "La reine Hortense et le prince royal, d'après des lettres inédites," *Revue hebdomadaire,* 26 Juin, 1909.

Gailly de Taurines, Charles. "La reine Hortense en 1815," *Révue des études historiques,* Janvier–Juin, 1913.

———. "La grande duchesse Stéphanie de Bade et la reine Hortense," *Révue Bleu,* 1 Novembre, 1913.

Jones, Ernest. "The Case of Louis Bonaparte, King of Holland," *Journal of Abnormal Psychology,* December–January, 1914.

Kerry, Earl of. "Le comte de Flahault et le coup d'état de 1851," *Révue de Paris,* 15 Septembre, 1934.

Marmottan, Paul. "Surveillance de la reine Hortense au château d'Arenenberg," *Nouvelle Révue Rétrospective,* 1894.

Masson, Frédéric. "Napoléon et Eugène de Beauharnais," *Revue de Paris,* Janvier, 1926.

———. "L'impératrice Joséphine et le Prince Eugène," *Révue des Deux Mondes,* Octobre–Novembre, 1916.

Pol, Stefan. "La jeunesse de Napoléon III," *Le Contemporain,* 1901.

NOTES

I   DINNER AT THE LUXEMBOURG

Eugène in his memoirs (T. I, p. 31) speaks of his dismay, when he realized that his mother was going to marry Bonaparte. Both he and Hortense tell a story that is also mentioned in the *Mémorial de Sainte Hélène* (T. I, p. 629). Napoleon, after putting down the insurrection of October 4, 1795, ordered that all weapons in private possession should be confiscated. Eugène came to see the General and asked to keep his father's sword. Napoleon was so impressed by the boy's spirit that he asked to be introduced to Eugène's mother. This may have been true, but it is almost certain that Joséphine had already met Bonaparte through Madame Tallien and Barras. She was on sufficiently intimate terms with him in October of 1795 to write him the letter quoted in the following chapter.

II   MARIE JOSEPHE ROSE

The nickname of "Puss in Boots" was given to Napoleon by the sister of Laure Permon, the future Duchesse d'Abrantès (d'Abrantès, *Mémoires,*

T. I, p. 113). The Permons were old friends of the Bonaparte family. The memorialist also tells how Napoleon proposed marriage to her mother, Madame Permon. He seemed to be more attracted by older women than by the fiancée whom his family had found for him, Desirée Clary, the sister-in-law of Joseph Bonaparte. Desirée later married General Bernadotte and became Queen of Sweden.

Joséphine's visit to the lawyer, Monsieur Rigaudeau, is told in the memoirs of Napoleon's secretary, Bourrienne (T. VI, p. 236). Napoleon never forgot Rigaudeau's slight, and sent for him on the day of his coronation. Pointing to his regalia, he said, "This is the cloak; this is the sword!"

III   A ROSE FOR VIRTUE

Madame Campan's *Mémoires sur le vie privée de Marie Antoinette* is much better known that her *Journal Anecdotique*, which has to do with her school. She was probably spared during the Revolution because her brother, Citizen, Genêt, was the republican envoy sent to the United States. James Monroe, the American Minister to France, sent his daughter Eliza to Madame Campan's school, where she became one of Hortense's life-long friends.

Hortense does not give the name of the poet who offended her at Versailles. He might have been Antoine Vincent Arnault, a great Napoleonic enthusiast and the author of at least one well known poem, "Le Feuille," which is supposed to have reference to Hortense. It was written many years later, when Hortense was an exile, blown hither and yon, like a leaf on the wind.

IV   THE CLAN

General Lavalette went to Egypt and later was put at the head of the postal service, which entailed keeping watch on the correspondence of important individuals and guarding much secret information. His memoirs tell of his courtship of Émilie (T. II, p. 259). When Joséphine had a household Émilie was appointed Mistress of the Robes and was given the hopeless task of keeping Joséphine's accounts.

V   TROJAN RETURN

Hortense makes no mention of her return with Joséphine to the rue de la Victoire. Her aim was always to shield her mother. Bourrienne, Madame d'Abrantès, and others fill in the story, which is also told in the *Mémorial de Sainte Hélène*.

VI THE MARRIAGE MARKET

The name of Malmaison is supposed to go back to the eighth century, when the site of Joséphine's house was a stronghold for invading Norsemen. Life there, during the Consulate, is described by many visitors, and also by Napoleon's valet, Louis Constant. The valet's ghost-written memoirs were published during Hortense's lifetime. Hortense's comment was that they had no value for public events, but were accurate in domestic matters.

Hortense, in her attempt to exonerate her mother from all blame, makes it seem as if it were Napoleon who arranged her marriage, though this the Emperor denied to Gourgaud and Las Cases, his confidants at St. Helena. Other authorities agree that Joséphine was responsible.

General Rapp was Joséphine's escort to the opera on the night of the explosion in the rue Saint Nicaise, and describes it in his memoirs (p. 23).

VII THE SACRIFICE

Bourrienne's memoirs, also ghost-written, appeared in 1829, and Hortense took a dim view of their veracity. She was particularly indignant with the account Bourrienne gave of her love affair with Duroc. Bourrienne says that Duroc wrote Hortense many letters, and that he was the one who delivered them. He also says that Napoleon offered Duroc Hortense's hand, but told him he would have to make up his mind at once. Duroc, offended, said, "If that's the way it is, he can keep his girl."

VIII HONEYMOON

Louis Bonaparte mentions his marriage in his *Historical Documents and Reflections on the Government of Holland* (T. I, p. 125). He gives the impression that he was bullied into a proposal one day and married the next, though there was actually a gap of three months between the announcement of the engagement and the wedding. Louis' book was written at a time when he was trying to divorce Hortense on the grounds that their marriage had been forced.

Lucien tells of Louis' coming to him for advice (*Mémoires*, T. I, p. 357). There was some thought, apparently, of marrying Hortense to Lucien, who had recently become a widower. Hortense says he asked for her hand, but was refused by Napoleon; Lucien says that the offer was made to him by Joséphine and that he was the one who said no.

Louis' health has been studied by Dr. Cabanès in his *Légendes et curiosités de l'histoire*. He has also been psychoanalyzed by Ernest Jones ("The Case of Louis Bonaparte, King of Holland" in *The Journal of Abnormal Psychology*, December–January, 1914). Louis is presented as a perfect example of paranoid syndrome—delusions of persecution and jealousy—caused by suppressed homosexuality. Though Jones thinks that Louis' rheumatism might have been gonorrheal in origin, he leans toward a psychic cause of his ills (p. 301) : "He sacrificed his health rather than his reason, and he had no energy left to make him a useful member of society." This study was made before the publication of Hortense's memoirs, in which there is much to fortify the diagnosis.

Madame de Rémusat (*Mémoires* T. I, p. 357) says that Hortense told her of the accusations Louis made against Joséphine. Hortense herself does not mention them, though they must have been one of her chief reasons for disliking Louis.

IX NAPOLÉON CHARLES

Caroline Murat was said to be one of those who spread the rumor of Napoléon Charles being the son of the Emperor. He denied it vigorously to Bourrienne and also to Las Cases at Saint Helena. The dates of his absences from Paris support his claim. The old story is revived by Pierre de Lacretelle in his *Secrets et Malheurs de la reine Hortense* (p. 48), his conclusions being based on the improbable supposition that Napoléon Charles was born several months before his birth was registered.

Napoleon's amours are fully described in Frédéric Masson's *Napoléon et les femmes*, Madame de Rémusat and Constant being heavily drawn upon. Madame de Rémusat, a lady in waiting from 1802 to 1807, is strongly pro-Joséphine and anti-Napoleon. Her memoirs, published in 1881, were written after the restoration of the Bourbons. It is said that she destroyed an earlier manuscript, thinking that it might get her into trouble because it was too friendly to the Emperor.

X "PRINCESS LOUIS"

The account of the death of the Duc d'Enghien is taken from Bourrienne (T. V, p. 296). Napoleon justified his action to Gourgaud, to Las Cases; and in his will, drawn on April 15, 1821.

Hortense mentions only briefly the dissensions in the Bonaparte family, before Napoleon's assumption of the crown. They are fully dealt with in volume two of Masson's *Napoléon et sa famille*.

XI THE LAUGHING CAVALIER

Françoise de Bernardy's interesting biography of Charles de Flahaut, which appeared in 1954, makes use, *inter alia*, of Gouverneur Morris' *Diary of the French Revolution*, of Baron de Maricourt's *Madame de Souza et sa famille*, and De Flahaut's letters and notes, published by Lord Lansdowne. There are also letters, in which De Flahaut and Hortense are mentioned, in *Le Portefeuille de la Duchesse d'Albany*.

XII IMPERIAL OVERTURE

Comte Rœderer recorded several conversations with Napoleon that are often quoted. It was to Rœderer that Joséphine made the remark that Louis Bonaparte "loved Napoleon as a lover loves his mistress." In his report of his talk with Napoleon, just before the coronation. Rœderer makes the mistake of saying that Napoleon was thirty-six, instead of thirty-three. Or was it Rœderer's mistake? At this time, Napoleon liked to make himself seem older than he was.

XIII THE EAGLE STRIKES

The description that Hortense gives of her visit to Boulogne is the only part of her memoirs to be published in her lifetime. She included it in an account she wrote of her travels in Italy, France, and England, in 1831. Her letters to Eugène at this time have also been used in writing this chapter.

XIV QUEEN HORTENSE

Hortense does not mention Napoléon Charles' recitation of *The Frogs* of La Fontaine. The account used here is taken from *The Bowood Papers* (p. 230). A somewhat different version is given by Madame de Rémusat.

XV THE KINGDOM OF FROGS

In describing her trip up the Rhine, Hortense first mentions her musical compositions. Her ballads were romantic and "nineteenth-century Gothic" in tone. Some were used as marching tunes. Her most famous ballad, "Partant pour la Syrie," became the theme song of the Second Empire. Hortense may have had help from her music teachers, just as she had help in her painting and sketching from her art instructors. She makes no great claim for the value of her work in any medium.

Charles de la Bédoyère seems to have rivaled his cousin, Charles de

Flahaut, as the ideal romantic lover. Since he was to have a tragic end and to be a martyr to the Bonaparte cause, he is often mentioned in memoirs of the period.

Hortense was rarely vindictive, but after her return to Holland in 1807, she dismissed, on score of moral turpitude, a Dutch lady in waiting, Madame Huyghens, who had been appointed by Louis. The incident caused unfavorable comment in Holland.

XVI FLIGHT TO THE MOUNTAINS

One of the books read aloud to Hortense at Laeken was Madame de Staël's *Corinne*, which had just appeared. When she met Madame de Staël later, in 1814, Hortense made the faux pas of asking a question that showed how little she had retained of the novel. She had interceded with Napoleon on Madame de Staël's behalf, but the latter refused to help her when Hortense was herself a refugee in Switzerland, after Napoleon's second abdication.

XVII PERHAPS DIVORCE

Hortense's travels have been minutely scrutinized by the enemies of Napoleon III, in order to prove that he was a bastard. A case of paternity is hard to argue, but the birth was obviously premature, and Louis, who seemed at first to have no doubts, announced it publicly in Holland; he was anxious to have the baby brought there for a state christening. It was only later that suspicion, the chronic symptom of Louis' psychosis, developed. Ferdinand Bac, in chapter one of his *Napoléon III inconnu*, brings forward the argument, for Hortense's innocence, that she was in no hurry to join her husband at Toulouse, but put the reunion off for several weeks; this would not have been the case if she had had intercourse with another man and wished to conceal it.

XVIII ONE FRIEND, MANY ENEMIES

The Bowood Papers (p. 232 & ff.) supply the quotations from the correspondence of De Flahaut with his mother.

Decazes, because he had seen Hortense in the Pyrénées, was one of the candidates suggested as the father of Napoleon III. Louis, however, recommended Decazes to Hortense, and retained him as a confidential agent in Paris for a number of years.

Charles's platonic flirtation with the Countess Potocka is fully described in the lady's memoirs. Charles's technique in wooing her was strikingly similar to that employed in wooing Hortense and Caroline.

Louis' letters to Napoléon Louis and Hortense are taken from André Duboscq's *Louis Bonaparte en Hollande* (p. 216, p. 219).

XIX THE DISINHERITED

The assassination attempt by Staps, which is only mentioned by Hortense and which is detailed by Bourrienne (T. VIII, p. 22) and Rapp (p. 123), may have hurried Napoleon's decision to divorce Joséphine and to produce an heir.

The aide who carried Joséphine to her room was General Bausset (Bausset, *Mémoires*, T. II, p. 4).

XX THE AUSTRIAN BRIDE

Authorities used for Napoleon's marriage are Frédéric Masson, *Napoléon et les femmes*; Jules Bertaut, *Marie Louise*; and the recently published *King of Rome* by André Castelot.

Hortense is quoted by Férdinand Bac as saying, in later life, that she reproached herself for having taken any part in the marriage of her mother's successor.

XXI SET FREE

The account of his struggles with Napoleon that Louis gives in his *Historical Documents and Reflexions on the Government of Holland*, published in 1820, is one-sided, but pitiful; there is no doubt of Louis' suffering and sincere wish to serve his subjects.

XXII A DAY OF GOLD

A long speech that Napoleon was reported to have made to Napoléon Louis, when he reached Paris, was printed in the *Moniteur*, in which the Emperor told the child that he must make up for his father's misdeeds by being a loyal vassal. It seems unlikely that the speech was actually delivered to an eight-year-old boy; this was a way of putting Napoleon's point of view across to the French public.

The seal that Charles gave Hortense, and that she gave back to him, was in the possession of Lord Lansdowne in 1925.

The memoirs of the Comte de Sainte-Aulaire, though only fragmentary, picture the imperial court at this period, as seen by a traditional aristocrat. Sainte-Aulaire, brought up, no doubt, on the legend of Versailles, was struck by the impersonal splendor of the Tuileries and Saint-Cloud. Though he was a palace chamberlain, he never saw the Emperor undressed, never saw him eat, and never knew where he slept.

XXIII   THE PRIME MINISTER

Hortense, of course, passes over in silence the birth of Charles Auguste Demorny; the correspondence in *The Bowood Papers* (p. 241) tells the little that is known. Since the baby's birth was registered in Paris, it was once thought that the future Duc de Morny was born there. The whole affair was kept so secret that there is not even a whisper of it in contemporary letters or memoirs. Jean Hyacinthe Demorny died in 1814, and in his will left the guardianship of "his son" to the De Souzas and Charles de Flahaut.

The memoirs of De Caulaincourt, latecomer to the Napoleonic canon, since they were not published until 1935, are used in this and succeeding chapters. De Caulaincourt was supposed, unjustly, to have had some connection with the death of the Duc d'Enghien, but Hortense is careful to exonerate him (*Mémoires*, T. I, p. 158).

XXIV   THE YEAR OF DEATH

Louise Cochelet's writings (1813–1820) supplement those of Hortense herself. Louise, a devoted friend, went into exile with Hortense in 1815, and died in Switzerland in 1835. Her unfinished memoirs then came into Hortense's possession, and were sent anonymously to a Paris publisher, who brought them out in 1836. How much editing had been done is uncertain, but Hortense, who did not want her own work to appear until after her death, saw an opportunity here to speak through another. She could not have taken too many liberties with the text, however, for Louise's personality—warm-hearted, naïve, and indiscreet—comes through completely.

XXV   MALBROUK S'EN VA-T-EN GUERRE

Napoleon's famous interview with Metternich at Dresden appears in chapter eight, volume one of Metternich's *Memoirs*.

XXVI   CATASTROPHE

At the Regency Council meeting at the Tuileries on the evening of March 28, 1814, Marie Louise was urged by a member of the council,

Moulay de la Meurthe, to imitate her ancestress, Maria Teresa, when Austria was invaded; she should walk through the streets of Paris, carrying her child in her arms, and rousing the city to resistance (Lavalette, *Mémoires*, T. II, p. 87). Joseph, on the other hand, had been told by Napoleon that he must not allow the Empress or the King of Rome to fall into the hands of the enemy. Lavalette, as well as Hortense, felt that the morale of the citizens was high and that the enemy could have been held off until Napoleon came to the rescue.

Charles's letters to his mother, from Fontainebleau, are given in *The Bowood Papers* (p. 248).

XXVII A KINDLY CONQUEROR

Hortense says nothing of De Flahaut's offer of marriage, for very obvious reasons. De Flahaut's biographer, Françoise de Bernardy, seems to have been the first to examine the dates of the letters in *The Bowood Papers*, and conclude that the offer was made at Rambouillet. One does not know whether Hortense was surprised, or whether Madame de Souza had managed to communicate with her.

Napoleon's suicide attempt, denied by earlier biographers as "not in character," is only hinted at in Hortense's memoirs, but a full account is given by De Caulaincourt.

XXVIII THE DUCHESSE OF SAINT-LEU

The police-bulletin account of Joséphine's death is reproduced from the French National Archives (A.B. XIX, 341). Hortense and Eugène wanted to write to Napoleon of Joséphine's death, but communication with Elba was already difficult.

Hortense says little of the visit of Madame von Krüdener to her at Baden; Louise Cochelet is more chatty. Hortense, in a letter to the Czar, told him of the incident at Saverne. This may have caused Alexander to think later that Hortense was privy to Napoleon's return.

XXIX THE LAWSUIT

Under the terms of Napoleon's treaty with the allies, Hortense and her children were to receive 400,000 francs a year, Louis 200,000.

The anecdotes of Charles de Flahaut's indiscretions are taken from John Cam Hobhouse's *Recollections of a Long Life.*

XXX FROM STEEPLE TO STEEPLE

Hortense's correspondence with Alexander, published in the *Revue de Paris* in 1907, contains a number of letters to Eugène, which, apparently, were never delivered. Hortense realized, perhaps, that even the Czar was not altogether reliable as a means of communicating with her brother. Louise Cochelet (T. II, p. 297) tells of Hortense's sending a letter to Eugène through the English embassy, concealed in a clothesbrush; it warned him of spies at Vienna. One of her letters that did get through (*Revue des Deux Mondes*, Juillet-Août, 1933) tells of Napoleon's arrival, and mentions a joke book she was sending to Eugène and Alexander; she thought they might enjoy it. This was a serious moment. One wonders if perhaps the joke book contained a secret message.

XXXI A CENTURY OF DAYS

Lavalette told Napoleon of Marie Louise and Neipperg, but Napoleon overlooked his wife's inconstancy and spoke of her with affection to the end of his life. Marie Louise had two children by her lover, before Napoleon's death in 1821.

XXXII IN JOSÉPHINE'S HOUSE

There are many accounts of the last days at La Malmaison. They all differ as to details. The color of the coat which Napoleon wore when he left, for example, is given variously as gray, green, or brown. Hortense is the only one who says that De Flahaut was one of the two messengers sent to Paris on the final day.

Maria Walewska's son was to have a distinguished career, but Léon Dénuelle was to be a waster.

XXXIII THE HUNTED

The Czar may never have read to its end Hortense's long letter of exoneration. It was found among the papers of Count Nesselrode (*Lettres et papiers*, T. V, p. 215).

Count Woyna was Metternich's choice as guardian of Hortense. He had also selected Neipperg to be Marie Louise's cavalier, and may have hoped that Hortense would succumb to the young man's charms and thus be brought under Austrian influence.

In 1814, Jérôme's wife, Catherine, was robbed of all the money and valuables she was taking out of France by an adventurer, so Hortense had reason to think that the same might happen to her.

Madame von Krüdener was appealed to by Charles de la Bédoyère's friends to save him, but, except for sending him a Bible, she did nothing for him.

XXXIV   A RESTING PLACE

Louis' letter to Hortense is quoted from volume twelve, page 307, of Masson's *Napoléon et sa famille*.

Hortense's return to the church was lasting. She made yearly pilgrimages to Einsiedeln, and her son, Louis, received his First Communion there. Later, after he had become Emperor, he sent the abbey a handsome gift.

Charles de Flahaut was reluctant to break with Hortense. He was not in love with Margaret Elphinstone, though he proved to be an attentive and considerate husband. Margaret had none of Hortense's social gifts; she was apt to antagonize people by her bluntness.

XXXV   HOUSES OF EXILE

Metternich's invitation to Hortense, asking her to come to Austria, may not have been entirely for security reasons. He admired her greatly and told his granddaughter, Pauline, that the Queen of Holland had the most perfect manners and was the most fascinating woman he had ever met, this in spite of the fact that he had been one of Caroline Murat's lovers (Pauline Metternich, *Souvenirs d'enfance*, p. 36).

Though Hortense's memoirs were finished in 1820, she was still revising them in 1830, when Valerie Masuyer became her secretary. There are a number of manuscripts in various hands, with notes in the margins by Hortense or by her son, Louis. Hortense read her work aloud to many of her friends, among them Madame Campan, Chateaubriand, Madame Récamier, and Alexandre Dumas.

The visit that Madame Campan made to Aix with Hortense, and her subsequent visit to Arenenberg were their last meetings. Madame Campan died March 22, 1822, at Mantes, where she had gone to live after the Restoration and loss of her position at Écouen.

XXXVI   THE CONSPIRATORS

The memoirs of Valerie Masuyer are invaluable, for Hortense's later years. Valerie was extremely exact, and her diary of the 1830 trip to Italy, France, and England is much more colorful than Hortense's account, which may have been toned down for publication.

In Italy, Hortense became intimate with Madame Récamier, whom she had known slightly, as a friend of Madame de Staël. They saw one another more or less secretly at first, for Madame Récamier was identified with the French Ambassador. The police kept close watch on Hortense in Rome, as well as in Switzerland.

XXXVII   ONE LOST, ONE SAVED

After the death of Napoléon Louis, his father was said to have written to the Pope, announcing his loss and adding "—as to the other, he usurps my name. You know very well, Holy Father, that, Heaven help me, he is nothing to me. I have the misfortune to have for wife a Messalina." The authenticity of this letter is doubtful. It was first quoted in a book reviling Napoleon III and published anonymously in 1874. *Le Dernier des Napoléon.* Joseph Turquan, one of the early biographers of Hortense, says that he attempted, without success, to find the letter in the archives of the Vatican. Though it is not impossible that Louis should have relapsed once more into suspicion, the phrasing of the letter seems oddly familiar in tone, addressed to a Pope; Louis never abandoned his claim to paternal authority over what he termed his "one remaining child." Hortense says that her husband and all the Bonapartes were indignant with her, because she deceived them about Louis, Junior's, going to Corfu.

In the introduction to Valerie Masuyer's memoirs, a letter is quoted that she wrote to her sister on April 19, 1831, from Lyon, while she was on her way to Paris. She describes a strange conversation she had with Zappi, who burst into her room and in great excitement cried out that he must tell her of something which had been weighing on his mind for weeks: Napoléon Louis had not died of measles, but of a wound. Because he had failed to lead his troops on Rome, the Council of the Carbonari decided that he must die. He was either shot or stabbed, and lingered for several days. The story seems improbable. Valerie does not mention it in her diary, but she had a life-long horror of the Carbonari thereafter.

XXXVIII   A LONG WAY HOME

Charles de Flahaut and his mother had known Louis Philippe when they all three were exiles in Switzerland, during the Reign of Terror. Charles was favored from the start of Louis Philippe's reign. He was sent on a diplomatic mission to Prussia, leaving Paris on the same day as Hortense, May 21, 1831. He had no inkling of her being in France, but had her interests in mind. He and his wife wrote to the governor of Corfu, a relative of Margaret, asking him to look out for the Queen and her son. When Charles heard that Hortense's banker in Paris had failed, he sent her a letter of credit on which she could draw. At this time, Charles hoped to get the embassy in London, the post held by his father, Talleyrand. He was never able to dislodge the old man; their rivalry brought a coolness between father and son that lasted for several years.

XXXIX HEIR APPARENT

Louis, Senior, not only disapproved of the writings of Louis, Junior, he considered Hortense's account of her travels a libel. Hortense's work must have been profitable; it was serialized in a newspaper and appeared in book form in several editions.

Hortense may have seen Auguste Demorny, as a small child, more than once, but of this there is no direct evidence; even the meeting at Aix is inferential. When, later, she corresponded with her son, it was always through a third party. The money that she sent him, 2,800 francs in 1818 and 40,000 francs in 1820, was sent to Madame de Souza's husband, as a gift to Auguste from "Henri de Morny."

Demorny was always proud of being his mother's son, and when later he became a duke, under the Second Empire, he used a hortensia in his coat of arms. The tradition of bastardry was carried over to a third generation. Fanny Le Hon later had a daughter, of whom the following verses were written:

> *Quel est donc ce visage blond,*
> *Qui ressemble à la reine Hortense?*
> *C'est la fille de Monsieur Le Hon—*
> *Morny soit qui mal y pense!*

Morny cheerfully recognized the situation by saying, "I call my brother sire, my father monsieur le comte, and my daughter madame."

XL GENTLE, BUT OBSTINATE

The account of the Strasbourg attempt is that of Louis, given in the first volume of his collected writings. He treasured Hortense's letter of farewell and carried it in his wallet for the rest of his life.

Hortense's doctor, Dr. Conneau, was the one called in when Hortense had a wounded refugee hiding in her Roman apartment, in 1831. Conneau later helped Louis to escape from the fortress of Ham in 1846.

XLI TO REMEMBER

The letters exchanged between Louis, father and son, were intercepted by the Austrian police and have been published in *La Revue des Études Napoléoniennes*. The letter of condolence, that Valerie Masuyer copied, was found among her papers, and appears on page 205 of Anne Leflaive's *Sous le signe des abeilles*. It has been assumed that the words of practical advice omitted by Valerie are those given in *La Revue des Études Napoléoniennes*, it being noted there that the police had not thought it worth their while to transcribe Louis' expressions of sympathy. Though the dates of the two letters differ slightly, one being October 12th, the other October 14th, they were probably one.

Valerie says that Louis did not know of the existence of his brother, Demorny, until just after his mother's death. They did not meet until Louis was President of France, in 1848. Though very unlike in temperament, they managed to coöperate closely thereafter.

Louis, who forgot none of his friends when he came to power, was particularly grateful to Valerie Masuyer. She had resigned her pension when Louis was in money difficulties, and in 1840 she gave him all her savings, 20,000 francs, to finance his attempted military coup at Boulogne. Until Louis could repay her, she supported herself by giving music lessons.

Louis expected from women the tenderness and generosity that he had always found in his mother. He was so devoted to Hortense's memory that the Empress Eugénie was jealous of the mother-in-law she had never seen.

INDEX